ARCHITECT

THE LIFE AND WORK OF
CHARLES W. MOORE

BOOKS BY DAVID LITTLEJOHN

FICTION

The Man Who Killed Mick Jagger

Going to California

NONFICTION

Doctor Johnson, His Life in Letters

Black on White, A Critical Survey of Writing
by American Negroes

The André Gide Reader

Gide: A Collection of Critical Essays

Interruptions

Dr. Johnson and Noah Webster: Two Men and
Their Dictionaries

Three California Families

ARCHITECT
The Life and Work of
CHARLES W. MOORE

David Littlejohn

A WILLIAM ABRAHAMS BOOK

Holt, Rinehart and Winston / New York

Library of Congress Cataloging in Publication Data
Littlejohn, David, 1937–
Architect: the life and work of Charles W. Moore.
"A William Abrahams book."
Includes bibliographical references and index.
1. Moore, Charles Willard, 1925–   2. Architects—
United States—Biography.   I. Title.
NA737.M65L5 1984   728'.092'4 [B]   83-18592
ISBN 0-03-063829-1

First Edition

Designer: Margaret M. Wagner
Printed in the United States of America
10 9 8 7 6 5 4 3 2 1

Portions of this book have previously appeared in
somewhat different form in the following
publications:TWA *Ambassador*; *Places* 1:2, MIT Press;
Smithsonian magazine; *California Living.*

The illustration on preceding pages is Condominium I,
the Sea Ranch, California (1965), view from Highway 1
(Morley Baer).

ISBN 0-03-063829-1

Contents

ARCHITECT
THE LIFE AND WORK OF
CHARLES W. MOORE

INTRODUCTION:
WHO IS CHARLES MOORE?

VERY few architects, however good, successful, or influential they may be, obtain much recognition outside their own profession. Historically, and elsewhere, there are those who have left a mark on the popular imagination: Bernini and Palladio in Italy; Wren and Barry in London; Garnier, Eiffel, and Haussmann (although the last two were not really architects) in Paris. But fame in our own time seems harder to come by. Of the millions of people who have visited the Sydney Opera House or the Centre Beaubourg in Paris—two of the most famous recent buildings in the world—I doubt that one in a hundred could name the men who designed them.

In the United States, a Bostonian may have heard of Charles Bulfinch; a San Franciscan, of Bernard Maybeck. Aficionados of old train stations or movie palaces, lovers of eighteenth-century townhouses or abstract modern art, may learn the names of architects associated with their specialties. The visionary may know of Buckminster Fuller; the shopping-mall developer, of Victor Gruen. Between 1979 and 1982, the U.S. Postal Service issued four sets of stamps, honoring sixteen distinguished American architects.[1] I would guess that the only ones known to the general public are Thomas Jefferson (because he did other things besides design buildings), perhaps Stanford White (because of his love life), and Frank Lloyd Wright—the one flamboyant exception to my rule, an architect of this (and the last) century whose name *has* become a household word: the unique and prototypical Architect as Hero.

PERHAPS we should make an effort to know our architects better. We may live in builder-designed houses and apartments, work in offices and schools put up from committee-drawn plans. But even these buildings are likely to bear the stamp or transmit the values of identifiable professional leaders.

1

Famous buildings, buildings that win their designers prizes and publication, are often imitated by other architects and builders almost instantly and spread new styles across the land. These styles will even reach to the drawing boards of the tract builder, the state architect's office, the supermarket chain. Famous architects like Charles Moore—or Stanford White or Frank Lloyd Wright or Walter Gropius—often teach others, who in turn teach others, who may have taught the person who designed your own barracks or brothel or barn.

Beyond their immediate or distant effect on our own living and working environments, major architects—by which I here mean the more fashionable, the more financially successful—are responsible for designing the built world we all have to look at, travel past, and frequently use. Anyone who makes use of an airport, a shopping center, a new college campus or museum; who has to travel past a housing project, or along a commercial strip, or go downtown to shop; who sees his city presented as a skyline; who goes to court in a new federal building, attends concerts in a new auditorium, is locked up in a new prison; who vacations in the Sun Belt; who goes to *any* major city, anywhere in the world, for business or pleasure, is submitting himself to the ideas of the more prosperous contemporary architects and having his life shaped, for better or worse, by their designs.

FROM 1940 to 1965, when a great deal of the urban and suburban world we know was built or rebuilt, the ideas and designs of the more prosperous American architects were dominated by what has in retrospect come to be called *modernism*.

Etymologically, all the word *modern* means is "current," "of today," or by extension, "fashionably up to date." During much of Queen Victoria's reign, for example, pointed arches and other medievalisms were properly regarded as "modern."

But after several centuries of being thus used—or of implying nothing more precise than "not ancient"—the word narrowed to signify all the rebellious, past-defying forms of art that grew up in Europe after World War I.

In architecture, what we now call modernism involved a rejection of historical period ornament and detail (frequently of *all* ornament); an aesthetic of simple, flat, or sparely geometrical forms that either were, or appeared to be, made and put together by machines, not by hand; a preference for new or factory-made materials (steel, concrete, glass, plastic) and components and for the color white; and a willingness to abandon many traditional elements of design—picturesque landscaping, formal symmetry, the closed-box room, discrete doors and windows, and other familiar and friendly archaisms (gable roofs with dormers and brick chimneys, paned glass and shutters, milled moldings and turned balusters) in the interests of a more liberated and rational design and the abstract play of line and form in space.

Much has been written of the triumphs and the failures of this period of architectural history. In its earlier days (from, say, 1919 to 1939), when it had to do daily battle with the established orthodoxies of historical period styles and accepted artistic forms, modern architecture seemed to its practitioners and advocates a necessary aspect of the world's coming of age. It was an essential part of mankind's emancipation from the oppressive prewar order, no less than airplanes and telephones, streamlined cars and their highways, servant-displacing machinery, short skirts, and the end of the class system. To these pioneers, what we now call modernism was thought of not as *a* style, but as the only valid style, and they promoted it with moralistic and visionary fervor. One of the most respected documents of the revolution, by the Swiss architect who called himself Le Corbusier, was entitled *Vers une architecture* (Toward an Architecture), as if there had been none before. Peaked shingle roofs and carved wooden moldings and Ionic capitals came to seem symbols of reactionary illiberalism and enslavement to the past, no less than miters and titles and the overseer's lash. If they called their work "modern," it was only in your basic dictionary sense—"proper for the time." Many simply called it "the new architecture" or (like Le Corbusier) "architecture." In 1932, one prophetic propagandist labeled it "the international style."

That first fervent flame came gradually to burn with less light and less heat. By 1940, what had once been radical and passionate was already becoming, in many hands, commonplace and cold. A new orthodoxy began to displace the old. If modern architecture triumphed after World War II, the reason was not only that it was the incarnation of mankind's aspirations or that it was helping us to a brave new world. It was also easy to design and cheap to build. It was admirably suited to large industrial institutions, to immense new bureaucratic systems, and to unskilled designers and work-men. Components, even whole buildings—given the machine aes-thetic—became endlessly replicable. Profitable new technologies and building methods made possible ever larger, plainer, and more rapidly erected structures.

AS an American architecture student in the 1950s, I felt consider-ably perplexed by all this. I studied, traveled to see, and tried very hard to design buildings in the ruling style favored by my class-mates and professors. On my first trip to New York, in 1954, I went at once to inspect the new buildings everyone was talking about: the cool blue-green slab of Lever House on Park Avenue, the glow-ing golden cube of the Fifth Avenue Manufacturers' Trust bank. I made serious intellectual efforts to understand and respect them.

A few years later, when I first went to Chicago and saw Mies van der Rohe's buildings at Illinois Tech and his Lake Shore Drive Apartments—the purest, most austere international-style monu-ments in America—I was less constrained by scruples. I knew at once that something essential was missing.

But in 1954–58 I was confused and unsure and prepared to con-clude that I was architecturally stupid. I was unable to come to terms with, or to derive more than a faint aesthetic charge from, the very finest glass-and-steel boxes—and some were very fine indeed. So I turned my attention to old buildings (which I could more easily enjoy) and to the written word. I was not to regain a serious interest in contemporary architecture until 1965, when I saw the new Sea Ranch Condominium in northern California, de-signed by Charles W. Moore and his partners—a building radically different from the modernist ideal.

Today, modernist forms and materials are so inwrought with contemporary economic forces that most large buildings continue to be designed in one version or another of the style. Whether or not people like them—and many people now claim *not* to like them—such things as real estate costs, building codes, and zon-ing; methods of taxing and financing; the power of the building-materials industries; the practices of construction firms and labor unions; and the existing systems of corporate and government de-cision making virtually guarantee that most new buildings larger than single-family houses and small businesses will continue to be "modern," in the architectural sense of the word: flat-topped, flat-sided, and undecorated; minimalist and functionally efficient; probably built of reinforced concrete or steel and glass. If we really wanted to get rid of them, we'd have to change society first.

Sometime in the 1960s, however, modernism both as a style and as an ethos began to lose its dominion over the hands of many architects and the minds of their observers. Journalist-critics like Ian Nairn, André Fermigier, and Ada Louise Huxtable, while still enthusiastic about the best modern work, began to point fingers at its more and more frequent failures: aesthetic failures, human and social failures, even economic failures. Many of these failures became famous: the Centre Point tower in London, the Défense quarter of Paris—in fact, most of the new skyscrapers of London and Paris; blockbuster office buildings in Boston, New Orleans, San Francisco, and New York; monumental culture complexes like Lincoln and Kennedy centers; the majority of subsidized high-rise housing projects in the United States and Europe; lifeless new suburbs; unworkable airports; Brasilia. An important early statement was Jane Jacobs's *The Death and Life of Great American Cities* of 1961, which defended the natural vitality of crowded old-city neighborhoods against the unnatural panacea of suburbanization and the megalomaniac schemes of the redevelopment agencies that had grown to power since World War II.[2]

In the 1970s, some authors began to assert that the entire modern movement was a failure, a crime against humanity, in excited books with titles like *The Failure of Modern Architecture, Crisis in Architecture, Towards a Non-Oppressive Environment*, and *Form Follows Fiasco: Why Modern Architecture Hasn't Worked.*

Since the clean, machined wall of international-style hegemony first began to crack about twenty years ago, architects have run in many directions in their search for new solutions. Anyone who contemplates the serious architectural scene since 1965 may well judge it to be chaotic. Critics lost without their labels have taken to calling this new scene *postmodernist*. But that phrase communicates nothing except what it is not, or what it came after. With the decline of faith in the modernist ideal, there is no longer any fixed center of value or style. Postmodern has come to mean almost anything goes.[3]

In the same cities that erect gigantic, blank-walled concrete bunkers and tombs (which often turn out to be art museums), mirror-sheathed office buildings and hotels rise in the shapes of pyramids, tents, clustered cylinders, trapezoidal prisms, black pianos, and blue whales. Buildings are turned inside out, with floors and walls (when there are floors and walls) hung from nude exterior skeletons. Heating, water, sewage, and ventilation pipes are defiantly exposed and painted bright colors. Gardens are planted on the roofs of underground buildings. Gardens are planted in the glazed cores of buildings overground. Windows are round or triangular or Palladian-arched. Vast atria and *gallerie* and wintergardens and radio evangelists' cathedrals are enclosed in crystalline prisms made of thousands of panes of glass. Avant-garde architects of the 1980s proudly design almost exact imitations of eighteenth- and nineteenth-century structures, as well as false-front historicist stage sets that "allude" to Versailles or the Villa Giulia. Others exhibit works that contain bits and pieces from all periods of architecture—columns and colonnades, arches and arcades, dormers, domes, pediments, porticos, deformed and disposed in whimsical ways. Old buildings everywhere are being "adapted" for "reuse." Self-effacing new buildings are slotted, almost unnoticed, into old streets. Other new buildings (sometimes by the same architect) shriek their unneighborly difference. Hotels, apartment buildings, churches, and opera houses assume the shapes of icebergs and the ships they have destroyed, pyramids rightside up and upside down, superimposed flying shells, spheres atop poles, tumbled piles of blocks, cubes plugged eccentrically into cylindrical cores, unbalanced piles of concrete slabs. "Woodbutchers," proud of the name, build themselves domes and dodecahedrons out of scraps. Fairs and airports blow up immense balloons into buildings. Experimental architects in the United States and Japan design metaphoric pods for their mothers.

Color is back, symmetry is back, peaked roofs are back, wood is back, brick and tile are back. At the same time, concrete, steel, glass, whiteness, flatness, and asymmetry have never gone away. Houses built of mud or plastic or sprayed metal mesh take the form of entrails or wombs. Others, of pure white wood and stucco, look like ingenious geometrical puzzles, waiting to be taken apart. Still others, in an architectural approximation of punk, smash corrugated metal into cyclone fencing in order to honor the ordinary and cheap.

Things fall apart; the center cannot hold. Nothing is simple or straightforward anymore in the academic and professional circles where people care about architectural style. Some of this chaos seems to descend directly from the modernist masters; some of it spits in their faces. Perhaps because of this confusion among the putative tastemakers and trend setters themselves, not a great deal of postmodern architecture has trickled down to everyday building—except insofar as you and I must occasionally travel past, or stop in, a mirror-walled cylinder or upended pyramid supported on red Tuscan columns.

THIS flashy, overrapid summary of twentieth-century architectural taste has obviously left out a great deal. Through these angry revolutions of ideology and style, a few distinguished American architects (and many lesser ones) kept to a determined and independent antimodernist course. In the 1930s, John Russell Pope and Cass Gilbert in New York and Washington, D.C., Arthur Brown, Jr., in Washington and San Francisco, and Mott B. Schmidt in and around New York continued to design impressive mansions and monumental buildings in traditional styles. (Much of Colonial Williamsburg, Inc., was built in the 1930s.) Skillful conservatives like Samuel Wilson, Jr., in New Orleans, Philip Shutze in Atlanta, O'Neil Ford in the Southwest, and John Barrington Bayley in New York have been able to maintain a lively connection with the architectural past up to our own time, undaunted by the modernist dominion. And as the average American home buyer (or restaurant owner), defying the tastemakers of the design schools and professional magazines, continued to demand Cape Cod or Spanish mission or Tiki-Polynesian, architects and builders across the country were found who were able and willing to give them what they wanted. The planners of the two most celebrated American "new towns" of the 1960s and 1970s—Columbia, Maryland, and Reston, Virginia—were obliged to offer prospective residents facades and rooflines in familiar early American styles in order to populate their adventurous schemes.

AT the same time that modern buildings were filling in or replacing much of our cities, a counterphenomenon of considerable significance was neutralizing some of their effect. Thousands of Americans were rediscovering the attractions of old buildings and neighborhoods, developing a new sense of their cultural, economic, and emotional importance.

One sign of this was the growth of America's National Trust for Historic Preservation. From an association of mostly upper-class, historically minded people in 1949, interested (like their British cousins) primarily in preserving distinguished old mansions and estates, it has grown to a 160,000-member national force that now does a very effective job of mounting and coordinating educational and political campaigns across the country, designed to preserve (i.e., protect from demolition, restore or upgrade, and recycle when necessary) everything from rotting but decent old inner-city neighborhoods to nineteenth-century breweries, Louis Sullivan skyscrapers, Art Deco moviehouses, and disused Victorian train stations and churches.

As the urban-renewal juggernaut tore down more and more impressive old buildings and genial old neighborhoods after World War II, and replaced them with modern-style structures of less and less charm (frequently by parking lots and garages, than which it is difficult to get more charmless), volunteer armies of resistance grew in city after city. By the mid-1970s almost every American city more than fifty years old had formed an education and pressure group for saving old buildings, along the lines of the National Trust. Ad hoc militias formed to fight for individual buildings— Penn Station, the Traymore Hotel, the Old Stock Exchange, the City of Paris store—to cite four of their notable recent defeats.

In 1975–76, an important crest was reached in the American movement for historic preservation, thanks in part to the country's bicentennial celebration. In city after city, preservationist forces began to win a few battles, and redevelopers to lose. Newspapers and civic administrations that had previously been 100 percent in favor of progress (in favor, that is to say, of displacing the old, however good, by the new, however bad) began to listen to, and even support, the Don't Tear It Downers.

The transformation of out-of-fashion or abandoned premodern buildings—some of them already under sentence of death—into successful new enterprises became one of the most newsworthy phenomena in American urban planning in the 1960s and 1970s (Ghirardelli Square, Quincy Market). In 1976, the American Institute of Architects, a professional organization very protective of its members' prestige and profits, began awarding separate annual prizes for preservation and restoration jobs, alongside those it had traditionally given for notable new buildings. Suddenly it was professionally O.K. to like—even to design—old or old-looking places.

The causes of this cultural turnaround are too complex to be reduced to any single explanation. Many sound old inner-city houses owe their survival to the growth of black power and of neighborhood politics generally. It is possible that most Americans had preferred premodern buildings to modern ones all along, but had been unable to communicate their feelings to people who made the big decisions about construction and demolition. Inflation, and the post-1973 energy crisis, frequently made restoring a good old building a bargain compared with erecting a new one.

But I think that much of the growing American concern for and love of old, unmodern buildings was simply a counterpart of the growing national frustration and disgust with the new and the modern. People began to feel they were missing something important.

IN the decade before the crack in the modernists' dominion over seriously regarded architecture (which I place at some time between 1960 and 1965), not *all* of the professional prizes and attention went to works of the flat-roof, glass-box, white-and-concrete persuasion. A few architects, in this country and abroad, were able to venture forward stylistically while still designing recognizably homey-looking houses with pitched roofs, natural-wood siding, brick-and-stone details; or churches, schools, hospitals, and civic buildings that left everyone feeling comfortable, both their forward-looking colleagues and their past-loving clients. The best known of these independents was a skillful and sensitive Finnish craftsman named Alvar Aalto, whose buildings—for all their sleek geometry and nontraditional asymmetry—cannot fairly be called modern, or at least not modernist, in style. In this country, something akin to his woodsy, subtle, people-centered approach was fostered by regional independents like Edward Larabee Barnes in the Northeast, Pietro Belluschi in the Northwest, and the prolific and respected architects of the Bay Region tradition of northern California, whose best known representative was William Wilson Wurster.

NOW that a distinctive break with the modernist faith and style has taken place (even though thousands of modern buildings are still being designed, built, and praised), critics and historians are attempting to name a date and identify a cause for the shift.

But this is like trying to explain by one cause, or pinpoint to one year, the nation's renewed interest in old buildings. Architects go on working in premodern, modern, and postmodern (and, if you will, late-modern) styles. Observers keep discovering antecedents for the latest innovations in the work of nineteenth-, eighteenth-, and seventeenth-century architects—in any designer who willfully broke rules and mixed styles before the present day.

The most identifiable evidence of this break or shift can be found in the places where architects talk about architecture to other architects: in the professionally accredited schools of design, and in the magazines and books written primarily to be read by design professionals. In these places, three positive, seminal causes are most often cited for the defections from the modernist creed over the last twenty years.

First, the teaching and influence of Louis I. Kahn, a respected renegade whose work in the 1950s and early 1960s (he died in 1974) looked "modern" enough to many people at one time, but who is now seen as someone metaphysically alien to the international style and the grandfather of many postmodern forms. It is difficult to sum up easily the intense and radical moralism of Kahn's approach to architecture. It demanded a constant return to first principles, beyond all styles and isms; a rage for formal order as fundamental as the Attic Greeks'; and a living awareness of other centuries and places—the earlier and more distant the better. His most impressive works, in India, seem at once timeless and twenty-first century, otherworldly and indigenous. Far more successful as an oracular force than as a politician or promoter, he never achieved a profitable practice and died in debt. Many of his sacred-seeming buildings may strike the observer as more Platonic than practical. But he, and they, represented a uniquely powerful alternative to modernism. He taught at Pennsylvania, Princeton, and Yale, and profoundly affected the thinking of many of the leaders of the "new school" (if it is one), often more by his ideas than by his actual buildings.

Second, the ideas—again, more than the built work—of Robert Venturi, a one-time student of Kahn's at Penn. His first book, *Com-*

plexity and Contradiction in Modern Architecture (written from 1962 on, but only published in 1966) was hailed by Yale art historian Vincent Scully, who has since become Venturi's chief advocate, as "the most important writing on the making of architecture since Le Corbusier's *Vers une architecture,* of 1923." With his second book, *Learning from Las Vegas* (1972, begun in 1968), written with Denise Scott-Brown (his wife) and Steven Izenour, Venturi—then teaching at Yale—extended his reputation as the most influential American polemicist *against* the modernist tradition; and in favor of the historical and emotional content, the readable symbolism, the willful vulgarity, and the agitated expressiveness of many buildings (new and old, vernacular and architect-designed, his own and others') that lay outside that tradition.

And third, the early completed work—primarily individual houses and vacation cabins, as well as one famous condominium—of the partners in a California firm called MLTW (Moore, Lyndon, Turnbull, and Whitaker); in particular, the work and ideas—insofar as they may be separated from the others'—of its senior member, Charles W. Moore.

IF I concentrate in this book on Charles Moore and his associates, it is not to belittle the work of Louis I. Kahn or the Venturis or any other causes that may be adduced for this revolution in architectural taste. Moore worked very closely with Kahn at Princeton in 1957–59, readily acknowledges the influence of his ideas, and (although few of Moore's completed works bear much resemblance to Kahn's) may be regarded in some ways as his most successful pupil. He has known Robert Venturi and his work since his Princeton days also, and though they are men of radically different temper, they share a number of central concerns. ("I like Venturi very much," Moore insists. "I don't *mean* to deflect attention from him.") As department chairman at Yale, and organizer of the competition, Moore strongly defended Venturi's controversial winning entry for the university's new mathematics building in 1969–70.[4]

But I think a strong case could be made that the writings and teachings of Charles W. Moore, and the design projects in which he has been involved, have formed the single most important positive influence in shaping new attitudes toward architectural design in this country during the last twenty years. I do not think there has been an American-born architect of comparable influence or importance since Frank Lloyd Wright. The Sea Ranch Condominium, designed by MLTW in 1963 and completed in 1965, became the most written about, most influential American building of its decade. Kresge College in Santa Cruz (completed in 1974) and the Piazza d'Italia in New Orleans (completed in 1978) each had a similar, revolutionary effect—and these are three very different designs. Through the 1970s, Moore attracted more attention in the American professional design press than any other architect. He has served as head of three major architecture schools; his original associates have headed four others. In more than one hundred completed building projects (most of them houses), designed in collaboration with many other architects, he has rarely repeated himself. In almost every one, he has introduced some new form or idea.

Many factors have influenced the new architecture of the last twenty years: fashion and publicity, new technology and new ideas, powerful individual figures. Without positing any simple equation between public attitudes and professional styles, one should also consider the immeasurable but unmistakable force of a surrounding *Zeitgeist*, or set of dominant feelings: feelings of faithlessness, cynicism, moral confusion, and fear of or disgust with the world we have made—the very opposite of the attitudes that fueled the modern movement. Any one of a dozen leading practitioners could be singled out to represent the transformations these forces have helped bring about since 1960.

But I do not think that the dizzying sense of openness and possibility that exists in the profession today could have come about without the radically independent and self-renewing presence of Charles W. Moore. In himself, he sums up all the elements of the stylistic revolution I have mentioned.

MOORE'S rejection of the modernist ideal is virtually absolute. He managed to obtain a rich architectural education between 1942 and 1959—the glory years of modernism—without once being either seduced by its creed or attracted to its forms.

His knowledge of and dedication to the buildings of the past are more secure than those of any other major practicing architect, with the possible exception of the Italian Paolo Portoghesi. His Princeton Ph.D. was a joint degree in both architectural history and professional practice. In a lifetime of indefatigable travel, he has seen most of the major and thousands of the minor interesting buildings of the world. He has written and lectured on the architecture of many different periods and regions.

He was, as I say, partly trained by Kahn and raised in the same air as Venturi. But independence is as significant as influence. Moore's affection for what his sometime partner Bill Turnbull calls "indigenous, nonarchitect architecture" (farmhouses and barns, Main Street shops, gas stations, amusement parks), for all-inclusive eclecticism, and for novel clashes of style can be traced to his remarkable childhood travels. It owes nothing to Venturi's *Complexity and Contradiction*, which appeared several years after Moore's first radical experiments in the new style. And some of these early experiments—mostly small houses in California—strike me as clearer and more interesting demonstrations of Louis Kahn's ruling ideas than many of the master's own buildings.

With the other successful opponents of twentieth-century orthodoxy—Maybeck, Aalto, the Bay Region school—Moore's awareness and involvement were early and close. In the years since 1959, he has been able to demonstrate, in building after building, humane and novel alternatives to a tradition that had come to seem, to him as to others, aesthetically bankrupt, perhaps even morally wrong.

THIS is not intended as a picture album of the work of Charles Moore. There are already four of those, plus a separate book on several early Sea Ranch buildings designed by MLTW.[5] But by studying the illustrations included in this book, the reader may recognize a few of the concerns, design ideas, and innovations of Charles Moore—even some of his whims and obsessions—that have become part of the common currency of American architectural design.

These include careful attention to the proper fitting of a new building into its neighborhood and site. They include a celebration of the *roof* as a satisfying and meaningful form outside, a rich organizing device inside, a building. (His roofs are almost never flat and rarely simply gabled.) On the underside of these provocative roof forms one finds high and unusual ceilings, which yield an extensive repertory of spatial effects. To home design in particular, Moore has brought a fresh approach to the concept of *rooms* and the lives we lead inside them. This has led him to design open-walled perches, obtuse- and acute-angled walls, columned caves, indoor courtyards and balconies, flying-bridge hallways, and an almost endless variety of indoor levels and paths. From this has come the return of the grand (or giddy) staircase as a major element of design.

His interiors are filled with heretofore unknown rainbows of color; a rich and eccentric play of light, both natural and artificial, from every possible source (including windows in unheard-of shapes and positions); and intricate, multilayered transitions between indoor and outdoor space. He has reintroduced visual wit and historical allusion into buildings, and has deliberately used cheap materials or things with "low" associations in highly sophisticated designs.

BY the main title of this book, I mean to suggest a significance in Charles Moore's character and work that goes beyond historical influence and stylistic innovation.

There are many different and defensible approaches to the practice of architecture. One may think of it simply as a practical planning and construction-supervision service that a trained professional offers to clients. He gives what they ask for as matter-of-factly as possible, by meeting their expectations and their budgets with detailed designs for structures that are buildable, usable, durable, safe, and unsurprising.

With more complex structures or more intricate programs—a hundred-story office building, a pipeliners' dormitory above the Arctic Circle—architectural design tends to refine itself into the art of problem solving. For many practitioners, this has a fascination all its own, the way complex equations have for mathematicians. Some of the mammoth projects undertaken by our larger design firms (whole cities in Arabia, new university campuses or research complexes) involve millions of computer calculations and engineering decisions, the most intricate systems analyses, work-flow charts and timetables that cover walls.

But architecture has also had a long history as one of the fine arts. There remain a great many critics, a fair number of professors, several practitioners, and even a few untrained users of architecture who continue to think of it in these terms.

This may simply be a matter of adding something "artistic" to a pragmatic design solution, the way Victorian architects attached temple or cathedral facades to the fronts of railway-terminal sheds. Even today, many American civic bodies are mandated to reserve 1 percent (or some such fraction) of their building commissions for "art."

The more self-consciously artistic architect—who is likely to have few, but distinguished clients and more than his share of publicity—may see his role as similar to that of the public muralist or sculptor, but on a grander scale, and his primary responsibility as that of creating autonomous and striking works of visual art. For a person so dedicated, such matters as budgets, users' needs, and integration with one's surroundings may take on relatively lower priorities.

This seems to me to have been the case with Jørn Utzon in the Sydney Opera House; Frank Lloyd Wright in the Guggenheim Museum; Luis Barragan in some of his spare, astonishingly colored buildings in Mexico; Philip Johnson in several elegant, smaller-scaled works; and a number of provocative young space sculptors and suave colorists working today.

This, the painter's or sculptor's approach, is most easily justified when what is wanted is a striking, symbolic monument—to the City of Sydney, let us say, or to the good taste of an enterprise of distillers—even more than a functional and satisfying place to be in. A more complicated version of this approach is the attempt, while meeting all the other requirements of a building program, to provide for life-enhancing experiences that are specifically architectural. In this case the architect will try to contrive delights that are not so much formal and iconic (like the pleasures one typically derives from the art in museums and other public places) as motor or kinesthetic, pleasures specifically derived from and involved in the very acts of being in or walking through a building, using it as it was meant to be used. To such architects, a building comes to life only as we move through it, as the text of a play is in some essential way lifeless until it is acted on a stage. The proper art of reference is not sculpture but choreography—except that here it is not the actors' motions that are designed, but the spaces and experiences they move through. The delights provided might include the pull of a satisfying perspective sequence or a changing play of light as one walks along a corridor or through a series of spaces; a satisfying bodily *and* visual sense, however achieved, of shelter or exuberance or the glory of God. Gothic cathedrals, classic Japanese pavilions, many of Frank Lloyd Wright's private houses provide pleasures of this sort, inseparable from their nature as architecture.

The line between architecture regarded as art and architecture based on theory is often indistinguishable. Many of the most interesting buildings of this century are a combination of the two. In both cases, the architect usually goes well beyond meeting the stated needs of a client or the solving of practical problems, and tries to impose a vision or embody an idea of his own. "Theoretical" designs include the projects of certain eighteenth-century French architects or the European expressionists early in this century, who tried to convey in the very plans or external shapes of their buildings a symbolic representation of their purpose. The Centre Beaubourg in Paris (by Renzo Piano and Richard Rogers) strikes me as more an ideological design than one that naturally evolved from the building's place and purpose. So do the more recent works of Italian "rationalist" architects like Aldo Rossi, and many of the current Japanese avant-garde.

CHARLES MOORE'S approach to the design of built places, although it contains elements of all these conceptions (in particular the provision of specifically architectural delights), seems to me more appropriate, more beneficent, and more defensible than any of these taken singly. His historical importance may be disputed, and the success of his individual works may be inconsistent. But his attitude toward the practice of architecture strikes me as exemplary.

To many people, some of his and his partners' celebrated buildings look very odd. Their forms, materials, details, and colors are often unexpected, and hence surprising. A common first response, therefore, is to consider them willfully weird or funny or just plain ugly.

But except for a few fantasy projects and follies (like the designs for a new world's fair, which we will observe in the next chapter), works whose very purpose is to dazzle or amuse, none of the buildings designed by Charles Moore and his partners was, I believe, intended to be a piece of "look-at-me" art. If they end up looking strange or surprising—and they often do—it is because other, nonformal considerations led to that result, or because many people are still unused to so open an approach to design. The model of naturally accreting forms, like those of an Italian hill town or an

old barn with its attached sheds and outbuildings, is more satisfying to Moore and his friends than the model of a single, admirable
object, self-consciously and primarily shaped to please or excite
the eye. Moore has mocked the idea of architecture as "frozen music or residable sculpture." He has decried the ill-fitting buildings
by other architects that "scream for attention as a shape, and not
as a place to be in," which surround his own work at the Sea Ranch
in California. He is as hostile to the elevation of architect to artist
as he is to the declension of architect into engineer.

One of the problems, in his eyes, with architecture seen as art is
that it tends to begin with a form—perhaps a beautiful form—and
then imposes that form on human users, who unfortunately come
in all shapes and sizes. He likes to remind lecture audiences of the
origin of the phrase "Procrustean bed." Procrustes, in Greek legend, was a cruel and kinky highwayman who kept two beds, one
very long and the other very short. He stopped passersby and
forced them to lie down in one of the two. Then, to make them fit,
he either stretched their legs or sawed their legs off.

As Moore sees it, this is the way a great deal of modern architecture has proceeded, from Levittown (and suburbia generally) to
Le Corbusier's Ville Radieuse and its thousands of tower-block
apartment descendants. He rails against the Cartesian tyranny of
"buildings arbitrarily aligned by the T-square," of all the pure geometrical forms into which human beings are stretched or chopped.

Theoretically, at least, a Moore (more especially a Moore–
Turnbull) design will begin by attending to, somehow yielding to,
its environment, whether natural or man-made; then proceed by
allowing the user's needs, peculiarities, and fantasies to shape the
emerging form, as the actions of a caterpillar or a bird determine
the form of a cocoon or a nest. Moore once praised a building of
Joseph Esherick's in San Francisco for being "dedicated to the
moving inhabitant, and not to the maker of forms."

Beneath the international accomplishments and celebrity of
Charles Moore, there remains a surprising degree of self-efface-
ment. He is, you will discover, a colorful man and an idiosyncratic
designer, aware of his skills and jealous of the privileges they have
earned him. But I think that in many ways he is a *non*egoist architect. His self-image is the very opposite of the Architect as Hero
(Bernini, Wren, Wright, Johnson). In a review of a book on the Aus-
trian emigré architect Rudolph Schindler, Moore defined the dis-

tinction between the "vulnerable" and the "invulnerable" creative personality and aligned himself with the former. *Vulnerable* means to him

open to all kinds of things (nobody is open to everything) in the world around. Rudolph Schindler seems to have been vulnerable . . . and I like to think I am. His vulnerability caused him pain, and lost him work, and created some terrible looking buildings as well as some of lasting power. In this respect Schindler stands not only for himself but for a great many other vulnerable architects as well—most of them summarily dismissed by historians as "derivative."

    Bona fide vulnerability, as I see it, involves caring about the specific things you find, and find out about, so much that you will change your position to accommodate them. Invulnerable architects see and learn things too, but they have a position, or a sense of mission, early arrived at, to which the learned and seen things contribute, without the power to change it. Moshe Safdie's *Beyond Habitat* is the proud story of an invulnerable who has seen and known and felt a great deal, to the greater glory of his steady vision. . . . I like to think that Bernini was invulnerable, and that Borromini was vulnerable. Some architects perhaps are vulnerable to a point, and then fix their positions. I am willing to believe that Louis I. Kahn's AFL-CIO Medical Center in Philadelphia was the work of a vulnerable, his Exeter Library of an invulnerable (this excuses me for preferring the former); Walter Gropius was the thoughtful arch-invulnerable, the International Style the temple of invulnerability.[6]

"Michelangelo was more invulnerable than vulnerable," he added later, in a public lecture. "Frank Lloyd Wright was hopelessly invulnerable."

    Humble is not precisely the right word for Charles Willard Moore. But there is about him a deep humanism, a receptivity to others, a Montaignean fascination for what he feels in *common* with the rest of mankind which distinguishes his approach to architectural design in a number of interesting ways.

    One example of this is his willing openness to, even his insistence on, collaboration with others, both with professional partners—who are often much younger than he, sometimes even his students—and with his clients. It is frankly impossible to apportion credit for their joint designs fairly among Moore and his collaborators, so genuinely interactive is their collaboration. The fact that writers and critics (like me) often adopt the convenient shorthand of calling the result a "Charles Moore building" may be unfair to the co-creators, but it is almost unavoidable. (I have tried to do these fellow workers justice first by showing a collaborative design project in action, then by letting his three original partners speak for themselves, explaining who did what and how.)

One of his clients—and they are frequently his most active collaborators—told me of her horror when Charles blithely began cutting up with a kitchen knife the cardboard model of her house-to-be the instant she even hinted at fancying something different. Another was astonished at his apparent glee on being presented with her family's list of dozens of warring demands.

An extreme of some sort is reached in the barely controlled chaos of several community design projects Moore and his colleagues have tried to orchestrate. Among these have been a park in Seal Beach, California; an Episcopal church in Pacific Palisades; a riverfront planning scheme for Dayton, Ohio; and to a lesser degree Kresge College in Santa Cruz and the new Hood Art Museum at Dartmouth. In these time-consuming, democratic participation experiments, a large number of potential users of the place—members of a parish, students in a school, university administrators, museum trustees—are invited to play dreamer-designer themselves, in a series of purposefully staged workshops. The architects then make up several models, incorporating the ideas that come out of these sessions. The laymen mess around with these some more, indicate their preferences, and send the models back to the architects. This process goes on until an acceptable preliminary design results, which Moore then tries to make "special." The results of these sessions may turn out looking like conservative compromises. But to Charles Moore, the user-involving process matters more than any preconceived form in the Great Architect's all-knowing mind.

Moore can listen to clients—at least to those he likes—remarkably well, rather like a good psychiatrist. This is particularly true when he is working on a house, trying to create a special and private place for identifiable people. (Unfortunately, his great public successes of the last few years, and the demands on his time generally, have made him less available to private clients.) In designing a house, he will try hard to discover not only such things as the clients' budget, space needs, daily round of activities, and conscious preferences, but also their *dreams*—the full array of their daydreams, memories, fantasies, and pretensions. Moore believes that the realm of the nonrational has been ignored by architects for too long, at severe psychic cost to the people who have to inhabit the places they design.

Ask yourself what your mind is really set on. Is it the hot sun of the south playing on white walls and bright flowers or the dark, cathedraled forests of your memory? Is cozy clutter comfortable, or do you need cool, elegant, unbroken surfaces? Do you picture the gleam of brass or of parquet, or the acoustical-tile ceilings and green walls of the apartment you lived in when you were nine? Does the snap of screen doors, the whir of the lawn mower, or the buzz of an outboard motor bring a flood of memories?

What places have lurked in the recesses of your mind since first you saw them or read about them? Are they secret gardens or labyrinthine mazes, arches of triumph or alpine waterfalls, latticed porches or patios cooled by the splatter of fountains? Or, if you must, are they penthouses spacious enough for Fred Astaire and Ginger Rogers to grace with an impromptu foxtrot or staircases grand enough for Scarlett O'Hara to descend?[7]

In the book from which this passage is taken, Moore and his co-authors describe Carl Gustav Jung's house in Switzerland, in which this wise pioneer explorer of the unconscious mind incorporated towers, a large stone, an enclosed garden, and other elements as he felt ordered by his prerational self. "It might be said," wrote Dr. Jung, "that I built it in a kind of dream." A few miles from one another in west Los Angeles are two Charles Moore–designed houses, built at about the same time for about the same cost, but as different from one another as fire is from ice. They grew in response to the dreams of two very different inhabitants. Places, Moore insists, should be psychically as well as physically habitable. He takes what he calls the "realm of dreams" very seriously indeed. He can honestly love a sentimental cottage *orné*, a Regency-Tudor-Mayan manse in Beverly Hills, a thousand-turreted Victorian pile (or for that matter Disneyland) because the illusions and pretensions each incarnates are so recognizably human and so vividly displayed.

Architecture, as he and Kent Bloomer defined it in *Body, Memory, and Architecture* (1977), is "the making of places . . . [to extend] the inner landscape of human beings into the world in ways that are comprehensible, experiential, and inhabitable." Their theory in that book may be seen as an elaboration of Geoffrey Scott's lucid defense of Italian Renaissance masters in *The Architecture of Humanism* (1926), where Scott pointed out how agreeably the best sixteenth-century Italian buildings correspond to the forms, proportions, and senses, the inner feelings of weight and pressure in the human body itself. Moore's best work pays attention to our psychic needs not only by evocative forms and cultural recollections, but also by such things as "choreographed" motion (the way a building seems to move as we move through it) and the changing play of light and space.

MOORE'S frequent reference to, or dependence on, architecture of the past in his work is one more example of his open and humanist approach to design. Some critics and observers have gagged over his free uses of the past in the Piazza d'Italia in New Orleans, which they regard as a decadent and offensive joke. But his historical recollections are never, I believe, just in-group allusions (the knowing professor and traveler showing off); or merely evidence of a passionate and personal predilection for buildings past (although they are also that); or an instance of trendy-chic "style" in the interior decorator's sense. His borrowings and recollections are based on a philosophical presumption (unshared by the pioneers of modernism) that our predecessors were people at core very like us; that what satisfied them for a long time is likely to satisfy us; and that in any case there is something decent, something warmly civilized about holding hands with the past by means of respectful allusions to its preferences and achievements.

This hands-with-the-past link was maintained through the nineteenth-century Beaux Arts tradition (for all its empty gestures and boring excesses) and into the early years of this century, through the craftsman and arts-and-crafts movements, and through such individual practitioners as Edwin Lutyens in England and Bernard Maybeck in the United States. Charles Moore believes that there *is* an evolved and autonomous life of forms in art, and that it was absurd of the early modernists to pretend it didn't exist or to sever themselves from it. Today, he is one of many architects who are trying to repair the broken connection.

The receptive, nonauthoritarian architect, then, will want to listen to the ideas and tap the unconscious urges of the people who will use his buildings—and then design places to accommodate them. But this isn't always possible. In the design of public places (housing projects, dormitories, condominiums, parks, and plazas) actual users may not show up until after the work is finished. In such cases, the architect is thrown back on his own resources and obliged to imagine what will best serve people he has never met. (For architects of the Procrustean school, this absence of visible clients is a blessing. They *know* what will serve other people best, and alternative suggestions only vex them.)

A more extreme case of working in an unpeopled vacuum occurs when one enters a design competition. Here the architect may have little more to go on than a site plan and a typed set of programmatic requirements—so many square feet of office space, so many toilets or parking places.

Charles Moore brings a great deal of his private reading of human nature to every design project he undertakes, whether or not there are potential users to talk to. In the case of the many competition entries he has worked on—the California governor's mansion, the Piazza d'Italia, the Tegel Harbor development for Berlin, plazas and apartments for Los Angeles' Bunker Hill, the Beverly Hills civic center—Moore's own dream life may predominate. He accepts the requirements of site and program, then goes on to create imaginary places *he* would like to be in. Whatever clients may ask for, Moore and his partners believe they can give them more.

The extra something that Charles Moore is expected to bring to a design project is, by many clients and co-workers I have talked to, referred to as "magic." There is obviously nothing supernatural about his contribution. But his particular offerings often derive from an exceptionally keen sense of the secret sources of human pleasure, so that the results appear as enchanting as they are unexpected. He understands the effect of a surprising and "excessive" fall or wash of light; the pleasure of looking *down* on life from overhead; the joy of cozy, body-welcoming spaces like bays or tents or niches. He knows the importance of transitional spaces between rooms, modulations between inside and outside; the many ways in which "senses are heightened and bodily responses are quickened" by great staircases and processionals or the carefree rapture of surplus overhead space.

Let me say something about that last idea. From the start of my exploration of his buildings, I was struck by the excitement of

Moore's extraordinary "gift" of empty space over one's head, breaking through all the places where ceilings ought to be. It is one of the most noticeable distinctions of his first identifiably different houses, designed in the early 1960s—breakthrough buildings, both literally and figuratively.

But only in reading a passage he and Don Lyndon wrote a decade later did I realize that there was a sound psychological theory behind what had all along seemed to me simply an instinctual sense of how to create emotionally satisfying places.

In the architecture, not only of houses but of churches and public buildings, the most dramatic examples of display are often overhead. From the elaborate ceilings of Japanese palaces or the palace of Versailles to the painted vaults of Baroque churches and the pressed-tin ceilings of old American stores, builders have sought to develop their imagery above, where it would not interfere with the movement of people. These ceilings remind us that the life of the mind is not limited to the realm of immediate actions, and they indicate usefully a means by which our imaginations can be enriched without clogging the flow of practical events. They suggest that it is often wise to keep the myth up off the floor, and, where possible, to build in such a way that the shapes which carry the visual imagery of a house can be largely independent of those which determine the actions of the place, except where those actions themselves can embody dreams.[8]

AT some point in the design process, Charles Moore feels the need to come up with a conceptually and visually unifying idea that can pull together all the varied things I've been writing about so far. Only this way, he believes (the idea was one shared by Louis Kahn), can he make each building he designs a satisfying and special place, with a life and an identity of its own.

Moore is usually able to find, often in the course of the design process itself, one organizing image or idea that will enable him to endow each new place with unity, identity, and specialness. Sometimes the idea may be obvious and formal: to borrow, very freely (as Moore recently did), from a nearly cubic sixteenth-century Palladian villa while designing a guest house for sixteen people at a Long Island conference center. In other cases the unifying image may be novel and intricate (as in the Sea Ranch Condominium or the Piazza d'Italia), composed of layers of meaning and different possible interpretations.

The primordial nub about which the emergent form crystallizes may come from a chance memory of, or an expression of preference by, the client. It may come from a floating image in the architect's mind. It is as likely to be a metaphor—a geode, a Russian Easter egg, a saddlebag, a crow's nest, a fort—as a specific response to the program or site. It may be born of nothing more intentional than a fortuitous shape that occurs when several pencils are set to doodling on paper. One may begin by imagining a large New England family house as if it were a sunny, southwestern village made up of separate buildings and plazas, all sheltered under one roof. One may proceed by deciding to save a giant spruce tree; then to celebrate it, open up the roof to accommodate it, design a whole building around it. A client may dream of a Japanese meditation garden or a stairway floating in space or a pioneer's log cabin. The architect may find himself recalling with affection a great eighteenth-century Virginia mansion or the miniature canals of an orange grove in Spain. Such vague but emotionally charged points of focus can grow into an idea and an image that embrace all the other requirements of a building and give it additional qualities of unity, coherence, and meaning.

Some such unifying concept is probably essential if a work of consciously designed architecture is to be wholly successful—as near to a work of art as a useful building ought to be. But the search for such concepts can be dangerous, too. I have been in (and talked to the residents of) Charles Moore buildings in which what looked like ingenious coherence in the plan—a set of five octagonal interior towers, let us say, imposed on a square—felt strained and unnecessary in the built and experienced fact.

Several of the houses Charles Moore has designed for himself (there have been seven so far) are by many people's standards unlivable, over-the-edge insane. But I have no quarrel with any of these. Second owners may have some problems, but the buildings were obviously true to their original owner's needs and dreams.

Some of Moore's public buildings have been based on or directed toward a theatrical, sentimental fantasy of the ideal lives that ideal people should live in them. Major works like Kresge College, the Santa Barbara Faculty Club, the Piazza d'Italia, and the Church Street South housing in New Haven suffer, I believe, from such an excess of idealism. In each case, the users have consistently refused to play the roles the architects have written for them. And there are a few cases, like the Gagarin house in Vermont, where I fail to detect *any* unifying concept and find the finished building troublingly incoherent.

But when one of these fortuitous unifying concepts works—as in the octagonal central temple of the Johnson house at the Sea Ranch—it can seem at once simple, fresh, and right.

FOR Charles Moore personally, the ideal design project seems to require the concurrent presence of a number of elements:

1. A congenial and open-minded client whom he can admire, creative in his own right, full of unusual ideas—but also patient; dogmatic clients fare no better than those who simply tell him, "Do whatever you want"
2. A good but troublesome site and (at least in his earlier days; he seems to be getting better at spending millions) an impossibly tight budget
3. A hopelessly clashing program or list of objectives to be accomplished, piled *on top* of the troublesome site and impossible budget
4. The point we have just been considering—some romantic ruling concept which is able to inspire both architect and client, to control and at the same time nourish the imagination.

Charles Moore typically enters this scene nowadays pressed for time and (if he is fortunate) aided by sympathetic young draftsmen and argued with by co-designers. Together, they begin to propose schemes designed to satisfy all the above requirements. Moore, all the while, is working to maximize the spatial play, the rich and varied light, the visual and tactile and motor delights in ways he uniquely seems to understand and presumes others will love.

If magic enters anywhere, it is here. I have seen, and colleagues have described, Charles Moore's wizard speed at architectural problem solving, the "laserlike" attention he is able to focus on a few square inches of plan, the Library of Congress resources of his private archive of remembered places.

When he moves into a design in progress, still at the pencil-sketch stage, Moore will frequently try to complicate it. Why not go high and lofty there? he will ask, pointing and doodling. Then you can go low and cozy here. Why not try a column or an ellipse or a winding stair or a thirty-degree angle or some detail remembered from the ceiling of an obscure Bavarian church?

He will then try to "massage" the resultant jumble back into unity; then complicate some more, unify it all again, each time at higher and more interesting energy levels, trusting to sheer instinct to keep it all one and right as he goes on varying and enriching.

He may decide to work with cut-out cardboard models instead of pencil and paper. Sometimes he opts for the total freedom of verbal metaphor, as opposed to the deceptively logical fixity of a two-dimensional line. This means that skilled assistants must be at hand, ready to cut and paste or to turn his poetic evocations into usable plans and perspectives.

Once construction begins, the surprised client may find that miracles (or at least changes) are still taking place. Found objects are suddenly turned into centerpieces, architects' and carpenters' errors (wood that shrinks or cracks, beams that don't reach) get themselves mirrored or painted blue and thereby rendered immortal. Moore loves to keep designing on location, with his own paint pots and saber saw, yielding to impulse and serendipity. This does require an understanding client. But how else can one know for certain how light will fall, colors sing, spaces bounce?

MOORE'S design for Leland Burns's house in Pacific Palisades, a hillside enclave just north of Santa Monica (once a haven for cultural expatriates like Thomas Mann) is as good an example as any of his manner of working. This house, finished in 1974, was the result of a harmonious and fruitful collaboration between architect and client. The client was a young professor of urban planning and land economics at UCLA, as well as an enlightened musical amateur: a single, gentle man possessed of considerable generosity, adventurousness, patience, and charm.

When he first met Charles Moore in 1972, Leland Burns owned another house higher up in the hills, in which he kept a prize eighteenth-century-style organ. He had decided to move, in part because of fire danger in the Los Angeles mountains. Like a number of other Moore clients I talked to, he had been induced to hire Charles by what he saw at the Sea Ranch.

Moore looked at three available Los Angeles building lots that Burns had discovered, including one seventy-five-foot square on top of a steep Pacific Palisades slope. The architect discovered that he could see sailboats in the Pacific Ocean from this site, across the mouth of Santa Monica Canyon. "He sat there singing to himself for a while, and then said, 'Buy this one.' So I did." For $25,000.

When Burns was driving him back to the LA airport that same day, Moore made an "absurdly low" estimate of $48,500 for the house he would design. He insisted that—whatever it ended up costing—he would take as his fee 15 percent of that sum. In the end it cost more than double his guess. (It is now worth a great, great deal more.) But Moore kept his bargain. Associates still bewail his cavalier way with contracts and dollars.

Fitting any kind of house onto this lot was going to be difficult. The front approach was too steep to use, so Moore decided to place the entry off the narrow back alley, already crowded with ordinary California-style houses. Then, on this site, and within— for Pacific Palisades—a relatively moderate budget, Lee Burns asked for (1) a large, separate, ideally designed performance chamber for his German baroque organ; (2) a swimming pool ("and regional tradition required that there be room to cavort around as well as in it"); (3) total privacy, in a fairly dense neighborhood; (4) a separate and secluded workplace; (5) the usual places to sleep, wash, cook, eat, and entertain; and (6) some unique and evocative kind of "Los Angeles statement"—by which Burns meant Hollywood fantastic as much as imitation Spanish colonial.

In one way, the Burns house was not a typical Moore project, any more than the Sea Ranch Condominium of 1963–65. At the end of a recession, two years after the near bankruptcy of his first Connecticut firm, Charles Moore had, for a change, relatively little work in hand. So at home in New Haven, during Sea Ranch vacations, and by way of monthly trips to Los Angeles, he was able to devote hundreds of hours to this one job—perhaps the last time he has been so free. Even so, Moore's very first design, concocted after his first visit to the site, was for a house in all essential ways the same as the one they ended up building.

Moore began not with fantasy, but—like a dutiful architecture student—with the law and other realities: setbacks mandated by the building code, places to park, angles of the sun. Many months were spent (primarily by Richard Chylinski, Moore's on-site agent) negotiating with the city over such matters, which shaved still further the buildable space.

The house that resulted I found impossible to comprehend from plans and elevations, so intricate is its interior geometry. Seen through binoculars from the south side of the canyon (the alley facade is a blank gray wall), the Burns house looks like a little village of diagonally sliced, many-windowed towers, faced in stucco and painted pink. Floating on one's back in the swimming pool, a sybarite's dream cut in the zigzag shape of an old Chevrolet emblem and enclosed by a walled court, it becomes clear morning sun playing over different shades of fading rose and mauve and ocher, persimmon and terra cotta (the wall colors change indiscernibly, like the colors of a sunset, every time a corner is turned), as innumerable windows reflect the sky. Pots of pink pelargoniums and a riot of bougainvillea outcolor it all. (These colors were all worked out on the spot *after* the house was finished.) Fitted into one edge of a compact hillside lot, this pool court provides the required "Los Angeles statement." A belvedere annex allows one to climb a few steps, in order to admire pool and house together. A crazy freestanding bent, like three sides of a huge picture frame, straddles the pool. "Charles never did explain that," Burns says. But it does block out the uglier portions of the view, buffer the winds, and provide at least an illusion of privacy. A trellis-shaded outdoor stairway descends discreetly from the owner's quarters above.

The music room is a gigantic box, sealable from the rest of the house by a high sliding door. Walled (for acoustic reasons) with a thick layer of white plaster, tile-floored, and with a sloping stained-fir ceiling, it was built around what Lee Burns calls the "Stradivarius of organs," built for him by Jürgen Ahrend in 1967. Standing on an altarlike platform, the organ produces a dry, strangely moving range of archaic sounds, perfectly carried and contained in this airy, slant-roofed cube. The room's secondary focus is provided by a Mexican balcony atop four hand-carved wood columns that Moore found in Guanajuato and insisted on fitting in.

Two sets of steps lead from the adjacent, brilliantly skylit entry hall down to the main living area, on either side of a third staircase that winds its way to the upper reaches of the house. Below that staircase Moore placed a low-ceilinged fireplace-and-conversation area filled with more Mexican collectibles and comfortable seats— including a sinuous, cushion-centered couch, like a pale orange velvet brioche, intended to evoke Hollywood and grand hotels. The whole ground floor, inside and out, is paved with seven-foot-square cast-concrete panels from Torrance, California, scored and stained to look like expensive, handmade imported tiles. The big Mexican front door arrived cracked, so Moore stuffed the cracks with some leftover wood scraps and painted them gray. Decorator tours love it. A number of accidentally exposed beams and superfluous joists were covered with mirrors and fancy moldings to celebrate the error.

At the dining end of this space—a table surrounded by comfortable Mexican *equipales* (chairs made of tanned pigskin and latticed cedar frames)—a few of the house's twenty-three French doors open onto the poolside terrace. The house is a security man's nightmare, a window freak's delight. The fake-Belgian tiles flow on out the doors. "We had been considering a round-arched arcade," Burns told me. "But then we saw some French doors we liked on a bank in Guerneville, so we decided to use them instead." The parade of French doors serves as their "abstraction" of a Latin arcade.

These interior spaces were originally even more dramatically painted than the rose-mauve-ocher south facade, which began as Christina Beebe's master's thesis project at Yale. The idea was to have the colors grow progressively hotter as they reached the center of the house. Slightly exhausted after seven years of the daily orange-and-yellow visual drama (and pressed to repair some sagging wallboard in any case), Burns recently asked Tina Beebe— who is still Charles Moore's color expert—to calm her inside sunburst into white, with some restful grays and blues.

The soaring, central book-lined staircase leads first to Burns's bedroom suite on the second level, then makes two obtuse-angled turns to his study a level above that (whence the tower silhouette). It came, I was told, by way of two simultaneous dreams. On the very night Leland Burns had dreamed of a high stairway to paradise, floating in space, Charles Moore had dreamed of high bookshelves rising alongside stairs. Given Moore's commitment to the realm of dreams, what could they do but build a combination of the two?

This steep and dramatic vertical sitting room became in the end much more than a staircase-library. At least as much as the Los Angeles statement of exotic colors and flowering plants over a pool, it is one of those unifying concepts that at once enrich a building, give it definition, and pull its separate parts into coherence. The high wall sections that embrace the stair ennoble the great wood-planked ceiling overhead. "That was Charles's way of keeping the organ room from overpowering all the other spaces in the house," Burns told me. "They're all so tall you never notice how tiny they are." The large and small voids, the cut-out holes and niches in the stairwell walls quadruple, octuple the light play of all the windows beyond and seem to send space or air flying about. The impossibly high top bookshelves, the cramped final jog up to the study, the toilet with a view are indeed images out of dreams— not *my* dreams, but (I presume) Professor Burns's and Professor Moore's. The sharp slopes and angles of this free-spirited flying stair offer romantic, logic-defying vistas—through the poolside windows, from the entry, from the seating area tucked under it— and vertiginous fantasies from above.

Charles Moore has probably designed fifty remarkable stair-cases, enamored as he is of the enhancement of bodily presence one obtains from processional movement up or down in open space. His own two most recent southern California residences are almost all stair. But Leland Burns's is one of his most extravagant. I honestly don't know how Charles Moore can figure out the spatial logistics of these free-floating, three-story, trapezoidal-corner-turning internal staircases he sculpts with such daring and finesse.

I found the experience of being in or outside this joyful house, like the experience of so many Charles Moore buildings, a genu-inely enhancing adventure. I felt sensually enriched and excited, a part of the greater imaginative, spatial, and visual range I inhab-ited and moved through. But what especially distinguishes the Burns house—apart from its warm and luxurious Los Angeles qualities—is the way in which such an intricate network of spaces, pathways, and openings, of so *many* novel ideas, is organized into a single and memorable place.

Like other Moore owners, Lee Burns admits that his building leaks in heavy rains (it's apparently hard to build complicated houses that don't), that his tower workspace can grow hot and confining, and that he gets tired of running up and down stairs. "But my main problem is leaving it in the morning to go anywhere else."

CHARLES MOORE'S is not the only (or necessarily the best) way to design buildings. It might not, for example, get one very far with a hundred-story office building. And not every thinking person is obliged to admire the results. Indeed, many thinking people (including many architects I respect) have told me they do not.

For all Moore's theories about universal emotional responses, each individual continues to respond out of his own private sense of what is appropriate, particularly in the intimate realm of the personal dwelling place, where many people are loath to break with old, to-them-comfortable ways. In such cases, the comfort of recognition may count for more than the exhilaration of surprise. One may well *need* box rooms with closable doors and have no desire to "celebrate" the taking of a shower.

Charles Moore's enriching and unifying imagination is rarely tranquilizing. He is often making a willful effort to wake up dormant selves and senses some of us may prefer to keep at rest. He seems to prefer (as you may not) the irrational to the rational, the unconscious and affective to the logical and clear—partly because he feels that rationalism has played tyrant over the world of architecture for too long. You may find yourself totally out of phase with his visions, disagree completely with his readings of human nature, and take profound pleasure in the austere and elegant modern buildings he derides.

I have chosen to write about Charles Moore because his work, his work methods, and the man himself interest me. I am not (as you will learn) a universal or uncritical advocate, but I find a great deal to admire in all three. In the course of attending closely to this man and his work for three years (after observing them superficially for fifteen), I've become as fascinated by the process of design as by the product. So I begin this portrait with a long dramatic sequence in which you will see and hear Charles Moore and some of his colleagues in the act of designing—specifically, designing some of the more festive portions of the 1984 Louisiana World Exposition in New Orleans. (I offer an updated description of this project later on.) This episode also serves to introduce other important elements of his life and work: collaboration, the use of history, his wit, and his temper.

This design session is followed by a descriptive tour of the seven houses Charles Moore has so far designed for himself. (He never stays put long.) This is intended to provide the reader with a sketch of his changing ideas, as well as a small but intense sample of his work over the past thirty years. After a digression on architectural ambition and fame in our time, I move to biography proper, told for the most part through the words of my subject and the people who have known him best. Quite apart from whatever inherent interest Moore's unusual life story may hold, this biographical sketch may afford some insight into the origin of his values and ideals. It is a portrait of a late-twentieth-century architect closely tied to the past and untainted by modernism; and, at the same time (quite unscientifically), the psychobiography of a creative genius, one who dreams of and designs "places to be."

When this chronological account reaches the breakthrough period of 1959–62, I yield the floor to Charles Moore's three original partners—Donlyn Lyndon, William Turnbull, Jr., and Richard Whitaker—in the hope that their words will communicate more than mine could of the complex reality of collaborative creation, help compensate for the injustice of my devoting a whole book to a man who often works as a first among equals, and shed some special light on their early years together, which did so much to change the course of American architecture.

In tracing, next, Moore's professional career after 1965, I shall have a few things to say about his work as a university administrator, teacher, and lecturer. The final chapter in this section fixes on his particular position in 1982–83, when last I took my snapshots and my soundings: the condition of his professional business, his relationships with colleagues and clients, his travels and his health, his plans and his personality, as seen both by Charles Moore himself and by several key people among his acquaintances.

In the second section I offer my own critical tour of his works, preceded by a small portfolio of photographs that illustrate them. But since my focus in this book is primarily on the practice of architecture and the origin and nature of the creative personality, as typified by Charles Willard Moore, words must count for more than pictures. Even in my critical tour, I have tried to let clients and tenants talk whenever I could and to *live* in the buildings I visited as well as to look at, photograph, and draw them. Good contemporary architecture, in the end, has more to do with people than with art.

THIS section concludes with descriptions of what I call "unbuilt and unbuildable" designs: doll's houses, theoretical works, a few major projects that never got built. In my conclusion, I try to sum up what seems to me special about Charles Moore's contribution to the architecture of our time.

Words are no substitutes for the personal experience of a place. Even plans and photographs may serve one better than verbal descriptions. But I like the challenge of trying to evoke nonverbal experiences in words. I like to read the works of those who can transport *me* to other places from words on a printed page, and I have tried to learn from them. The illustrations in this book may help give you your bearings for some of the descriptions in Part Two. But they represent only about a quarter of the buildings I refer to, and of these only one static, two-dimensional aspect. I hope that my verbal pictures will evoke other aspects and dimensions and help to re-create for you some of these extraordinary places.

My critical tour of the works is an account, for the most part, of my own experiences of them: of what I felt and thought while looking at, being in, moving through these places. I was favorably impressed by some, disappointed by others. To balance my own responses and tell the story of how some of these buildings came to be, I have often quoted the people who commissioned them, or who live or work in them now, or who helped design them, or who have written of them before me.

I am, in almost every case, describing the buildings or building projects as they appeared at various times between December 1980 and February 1983, when I did the work that resulted in this book. Owners, aspects, and the fate of uncompleted projects may have changed by the time you read this.

Part One   THE LIFE

1 / DESIGNING A FAIR

THE sharpened point of a brown pencil (Eagle Drafting, #314) hovers over a sheet of pale yellow tracing paper, eighteen inches wide and about the consistency of cheap British toilet tissue. The pencil's point circles over the area of a small abstract sketch. Underneath the torn-off sheet lie two others, similarly drawn on. At the bottom of the pile is a large sheet of blueprinted plans. Although the drawing on each layer of yellow tracing paper takes its bearings from the drawing beneath it, the sketch on the uppermost sheet now bears very little resemblance to the plan at the bottom.

"It's interesting. It's not right, but it's interesting." He smirks, then squints—the large, balding man who is holding the hovering pencil. "What happened to all our gorgeous curves?" He sighs. "If only we could get one we believed in." He stares at the paper, momentarily lost in this drawing of an imaginary place: "I can't find the center."

Simultaneously, three identical sharp-pointed Eagle 314s dart in, one from the north, one from the east, and one from the west. (The big man is sitting south.) For one second the four pencils form a precise orthogonal cross about some imaginary central point on the yellow trace.

The large blueprint, which covers about half of a pine dining table, represents a plan view of the grounds of the 1984 Louisiana World Exposition. Twelve hundred miles away from this tableau, the organizers of the fair, a committee of Louisiana businessmen and politicians, have put together a parcel of eighty-two acres of riverfront land in the old warehouse district of New Orleans, downriver from the Vieux Carré between the foot of Canal Street and the Pontchartrain Expressway, which now extends into the new Mississippi River Bridge. This fair is expected to cost about $350 million and, like all such expositions, to bring a cornucopia of benefits to the people who host it.

To pass as an official world's fair, such an event must be sanctioned by the Bureau des Expositions Internationales in Paris, which divides world's fairs into two categories. In those of the *catégorie universelle* (Brussels, Montreal, New York), traditionally limited to one every ten years, all member nations of the bureau are obliged to participate and to erect their own pavilions. Those of the *catégorie speciale* (Spokane, Knoxville, New Orleans) are really more national than international in scope. In these, only the host nation may put up its own pavilion. Exhibits from foreign nations are housed in common shelters provided by the host.

Most world's fairs leave behind some civic monument or urban space—a Crystal Palace or an Eiffel Tower, Flushing Meadows or Treasure Island, Habitat in Montreal, the Space Needle in Seattle. Around the monument, or upon the space, are built the temporary exhibit pavilions—national, regional, thematic, or commercial. In recent expos these pavilions have tended to form an uncoordinated display of avant-garde architecture (or topical-regional kitsch) designed to attract fairgoers for six months or a year and then be taken down.

The 1984 Louisiana World Exposition, for reasons of economy and energy efficiency, is intended to be somewhat more lean and coherent than most of its predecessors. A new glass-roofed conference center (the fair's legacy to New Orleans) will house state and industry exhibitions. Twenty-five existing old warehouses and industrial buildings will be renovated for restaurants, shops, and displays. A few corporations will be able to design and build pavilions of their own around two artificial lakes. But design of the fair as a whole has been assigned to a single architectural firm: Perez Associates of New Orleans.

In an arrangement that appears to be unique in American architectural practice, the large firm of Perez Associates (110 employees, including 85 design professionals) makes regular use of the services of one of the world's most famous architects, on a more or less free-lance basis. In 1974, Charles W. Moore—then based in Connecticut—entered a competition to design a fountain and piazza for the Italian community of New Orleans. Two young architects working for Perez—Allen Eskew and Malcolm Heard—entered the same competition. To the dismay of some critics (and the delight of others), the Perez Associates' relatively conservative scheme came in first. Charles Moore's astonishing conception, which involved ellipses, towers, arcades, and islands, was declared runner-up. In the end, the two firms were persuaded to collaborate on a single design. The result was one of the most original and controversial concoctions of what has come to be called post-modern architecture, in which Greco-Roman orders mix with Hollywood-set colors, lights, materials, and (occasionally) running water.

Partly because he got along so well with Eskew and Heard, partly because he loves New Orleans—and partly because playing visiting guru to a large commercial firm spares Moore the griefs of running an office of his own—this unlikely relationship has been maintained ever since. After the Piazza d'Italia was finished, Moore collaborated with Perez Associates on another plaza in Gulfport, an exuberant hotel remodeling in Natchez, a projected building (which never materialized) for the Italian-American Renaissance Foundation alongside the piazza—and, for the last two years, the 1984 Louisiana World Exposition.

Charles Moore's role in the giant project, like all his work at Perez, has never been closely defined. He has no more power at the office than he can win by the force of his celebrity and the success of his ideas. Allen Eskew, thirty-three years old at the time we are observing, architect in charge of the Louisiana Exposition, has the right to reject anything the fifty-six-year-old Moore proposes—or to force him off the project altogether. On the basis of past experience, however, it is presumed in the Eskew atelier that Moore can add something magic to any design his pencil touches. So he has been granted free rein to propose whatever he likes for any aspect of the fair—to make suggestions on what are, ostensibly, other people's assignments. And he has been given primary responsibility for designing the most festive and symbolic portions of the grounds.

Out of this particular design session, held over several days at Moore's redwood-and-glass retreat on the north California coast, are supposed to emerge specific ideas, plans, and drawings for the main entry and approach road; the lake area, which is to serve as the exposition's central image; and a dizzy Wonderwall, which is to extend down the major boulevard and parade route of the fair. Back in New Orleans, less fanciful souls are working out the mundanities of engineering, structural details, crowd control, and commercial viability. For Charles Moore and company, trapped at the Sea Ranch by California's "killer storm" of January 1982 (which has cut off all exit roads), it is a week free for dreaming.

Already they have made a number of tentative decisions. For the Wonderwall, Charles Moore has made a pen-and-ink sketch on a paper napkin of various fragments of architectural history jammed together—arches, colonnades, little temples set askew. This idea he adapted from one of Giovanni Battista Piranesi's eighteenth-century fantasy engravings of Roman antiquities, which shows a road lined with half-ruined pieces of ancient Rome: statues, obelisks, sarcophagi, columns. The napkin—Moore's napkin sketches are collected by connoisseurs—and the Piranesi engraving keep resurfacing atop the unrolling yards of yellow tracing paper. Taking a cue from the gardens of the New Summer Palace outside Peking (rebuilt by the Dowager Empress Tzu-hsi around 1900), Dmitri Vedensky, a friend and sometime collaborator of Moore's, suggested earlier in the week that the architects provide a covered and colonnaded walkway, which would meander along the north side of their lake. The theme of this fair (all fairs must have themes) is to be Rivers of the World, represented by the adjacent Mississippi as well as by an artificial river that will run through the fairgrounds. In place of the theme building they were originally assigned—a glass pyramid up on poles, now abandoned by Perez Associates—Moore and company are planning to erect a series of little "pavilions of the river gods" along the shores of their lake.

Seated opposite one another at the dining table, William Turnbull, Jr., and Charles W. Moore (who were partners from 1961 to 1970 and who still work together from time to time) now begin scribbling alternatives for a curving, Colosseum-like wall of arches that may become the entrance to the fair. At the moment, they are trying to make it loop out of a row of ticket booths to the right, and then somehow roll suavely into the Wonderwall to the left. One draws; the other criticizes. The critic then pushes in a pencil and draws over the lines of the draftsman. Whenever the sketch becomes so muddled as to be illegible, they tear off another piece of tracing paper, redraw what's underneath it, and start precisely from where they left off. Arthur Anderson and Leonard Salvato, two young designers from the Perez office, watch from opposite ends of the table and contribute when they dare. Burwash, Bill Turnbull's moplike, twelve-year-old Columbar spaniel, schlepps arthritically from one napping place to another. His claws click on the wooden floor.

"I AM thinking—as Paul Klee says—of taking zees line for a walk." Moore plays with lines and loops. "Though perhaps what we really want to do is a kind of *varsovienne*, here." He indicates the large entry fountain they have taken to calling their Mississippi Trevi.

"Isn't that supposed to be the home of the river gods?" asks Bill Turnbull. "Sam and Myrtle and Ethel and George?" Moore is clearly growing more and more pleased with the shapes on the paper.

"You know, if it weren't quite so awful it'd be interesting."

They laugh, and go on drawing, erasing, and drawing in silence, trying to reduce the awfulness, to increase the interest. Gradually the various pieces they are designing take on more of a family resemblance, the lines that connect them begin to seem more natural.

"I like the way this stuff talks to this stuff," Turnbull says, pointing from Wonderwall to entry loop to ticket booths.

"Yes! Now *these* pieces are a broken version of what goes on over *here*." .

"It's all the same thing."

"It gives us the chance, after this line leaves the buses, to build those arches up into an actual wall."

"Which is nice."

"And to head off *this* somehow—which is not very beautiful."

"Why is the work we do always so defensive?" Moore asks. "We're always hiding views of other people's shit that we don't want anybody to see. So they'll look at our shit instead."

"That's why you're a facade architect, Chuck."

"Do you realize," Moore asks, speaking to the company at large, "that 'facade architects don't have any social conscience'?" He is quoting a well-known Marxist architectural critic.

"Somebody's been damning you again?"

"I presume so. Probably for my relation to the Shah of Iran. Did you ever read those letters that came in when the piazza was first published?" he asks. "One of the letters linked me with the Shah of Iran, for dealing in unsocial things like fountains in the first place. Another one said I was responsible for the *fall* of the Shah of Iran."

"You out-Shah'd him."

"Riding rough-shah'd."

"Shah Na Na."

Enough silliness. "O.K. How we gonna get the folks in?"

"They buy their tickets where?"

"They buy their tickets in that line there." A pencil points.

"And this is just a great big open space." They are now walking into their paper fairground, at a one-inch-equals-forty-feet scale.

"Which they could reach after walking along here."

"Could we come in behind them with some trees?"

"We don't have time. Remember how small those trees in the piazza were after five years? They don't grow fast enough."

"Bananas. We could have bananas."

"We could do trellis. Should we bring out that Schinkel drawing we were looking at last night?" Moore asks. This is his polite way of ordering someone to find it. "For een-speer-ay-shun?"

"If we went soft here, we could go strong there. That part's lit all the time. Soften the back, and pull 'em in. Use this knuckle as . . ."

"Knuckle?"

"Isn't that the Trevi?"

"The Trevi knuckle? No, it's the Navona knuckle." Turnbull continues to draw, but Moore is now engrossed in the exquisite plates of his new $450 Karl Friedrich Schinkel portfolio, the drawings of an early nineteenth-century Prussian architect, a romantic classicist now back in vogue and very much to his taste. He finds what he is looking for—an engraving of the queen's trellised loggia at Charlottenhof.

"That's it! That's it! I think we've got it." The plate is handed around. The others are not quite sure what to make of this neoclassical, vine-entwined folly.

"It would only cost about forty million . . ."

"A little Piranesi here, a little Schinkel there . . ."

"A little Borromini . . ."

"And a little Charles Gwathmey." (The last reference is to a younger contemporary.) At this Charles squawks, but he remains genuinely entranced by the engraving. "This is *it*, if we could just get our language right. Look: that tree isn't going into trellis. It's holding it *up*. It's a column. It's fake!"

"Holy shit." (A classic Turnbull response.)

"Boy, that man knew. Oh he knew. We've got to have some columns like that. I'm sure we can get them. With a lotus capital, and a herm . . ."

"Herm and Myrtle."

Schinkel is laid aside. Moore turns back to the emerging plan. "So if this back edge softens itself . . ." Turnbull goes on with his interrupted proposal.

"Softens itself how?"

"With vines, or kudzu, or bananas. So when you pass through it, this is all strong . . ."

"And this is all soft?"

"This is all soft. Soft here, and hard there."

Moore breaks into song: "Round in the end and high in the middle, is O-Hi-O."

"This then becomes just a big series of gateways. And somewhere you gotta be able to see through that. 'Cause you've got the sparkle of the big fountain, and the river gods, and the Mississippi gods . . ."

"So you see this as being . . . ?"

"Water. The Mississippi Trevi. You see a piece of it as you move up here, then you see more. This is all quite transparent and open."

"But this is where you pay your money, where the barriers are?" Someone pencil-points to a closed semicircular line on the plan.

"No no no. Those lines are just overhead structures, colonnades. You shouldn't see them as walls."

"Somewhere in here there should be water."

"Oh, I don't think we want water yet."

Charles Moore tears off another trace and starts again. "Look: this isn't necessarily right, you understand . . ." He redraws the whole thing very quickly.

Bill Turnbull points his pencil to the edge of the entrance plaza. "Now the edge of the water, Chuck, is there, in your mind?"

"Well, that's where it is on the drawing underneath. That doesn't mean it is, necessarily. Actually, I think this has to be a place where people can stand. There can't be water here."

"It's also where you board the monorail."

"If this is the monorail—which it might well be—I think it'd be fun to have a monorail going along the back of the Trevi." He draws that. "And this is whatever you need to get up to the platform where you board. This is a colonnade, from here to there, and then the water could be just on the other side of it. This is our shore-line." He quickly draws each of these elements. "And then you would go here, and what I was *hoping* for—I admit I didn't draw it very well—what I was hoping for is a scene where as soon as you came around here you saw this magic shot of fairyland—Whoopee! Wow! Smash!—and then" (he quickly draws in the river-god pavilions around the lake) "you saw the Nile, and the Ganges, and the . . . Housatonic, and the . . ."

"Ohio . . ."

"the Eel . . ."

"What I'm trying to figure out is how to get that element of sur-prise. You've got an object that attracts—the Mississippi gods—and then you come through, and you want the view to be blocked, partially. You can see *something*, but you've almost got to get up in this space before you can see what it is.

"My guess is that the inside of this is going to have to stay fairly open, because you're dealing with lots of people. You've collected them across this vast plaza—with a detour here—to *this* point, and you're letting them into the fair. There's this old idea about car-nivals—which should apply to world's fairs too—that the first thing inside the gate nobody goes to, cuz they're all anxious to get on with it, get to Where It Is. It can't possibly be *yet*."

"It's where you are already."

"So this," Moore says, moving his pencil along from site to site, "I don't think that this thing . . . and surely not this . . . and I don't think even *this* are in a position yet to be wonderful. Nothing won-derful at a fair is ever just inside the gate. The Trevi here ought to be wonderful, of course, but it's a throwaway. And *this* ought to be wonderful, but it's a sort of Piazza del Popolo. It's just the Some-thing at the Beginning."

"Piazza del Banana Republic."

"But from *there* you get vista A, across the lake; and from over *here* you get vista B, of our Wonderwall."

"Hey. That's the watercourse, remember. You're putting the monorail on top of the water."

"I am worried about that. There will be mobs of people here, and they're going to push each other into this thing. We're really deal-ing with all those people who for a year or two *didn't* go to the fair in Knoxville."

Talk turns for a while to the 1982 Energy Expo in Knoxville, which they evidently expect to be a failure. Moore notices a new drawing of Turnbull's.

"Why did you decide to make it so ugly, Mr. Turnbull?" he asks, in his ingratiating way.

"I'm just following the lines you put down, Uncle Chuck." Turnbull is moving the plan on further, trying to work out paths and sight lines from the entry plaza down to the corporate pavilions alongside their lake, the riverside beer gardens, and the state pavilions on the other side. Now he is drawing like crazy. "Let me try this one on you. If you brought your bus in here and angled it in, through a sort of mini triumphal arch . . ."

"Triumphal arches of the world!" Moore breaks in. "Our new theme!"

Turnbull picks up on the Moore-ish whimsy. "Meet me at the Egyptian triumphal arch at two o'clock, Myrtle. That's when our bus leaves."

"Which one is the Egyptian, Herm?"

"The one with the Ionic columns."

"How the hell am I supposed to know what an Ionic column looks like?"

Turnbull returns to a semiserious note. "I see it as a sort of Porte Cochere of the People."

But Moore will not be tempted. "Ugh. More aristocratic-Marxist concepts." He is examining Turnbull's sketch. "Bill, this is *awful*. This is just terrible!"

Turnbull leaves Charles and the boys to play games with their pet Wonderwall, while he doggedly measures out diagonal stalls for buses, each with its own mini triumphal arch. "This is *boring*," he protests, as he sizes out bus stalls. Everyone begins singing verses from all the songs they can remember about rivers. Out the window, a ship moves slowly along the Pacific Ocean horizon. In the end, Turnbull is proudly able to display the requisite number of spaces dictated by Perez Associates, splayed back so as to leave a broad, clear pre-entry plaza where seventy thousand Herms and Myrtles can mill about each day before buying their tickets.

"Look, Uncle Chuck. I think I got us a bus park. If you take this corner tight you can get in all twenty-six."

"Hmmmm. There's something very appealing about that whole mess."

As the design process progresses, fueled by pots of tea, Charles

—who is clearly the leader—keeps shifting his attention from one area to another.

For a while everyone doodles around the lagoon, devising spaces for the corporate pavilions, which (since they will be designed by other architects) everyone presumes will be irredeemably atrocious. Bill Turnbull manages to find room for about fourteen, which they hope will be enough for Perez. Moore is determined to avoid what he calls "the chaos of Brussels."

"Let the corporations build their slew of little turds sitting out in a field. What *we* have to do is provide so attractive and so desirable a setting that no one will even notice them." They take to calling the whole corporate precinct the White Elephant Park and fantasizing a particularly gross IBM pavilion to fit on a quarter-acre site. Charles Moore has had very few corporate clients.

In a book on which he collaborated in 1977, Moore cited a theory of the Greek planner Constantinos Doxiados, which held that the buildings of the Acropolis were consciously organized in precise thirty-degree-angled segments from an entry point just inside the propylaeum, to compose a closed, rational, and satisfying vista. He is determined to achieve something like this with the buildings around his New Orleans lake—all the more reason to screen out the corporate turds. He proposes building a little viewing platform at the head of the lake ("an aedicule for Instamatics"), just inside the main entry. Then he keeps rearranging the shoreline, and the placing and shapes of the five river-god pavilions that project into it, until they compose into precisely the pattern he wants (which also has something to do with the Temple of Ramses II).

Arthur Anderson suggests that they make the more distant pavilions taller than those nearer. That way, when they are seen in perspective from the vista point, they will all appear to form a unified whole, with a common roofline. He starts drawing out his idea. Charles is impressed and helps him finish his drawing.

"River gods of the world, unite!"

Charles, in fact, is delighted. The vista now totally excludes the White Elephants. "Great! We'll make it so bizarre and recherché and arcane those corporate bozos won't be *able* to fuck it up."

Leonard Salvato, meanwhile, has been playing around with appropriate designs for each pavilion—onion domes for the river Volga, lotus columns for the Nile, an African tree house for the Congo. Charles looks over his sketches.

"Let's not get *too* hokey, Leonard, too Disneylandish. But do save all these sketches. We'll need them for the Wonderwall."

Eventually each pavilion is pulled out onto its own little prom-ontory, with coves and curving walks in between. As two of them, reaching from opposite sides of the lagoon, begin to approach one another, someone proposes building a bridge between them. "A cunning little footbridge," says Charles, "into our White Elephant Park."

"Yes. An Elephant Bridge."

This leads to talk of possible boats or barges, on which fairgoers could float about the lagoon. Boston swanboats, Tivoli bumper boats, a marble boat like the dowager empress's. Suddenly every-one is designing Cleopatran barges, "evoking" one river or another. The barge de Nile, the barge of the Susquehanna.

Charles has somebody fetch one of a pile of his unfinished Christmas cards. (Two weeks after Christmas, he is still trying to finish these hand-drawn fantasies: they are all inked, in giddy lines and dots and scribbles, but wait to be watercolored.) This year's card depicts an impossibly steep floating island-palace in car-toonlike elevation, covered with a forest of little rococo roofs: curved, mansarded, peaked, towered, domed. From atop every roof rise finials or crockets or ironwork or tall flagpoles or weathervanes with long flapping banners. (All Moore's fantasy buildings have long flapping banners, inevitably blowing to the right.) Mock-heroic statues stand inside arches or atop high plinths. Thin columns, round and oval windows turn the walls transparent. Pa-vilions in one style perch precariously atop smaller pavilions in another, while swooping Arabian awnings and cascades of broad steps weave between the wings. The whole topheavy pile rests with comic-opera stateliness on slender arches and footings, floating over an ink-dotted lake of its own reflection. Tiny boats are moored to its landings. In between work on his slightly more buildable projects, Charles Moore has drawn scores of these fantasy struc-tures. Most—like the Christmas cards—are designed for friends and relatives. Those that escape into commercial galleries sell for up to $2,000.

"You want us to design barges like *that*?" asks one of the team.

"Well, not exactly. I was just trying to offer you some inspi-ration."

As he frequently does, Charles lets the talking and drawing go quite mad for a while. The release is relaxing, and there may always be a usable idea on the other side of sanity. They talk of setting one cove on fire, to represent a polluted eastern river; of allowing tourists to leap across the water on imitation ice floes.

"Like Eliza crossing the ice."

"Who's Eliza?" asks one of the youngsters. It's one of the first historico-literary allusions that anyone has missed, out of hundreds—one of the first allusions that anyone has *acknowledged* missing—in forty-eight hours. Charles explains, by acting out a scene from *Uncle Tom's Cabin*, who Eliza is.

From there they conceive of an underwater contour map of the world, to be built in the largest of the coves. Someone finds an ancient encyclopedia in a closet, in order to draw the world in its proper shape. Somehow dancers are to perform on top of all this— perhaps leaping from mountain range to mountain range in galoshes. On these contour-map islands, the rivers of the world will be lighted, under water. Crazy as it sounds, the idea stays in.

On about the fortieth redrawing of the whole area, Bill Turnbull comes up with a wizard idea everyone agrees to at once. At the head of the lake, by the Instamatic aedicule (an *aedicule* is a little shelter made of a roof on columns, like a small portico or pavilion), he proposes placing a great fountain of the rivers which will send out jets of water in sine-wave curves at five-foot intervals, creating perfect and regular waves the whole length of the six-hundred-foot lake.

Whenever he grows tired of playing with the curves and complexities of the entry and lagoon, Moore thinks some more about his Wonderwall. This fantasy structure at least fifteen hundred feet long and twelve to twenty feet wide will run down the median strip of the Front Street mall (the main north-south boulevard of the fairgrounds), where it will obviously serve as his signature. Along the top of it—"A Beaux Arty narrative number, but with palms and glitter"—he hopes that a monorail or people mover will run along one section of its fair-encircling course. Below the monorail, Charles would like to have a watercourse of some sort and period-style arcades people can walk back and forth through, alongside neoclassical booths for cotton candy and souvenirs. Exactly what this wall will end up looking like (beyond the tantalizing napkin sketch) is, at this stage, anyone's guess. I find myself imagining a sort of Son of Piazza d'Italia, with the curves and mock-historical motifs of the piazza—only three blocks away from the fair-grounds—pulled out into a long, thin history-of-architecture stage set that will probably offend and delight even more people than its parent. (Six months later, it is a permanent part of the plan. A New Orleans newspaper refers to it as "the Great Wall of China as built by the Marx Brothers.")

After it loops around the entry plaza in that colosseum arc, the site plan shows the line of the squashed classical Wonderwall splitting in two. One branch is to turn into the orderly lines of the dear dowager empress's covered promenade, then head along the lakeshore toward the riverside beer gardens. The other is to diminish into a row of ticket sellers' kiosks outside the gates. Charles wants these kiosks to "recall" various pieces of his three-dimensional collage on the Front Street spine. The actual configuration of this important junction grows out of yet another art-historical recollection.

"I was wondering," Bill Turnbull suggests, as he lays in more pencil lines on the uppermost of a dozen drawings, "if maybe you wanted to do something like that Florentine thing, where the two passageways split?"

"What Florentine thing?"

"You know. Where you come out past the David statue, and that gallery splits going down to the river."

"The Uffizi?"

"Yeah. Because that would give you the space on the axis, and the beginning of the Empress's Walk as something very special on the inside."

Moore adds some more lines to the sketch.

"Is this what you mean?"

"Something like that. And then the back does . . . whatever the back does. We could just use the wall of whatever White Elephant was next to it." Turnbull draws some more.

"That's quite amusing," Moore concedes.

"Now *this* could be solid." Everyone is now either drawing or watching others draw.

"And this would be what you'd do with the steps."

"You know," Charles says, after a significant pause. "I think we've hit on one of the eternal verities."

From that moment on, this cleverly splayed intersection, which connects Charles's trash-compacted Piranesi Wonderwall with

Dmitri Vedensky's dowager empress's promenade, is locked into the design. Charles refers to it as "Bill's Uffizoid effusion." The wanton, eclectic mining of historical sources, long a staple of Victorian architecture (then abandoned in disgust by modern architects), is obviously, in some circles, back in force.

Attention shifts to the aqueduct, the twelve-foot-wide sluice which is to run along the top of, or through, the Wonderwall, at a different level from (but if possible visible from) the monorail. At the point where the monorail is to make its great entrance loop around the ticket takers' Piazza del Popolo, Bill proposes that this aqueduct spill over in a great waterfall, either into or near the Mississippi Trevi Fountain: perhaps a shower people can walk under, like Niagara Falls; perhaps a cascade running alongside the stairs down from the monorail station. Bill draws. Charles says nothing. Bill finishes; stops; looks up.

"You don't like that idea?"

"Don't like it? Oh, no no no. I love it. It's strong, brilliant, exciting, moral; American. You go through the rotunda rocks and then have all this water pouring down in front of you."

"Like at the Villa d'Este."

They next debate about hiding the monorail pylons behind various period-motif structures. ("You can sell hot dogs and hamburgers in the arches.") Charles wants to cover the rail line with an egg-and-dart molding and a frieze. Leonard draws a possible pylon-camouflaging tower.

"That's nice," Charles says. "It's got a kind of post-Mayan cleanliness." A high-tension power line loops down the center of Front Street, which all their constructions must be careful to clear. Bill wonders if they could feed off it for a twinkling swarm of fairy lights.

Halfway along the Fulton and Front Street malls, the original scheme called for a second loop of the monorail, to surround a spectacular Eiffel-type tower of some kind, which would also contain a Coney Island parachute drop. But bids on the tower came in at twice the architects' estimates ($30 million instead of $15 million), so now it appears to be out. Anderson and Salvato are anxious to leap into the breach and seize the now-vacant St. Joseph Street loop for Charles Moore's fantasy-making team. Moore demurs.

"You guys decide on St. Joseph Street. I have no opinions. It's not ours."

He retreats to the ocean-view corner of his condominium to go over the manuscript draft of one of his four books-in-progress with another assistant, who is part of this floating work party. Outside the glass a primal spectacle is taking place. With a dulled, inexorable roll, gray Pacific waves surge, crash, and break in ceaseless slow motion (about once every ten seconds), spewing with murderous slowness up fecal-brown rock islands. The wild spray then spills back in runnels and waterfalls down the ridges of the rocks. The lower rocks are covered with foam all the time. Strong winds blow spray in every direction; flotsam and sedge accumulate in the coves. It is the wettest winter here in anyone's memory.

By the time Charles gets up and looks in next at the dining–drafting table, Arthur and Leonard have fitted a huge carousel and a Ferris wheel (of the same diameter as a carousel, tilted up ninety degrees) into the St. Joseph Street loop. They are toying with the idea of having passengers for the Ferris Wheel embark from the monorail level of the Wonderwall.

"Nifty!" says Uncle Chuck. This, too, is high praise.

Charles rejoins Arthur and Leonard at the table, three pencils at the ready, to play some more with the far end of the Wonderwall, on past the now-interesting St. Joseph Street loop. All three think on paper.

"Maybe we could space the bits out further and further—as if it went on to infinity?"

"Or have it end at a giant mirror."

"Or in a grotto, underground." Pencils flash like calligraphers' brushes.

"I can't seem to get it right."

"Something *special*."

"Could it go meandering romantically to its end, with little garden pavilions at the close? Something like this?"

"Maybe it could just fray off across the last pavilions, end with an obelisk or something at the door to the museum."

"How about another river-gods' fountain? Like the Piazza Navona?"

For inspiration, Charles fishes out the napkin, with its Hadrianic bibelots set at forty-five-degree angles, its Bolognese late-Gothic portals in exaggerated perspective—all squeezed to fit in the median strip. He is still obviously very proud of his idea.

"Where it succeeds, I think, is in the concept of design by Trashmaster; composition by smashing. You march along the ages as you walk along it—but not in chronological order. The ascent of Assyria, the best of Babylon; then something Egypto-Mayan . . ."

Eventually, they have to worry some more about how and where to get people in—the one serious, nonfantasy job (along with bus parking) they take on during this long surrealistic *charrette*. How many ticket booths do you need to serve seventy thousand people a day? How large a radius must the colonnade–monorail loop have to enclose the proper number of people, in this outdoor *salle des pas perdus*? Moore and Turnbull shift for this stage of the work from soft drafting pencils to plastic needlepoint pens, one black, the other red. Leonard and Arthur get out French curves, templates, prismatic three-sided architect's rules.

GROUPS of friends working together, particularly under pressure (the M*A*S*H syndrome), often develop a peculiar private style that may seem to the outsider manic, cryptic, giddy, and irrational. Turnbull and Moore have been drawing plans for buildings together on the same sheets of paper since they were at Princeton together in the late 1950s. Other architects who collaborate with Moore adapt, perforce, to his working style. It is at once a verbal-historical shorthand, involving rapid data retrieval from a common bank of ideas; imaginative search and play; a subtle jockeying for place (who is closer to the master?); and an emotional release.

Because so much of the time is spent drawing, there is, to begin, a great deal of silence. At this early stage of the design process much of the sparse talk seems metaphoric or allusive, surreal scenarios that bubble up from the depths, rather than any actual description of possible finished buildings. There is also a jargon of the mystery that may appear arcane to outsiders: traditional designers' vocabulary, architecture-school lingo, current vogue words like *contextual* and *layering* that professionals like Moore and Turnbull first coin and then mock. More interesting are the metaphysical references that provide occasional glimpses into the thought processes behind the moving pencils: the evolving plan seems a Ouija board that forces their fingers this way or that. "I see this getting transparent." "It wants something over here that talks to this space." Allusions, both verbal and visual, to the entire sweep of architectural history are indispensable food and fuel to this group. These are not so much professional art historians talking as people who know and *use* art history, who strip-mine it for ideas.

The power playing is tangible, but less easy to analyze. Secret points are gained or lost, one feels, whenever suggestions are accepted or rejected by the team captain. The Moore–Turnbull relationship ("Mr. Turnbull"; "Uncle Chuck"), in which the junior "equal partner" mixes deference and defiance, has the devious intricacy of a long-established marriage between two harmonious but very different souls. Charles Moore, in the company of other designers, can be a very tough cookie. One must obviously share his taste for historical allusion or fantasy, or simply drop out of the game. He proposes ideas with a regal assurance, presuming they will be accepted (the sacred napkin). He seems easily offended (into silence) by criticism, or even *lèse majesté*, but is fairly free with his criticism of others. One must be very sure of oneself, or know Charles Moore very well, to disagree. And one is expected to serve. (These rules, I should add, do *not* apply to clients, before whom he can become all deference and grace.)

"Is that dimension, gentlemen—I hate to be *pedestrian*—adequate? It would be nice if things fit."

"Mr. Turnbull, you were about to say something very important?"

"I'd like a little tea, very weak—if it's no great pain."

The "craziness," always orchestrated by Moore, is perhaps the most agreeable aspect of his drafting-room style, although even here there is a trace of unacknowledged and sometimes exhausting competitiveness (who can come out wittiest, gooniest?). For no discernible reason, one, then another, will shift into a broad French or Spanish or German or Italian accent; old teachers or other architects are being imitated. Digressions can carry talk far away from the design at hand (as long as the topic of the digression interests Moore): to Vita Sackville-West's love life, to lesser-known Cole Porter lyrics:

> You're the top
> You're the steppes of Russia;
> You're the pants
> On a Roxy usher.

Earlier this same week—for even under deadline, there is life beyond drafting—"the pants on a Roxy usher" had won for Charles Moore a raucous round at charades.

THE telephone rings about once an hour. Berkeley, New Orleans, Los Angeles, San Francisco, Houston, Aspen, New York, Connecticut all keep in touch. One afternoon a knock on the door announces the man from Federal Express, arriving heaven knows how in a place supposedly cut off from the world by water. He bears, in a mailing tube, the most recently revised plans for a new art museum Charles's Connecticut office is doing for Dartmouth College.

During breaks—Charles announces nap time like a nursery-school teacher—people sleep or watch the waves or page through one of the many new books piled around the house, mostly on architecture.

Food and drink are no problem. One may be working very hard, and isolated by the elements, but creature comforts are provided. Each morning, Charles Moore does his scrambled-egg act. Others do toast, bacon, coffee, juice, and the dishes. The fridge is packed solid with liter bottles of white wine and enough leftovers for a week of lunches. A pregnant young woman drives down from her cabin in the woods each afternoon (when the roads are open) to prepare a gourmet dinner for whatever number are staying. In her absence, or for variety, Moore and company eat at the Sea Ranch Lodge just up the road. The bar chez Moore is well stocked, and the cocktail hour is sacred: all work stops for that.

The weather outside being what it is, no one is tempted much further than the lodge. But one afternoon the sea grows calm, and the sun breaks through, so Charles drives everyone up the road to a swimming and tennis club he and his partners designed in 1971, hidden behind the Sea Ranch stables. The energetic play tennis or swim in a long blue pool overlooking the ocean. Charles, who is no athlete, holds court in the sauna—one of his favorite conversation places. After a long nude sweat, he cold showers, and emerges pink and refreshed for an evening of good drinks, good food, and good fellowship. That night, he wipes out the house with the names of obscure artists in a game of Botticelli.

After the better part of three days (this is atypically slow progress; Turnbull tells me later: "We can hammer out a house design in hours"), Charles Moore calls a temporary halt to designing and proposes that a composite drawing be made, incorporating everything they've decided so far. He and Bill Turnbull redo the shoreline of their lagoon; two pencils and one eraser needlepoint back and forth. Suddenly, the shoreline curves turn crystalline, angular. They begin to add colors. Leonard and Arthur are given the job of drawing up all the adjacent streets and buildings to scale, along with whatever else they've definitively added. "Feel free to beautify it," Charles instructs them. In the midst of their efforts, one of them wonders whether they should continue the monorail line along the top of the lakeshore promenade.

"*Horreur!* The Dowager Empress's Walk? *Jamais de la vie.* It's much too profound and serene. Don't monorail it; Uffizify it. Anyway, stop talking and draw."

The two seniors withdraw to one of the ocean-facing window seats, to mull over the latest changes ordered in a country club they are designing for a Houston developer. Back after an hour to examine the results of everyone's combined labors, Uncle Chuck gives a pep talk. He reminds them all of the fragility of their efforts. The people at Perez can still say no to it all.

"We've lost the St. Joseph Street tower. Someone else has the beer garden. Someone else has the other end of our *spina*. That's O.K. with me. We still have the long mall, the corporation area, and the lagoon, and maybe the bus and ticket entrance—*if* we come up with something they like. We can still do something dazzling and memorable.

"We no longer have a theme building, so *this* has to be our major architectural statement: our Eiffel Tower, our Palace of Fine Arts. It has to have some sort of overall gorgeousness about it, especially when it's lighted at night. I want that water axis vista to be *the* magic moment of the fair."

He worries whether they have done sufficient justice to the river theme. They now have the great Mississippi Trevi at the entrance; the pavilions of the river gods around the lake; the lighted rivers on their underwater world; the barges, the fountain, the Wonderwall watercourse with its cascade. Is that enough of rivers? Enough to satisfy Perez and the fair commissioners? Charles rereads the official background paper, which is very insistent indeed on the significance of rivers. In this place, at this time—the rain has been pouring for days—it seems odd to be worrying so much about an insufficiency of water.

But now the sky is clear, the streets are drying out. Three days of storm-enforced isolation are ended. The tempest—the area's worst in thirty years—has hammered on Charles Moore's roof, beat against his windows, churned the ocean at his feet into fury. The bridge at Bodega, forty miles to the south, is cut in two. Trains, buses, and subways throughout northern California were stopped, as well as cars. The Golden Gate Bridge is still closed by mudslides and flooding on Highway 101 to the south. Hundreds of homes in Marin and Santa Cruz counties have been ripped off their foundations or buried in mud. Acres of farms and suburbs are still under water.

But now the Richmond Bridge, which crosses San Francisco Bay north of the Golden Gate, has been reopened. One lane of the ravaged Coast Highway down to Jenner has been scraped clear of mud, its worst holes refilled. East of Jenner, the Russian River has receded just enough to permit drivers to crawl carefully along the River Road. It is possible, once again, to get from the Sea Ranch to San Francisco.

Bill Turnbull must fly out to meet a client in Colorado. Leonard Salvato and Arthur Anderson are needed in New Orleans. The Los Angeles team of Charles Moore's associates (who have been telephoning twice daily to learn of road conditions) is due in tomorrow to work on other plans, for other projects. This particular work party is about to break up.

Before he takes temporary leave of the Louisiana fair, Charles Moore has one last assignment for the group. Everyone is to draw up a collection of his favorite historical facades at quarter-inch scale. They can then be cut out and sliced up and pasted back together in a fifteen-foot-long row, to make a model of the Wonderwall that will dazzle the folks back in New Orleans.

2 / A PLACE OF HIS OWN

UNIT 9 of Condominium I at the Sea Ranch, California—where all this took place—is one of seven residences Charles Willard Moore has designed for himself since 1954.

The first Moore house he actually designed for his mother, a merry Michigan widow ("she could drink us all under the table") who came out to California in 1945 to be near her two children. In 1953, her daughter Miriam (Mimi) was married to a navy lawyer stationed at Monterey, for whom Charles designed his first California house. Driving up on weekends from Camp Roberts, where he was serving in the U.S. Army Corps of Engineers, Lieutenant Moore (then twenty-eight) supervised construction of this small, inexpensive, California modern house in the hills of Pebble Beach for his sister. A year later, after his discharge, he designed a second one for his mother two blocks away. His mother's house, just inside the guarded upper gates to this golf-and-country enclave, served as Moore's own California home (during the few years he *was* home) for the next five years.

Mother's House—Moore #1—cost $8,500 to build. It is a simple rectangular wooden box fitted into a steep lot with a view through the pines down to Monterey Bay, austere and vaguely Japanese. The architect had just returned from ten months with the army in Korea and Japan; several of his early houses look "vaguely Japanese." A sheltered walkway leads to the door, past a small, enclosed, gravel-floored Japanese garden carved out of the slope. From one of the very few right-angled, flat-ceilinged living rooms to be found in a Charles Moore house, a west wall of glass looks out to redwood decks that terrace down the hill. Because of the chill fogs that frequently cover the upper slopes of Pebble Beach, the decks are rarely used. In a straight line off the living and dining room, a corridor with shoji-screened cupboards ran past the eight-foot-square kitchen (since enlarged) and bathroom, to Charles's and his mother's bedrooms; this is why the house fit so tidily into its elegant little matchbox. The plan is similar to those of two Frank Lloyd Wright–inspired Houses in a Desert Charles had designed as a boy of fifteen.

Since 1974, Charles Moore has rented the house to Roger Bailey, his design teacher at the University of Michigan (1942–46) and later his boss at the University of Utah (1950–52), where Bailey founded the school of architecture and invited his prize pupil out to teach. Bailey and his wife have furnished the small house, which looks like a hundred thousand others in California, with comfortable, conservative good taste. On the walls hang some of Roger Bailey's watercolors of his European travels.

Roger Bailey is a suave, sharp gentleman with a wonderful head of wavy silver-white hair, who mixes and pours substantial martinis. Looking out into the Monterey fog, he recalls in happy detail his and Charles's years in Ann Arbor and Salt Lake City. Like many other old friends who have followed this enchanted child's work through two or three decades, Bailey detaches himself from some of his protégé's recent unusual projects.

"Sometimes I really don't understand how he got to be so famous. He's *playing* with architecture. I don't like the stuff he's doing now. That thing in New Orleans!" The thought of the electric-eclectic Piazza d'Italia leaves Charles Moore's old teacher lost for words.

"He used to be a lot harder headed, I think, about what was good and what was bad. He made line-drawing perspectives of this house; did you know that? They're on file with the county. He worked a lot harder then. Now he can be as irresponsible as hell."

Bailey points to a giant hollow iron hemisphere that disfigures his back garden—one of a set of submarine net buoys that Charles impulsively bought from the navy and had sawn in half, with the idea of turning them into cheap fountains for public housing projects. That idea failing, he offered them to clients. "The damn thing never worked. It tipped over sideways, and it fills up with needles from the pine trees. We asked him for something that would make a little water noise to trickle down the terrace—and instead he gave us *that!*"

New Orleans and navy surplus fountains aside, there can be no doubt of Roger and Betty Bailey's devotion to their prodigy-protégé. "Our friendship with Chuck has been long and happy. He is about the nearest thing to a son we ever had."

(Moore is "Chuck" to many older friends and pretend-intimates, "Charles" to most newer acquaintances. "People in the East think 'Chuck' is something you call your horse," was one friend's explanation of this double identity. Some of his closest friends, oddly, always call him by both names, "Charles-Moore," as if it were a double-saint French *nom de baptême*, like Jean-Luc.)

Moore, on his part—though he has long outgrown the visions of his former mentor—refuses to let go of people who have been important to him in the past. "I think the secret of all his projects nowadays is the way he can inspire a lot of helpers," says Bailey. "So many people are devoted to him. He never says or does anything to make people dislike him. He can do lots more with all these collaborators, because they let him avoid the time-taking work. When I think about it, that may be the breaking point between Chuck's more thoughtful stuff and his slapdash style today. The way he travels around now, I don't know how UCLA keeps him on the payroll."

Two months later, Chuck/Charles himself—sometime professor/chairman/dean of architecture at Princeton, UC Berkeley, Yale, and UCLA—is in Monterey for three days, to address a conference and receive an award, two things he does a great deal. Roger and Betty Bailey have invited him, his sister, and other distinguished guests at the conference for cocktails at Moore–Pebble Beach, as their house is called in the *catalogue raisonné* of Charles's *oeuvre*. The week before, he was in New Orleans, Indianapolis, and Houston, working on elaborate projects he has going in those three cities. The next day he is flying off to Berlin, to try to placate the city fathers there, who are dissatisfied with a giant urban design scheme they have commissioned from one of his several firms. During the party, he asks his sister Mimi if he can run his dirty laundry through her washer and dryer up the hill, so he can be ready for his 7:50 A.M. flight.

Roger Bailey mixes and pours, compares notes with visiting professors of architecture. Betty Bailey passes hors d'oeuvres, recommends restaurants in Monterey and Carmel. The strikingly handsome co-guests of honor, Mexican architect Ricardo Legoretta and his wife Lala, sit on low stools by the fire and listen to an attractive Englishwoman who is proposing places for them to go on a holiday in Wales. Charles Willard Moore, mustachioed moon face atop football-shaped torso, six foot three and two hundred-plus pounds of rumpled architect, ambles amiably, shyly about the living room of Moore #1. He moves from couple to couple, talking now of the Berlin project, now of New Orleans, now of old days in Ann Arbor or Monterey, now of the conference just ended; now worrying about his plane or his laundry; now correcting some of the stranger stories I have been hearing from his friends and enemies in LA.

MOORE #2 (Moore–Orinda in the listings) is a unique one-room pavilion in a small circular meadow populated, even in decay, by jolly ghosts and happy memories. It was built over two years as a communal exercise by Charles, his friends, and his students at Berkeley, after he joined the University of California architecture faculty there in 1959. Many of them still recall design classes or weekend parties spent mortaring bricks or nailing beams for what was to become one of the most honored, influential, and written-about buildings of the early 1960s. Others recall great parties that took place here after it was built, hosted both by the architect and its subsequent owner, which gained the house a racy reputation among its peace-loving neighbors. In time, a swimming pool was added, as well as a lumpy-organic, mud-formed guest house and wine cellar built on the edge of the creek, the master's thesis project of one of Moore's students.

Orinda, like Pebble Beach, is a protected and restricted upper-middle-class town, proud of its natural setting, its large California ranch-style houses, and itself. Less than twenty minutes' drive from the University of California at Berkeley—and thus an easy commute for the new associate professor—the tunneled hills that divide the two towns divide worlds. To the east, particularly in 1960s, lay an often hectic arena of free spirits, political adventurers, and intellectual overachievers. To the west lay northern California suburbia all clipped and trim and comfortable, defined by and prized for the fast and tasteful things that new dollars could buy.

Charles Moore defied Pebble Beach by giving it two cheap and ordinary houses and designing one of them for its first-ever Jew (his brother-in-law, Saul Weingarten). He outraged portions of Orinda by falling in love with, and then impulsively purchasing, a wonderful one-acre glen, looped by a fern-bordered creek and surrounded by a thick screen of bay trees and oaks. Here he proceeded to build the absolute minimum house county regulations would permit, in a style that was definitely not California ranch.

For $11,000 (lot included), he got a 720-square-foot house with no internal doors (well *one*, to the toilet), no corner posts, virtually no walls (framed sheets of three-quarter-inch glass roll away from the corners on overhead barn-door tracks), a brick floor, and two odd interior templelike things on ten-foot-high pine columns, under one of which sinks a large Roman bath, whose occupants float open to view.

It is difficult to convey today the excitement this strange building created in professional circles (in the United States, Japan, Britain, France, Germany, Italy) when it first became known. Few houses had caused such a fuss since Philip Johnson's Glass House of 1949 in New Canaan, Connecticut—a comparable transparent-walled showcase of ideas designed by an older bachelor architect for himself and an admiring world. "It was such an enormous risk at the time," declares one of Moore's early associates. "It gave us all courage, just to think you could *do* something like that."

Like two then-bizarre, now-famous vacation cabins Moore and his friends were designing at the same time, the Orinda house broke many existing aesthetic norms. By introducing a new set of design possibilities, it opened up new definitions of "beauty."

Reached at the end of a narrow, winding drive, the Orinda house poses like an ideally formed Japanese pavilion—an object of worship, almost, so perfectly is it shaped—in the center of its knoll. Directly above the dissolving, sliding walls (the house is exactly square in plan) rises a steep-pitched symmetrical shingled roof without eaves. From then on the eaveless, prismatic roofline was to be a Moore signature. Where the four hipped roofslopes meet, a high light box crowns the whole like a cupola (another Moore signature). It contains a trussed plastic skylight designed to institute provocative games of illumination within. Light from this box is transferred and filtered through two interior, open-topped roofs beneath the roof, each resting upon four wooden "Tuscan" columns Charles Moore salvaged from a burned-out nineteenth-century hotel in San Francisco—and which, incidentally, support the roof. (The charred remnant of a ninth column stands as a found sculpture in the yard, along with two clay waterworks molds.) Four of the columns define a twelve-foot-square living area, decorated (at least in early publicity photos) with leather chairs, interior plants, a bright Mexican rug, and a goatskin throw—all of which objects one can find in photos of other early Moore houses. The four remaining columns enshrine the sunken tub. A ceiling-high bookcase separated two beds—the owner's and a guest's—which were otherwise unenclosed. A baby grand piano stood for a while "in exhilarating jeopardy" (to quote the architect) in one of the transparent corners. The "kitchen" was a study in minimalist design, suited only to someone who lived on snacks or expected guests to bring their own food.

What excited the architectural community, and particularly early Moore cultists, about this and similar houses were a number of unorthodox and novel ideas. Out of either perversity or deep personal conviction, the designer of this curious sport appeared to defy the modernist creed and to reintroduce into serious architecture a number of formal, emotional, sensual, historically recollective, and just plain comical elements and pleasures that had long been banished or forgotten.

The exterior was willfully shacklike, "aggressively nondescript," one critic called it—not *quite* an old barn (the forms were far too refined and generated by a complex geometry), but not self-consciously elegant either. In no way did it hint at the surprises within. The steep shingled roof was something from another time altogether. In it, observers saw—as Moore intended—Javanese huts, early California farm structures, medieval reliquaries, other times and other places.

Inside, the four-poster pavilions were obviously jokes (a temple over a bathtub? in a house this size?), as well as serious evocations of primal order and shelter. Moore had bought the columns—he remains a compulsive scavenger of building fragments—for two dollars each, then painted the simple capital fillets mauve and terra cotta. They were designed to give this tiny house a sense of grandeur; to filter and focus daylight in different ways at different hours; to enhance the inhabitants' sense of their physical selves; and to "recall"—how quickly the word reentered architectural criticism!—Roman baths, baroque baldachinos, toy houses, stage sets, the little "temples" erected over icons and idols; to evoke the atavistic pleasure Moore believes all people take in being enshrined under small, sheltering roofs, whether children playing house under a dining-room table or emperors parading under a canopy. The complex play of light, the wondrous overhead and out-reaching space, the density of cultural memories in this small structure—especially when its walls were thrown open to the surrounding green and sky, with no intervening sill or surplus frame—seemed to many observers more rich and humane, more defensibly thought out, than what contemporary architecture had been offering for years. Others responded to the happy novelty of it, so charmingly contrived and so ingeniously contained.

Twenty years later, Moore–Orinda—now the Moore–Heady house (architectural historians identify provenance very carefully: there are landmark residences in Boston and Savannah with triply hyphenated names)—had become as much an architecture student's pilgrimage site as Wright's Fallingwater or Jefferson's Monticello.

"I was just getting out of bed one morning," said the genial, long-haired construction worker who recently rented the house for three years, "and was standing there in my bathrobe making coffee. Suddenly down the road come these fifty Japs with their cameras. Their bus had stuck at the top of the drive. They had all bought tickets for this tour in Tokyo, which promised to take them to Charles Moore's house in Orinda! Nobody ever told me.

"Then there was this French architecture student with his knap-sack and camera, a real pilgrim. He had flown all the way from Paris to San Francisco, then took BART to Orinda, and walked out the rest of the way on this superhot summer day. He didn't know a word of English. He had come all that way just to see this house. We felt so sorry for him. I gave him a beer and drove him back to the airport." (I was to hear of this same French student from owners and tenants across the country.)

Students on study tours from American universities, architects and art lovers from Germany, Belgium, Australia, all find their way to 33 Monte Vista in Orinda to take pictures, do homage, check out the poles. For them, the effort is worth it. That perfect little pavilion in its meadow (with its two little pavilions inside) looks just like all the illustrations they've seen in the books and magazines.

The current tenants weren't so sure. "My friends ask me," Mark Smith said, "'What would you do if you ever met this guy Moore? Hit him?' Or else they say, 'It's bizarre, all right. But I couldn't live here!'"

Mark and Leslie Smith first saw the house two years before they moved in, when they were invited to a Fourth of July barbecue given by the previous tenant. When they married in 1980, it seemed the ideal honeymoon cottage. So when their friend moved out, they moved in.

"It'd make a perfect beach house, for somewhere like San Diego—if you could just move it there. Up here it leaks terribly every winter, and it's a sweatbox in summer. The temperatures get down to seventeen above, and all he had to heat was that dinky electric heater. I had to put in that iron woodstove and chimney just so we could survive.

"The place is a real wind trap, too. The whole front opens, all the corners open up. The winds come in over the reservoir and swirl all around—Charles Moore just wasn't aware of all that. The whole place is pre-code. All the wood frames on those sliding glass doors are rotted at the bottom. I jacked up all the glass with stirrups. There's a half inch give on those rollers at the bottom. You get six-by-seven-foot plate glass banging and rattling at night in a high wind, it gets pretty spooky." ("He sleeps like a rock," his wife Leslie puts in.) "The rain pounds on that plastic sheet on the roof, the wind blows in through a hundred wind leaks. That big Mexican tapestry" (which they hung to help wall off the living area) "flaps around at night like a flag. A bird flew into one window and broke it. I replaced the glass, but the frame is still totally rotted. When you water the lawns, the water stays in the cracks in the glass.

"When the skylight gives, it rains as much inside as out. Those bowed pieces of Plexiglas, you just can't make them watertight." A great transparent sheet now disfigures the roof. "Jim Heady [the owner] and I cut that plastic sheet to fit, put it over the skylight, pulled it taut, and nailed it down with wood strips. We wanted to leave the house as open as we could. But it leaks like crazy. My wife's not as hot for it as she was originally. Les is gone on seven months pregnant, and this is no kinda house for a kid. I think we'll be moving out soon."

It can't be soon enough for Leslie, a short, round, red-cheeked young woman. "See that?" she asks, pointing to a pile of clothes in one corner. "That's my closet. You can't leave dishes in the kitchen. 'Doors?' I ask my friends. 'Rooms? What are they?' We have to store our stuff in the shed."

So little of the famous Morley Baer–photographed interior

is visible that the architectural pilgrims are often perplexed. " 'Where's the piano?' they all ask. I don't think there's been a piano here since they took that damn picture." The aedicular columns are badly split, with ugly wood putty in the cracks. The blue of the fascia, the mauve and terra-cotta fillets of the capitals have nearly faded away. A big squashy double bed on a storage platform has replaced the trim pair of bookcase-divided singles, and the sunken, step-down tiled tub—shrouded by a palm-frond shower curtain—now serves as a drainage pit for a yellow automatic clothes washer perched on its edge. The place, frankly—with a big old Philco radio, a set of Britannica, the couple's seven guitars, and a lot of second-hand furniture—looks like a dump. It is not easy to imagine the visual joy this small building once afforded, or the revolutionary genius that went into its design.

"We thought of adding a loft over the bed, with a ladder up to it," Mark says. (Something like this was recently done to another famous Moore house of the sixties, totally eliminating the vertical space that made it famous.) "But what's the point? Clean it out, fix the roof, replace the rotted wood, heat it correctly—even the drainage here is so bad the lawn just erodes away, and the deck and frames keep on rotting." For all its faults, though, the tenants—who had never heard of Charles Moore when they moved in—don't regret their adventure in Moore #2. "Basically, it's been fun."

The house's current owner—a wealthy young contractor, who now lives with his wife in a lavish Japanesey-decorator spread up the hill—admits that the Moore place is a bit run down. He and his wife lived in the house happily enough for fourteen years, he insists, letting the sunlight wake them "naturally" at 6:00 A.M. They took quick Japanese-style baths together in the sunken tub. ("You had to be quick. The place wasn't insulated, and the cold ground sucked the heat out of the water in five minutes.") They depended on electric blankets for heat in the winter and watched wine bottles burst in the summer heat. But they relished the "oriental," open-walled life on warm days in their fine and private space. "You lived the way the house forced you to live. It was good."

Jim Heady and his wife added a pool, a decent road in, and landscaping. For many years, they considered building additional Charles Moore–designed pavilions to house real bedrooms and a human-scaled kitchen. But they kept putting it off, partly because of business reverses, partly because of their distrust of the young associate Moore sent up to finish the job. In the end, they decided the time had come for a change of "life style."

"We wanted something less sixties-ish. We were more into *quality* now, you know? More *restraint*: more like *Architectural Digest*, Paige Rense and those. I really identify more with that now."

So they moved up the hill and personally remodeled a much larger house around their accumulation of art, antiques, and miscellaneous collectibles. In 1980, they put the $11,000 Moore–Orinda house, with its very desirable acre of ground, on the market for $300,000-plus. "But it would have to go to somebody who'd appreciate it," Jim Heady assured me. "Somebody like us, who'd leave it as Charles first designed it."

MOORE #3—actually one-tenth of a vacation condominium—is Charles Moore's own favorite, the one place he has felt at home in since he left Battle Creek, Michigan, at the age of sixteen. It was the setting for the New Orleans fair design session we have already observed. After eighteen years (it was completed in 1965), he still depends on it, emotionally, and returns to it whenever his professional and academic obligations, and his own obsessive travels, permit.

It is by far the best known building he or his partners have ever designed. There are times, in fact, when they grow weary of being identified or introduced as "the men who designed the Sea Ranch."

The building is officially known simply as Condominium I. It was designed as part of one of the most utopian schemes in American regional planning. Fifty-two hundred acres along the north coast of California, fronted by ten miles of one of the most soul-stirring shorelines in the world, came on the market in 1962, when the Ohlson brothers decided that, after twenty-one years, they had had enough of unprofitable sheep farming.

Alfred Boeke, an architect and planner from Los Angeles, who was then an executive for a Honolulu developer, learned of the Ohlson brothers' plans and persuaded his employers (Oceanic Properties, Inc., the real estate subsidiary of Castle and Cooke Corporation, one of Hawaii's "Big Five" entrepreneurs) that the land could be transformed into an ideal and profitable vacation-home community of four to five thousand homes, and yet be left virtually untouched. Despite its rugged terrain, its frequent fogs and high winds, its distance (110 miles) from San Francisco, Boeke was convinced—and managed to convince Castle and Cooke—that the Ohlsons' Rancho del Mar would, if developed with proper respect, attract enough northern Californian second-home owners to justify what turned out to be a $4.7 million investment.

As things turned out, Boeke was wrong. Corporate greed, individual intransigence, too many compromises, and too much politics conspired against his utopian plan. After five years of euphoria came fifteen years of reality: design revisions, lawsuits, and ill feeling. Even so, the Sea Ranch today remains one of the more affecting and memorable unions of land and water forms under the sky, here graced, there disgraced by the relatively few homes that have been built since 1963. (At my last count, in mid-1982, there were 548. A total of 1,800 lots had been sold.) Al Boeke, disappointed at the result, soon left the enterprise. He now lives on a farm near San Diego. All Oceanic Properties hopes is to cut its losses as much as possible.

Very early in his planning for the property, Boeke called on the services of an even more idealistic thinker than he, San Francisco landscape architect Lawrence Halprin. With his wife, the dancer and choreographer Anna Halprin, he had been one of the prime shapers of, and spokesmen for, what might be called the California New Thought of the early 1960s. He was one of the first people to bring the word *ecology* out of the agriculture textbooks and into coffee houses and political platforms.

Boeke and Halprin led a team of like-minded spirits, who devised for the Sea Ranch a master plan of perfectly positioned, almost camouflaged worn wooden houses, houses which were to be either nestled in the sixty-year-old windrows of Monterey cypress that divided the grassland meadows near the ocean, hidden among hillside evergreens to the east, or clustered into tight, congenial groupings that would leave two-thirds of the land unscarred. It was to be "an environment in which Man and Nature, with mutual respect, look after each other in a biologically ordered way." A new-old coastal village was to grow at the north end of the site. People of every age and income would live happily together. Nothing at all was to be built on the far edges of the ocean-fronting cliffs, in order to preserve the most spectacular aspect of the site.

(The village became a golf course. Shoreline lots turned out to be too valuable not to be sold. Prospective buyers insisted on large separate pieces of land—which earned land salesmen higher commissions—instead of unified clusters. Individual lots sold for $100,000. The last condominium to be transferred went for $200,000. Utopia became Utopia, Ltd.)

Lawrence Halprin: "Al Boeke called me one day and said, 'I have this ten miles of coast that I need a plan for. Would you be interested?' That was the first that I had heard of the Sea Ranch. When he told me where it was, I said, 'Gee, I'd love to.' I had spent a lot of time there; I love it very much. I like it better than Big Sur. There's a 'boutique' quality of people down there who haven't come yet to the north coast—at least not when we started the Sea Ranch. There's an Indian reservation, local foresters and sheep ranchers and fishermen. I enjoy all that very much.

"And so I said yes, indeed. And then we talked a little about it, and I said there are two things I would like to do.

"First, I said, could we possibly look at this not just as one more planning issue, a question of land use—but in terms of a whole new approach to land planning, which would have to do with the ecology of an area? That was a new word for most people at the time. But I had basically started out as an 'ecologist.' Right out of prep school I went to Israel and worked on a kibbutz. I lived there for a long time, right on the Dead Sea. I came back a raving Zionist. (I still am.) I went to Cornell and took courses in agricultural sciences, always with the idea of going back to Israel to live. I took courses in the relation of plant and animal life—in 'ecology,' in fact.

"But the war came along, and I decided somewhere along the line I wanted to be an artist as well, and I ended up in California. When this thing came along I said to Al, 'The first thing I would like to do is apply some of these principles to your ten miles of coast. I would like us to look at this land in a fresh way, as if it's a raw material we really treasure, and that we want to use in the best possible way.'

"And he said, 'Fine.' He was a really creative client, a collaborator. And Fred Simpich, the president of Oceanic, was very enlightened too. He had a profound love of land, of landscape; he wanted to do good things. As luck would have it, I had this pure ecologist on my staff, who could handle all the technical aspects—

soil and drainage and so forth. So we were set. What Boeke wanted most was *not* to suburbanize the place. In that sense I didn't have any problem. We were on the same side.

"So we embarked. And my second request was: could I please get some architects on board who were really sympathetic? Because if we didn't do that we were going to be dead ducks. All the planning in the world isn't worth a damn unless you get it articulated right.

"He said, 'Sure. Who would you like to have?' And I said, 'Joe Esherick and Chuck Moore.'"

Joseph Esherick was and is the most respected living practitioner of the Bay Region style of domestic architecture, chairman of the department of architecture at Berkeley after Moore, chief inheritor of the Bernard Maybeck–William Wurster line. He had been a frequent collaborator with Halprin in the past. But Lawrence Halprin had never met Charles Moore when he first proposed his name. A few months earlier, he had been on a design jury to decide on the *Sunset* magazine–AIA Western Home Awards (which count for a good deal among western architects). Among the 325 entries, he had been so impressed by two little cabins Moore and his new Berkeley partners had designed (about the same time as Moore–Orinda) that he politicked among unsympathetic fellow jurors to get these rule-breaking, avant-garde shacks into the winners' circle. (Within a few years, there were so many Moore-ish shacks and Sea Ranch clones among the *Sunset* winners each round that some jurors protested.)

Moore, who was then thirty-eight, had founded a partnership in Berkeley a few months earlier with William Turnbull, then twenty-eight, of New York; Donlyn Lyndon, twenty-seven, of Los Angeles (the trio had become close friends at Princeton in the fifties); and Dick Whitaker, thirty-four, a former Berkeley graduate student. MLTW they decided to call themselves, democratically and cryptically.

Since that time, M, L, T, and W have designed dozens of prize-winning buildings, separately and together. Three of them have, at one time or another, served as heads of seven important architectural schools. Turnbull now has a successful San Francisco practice. Lyndon, a professor at Berkeley, maintains an office there. Whitaker is a dean at the University of Illinois' Chicago Circle campus. Moore is everywhere, doing everything.

But in 1963, they had nothing but time. They were overrich in ideas, but poor in commissions—two $10,000 cabins (and Charles's own house) hadn't paid many bills—and they wanted very much to make a mark. So they snapped at Halprin's offer to design a model set of clustered residences on one of the more awe-inspiring bluffs. Oceanic Properties would then use their building to show prospective buyers how chic a Sea Ranch vacation place could be. Esherick's office, meanwhile, was planning a model series of detached single-family houses tucked under a windrow nearby. The two firms worked independently, but the results came out looking astonishingly right and alike. Together they helped to establish the Sea Ranch idiom as an international mode.

M, L, T, and (to a lesser degree) W—with Moore as the first among equals, and a lot of help from their friends—devoted several unbroken months of their combined and harmonious skills to this dream project, on a dream site, for a dream client. The result, both Lyndon and Turnbull now believe, was "the best thing any of us has ever done." They played with sugar cubes on cardboard contour maps, drew up lists of ideal objectives, and juggled around all the radical, antimodernist ideas they had been toying with since Princeton and had experimented with in the few buildings they had actually managed to get up.

The result is at once astonishing and fitting. It achieved all of Boeke's and Halprin's utopian goals—and Oceanic Properties' worldly goals as well: the ten units in the cluster sold quickly. In the process it created a new ethic and a new aesthetic for American architecture. Suddenly it was O.K. to do serious buildings that were cheap looking, shacklike, defiant of symmetry and right angles, because they *worked*, and could—if you looked long enough—come to seem beautiful.

Condominium I at the Sea Ranch won several prizes. It was published in scores of magazines, newspapers, and books. It was imitated thousands of times. Partly in order to earn a return on their $5 million, but partly also because soon it became clear that they had fortuitously underwritten something historic, Oceanic Properties hired a skillful press agent who was able to persuade representatives of the national and international press to fly out to San Francisco. She met them at the airport, drove them up the coast, and sent them home searching out new metaphors for this instant classic structure: "perhaps" (wrote *Fortune*) "the roughest hewn and most romantic building since Fort Laramie." Values in American architecture have never been quite the same since.

Condo I came in at $250,000—$110,000 over budget, partly because of some overengineered superbeams the architects didn't *need*, but simply liked. The four partners shared 10 percent of that sum and paid off their draftsmen and assistants at about seventy-five cents an hour.

Charles Moore decided to buy the northwesternmost unit, with a vista of Pacific waves breaking over dark brown rock islands directly below its corner window, after it had served its time as a model home. By doing this, he guaranteed Unit 9's availability for publicity photographs, visiting architects and critics, and Charles's own students and guests.

He spent the summer of 1966 living in it himself, as he worked on plans for a faculty club for the University of California's Santa Barbara campus. Bill Hersey, his favorite draftsman, kept him company; Donlyn Lyndon was living at the time in another unit of the condominium; Bill Turnbull drove up from his home in Sausalito to join in design sessions. In 1970, Moore spent another summer at the Sea Ranch, this time with Turnbull, Lyndon, and Gerry Allen (one of his Yale students), working on a book they did together called *The Place of Houses*. Tina Beebe told me that Bill Turnbull, who did the book's marvelous drawings, "would come in at six A.M. and sit in the corner and draw his eyeballs out." (She had come to help with the book too, but ended up mostly cooking. "I made lots of blackberry pies.")

Charles Moore comes to the Sea Ranch nowadays four or five times a year for short stays, either driving all the way up from Los Angeles—his current base—or flying in to Monterey or San Francisco and then driving from there in a rented car. There is usually a gathering of the clan in December–January, when the whales are swimming south, sometime after the Charles Moore Memorial Birthday Party in Santa Monica, and Thanksgiving or Christmas at Saul and Mimi Weingarten's in Pebble Beach.

The trip up, by whichever route one takes, involves at least a last twenty-five miles on the cliffside curves of California's Highway 1. In thick fog, when only the yellow center line of the road is visible, the narrow uphill-downhill bends can be a nerve-straining ordeal. In clearer weather, the Pacific Ocean is almost always one's immediate companion, a vast spread of hammered gray or glittering blue that pulls one's eyes constantly from the road, roaring dully as it breaks against the rocks and islets in its midst, eating away with its white-edged tides at the steep western edge of America. Occasionally the road itself is hooded with foliage. After the 1982 and 1983 storms, long stretches were buried in slid mud, and chunks of its western roadway fell into the sea. North of Jenner, a hillside and seafront town at the mouth of the Russian River, a few farms, crossroads stores, and resorts interrupt the landscape with buildings. Cows and sheep still graze in the long grasses of the meadows and the rolling hills, which rise rapidly into forest on the east.

However much one expects it, the first glimpse of the now-famous silhouette comes as a surprise. The MLTW condominium rises from its oceanfront cliff like a more shapely cliff itself, answering the land forms, a cluster of deftly tumbled rocks half a mile across a cove of the sea. The shape, dominated by the sliced tower of Unit 10, the echoing angles of its eaveless prisms, and one long downsloping roof, is at once commanding and discreet, ordinary and refined. There is much about it in common with neighboring barns. Its dark weathered shapes seem to have grown naturally, like the outbuildings of a farm—when you need a shed, you add a shed. In the right light, the building (silent, dark, totemic) looks as if it had grown there, like a tree, or had been built ages ago—until one realizes how artfully, and with what conscious care, these lines, planes, and volumes have been disposed.

Condominium I is the first building of the Sea Ranch seen by drivers from the south. (The Halprins' five-acre estate commands an even more spectacular view, but is invisible to passersby.) Along with the sign of a stylized ram's head, it announces one's entry to this compromised utopia. The private drive, winding down past the buildings of a small store and lodge, ends inside the palisaded shelter of a parking court, where the owners' cars are hidden from view. A further, ruggedly landscaped interior courtyard slopes steeply down to an opening onto the sea. Most of the individuated residences present their blank, Fort Laramie walls to this, their private space; their windows face the ocean.

Charles Moore's "vacation" home is the first on your right inside the parking court. A high blank redwood wall conceals a small entry court. Opening the door to the house reveals astonishing space games that are repeated, with variations, in all ten units of the complex.

Twenty-four-foot-square boxes, framed in rough, massive ten-by-ten-inch timbers—which occasionally cut diagonally through space—rise to whatever height the great oversloping roof allows. The high and low spaces this yields are then punched out for windows, projecting bays, window-seat alcoves, and solaria, positioned to seize most felicitously the sun (when there is sun) and the rampaging sea. Inside the high box are set two almost free-standing pieces of architectural furniture: a floating, unwalled bedroom loft raised on four wooden columns, which shelters a fireplace nook underneath; and a two-story "cabinet," into which Moore deftly fit a kitchen below, bath and storage above; a tight, steep stairway joins the two. (Higher still, up a ladder, is a sleeping loft.) Minute balconies and bridges link the upper levels of these two things. Depending on where they are set inside the box, these units (which are sometimes brightly painted, to assert their status as "furniture") carve out the interior space, direct the changing views, and define one's movement and experiences inside.

Not everyone confronting the building the first time feels pleased or at ease. A group of college freshmen I took to the Sea Ranch in 1978 admitted to a wide range of emotional responses:

The Sea Ranch buildings on the bluff fly in the face of nature [wrote one], and therefore common sense. They jut into the air where nothing else does. They have sharply angled corners and flat surfaces where everything else is gradual and rounded. They use wood where only sod and stone exist. The Sea Ranch buildings are no more appropriate on that stretch of Sonoma coastline than tin conning towers are at the South Pole. The only satisfactory sight of that coastline would be an uninterrupted one, just as the only reasonable sight of the South Pole would be white.

As I roamed about the lower level and around the upper floors via narrow passageways and steep ladders, I felt the way a mouse must feel wandering through a maze. The Moore house is simply not livable.

At times my eyes caught stagefright. The house vacillated between being playful and nightmarish, like a disorienting labyrinth or a "fun house" at an amusement park. Once within the walls of weathered wood, under the heavy beams, I could no longer feel where I was in space. With the entry as the only door, I felt a sense of entrapment in all this seeming spatial freedom.

There were no doors (except to the bathroom) to separate the different living spaces. At first I found this disturbing, even threatening. But when I started crawling into the cubbyholes and climbing up to the sleeping loft, I got the feeling that I was in a playhouse or a treehouse, and that this was another adventure. These spaces act as vehicles into a fantasy world: Moore's "master bedroom," with its canvas drops and ropes, might be a ship sailing on the sea, or a mountain high above the world. Everything above the ground floor feels like islands in space, instead of com-partments.

One of the things I like most about Moore's house is its playfulness. I spent a lot of my boyhood building forts in trees, under tables, in old barns, in rock quarries, anywhere. There's something about the steep lad-ders, the high little nests, the dark hatches covered by sliding doors, and the floating, crow's-nest bedrooms that recalls those early magic, fantasy feelings. Have you ever seen the Swiss Family Robinson Tree House at Disneyland? It has exactly the same kind of appeal—like living in a jungle gym.

Fantasy, playfulness, freedom: Moore's houses are more free than any-thing I've ever lived in. They're uniquely liberated and liberating.

In 1982, four of the original ten owners (including Charles Moore) still held on to their condominium units. Most residents, new or old, profess an almost sacred dedication to the place. They tend to be ardent devotees of the original Sea Ranch ideal. Several bear emotional scars from the long fight against the developers, who at one time proposed crowding fifty-six identical units alongside theirs, and the California Coastal Commission, which has ordered Sea Ranch residents to provide public access to "their" bluffs and beaches. Unit 10 caught fire recently; dry rot and moles invaded from below. One window in Unit 4 cracked in a storm; there have been some leaks. ("Don't all prize-winning buildings leak?" asked owner Bill Clement.) In 1982, owners paid $100 a month (in addi-tion to $35 a month Sea Ranch Association dues) for maintenance and services. But according to Clement, "the building has never been in better shape."

One traveling house party, leading up to one New Year's Eve, can stand for a great many. The editor of the *New York Times* Home Section is supervising a radical, but apparently ineffectual job of housecleaning and closet clearing, trying to empty the place of all sorts of baskets, toys, puzzles, and junk. Things she believes would fit better into Charles's current Los Angeles perch (Moore #6, described later) she directs a visiting student to carry out to the architect's beat-up Pinto. A former student, now an architect in New York, arrives with a load of metal light fixtures he has designed, for everyone to admire. Lee Burns, the owner of Charles's prize Los Angeles house (and a colleague of his at UCLA) has commanded one of the window seats overlooking the rocks and foam. Four of Charles's fantasy landscapes are being handed around—flying pennants on steep turrets, fairytale bridges to gemlike islands. One, already watercolored, will go to his sister and brother-in-law as this season's holiday gift, to join a series of dream landscapes on their living-room wall.

The ostensible host stands in the middle of it all, looking a bit lost. He makes futile gestures of help with the housecleaning, joins in half a dozen conversations, makes and receives numerous calls over a phone with a very long cord on the kitchen counter.

"The Rome Prize on the sixteenth? They told me the thirteenth. Tell Giurgola I'll be in Berlin. Let me see: Frankfurt the fifteenth, the sixteenth is a Friday."

"It's that Frenchman. You know, about that place the Arabs wanted in the Bahamas? Well, if he didn't call back, it's too late now. He'll arrive and we'll all be gone."

"Right. The PSA pick-up area. Sixth to the ninth. I'll be there with Dona."

("We refuse to have a telephone at our cabin at the ranch," Larry Halprin tells me. "But Chuck is different. He couldn't live without it. His phone rings like crazy when he's up there." "He can't relax," said another sometime partner. "Even at Sea Ranch there are always ten other people around and fifteen phone calls a day.")

More guests arrive, bearing food, wine, gifts. An old Princeton classmate, with his new poet-wife. (She is later to sprain her ankle falling down the precipitous stairs to the upper reaches of the house.) A professor of architecture from New Mexico, and his wife, arrive. A distinguished Berkeley architect—slim, southern, dressed in determinedly electric colors—arrives with his banker-friend. They bring champagne, a ham, a turkey. The Berkeley architect nips into the tiny kitchen to make his special mayonnaise, which is a signal for the whole company, directed by the *Times* editor, to sit on the floor and begin cracking and then eating a mountain of fresh crab. They wolf down salad and French bread spread with Stilton butter, empty bottles of white wine, pile up crab shells on a cloth. The talk is personal and professional, wide ranging and allusive, with little darts tossed now and then at Graves, Meier, Eisenman, Frampton, Venturi—the current East Coast architectural elite.

(Mimi Moore Weingarten remembers the time Charles invited her family—"all six of us"—to use his Sea Ranch place for two weeks. "When we arrived there were already three or four others, all staying over. Then *eighteen* more arrived while we were there. Tina came down from Oregon with her owl. He took them all out to dinner at the Gualala Hotel. It must have cost thousands!")

After this particular midday feast, most of the men in the crowd head up the road to the Northern Recreation Center, to swim in the turquoise waters and sweat in the sauna. Inside the sauna, the talk is of a pink villa in Cuernavaca, audiences in Barcelona, plans for an exhibition in Frankfurt. Arrangements are made to stow surplus guests at a friend's house up the hill. Back at Unit 9, the nonathletes have prepared a second feast: baked ham and potatoes au gratin for seventeen. Champagne is opened to celebrate the New York editor's birthday.

After dinner—the guests cook, the guests clean up—Charles is presented with a gift of an old geography-class chart of land forms, rolled on a stick. It is instantly hung near the door. Later, sitting on chairs or the floor near the window-seat corner, most of the company stay up till after 2:00 A.M. drinking more wine and singing old songs, the words to all of which Charles Moore knows by heart. Some of the singers are drunk, some glowingly near. The younger members of the party look on in silence. Moore and his friends work their way through the more obscure airs of *Kiss Me, Kate*, Noel Coward classics, the "Marseillaise," two Shirley Temple hits (which Charles does in a Shirley Temple voice, with coy winks and gestures), college fight songs, Christmas carols, Irish ballads, and propaganda hits from World War II ("I drill the rivets! I buy the bonds!"). Charles Moore is sitting cross-legged like a Buddha, back against the view window, happy to be onstage among his friends. The Pacific Ocean keeps crashing below, moonlighted. Ever genial, ever deferential, Charles accompanies the uphill contingent to their quarters for the night, leaving his own bed for other guests.

HOUSES 4 and 5 (Moore–New Haven and Moore–Essex) were both built long before Charles Moore was born in 1925. In each case, what he did was to buy an ordinary little nineteenth-century house and then remake the interior into something entirely his own.

In 1965, Moore was persuaded by President Kingman Brewster of Yale to leave Berkeley and become his department chairman in New Haven. Moore's first year in Connecticut was spent in a rented modern house designed by one of his new colleagues. "It was definitely not me," he admits. "Very . . . architectural. I hated it." He was also fed up with commuting and wanted to live within walking distance of his office in the ponderous gray fortress of the Art and Architecture Building, designed by his immediate predecessor as department chairman. A real estate agent found him a narrow clapboarded box circa 1860, at 403 Elm Street in New Haven: two full stories, plus attic and basement, a nice Victorian-federal porch directly onto the street, and a minuscule backyard "with its panoramic view of the adjacent Holiday Inn." It looked (Charles has written) exactly like a typical child's drawing of a house: high and narrow, with a single-peaked roof, a brick chimney on top, a real and obvious front door, and large-paned, double-hung windows set where they ought to be. The poor old lady who had owned it had died, and Charles got the house by offering the full asking price: $14,100.

Inside, he created an illusionistic fantasy-fun house no one passing by 403 Elm could ever have imagined. For five years of Yale students and friends, "Elm Street" came to mean this wild and crazy house they helped Professor Moore to build, or partied in after it was done. Actually, it was never "done." He kept changing it as long as he lived in it—sometimes *during* parties—using the house as a full-scale laboratory for experiments in space, color, optical effects, and visual wit.

At first, he left the house alone. "It was pleasant the way it was. I wasn't at all sure that I would do very much to it. I didn't want to gut it and make a Mies van der Rohe out of it. I wanted to have that funny little old house and play with it."

But after six months he had decided the ceilings were too low. With them in place, there was no way the house could yield the kind of celebratory vertical space, surplus *overhead* space (as well as the visible play of levels) he had come to need. So rather than tearing out walls, he punched great holes in the floors and ceilings and inserted three vertical tubes, or "interior towers," seven or eight feet square and twenty or more feet high. Two of them descended to the basement. One rose the full height of the roof. All were walled in double layers of plywood, which was cut out in fanciful shapes, so that one was always looking from one strange space into parts of several others. Two of the towers were skylighted. Together with the house's original large windows front and back, and a dazzling array of light fixtures inside, this allowed for a spectacular and constantly changing play of light over the interior spaces.

Interior Tower 1, originally painted metallic gold and named Howard ("after a dog I once knew in New Orleans"), plunged from the main floor, just inside the entrance, to Moore's office and studio below. Through cut-out sections of gigantic circles, the visitor could peer down at the bald dome of the architect at his desk. (Or, when it was hung up, at him lying in a rope hammock. "I hardly ever used it. You were too much onstage.") Some of the curves were cut to an eighteen-foot radius. The idea was to imply almost infinitely expanded space.

Along one foyer wall, colossal cutouts of numbers (1 through 6) could be moved back and forth in front of a window on sliding plywood panels. Why? Because cut-out numbers had appeared to one of Moore's students in a dream. Down below, the master of the manor—stared at by a life-sized Shirley Temple cutout—had the exhilarating luxury of all that overhead space, where his ideas and imagination could literally soar aloft. Below one segment of a circle, he hung the portraits of two eighteenth-century Vermont ancestors that he carries about from house to house.

Interior Tower 2 was called Berengaria—after the unhappy wife of King Richard the Lion-Hearted (or an early Cunard liner named after her, or one of Charles's cats). It rose, silver-lined, over a back corner of the living room to the full height of the house, punctured by fifteen openings and a skylight. Some of the openings were glazed, some were nothing but cut-out voids that stood behind the old house's own windows. Others served as niches for Moore's models and toys. One large opening was filled with a wonderful piece of leaded stained glass. The whole high space could be set shimmering into multicolored light effects by a wired eighteenth-century Mexican lantern that hung from its peak. One reason for giving these spaces fanciful names is that no functional name (loggia? sitting room? conservatory?) made any sense. They served no practical function.

Interior Tower 3, Ethel—I don't know who Ethel was—rose over a basement-level breakfast area and alongside a new kitchen, at the rear of the house. Light poured in from a bright array of windows, glass doors, a small skylight, and a greenhouse roof over the garden stairs, then reflected off walls painted yellow and orange. This tall box was cut open for a large curved and angled opening to the stairs, circular cutouts between the inner and outer plywood layers, and miscellaneous shelves. The stairway alongside became a game of its own. At the landing, a crouching oversized figure of a man cut from a Volkswagen billboard stared out the window; chunks of Victorian architecture sat in pure white spaces; a diagonal crossbeam stopped in midair halfway across. Between the kitchen tower and the adjacent lower-ceilinged dining room stood two five-foot-high classical columns, their composite-order capitals originally studded with red glass bicycle reflectors. They were there to prop up an old overhead joist (which was only discovered when Ethel was cut: "We liked it, so we left it"). But since the columns didn't quite reach the joist, adjustable house jacks, or Lally columns –which look like skinny telescoping metal pipes with flute holes—were inserted between the tops of the columns and the bottom of the joist.

This eclectic, disorderly kind of what-the-hell inclusiveness, regardless of periods or "appropriate" styles, marked a new, slightly manic turning in Moore's approach to the making of places, which not all his previous admirers were prepared to accept. At the time, it seemed of a piece with a great many other willfully shocking manifestations of the mid-1960s. Like many of them (pop and op art, "happenings," radical-chic costume), Moore's "supermannerism," as the critics came to call it, quickly degenerated into trendiness, until the whole once-radical effort came to seem a transient and superficial kick. But 403 Elm Street—which, as Moore rebuilt it, no longer exists—was at heart as important an experiment as Sir John Soane's 1834 house (now museum) in Lincoln's Inn Fields, London. The Soane Museum is a very personal "statement" (as architects now call their more distinctive works) not unlike Moore–New Haven in its vertical space games, its illu-

sionistic trickery, and its loving incorporation of historical fragments. But 403 Elm was definitely gaga as well, a fun house in the
amusement-park sense.

"Bob Rosenblum came when it was first being finished and announced that it was a piece of contemporary sculpture and not
architecture at all," Moore said to an interviewer in 1972. "Those
plywood walls, with all kinds of shapes and colors, are not very
serious. They're made fairly cheaply and very quickly. We just
opened them up with a saber saw. They are not travertine, they're
not pigskin like Philip Johnson's bathroom. They are statements of
pleasure and prejudice. It really becomes important just in terms
of my style and pocketbook. They don't represent a big investment
of concern, but are a response to fleeting things, light and air. And
when they don't seem to be accurate responses anymore, they can
be torn down and replaced easily. I like to think that this house is,
in the best sense, trivial."

In 1969 *Playboy* magazine sent out a team of models ("the ones
who kept their clothes on were more interesting to talk to than the
ones who didn't," Moore remembers), to help them illustrate an
article entitled "A Playboy Pad: Amid Connecticut's Early Americana, a Bachelor Architect Fashions a Flipped-Out Domain."

Playboy made much of the light shows, the huge neon 42 (a birthday creation) over the sink, the elaborate sound system (including
an antique juke box stocked with vintage 78s), and the bachelor
architect's spectacular third-floor bedroom. The bed was enclosed
in a star-spangled wooden box. Lying on it, one stared up, at first,
into a painting of angels floating in clouds. Then that was replaced
by a photocopy of a Giovanni Bernini drawing of the interior of a
renaissance dome. A nude model was photographed relaxing in
the adjacent sauna, as if she were a typical member of Professor
Moore's entourage. "All I need to do is set out the ice and glasses
and the house seems to do the entertaining for me," *Playboy*
quoted the professor as saying.

Partly because Moore himself has since turned to more tranquil
spaces and colors, and more conservative uses of the past ("He's
been mellowing out beautifully," said one friend; "he's almost
serene"), his first Yale house, along with a few similar gut-'em-and-
gaud-'em experiments, may end up being seen primarily as evidence of his participation in the psychedelic, anything-goes aspect
of the sixties. It now seems of a piece with his rococo mustache of

the period (a bald forty-year-old's version of long hair?) and the liberal do-gooder work he and his Yale students performed, designing and building camp shelters and community centers in poverty pockets about the East.

The little house at 403 Elm is still there, looking from the outside much as it did during its heyday. Charles Moore spent, he estimates, about $7,000 on its sculptural innovations, then sold the house (for about what he put into it) to a young couple. "I think it saved their marriage," he says. "At least, they had their first baby there."

But then they resold it to a man less entranced by neo-Mooreishness than were they (or *Playboy*, the *New York Times Magazine*, *Progressive Architecture*, *Art in America*, *House and Garden*, *Realités*, *Deutsche Bauzeitung*, *Kenchiku Bunku*, and *Design Quarterly*, all of which had honored his "hip-baroque" landmark). "Why on earth he bought it I'll never know. He spent more money undoing my work than I ever spent doing it."

A few traces still remain—a Vasarely-like op-art 3 painted on the back fence, Fred Hearst's yellow metal pipe sculpture in front, the stained-glass window in Tower Howard. But the new owner, in June 1981, insisted to me over the phone that the house was no longer worth my visiting. "It's been totally gutted and redone. I'm trying to get it back the way it was. It was impossible—like living in a stage set." When I mentioned the visible traces of 1966–71, he all but apologized. "I haven't been well the past two years. Otherwise I would have finished de-Moore-ing it."

ONE reason for the exaggerated joyfulness of 403 Elm (according to *House and Garden*) was "to separate you from the barren urban setting." Much as he loved the house, and many of his Yale students, Moore came to despise New Haven. He left the city in 1971 to move to Moore #5 because the neighborhood itself had grown too depressing. Over one period of four months, the house was broken into eight times. Ron Filson, then a Yale student and Charles's live-in caretaker, was sleeping in the little guest cove over the sauna one night in 1969 (Charles was in California) when he was awakened by a shoe kicking at his head. After a short fight he pretended to be knocked out, while four burglars ransacked the house. Then one of them decided Filson would be able to identify them. So they tore out the phone, came back to the bedroom, tied him up, and debated whether or not to kill him. In the end, they decided just to tear gas and knife him.

Dona Guimaraes once stayed at 403 Elm for a weekend with a friend. When they walked in—Charles had left a key under the mat—her friend (a *House and Garden* editor) was enchanted by the new casual oriental decorating scheme. "Silks, carpets, scarves were tossed all about," said Miss Guimaraes. "That looming creature from the Volkswagen ad was lurking in the stairs. The famous family portraits were ever so slightly askew. Instead of fifteen little toys on the table, there must have been fifty. One perfect orange had been left on the marble slab. Denise thought it all so luxurious, so Asiatic, so *raffiné*. She was convinced it was a new decorating phase Charles was going through, but she wondered how on earth her photographer could get it all in."

"I didn't leave it this way!" Charles burst out when he arrived later that evening. "My God. I've been burgled again."

The thieves had borrowed, then replaced, the key under the mat and had helped themselves to (among other things) Aunt Bus's silver. In the process, they redecorated a house already so delirious that it was hard for outsiders to tell whether or not it had been ransacked.

So when Bill Grover, a student-become-partner at Charles Moore Associates, discovered a disused 1874 wood-boring-equipment factory in the village of Essex, Connecticut—a tranquil, leafy crossroads forty miles east of New Haven—he began to lobby Charles to buy the old brick building and move the whole enterprise there. ("Everyone wanted to get out of ugly New Haven," Moore recalls. "Bill thought we could be lords of the manor in Essex.") The original two-story brick building had huge loft spaces that could be converted into a design studio. Downstairs worked a classic New England woodcrafter. "I thought that would be just great," said Grover. "He could just mill us out a molding any time we needed one." The rapids of the Falls River run behind the building. One of Bill Grover's dreams was to get the old water-power turbine running again so that the property could produce its own energy; but a serious flood in 1982 damaged the back of the building and put an end to such plans.

Along with the old factory, Charles Moore purchased the quaint Victorian houses that stand at either end of it, bookend fashion, completing the block. The two at the east end he rented out. The one on the west end—which had served variously as a residence, lawyer's office, union hall, and storeroom—he eventually converted into Moore #5.

As at New Haven, he left the exterior almost alone. Even more of a dollhouse than 403 Elm Street, Moore–Essex is a two-story gabled cottage sheathed in wood clapboard and fishscale siding, with some intricately milled bargeboards under the eaves, and a jolly wooden finial at the peak. Some windows were enlarged, and the whole was painted a combination of soft pink and plum.

Between the cottage and the factory ran a tall shed, which Moore gutted in order to fit in one of those vertical, self-contained pieces of architectural furniture he so fancies. This one comprised a tiny kitchen and study alcove below, and an open bathroom above; even the toilet enclosure had an interior window. These functional spaces fitted around a mock-monumental staircase, decorated with red, white, and blue stripes and large appliqué stars. Alongside the entry vestibule was an unusable open space, a sort of light well about six by seven feet across, squeezed in between the shed and the neighboring factory building. Moore opened sliding glass doors onto this diminutive space, floored it with pebbles, and painted the opposite concrete block wall with a noble trompe l'oeil copy of one of Giulio Romano's sixteenth-century Mantuan windows. (The palazzo from which the window was borrowed is full of similar illusionistic frescoes.) With its oversized, rusticated surround, the make-believe window enhanced and enlarged the tiny "court"; but it remained primarily a wry art-historical conceit.

From the top of the stairs, a ramped balcony led to the real booby dazzler of the house. Nothing in Moore #5 was quite as outrageous as the vertical tubes of Moore #4, but the Pyramid Room came close.

If you look at the back of a dollar bill, you'll see in the left-hand circle the obverse side of the Great Seal of the United States, which was adopted by the Continental Congress in 1782. It's a weird, occult-looking thing, more Masonic or Rosicrucian than early American. A stone pyramid (inscribed MDCCLXXVI) stands in a vast, empty field, sliced off about one-fifth down from the top. In place of the missing peak, a triangle hovers in the air, framing one huge eye, and surrounded by rays. Above it are the words *Annuit Coeptis*

(Favor Bold Undertakings). In a scroll below are the words *Novus Ordo Seclorum* (The New Order of the Ages).

Upstairs in an old house, in this peaceful corner of New England, Charles Willard Moore decided to rebuild this pyramid out of wood. Very large, very green, and very strange, it sat in the middle of the upper room of his house in Essex, rising about twelve feet toward the planked and steeply sloped ceiling. The words of the Latin inscription were painted on the ceiling, over the missing apex of the pyramid. In place of the eye in a triangle, Charles hung a golden-ball light fixture inside a transparent plastic "point."

Having contrived his U.S. Seal pyramid, Charles then proceeded to slice it open. On one side it was opened up to enclose and half hide his huge, often messy bed. On the other—the "living-room" side—it was cut open to reveal, as if in section, its own interior: a magical display case for some of the owner's toy trains, Kachina dolls, ceramic horses, and Mexican models. Dozens of toy soldiers stood on the floor of the pyramid, or marched up and down the tunnels and caves cut into the interior wall, like the tunnels and caves of an ant farm. (The reference Moore had in mind was to the Great Pyramid at Gizeh.) The whole thing was then painted "like a watermelon"—watermelon green outside, watermelon pink inside, and lighter tones of rose, white, and soft green as one moved from flesh to rind.

Shelves, baskets, hooks, and alcoves throughout the room contained more of Moore's treasures. The whole house seemed a minimuseum of his obsessions. One recognizes in photos many of the characteristic *objets* and appurtenances—the phone on a basket, the draftsman's lamp over the bed, the chests and skins and pottery churches—that go with him from house to house.

The firm of Moore Grover Harper—in which Moore eventually became one of seven equal partners (although less actively involved in most of the firm's work than the resident six)—still operates, happily and successfully, out of the reconverted factory in Essex. A giant moosehead, gift of a happy client, presides over the stairs, and an icon of Dr. Charles Willard Moore, F.A.I.A., is enshrined in the toilet, behind the glass of an antique fortune-telling machine. For many years, the drafting tables were pushed back every Halloween, the studio was decorated like Mr. Fezziwig's warehouse, and another festive Charles Moore Birthday Party was held, whether the master was in residence or not.

But the watermelon-colored pyramid and its tiny inhabitants are gone. The little pink house, stripped down and restored back to normal, is now rented to tenants.

CHARLES MOORE'S current residence is the front third of an ingenious tile-roofed triplex, stuccoed in soft ocher yellow, which stands across the street from the parking lot of the Mormon Temple in Los Angeles. Elsewhere this building might look unusual; but seen in the same coup d'oeil as the temple—a Wizard of Oz palace of pointy white towers with gold trumpeting angels at the top—the Moore–Rogger–Hofflander condominium looks positively Georgian.

Private houses near the UCLA campus in west Los Angeles—where Moore has been on the architecture faculty since 1975—are as expensive as any in the United States. Vacant building lots are nonexistent.

During his first three years in Los Angeles, Charles Moore lived in a series of rented apartments, each filled to overflowing with his library, his papers, and warehouse loads of treasured trivia: the toys, the models, the Mexican ceramics, the tin soldiers, the wooden chests. This 50-by-125-foot lot on Selby Avenue became available when the house on it was demolished "by accident." Moore purchased the lot for $82,500, and persuaded two other UCLA faculty members and their wives to come in as partners on a building he would design to house them all.

The plan he came up with managed to fit in three separate and very different residences—plus little gardens, the mandated setback, and a space for six cars—by interlocking rooms, stairways, passages, and levels like a Chinese wooden puzzle.

A wrought-iron gate, in the pattern of an off-center sunburst, leads to a walled courtyard concentrically paved with brick. From a long single slope of tile roof project windowed cubes at three different levels, hinting at strange goings-on within. Paired chimneys reach dramatically skyward. The sliced stucco face of the house nearest the court is punctured by an attention-seizing arc of triangular windows—"falling windows," Moore calls them (he has repeated the idea in two other houses). Askew and incomplete, they evoke fanlights, or arches, or something vaguely Roman.

I first visited Charles Moore's Los Angeles house during a happy birthday party for one of his associates. (He was, as usual, away.) Entering through a tiny enclosed porch (officially a parking space)—in which stands one of those mammoth sliced-in-half iron submarine buoys Roger Bailey disliked so much—one has immediately to climb a steep set of stairs, which leads, after a landing (kitchen to right, dining alcove to left) to another, wider set of stairs (living room off), which leads to yet another set, inside a strange sort of library-loft. Bedrooms, bath, storage spaces are all hidden away.

Guests were standing and sitting, eating and drinking, at all levels of these stairs, along which Moore had poised hundreds of tiny fragile objects, which seemed doomed to be brushed off in the crush. Many of them are the same toys that once filled Sea Ranch corners, New Haven niches, the green pyramid in Essex. They seem to copulate and proliferate when one's back is turned. In this mountain pass of a building, at once soaring and cramped, the found objects include chunks of Victorian architecture set into the very structure: an intricately scroll-cut wooden bracket supports a transverse beam; the stairways mount dynamically toward a voluptuous arched pediment, salvaged from an Oakland convent, framing nothing but space (and a section of bookshelf).

Since that evening, I have identified the triple-decker pad with the conversations that surrounded me—thin and brittle, knowing and allusive—which seemed to fit perfectly into this vertical museum of effects and *objets*. Even empty of people, Moore's third of the Selby Avenue triplex giggles, weeps, sings, and (from some angles) threatens. It appears to defy repose or domesticity and offers very little clear working space, unless one works in bed or at the dining table. It is hard to believe that many buildings have been designed here, many articles and lectures have been written here, many guests have been welcomed.

The whole three-household building cost around $300,000—a bargain for the place, space, and time. Construction was hamstrung by intransigent building inspectors, who refused to believe that anyone actually wanted to erect anything so defiantly odd—even in west LA. They insisted on extravagant safety measures more suitable for a three-hundred-unit apartment house than a triplex; contradicted their own orders with others still more strange; canceled the large overhead light shafts ("fire traps!"); and forced Moore to build a separate enclosed staircase, which he uses for storage shelves, alongside the illegal one that virtually forms his home. The wife of one of his Selby Avenue partners had to use her influence at city hall to get the thing built at all. More recently, Partners Three decided they could no longer stand their third of all this spatial excitement, so they had their unit totally gutted and de-Moored, redone "tastefully" and traditionally by somebody else.

How much can one learn of a person from his private quarters? Some of Charles Moore's homes seem to have had no private space—the bathtub open to view, the bed perched up on poles or tucked into hollow prisms—except as the whole house was demonstrably "his." But Selby Avenue does have its inner sanctum. Totally hidden behind a galvanized-metal box (which turns out to be his closet) lies a perfectly ordinary bed-and-bathroom suite. One squeezes sideways through a door in the metal box, then walks through his clothes to enter the room. (The closet, open to the bedroom, contains an extensive but conservative wardrobe in extra large, plus a dozen pairs of shoes. Moore—no fashion plate—dresses up in a blue blazer and gray slacks, dresses down in tan chinos and a striped Oxford shirt.)

A dark-wood five-drawer chest with intricate ring pulls holds piles of clean shirts and underwear, ready to be stuffed in a suitcase for tomorrow morning's plane. A double bed rests on a box platform (blue sheets, hand-woven orange throw). Over it hangs a collage of newspaper-printed cloth strips and half a real yardstick. To the left of the bed—the working side—is a marvelous cabinet of twelve narrow glass-fronted drawers full of tiny cars and people, beads, cookie cutters, stationery, and correspondence, with surplus correspondence piled on top (under an electronic take-your-own-blood-pressure kit). On two big baskets alongside the bed rest two telephones—one private, one office—and the current unopened mail, brought up by the young house sitter–assistant whom Charles keeps on as guard, host, and general factotum, and who lives in a separate room under the stairs. A large draftsman's lamp swings over the bed from the bookshelf wall to the left, which holds a basic library on architecture of perhaps five hundred books, as well as volumes on travel, gardens, and model tin figures. (The shelves at the upper end of the main house hold another fifteen hundred books.)

On the right side of the bed (from the sleeper's point of view) another wonderful trunk with many cleverly fitted wooden drawers rests atop a carved Mexican chest. A chair, a wastebasket. Outside a glass door, a canvas deck chair invites to a small balcony over the court. At the foot of the bed, three smaller chests. Along with Mexican folk pottery, model buildings, toy animals, and tin figures, wooden chests are evidently one of his collector's obsessions. On a shelf above the clothes chest are ranged binders full of lecture notes and unfinished manuscripts. Where these get written I cannot conceive.

A long separate room, hidden above the building inspector's side staircase, contains the fifty thousand-plus colored slides Charles is forever adding to and hiring new people to try to organize. It is, obviously, a hopeless task.

The correspondence that piles up alongside the bed comes to Moore from all over the country and the world, channeled to his latest home address from UCLA, the Urban Innovations Group (a professional design unit created by the university, where some of his design projects are based), Moore Ruble Yudell (his Santa Monica partnership), Moore Grover Harper in Connecticut, and his collaborators in San Francisco and New Orleans. A tiny fraction of it gets answered. A small part of it deals with actual business affairs: design competitions, scheduled lectures, work in progress, happy and unhappy clients. Some of it is like everyone's mail—bills, rubbish, subscription and membership renewals, cards and letters from genuine friends. Most of it is fan mail or requests for free services from some of the thousands of people who have met, known, or admired him—students, clients, colleagues, hosts, people who have heard him speak, or read something he wrote, or fallen in love with him or with one of his buildings.

They want him to write letters of recommendation for fellowships and teaching jobs, lecture to their gatherings, sit on panels and design juries, read their manuscripts and books, come to their exhibits and parties, donate drawings and design posters. Drop by for dinner next time you're in town. Find my daughter a place to stay in LA. Lend me some slides of your work. Approve of my new translations. Let us use the Sea Ranch condo. Get us into the Krishnamurti house. Stay with us in Italy. Write me an introduction. Sign our petition.

MOORE #6 is not likely to be the last in the series, or the archi-tect's permanent resting place. For the last two years, he has been building a cabin in the mountains north of Los Angeles, which he will share with his second cousin, Martha Kirkpatrick; and he has been searching for a New Orleans pied à terre, which he will share with Arthur Anderson, the twenty-five-year-old architect from Kan-sas City who worked with him on the world's fair design.

Aware of my mixed feelings about the hyperverticality of his Los Angeles aerie, Charles Moore defiantly boasted that his and Mar-tha's cabin near Tejon Pass (about seventy-five miles from UCLA, on the way to Bakersfield) was "the stairiest one yet." Indeed it was. Only sixteen feet wide, by about forty feet long, it descends a steep hillside site between tall pines in a series of four-foot stages, with decks projecting on both sides for the Piños canyon view.

The front view is of a plain wooden box rising abruptly out of a nearly unclimbable slope. Two simple window squares and a metal chimney flue recall little Moore houses of twenty years before. From the road below, forty-four unrailed outside wooden steps (in two switchbacks) lead to the front door and a small living room with built-in couch and black metal fireplace. Two more sets of stairs inside, along the left wall, expand curiously outward as they rise, like a row of books of increasing *width* as well as height. These are gray-carpeted down their side edges as well as on the treads, and railed by two freestanding chrome bars. These two Art Deco gray-and-silver piles are precisely mirrored in form by matching sets of plain wooden stairs outside, moving from deck to deck.

The first set of eight inside steps leads up to a dining area, partly opened at the sides. The next leads to a kitchen and bath, with a rubberized "bathmat" floor. From the kitchen level a third set of steps—this makes seventy in all, from car door to bedside—dou-bles back up to a pair of bedrooms (Charles's and Martha's) over the dining area, which project slightly beyond the side walls of the box. The shed roof (made of corrugated asphalt) follows the steep hillslope to the upper bedroom wall, then turns back down in an abrupt, uneven gable at the kitchen–bath level.

The interior particle-board walls (somewhat crudely installed) are painted in wide bands of what Moore called "bad Victorian" colors, inspired by painter Frederick E. Church's exotic dining room at Olana on the Hudson (1874). As the house levels rise, these color bands maintain their horizontal places, beginning with a two-foot stripe of spicy rust at the bottom, past a three-foot mud-colored band, to a four-foot band of gray, then to a grayish blue-violet that rises to the roof peak: from warm earth to cool sky, each band separated by a narrow chrome strip, repeating the sleek line of the handrails. The transverse partition walls are bluish white, the kitchen a softened brick red.

As domestic experiments go, the Moore–Kirkpatrick cabin is fairly tame—perhaps to suit the co-owner—with very little of the space-and-light adventures or conscious dreamstuff of Moore's earlier small houses. The play of chic colors and chrome inside a raw wooden box seems, here, more decorator-like than thoughtful. If one *must* choose so precipitous a site, then all the steps, the up-and-back design make some sense. The through-the-looking-glass image of sweet against sour stairs is quite winning. But the actual spaces yield little joy. Compared with half a dozen similar small houses and cabins he helped design in the sixties, this cabin, high in its private mountain precinct, counts for very little and marks no discernible step forward.

IN early 1981, tempted by offers from Tulane University as well as Perez Associates, Charles Moore began considering a move of his permanent base of operations from Los Angeles to New Orleans. With young Arthur's help, he began looking for a studio-residence somewhere in the French Quarter—preferably with a secret garden and authentic old iron on the balcony. Moore-ified within, that would become Moore #8.

Two years later, Charles had become (at least temporarily) reconciled with Los Angeles, but he and Arthur were still looking for a New Orleans pad. The plan was to buy a classic "shotgun" house—room following room without a hallway, so that a shot fired through the front door would blast out the back—with a small garden and a "slave's quarters" out back. Then they could rent out the main house, carefully preserved and properly decorated, and do wild and wonderful things to their own quarters in the rear. For a year or so, in the meantime, Charles had rented a one-room apartment for his trips to New Orleans ("with *two* gardens") for $225 a month.

3/MAKING IT, ARCHITECTURALLY

C HARLES MOORE designs many things besides houses for himself and the occasional world's fair. During that storm-battered week at the Sea Ranch, when he and his mates were sorting out river gods and Wonderwalls and White Elephant Parks on a mile of yellow trace, Charles was also going over plans for the new art museum at Dartmouth; the country club near Houston (and a park full of condominiums across the street from it); a large house near Washington, D.C.; and an elaborately arched and pilastered facade ("they only hired me to do the facade") for a fourteen-story apartment block in Battery Park. He was also, with the help of his editorial assistant Peter Becker, revising drafts of two books.

A few famous artist-architects of the last twenty years—including several with whom Moore is often grouped or compared—have earned considerable reputations on the basis of work less bulky or troublesome than actual buildings. They have grown famous for their writings and their lectures, their theories and critiques. From time to time they design imaginary buildings for real or imaginary clients. Every so often, one gets built.

But Charles Moore has taken a major part in the design of 107 completed works in the last thirty years. These include 65 private homes and 14 multiple-unit residences; commercial or office buildings, clubs, recreation buildings, public buildings, and urban parks or plazas. Independently, or in association with one of five different firms, he had in hand early in 1983 a resort hotel, a civic center, an art school, an auditorium, a park, another country club, some university buildings, a skyscraper project, some luxury condominiums, another museum, three more houses, and a redevelopment scheme for a whole district of Berlin—in addition to the jobs he was working on at the Sea Ranch in January 1982. He has led design teams on dozens of other building projects that, for one reason or another, were never realized: unsuccessful competition entries, projects for clients who changed their minds or for developers who ran out of money. A few of them, by virtue of their innovativeness and wide publication, have been almost as influential as his best completed works. One measure of the attention paid to his work (and of his remarkable success as a self-publicist) is that almost every one of these designs, built or unbuilt, has been published in the professional, and frequently the nonprofessional, press.

Given the relative inaccessibility of private homes and housing projects located in widely scattered parts of the country, favorable attention paid to one's work in the magazines—preferably accompanied by photographs, plans, and prizes—is a reward highly sought after by ambitious architects. It is the surest way (short of winning commissions for big buildings in big cities, which usually get published in any case) of making oneself known, and hence building a practice, in a profession that is still too discreet to advertise directly.

For an American architect, the major plums are the regional and national awards given annually by their own professional organization, the American Institute of Architects (for completed buildings), and the design awards given each year by juries selected by certain magazines. The most important prizes, in terms of publicity, tend to be those awarded (for commissioned work in progress) by *Progressive Architecture*, which has the second widest circulation among magazines directed to design professionals in the United States. Even so, its January awards issue inevitably provokes a rash of apoplectic protests from readers, who regularly accuse its editors and jurors of irresponsible trendiness and novomania.

The P/A Design Awards program has become a self-serving and predictable insidious recurrence. For many years it was Moore and clones, now it is Graves and clones, with the ethic clearly being, "the more eclectic, decorative, and unbuildable, the better." What a comment!

Charles Gwathmey
Gwathmey Siegel & Associates
New York, N.Y.

Among house architects, the annual honors handed out by *Architectural Record* (circulation 70,000) and *Housing*, formerly *House and Home* (circulation 89,000); and the biennial Western Home Awards given by more consumer-directed *Sunset* magazine (1,400,000) are also important in building reputations. Other specialized prizes are given by industry groups (the Redwood Association, Owens-Corning Glass, Reynolds Aluminum, etc.). In between awards issues, these and many other magazines, including general-circulation publications such as *Newsweek*, *Time*, and the *New York Times Magazine*, look for new and significant buildings to write about and photograph. Many times mere publication, with appropriate prose and illustrations, can be as important as any prize. In lieu of advertising, architects may order and distribute reprints of articles that deal favorably with their work, or hire press agents to spread the good word.

Best of all—especially for a relatively less well-known firm—is to enter and win a major design competition. Capturing the Boston City Hall competition "made" the fledgling firm of Kalway, McKinnell and Knowles in 1969. Beyond that, immortality of a specialized sort can be won by achieving international publication in the architectural magazines of Great Britain, Italy, Germany, France, and especially Japan; by citation in book-length surveys of contemporary architecture; by museum or gallery displays; and by the publication of a monograph devoted entirely to one's own work.

Within eleven years after leaving Princeton, Charles Moore had climbed all these peaks.

Every one of his early associates I talked to remarked on how well Charles Moore knew how to stage manage his (and in the process their) reputation. He would skillfully arrange the presentations of their projects for the editor or jury in question, spending many hours on a model or a rendering. He insisted on hiring the best architectural photographer in California, whose judgment was trusted by a number of key editors, on their very first projects. "We hired Morley Baer specifically because of his contacts with the trade," admitted one of Moore's early associates.

One client recalls architect and photographer arriving with a truckload of their own furniture, which they believed would photograph better than hers. (The same Moore–Baer wolfskin throws and Marimekko wall hangings can be traced through published articles on several of his early houses.) On this particular occasion—because the day was overcast and the landscaping not yet in—the two men brought along aluminum screens, sun lamps, and giant trees in pots, which they dragged around from window to window as they took their shots. In the end, Moore forgot to take home his dining-room table. The owner still has it.

This may all seem very unartistic and careerist. But Charles Moore knew that the hidden-away cabins he and his partners were doing in those early years, however novel and wonderful they might be, were never going to come to anyone's attention without a little help from their friends. "We were nobodies," says Bill Turnbull. "Four kids out of school, doing ten-thousand-dollar shacks for our friends from a leaky basement in Berkeley. We knew what we were doing was great. But nobody else did. Chuck thought the whole world ought to know, and he figured out a way to tell them."

Each year, Moore would organize a specific campaign to win them at least one major prize, and then dedicate carefully focused energies to that end. In 1961, he and Richard Peters won their first, a *Sunset* Award of Merit for a house near Salinas (photographed by Morley Baer), which went on to become a 1962 *Architectural Record* House of the Year. "After that we were really flying high." The next year he decided to blitz *Progressive Architecture* (or P/A, as it likes to call itself) with three entries. "We wanted a P/A Design Award in the *worst* way," he told an interviewer in 1975. "We spent the whole summer of sixty-one on those submissions."

The jury debated for two hours and ended up giving a citation to Moore's own house in Orinda. Within two years, that house had won an AIA regional award as well as publication in eight other places—including British, Danish, German, and Italian magazines. Both of the now-famous little northern California vacation cabins won *Sunset* awards in 1963. The Jobson cabin near Big Sur had been picked up by *Progressive Architecture* in June of that year and won a *House and Home* First Honor Award in July. The Bonham cabin at Boulder Creek made *Progressive Architecture* in May 1964. In that article, the editors summed up the way this infant Berkeley firm had taken the profession by surprise—and, incidentally, the success of Moore's salesmanship:

In 1962, the P/A Design Awards jury deliberated among three Charles Moore houses, finally selecting one for a citation. In the 1963 judgment, a Moore project for a condominium apartment was premiated after a lengthy debate. And only several months ago, in the 1964 Design Awards program, a third jury selected a third work by this office. "Moorishness" is a force to be reckoned with, they seem to be saying.

In fact, the firm won a fourth P/A citation for another house in Orinda in 1964. Never had so small and so young an architectural office won four design awards in a row, from four different juries. In 1965, the Sea Ranch Condominium made it five; in 1966, the first Sea Ranch Recreation Center made six.

It was in 1965 that the floodgates burst. The impeccably managed publicity campaign of Oceanic Properties, Inc., orchestrated with great finesse by Marian Conrad, managed to get the Sea Ranch idea (and Condominium I) into the pages of at least forty-six magazines and newspapers within eighteen months. *Newsweek* took note, then the *New York Times*, *Life* and *Fortune*, *Paris-Match* and *Elle*, *Horizon* and *Sports Illustrated* and the in-flights. In 1965, too, the first retrospective articles began to appear: in *Perspecta* (a design quarterly published at Yale) and *Japan Architect*—retrospectives on a career essentially all of five years old. In the end, the Sea Ranch Condominium captured an AIA National Honor Award in 1967—by which time Moore was already running the program at Yale.

Even the decision to go to Yale was career-strategic, a public-relations move on behalf of the firm. "I was having dinner at my sister Mimi's with Bill Turnbull," Moore told me, "and the phone call comes from a Mr. Brewster in San Francisco—the only Brewster I could think of was the president of Yale—and so he said he would like to see me about the chairmanship. And I expected Mimi and Bill to say, 'You don't want to do that! That's terrible! That dirty old place, all that sludge?' But no, that's not what they said at all. They said, 'What a wonderful idea! Go see Kingman! Whoopee! How exciting!'"

"That's right, more or less," Turnbull confirms, when I relate to him Charles's version of the evening. "Basically Mimi and I sat down that night at the dinner table and said, 'Hey, look. Look at Rudolph coming out of Florida. And look where he was.'" Paul Rudolph, Moore's predecessor as chairman, had expanded a strong regional reputation into a major national one only *after* taking the job at Yale in 1958. "'And then look at what we're doing now. We've had a couple of good buildings, but we're not going anywhere. We're still doing houses. Economically it's to your advantage to go; professionally it's to your advantage to go. It's the only way to get your name *known* by the New York crowd. Do it, Chuck,' we told him.

"Oh, he was mad at the Berkeley administration over one thing and another right then, too. But that was the real reason he left. It was that rational, that cool. It's about the one time I can remember doing any real career strategy. It was a gamble. It was, 'Let's roll the dice for the Big Time.' I said I'd hold down the fort here in California and move east if that seemed in the cards. But let's go for it. Let's go for the brass ring."

The wisdom of the advice soon proved apparent. Once at Yale, Moore was a certified celebrity. Virtually everything he did got into print. His first-year students' design project—the boys designed and built a community center in Appalachia—became a cover story in P/A. All the housing projects were duly noted, as well as the large New England mansions he was now asked to design. *Playboy* dropped in. The flashy faculty club in Santa Barbara made the cover of *Architectural Forum*, at the time a more serious and critical publication than P/A or *Record*, now unfortunately defunct. Kresge College in Santa Cruz won the bicoastal firm a prize four years before it was built. Special issues of many magazines, domestic and overseas, were devoted to the Moore phenomenon, often graced with the chairman's smiling face, framed by sideburns that flowed into a voluptuous handlebar mustache. According to the editors' count of angry letters, the Piazza d'Italia in New Orleans was the most controversial single project published in *Progressive Architecture* in a decade.

Progressive Architecture has now seen fit to publish and, indeed, to praise the Ultimate Horror ("The Magic Fountain," Piazza d'Italia, New Orleans).

I shall request that my subscription to P/A be cancelled forthwith. If I should be so fortunate as to receive a refund I shall at once apply it toward a subscription to *Hustler* magazine instead. If I am to read pornography let it at least be honest and not under the guise of architectural criticism.

David P-C Chang, Architect-Planner
Cold Spring Harbor, N.Y.

The ten-by-fourteen-inch albums in the Japanese series called "Global Architecture," each devoted to one or two famous modern buildings, do not so much win recognition for their subjects as certify it: there are few surer signs of critical approval. In 1970, after devoting numbers 1 and 2 in the series to classic buildings by Frank Lloyd Wright, Yukio Futagawa—whose elegant photographs make up each volume—decided to devote number 3 to the Sea Ranch. "He came to us," Bill Turnbull insists. "We never approached him." This was followed by four other books on their work: one in 1975, one in 1978, and two in 1980. In December 1979, to answer the critics who had accused them of favoring certain architects at the expense of others equally good, *Progressive Architecture* surveyed the amount of space it had devoted to each firm for the past ten years. Charles Moore and his several offices came in first—which may have proved the critics right.

Such are the cycles of anxious fashion in architecture that already a degree of reaction has set in. Protean as he is, Moore's designs cannot change course rapidly enough or often enough to satisfy the insatiable need for novelty among editors, who are trend spotters by definition. He remains one of the dozen first-magnitude stars of international architecture. But other men, who are designing things defiantly more unusual than his—more cerebral and geometric, or more witty and conceptual, or more funky, or more gaga, or more return-to-the-past traditional, are now capturing the pages and the prizes. And while Moore has been turning toward a (for him) relatively benign and palatable historicism, his current U.S. rivals for stardom (Frank Gehry, Romaldo Giurgola, Michael Graves, Charles Gwathmey, Hugh Hardy, Richard Meier, Cesar Pelli, Richard Stern—to mention only the heads of some of the smaller and younger offices) continue to surprise and impress the profession with their novel and assertive work. Even so, in October 1982, Charles Moore and UIG won a dream commission to design a new civic center for Beverly Hills, competing against five major firms. A month later, in competition with Robert Stern, Robert Venturi, and TAFT Architects of Houston, Moore Ruble Yudell was awarded the job of designing a new art school for San Antonio. In January 1983 (to his glee), Moore beat Michael Graves to a $20 million condominium project for Dallas.

There is no question that most, perhaps all, of the top architects in the world (the most often published, most often premiated) keep alert to the work of their peers. The intensity of frequent one-on-one competitions and the status anxiety built into this hybrid profession (artist-engineer-businessman-decorator) lead to an extraordinary degree of what sounds to the outsider like superfluous meanness. In my conversations with architects, I was struck by the frequency and cunning nastiness of their digs at one another, however much they may profess, in public, to admire one another's work.

All this may seem trivial and decadent to the average citizen of the republic, who may never (or rarely) have heard of any of these people or knowingly seen any of their work. But prizes make reputations, earn their winners professorships, commissions, and publicity. Architectural students (and less famous architects) attend very closely to what the top people are doing, and they often end up doing similar things. Thus a trend (sometimes even a style) is born. Innumerable copies of the Sea Ranch Condominium sprouted up all over the United States within a few years after it was built, praised, and publicized—whether or not heavy timbers, rough wood siding, shed roofs, oddly punched windows, and jutting bays were suited to the site and program. "I'd drive up a rise in some dead straight Kansas highway," says Turnbull, "and sure enough, there it would be: another Sea Ranch condo, out in the middle of the prairie where *none* of that stuff made sense." Hungry for a domestic style that could be at once more cozy than white-stucco-and-sliding-glass modern, and more advanced than suburban colonial, many architects seized on this mode—especially since it fit so well with the inflation-fueled demand for cluster housing and looked, in some way, acceptably "ecological." Given the seal of approval not only by Moore, but also by other celebrity architects, critics, and the professional press, designers across the country began, first, to play pop games with colors, light, graphics, and found artifacts; then to go in for conscious imitations of historical styles.

The celebrity stakes among design professionals eventually affect the world many of us inhabit. The visible turning away from rectilinear, straight-up-and-down buildings in U.S. cities; the vogue of the two-story living room overlooked by bedroom mezzanines; large, high light-trapping windows and skylights; and a new acceptance of cheap materials and historical recollections in serious architecture are all evidences of a trickle-down phenomenon in building design. You may not *know* you are beginning to live among the ideas, interpreted at third and fourth hand, of Louis

Kahn or Robert Venturi or Charles Moore or Michael Graves; but you are.

ONE of the many remarkable things about Charles Moore is the degree to which, through forty years as a student and practitioner of architecture, he has remained proof against fashionable styles (other than those he himself has invented). Not once—as a student at Michigan and Princeton, teaching at Utah or Berkeley or Yale, practicing on the West Coast or the East—has he been tempted by or interested in classic modern architecture, although for many years it was virtually the air one breathed in professional circles.

Yet neither was he any recognizable kind of traditionalist. He liked the best work of the eclectic, academic Beaux Arts tradition, which dominated serious Western architecture for a hundred years before the modern movement. But then he liked so many unfashionable things: wooden sidewalks, Edwardian hotels, weathered barns, neon lights, fantastic gardens, the architecture of Asia. For a long time he regarded himself as an architectural historian at least as much as an architect, and he felt free to invest his affections in the buildings of other centuries and civilizations than his own.

Although his degree of cultural independence is common enough today, it was rare twenty or twenty-five years ago. Moore is squarely in the tradition of eclectic freaks: of architects who were history loving but antiacademic; originally unfashionable, and apparently *sui generis*—the tradition of architects like John Soane, Karl Friedrich Schinkel, Bertram Goodhue, Bernard Maybeck, and Edwin Lutyens. All these outlaw architects have won Moore's affection. All have recently been upgraded by art historians. In each of their cases, one must turn to biography rather than to theory to understand the springs of this strange creative autonomy.

4 / FROM BATTLE CREEK
TO KOREA

S EATED at the Sea Ranch dining table one afternoon, Charles Moore tells the story of how he became an architect—and, more particularly, the kind of architect he is. Despite a veneer of nervous self-efface- ment, he is a skilled and easy raconteur and a clever (if sometimes deceptive) self-dramatizer. One senses that he has told this story before, to other audiences and other interrogat- ors—often enough, in fact, for it to have taken on the shape of semifictional myth. It may be an artful way of eluding deeper truths.

His voice is thin, high-pitched, and gentle, with a faint mid- western twang. He pauses every few words, constructing long sen- tences with a precisionist's syntax and diction, intercutting for effect, or by nature, with earthy expletives and schoolboy slang. He slips in parentheses and subordinate clauses and often saves the key ideas of a sentence for an apparent afterthought, inevitably and sometimes acidly clever. Despite his honors and his entou- rage, he gives off a disconcerting sense of shyness, real or pre- tended. The little voice and 1940s adjectives (creepy, swell, groovy, goofy) hint at boyishness and timidity; but this is belied by the apparent candor of one above ruse and pose and by the self- conscious wit. He studiously avoids any overt display of egotism; a droll self-deprecation, in fact, has become almost automatic, even when he is recalling one of his triumphs. People in his disfavor may be either dismissed by understatement ("not one of my favor- ite people") or theatrically trounced ("that sniveling, subservient little creep!").

As usual when Charles is in residence, Unit 9 is full of retainers. But today most of his houseguests are off for the afternoon, hiking along the bluffs, self-indulging at the swimming and tennis cen- ters, or driving further up the coast. A couple of sedentary types, feigning mild convalescence, comment from time to time, correcting or adding to his recollections, or drawing his attention to the flumes and the arching backs of gray whales heading south, for which the window seats of the condominium offer a perfect point of view.

Charles Willard Moore takes his ancestors very seriously, the Willards even more than the Moores. He announces himself on the telephone—even to old friends—by saying, "This is Charles *W.* Moore." In each of his houses, he has tried to find a place for portraits of a pair of his eighteenth-century Willard ancestors from Vermont who were related to Emma Willard, the pioneer poetess and women's educator. Charles has traced the family line back another century to the Isle of Man, but much of the Willard character, and most of its property, derived from Allen Willard (1794–1876), Charles's great-great-grandfather, who was born in Vermont, grew up in New York state, and moved to a homestead near Battle Creek, Michigan. Beginning as a modest farmer, he earned a fortune in business and ended up a local philanthropist. He gave Battle Creek a library and endowed the Baptist College at Kalamazoo with a chair of Latin and literature. Charles was brought up across the road from a beautiful Greek Revival house his great-great-grandfather Willard built in Battle Creek, four years after the first settlers had driven off two Indians to establish possession of the land.

Allen Willard's son George (1824–1901) was for fourteen years an Episcopal minister as well as a farmer, until one day he decided he had had enough of the ladies of the church. He kept his farm notes in Latin and his personal diaries in Greek. Long the editor of the *Battle Creek Journal* and an ardent abolitionist, he was elected first to the Michigan state legislature, then (1872–76) to the United States Congress. Late in life he introduced co-education to the University of Michigan (the first in any American state university) by means of a Latin resolution "so high-sounding that it was approved before anyone found out what it meant."

Congressman Willard's younger daughter Lilla married Ephraim Moore (Charles's grandfather) of Rochester, New York, in 1877. He inherited the Battle Creek paper and bought and sold a string of others in southern Michigan. His 1904 Oldsmobile was the first car in Battle Creek. By the time Charles was born in 1925, his grandfather had moved out of the newspaper business and into real estate. The family homestead became a country club.

Charles's and Mimi's father (there is a stepsister Lilla, twenty years older, from his first marriage), Charles Ephraim Moore, seems to have been something of a loser: a man who drank too much, mishandled (or ignored) whatever real estate or newspaper business Grandpa Moore passed his way, and died—not particularly mourned by his son—when Charles was seventeen. He had married, *en secondes noces*, Kathryn Almandinger, a schoolteacher, in 1918, after an unusual "honeymoon" trip on a houseboat in Florida. ("They were actually living in sin," Charles footnotes.) Mimi thinks of their parents as free spirits, who did pretty much what they wanted. "Mother was the first cheerleader to do a cartwheel right up in front of everybody." Charles Moore remained devoted to his widowed mother, particularly in the times when they shared Moore #1 in Pebble Beach, until her death from cancer in 1958.

The Battle Creek of his childhood was a thriving two-company town, the fiefdom of cereal kings C. W. Post and J. H. Kellogg: you could smell the roasting wheat for miles. Grandpa Moore and his second wife, Aunt Bertha, lived in a big house in Benton Harbor (where Charles was born), a Lake Michigan resort town seventy miles from Battle Creek. The family visited them almost every weekend, traveling in a high old Franklin with horsehair seats. They lived much of the year on the lake, sailing or canoeing in the summer, iceboating in winter. Chuckie, a genuine prodigy, who could read at two and learned Latin very early, was a nervous, frustrated, unsocial child, intolerant of the grosser, slower children around him. Although he did have a couple of good friends, according to his sister, most of his time he spent alone or with his family. Photographs show a handsome little blond-haired boy of five or six, with large, down-drooping eyes, maturing into an awkward and frightened-looking youth, his hair thinning early to reveal a large dome of a forehead. His eyes look anxious and intense behind glasses. He wore a crew cut for a black-tie senior-prom picture ("He went with my friend Mary Jane," Mimi remembers; "but nothing came of it"), but was soon back to neatly combed short-back-and-sides.

Charles remembers taking it for granted that he would grow up to be a newspaper editor like his legendary grandfather, "whom I adored." He doesn't recall even thinking much about architecture until he was thirteen, when a new room for him was added over the family garage. He watched with fascination and assisted the young man who designed it: what a wonderful thing to be able to do! This was at his parents' 1932 colonial-style house overlooking Goguac Lake. A much grander house had been planned—"Monterey style, with balconies and all"—before the family fortunes sank during the Depression.

The plans for Room of Charles Moore, Designed by Charles Moore (including details of built-in cabinets for "souvenirs, projects, collections, and junk") have been preserved in a wood-bound scrapbook, along with plans and drawings of twenty-four buildings he designed—some for a high-school drafting class, most just for himself—between the ages of thirteen and seventeen. A few of these were done in traditional styles, but the majority were simple and modern. A department store and a hotel for Battle Creek made use of bands of *moderne* fenestration. A second plan for the hotel (dated 1940) shows an oval lobby unique in this portfolio of rectilinear rooms. Most of the plans are for houses, a majority of them Sun Belt fantasies: Home in Arizona, Casa Desierto, Las Palmas, Adobe, House in the Desert. They have low-pitched or even flat roofs, horizontal Frank Lloyd Wright–like elevations, swimming-pool terraces, breezeways, and badly drawn palm trees and cactus. The floor plans are logical, workable, and austere. (He did minimal kitchens and baths, even then.) Some of the schemes resemble those published in house magazines at the time. Wright-like details include bands of casement and clerestory windows, rows of French doors, open plans, long built-in couches near big fireplaces, and terraces that flow through the house. Moore acknowledges the influence—in particular that of Wright's 1940 Pauson house in Phoenix, and others like it.

Most interesting to me was A Vacation Cottage with a Choice of Exteriors dated February 1940, which offers the same simple floor plan with three different facades: one for Arizona (cactus, projecting vigas, flat roof), one for Michigan (evergreens, wood siding, pitched roof), and one for Florida (palms, extra windows, tile roof); Charles Moore, Jr., facade architect at fourteen. His spacious July 1943 House in the Sun included Moore's first two-story living room (with a giant window divided in four) and a spiral staircase to the mezzanine bedroom, as well as his first pair of opposing single-pitched roofs. The scrapbook concludes with a questionnaire concerning his "vocation" that he filled out in his last year of high school.

How much money will I make? Depends entirely upon business. Usual rate 6% of cost of buildings designed.

Where will I go to school? University of Michigan, Massachusetts Tech, Georgia Tech.

How many hours a day will I be working? Depends upon business. Irregular.

Where would be the best place to practice my vocation? A town slightly larger than Battle Creek.

Mimi Moore Weingarten remembers her brother publishing and printing his own newspaper as a boy and later editing the high-school paper. But she also recalls towering structures he built out of blocks at Grandpa Moore's and the secret houses they made out of tipped-over chairs with blanket roofs whenever their parents went out. He made fussy little copper-wire sculptures for Valentine's Day gifts and devised a wonderful waterfall by running hoses down the hillside path from their house to the lake—a sequence of ponds, stone steps, and underground streams. Mimi, a cousin, and a girlfriend helped him build it; teachers came out from school to marvel.

"Water in Architecture" was the title of his Princeton Ph.D. dissertation; he is still working on a book version of that project. Very few of Moore's buildings do not include, or overlook, moving water. The intricately stepped fountains at Portland and New Orleans, the rivers and lagoons of his projects for Tegeler Hafen in Berlin, and fairgrounds for New Orleans and Indianapolis may all have had their origins in these homemade hillside waterworks at Battle Creek (or whatever inner impulse led to them).

The most significant influences on his later life and work were the annual trips his family took, in the old Franklin car—four-month-long trips, usually from November or December to March or April—to Florida or California. Except for a two-year break during the Depression, these journeys continued right up to the time Charles finished high school. His unorthodox parents had been driving cross country ever since their marriage in 1918 and took this annual displacement for granted. ("My mother kept a diary of that 1918 trip from Michigan to Pasadena. . . . Forty miles in one day through the mud of Missouri, backtracking through endless desert roads.") Grandfather Moore and his wife Bertha went out first, usually either to Orlando, Florida, on one coast or to Pasadena on the other. ("I was conceived in Pasadena," Charles confessed.) Grandpa bought little newspapers on the Coast, as he had back in Michigan, in the hope that Charles's father would one day settle down and run one intelligently. On the whole, Grandpa Moore preferred Florida to California, which he regarded as a "land of liars and little oil stoves," an Eden full of snakes.

"We tended to go to St. Petersburg, or sometimes Orlando; or else Hollywood, or sometimes Pasadena. My mother wanted to go to California every year, and my father wanted to go to Florida. And so some years they would do one and some years the other. The year I was fourteen we did both. We'd move close to Grandpa and rent an apartment. Since my father didn't have a real job anyway, it was no problem for him to leave.

"Fifth grade in St. Pete I went to school, and the sixth grade in Orlando—although they put me in seventh; but after that I announced that I was not going to do that anymore. So seventh, eighth, ninth, tenth, and eleventh, I just didn't go to school from November to April. It became an annual scene. One day in November I'd go in and say to my teachers at Lakeview Junior High School, 'I'm going away now. May I have all my assignments to the first of April?' And then these cheats would tell me the books I had to do the lessons in, and the Caesar I had to read or whatever, and the algebra, and I would do it all. And I'd get back, and it would turn out that all the people in school were months behind; they'd got about a third as far as I had. And then I'd sit around for the rest of April and May, integrating badly into the scene. We could do extra problems to get our grades up over one hundred percent, and my grade ran about one hundred seventy. Which didn't make me very popular at school."

("He had the highest grades ever given at Lakeview," Mimi boasts. "An A-plus average. It was hard having to follow that three years later.")

"My sister didn't groove on these trips at all. I think she would far rather have had a normal life, staying back home in Battle Creek—which I hated." ("I was carsick the whole time," she remembers. "The car had these scratchy horsehair seats and high windows I couldn't see out of except the telephone poles. Chuckie could do all his lessons so easily, but mostly I had a tutor. I just tried to be a good little girl.") But her brother was very glad to be in

Orlando or Hollywood or wherever they were. They took day trips to Santa Barbara, Ojai, Key West; they went to the beach.

"From the time I was maybe twelve I got to plan our route. I'd go down to the Automobile Club and get sheaves of maps and tour books and decide whether we wanted to drive to Florida this year by way of Covington, Kentucky, or Knoxville or wherever, and then work out exactly where we were going to stay and make hotel reservations. I got very fond of middle-sized cities. Going to somewhere like Knoxville or Cincinnati was a real treat. These trips were enormously important for me. I'd sit around for days, planning and replanning, figuring out what would happen if we took Route 25 instead of Route 26. Would we make it to Lexington in time for dinner?

"I've still got boxes of stuff from the Will Rogers Museum and the Cyclorama in Atlanta, Georgia. I don't throw anything away. Oh, I just thought it was wonderful, the whole business of standing on the steps of the capitol of the Confederacy.

"By the time I got to architecture school I had a well-built-in sense that cities, the way they were constituted, were very interesting places and that I enjoyed going to see them. I was a full-fledged tourist, had been for a long time. Seeing things that were special and unique—going to the Palmer House in Chicago for a couple of days' outing in the summer, for example—that was all built into me, a part of my urban and rural experience. I never understood the modern revolutionary notion that it all had to be swept clean, that we had to tear it down. I *liked* what was there. Especially places that were very different from one another. The first time I went to Yuma, Arizona, and found out it had wooden sidewalks, I thought that was heaven."

On a trip to Mexico with his mother and sister in 1942, Charles had picked up a strain of malaria sufficient to keep him out of the army. When he entered the University of Michigan's architecture program later that year ("It was as far away as I could get, with the wartime travel restrictions"), he was one of only about a dozen majors in the department. "It was a good time to be there," he says. "There were four male civilians in my class and the class before me, maybe four or five girls. It was as intimate as any Ivy League school. Of course, it all ballooned again in forty-six when the vets came back. But I was established by then."

One thing that helped establish him was his friendship with Roger Bailey, his design instructor, who had set up a professional practice in Ann Arbor "to give the boys something to do." Charles's own father died in 1943, and Roger and Betty Bailey played part-time parents during his college years, having him to dinner, going with him on trips. "That got him out of lots of drafting," Bailey recalls. "We all worked in one room over a movie theater around one huge square table, so close to the walls you couldn't open the drawers. Chuck would just put his feet up while the others were drawing like mad. He wasted reams of paper designing one house for a client, but it got too expensive and had to be abandoned. But he was brilliant. No question about that."

"I got very fancy grades and all," Moore admits. "My memory in those days worked very well. It caused me to get an A in any academic course I ever took. I managed to get A's in design courses too, but only with intense cliff hanging. After the insecurity of design studio, the academic courses filled me with great pleasure and self-assurance." He used to set his alarm for 4:00 A.M., so he could work from four to seven on classwork, then stay up drafting till late at night. Dona Guimaraes, daughter of a Portuguese doctor from Dearborn, took a memorable course in classics with Charles Moore and recalls sharing his disdain for their simpleton classmates. ("We obviously knew more than anyone else.") Halfway through the program, prompted by the easing of travel restrictions and his own obvious superiority, Charles considered transferring to Harvard. But (as he tells it) he was talked out of moving by Harvard's own dean, Walter Hudnut, who disliked what Walter Gropius and his German modernist colleagues were doing to his school.

"There was very, very little of the Kraut-ish persuasion at Michigan," according to Moore. Roger Bailey's own professional career (Cornell, Prix de Paris) had been urban-eclectic and included elegant Park Avenue co-op apartment buildings "with chaste Italian Renaissance facades" and a grandiose war memorial for Chicago that never got built. He tolerated the modern movement only as far as Louis Sullivan ("Which was fine with me," Moore declares). Bailey's wife was a niece of George Elmslie, one of Sullivan's most successful apprentices. Eliel Saarinen—"the good Saarinen"—had come to the university before settling at nearby Cranbrook

Academy in 1925. The rest of the faculty still included some "woodsy Finns," Moore recalls. But the curriculum was essentially untainted by Bauhaus ideas or ideals.

For his senior thesis, Moore wrote a study of college dormitories and designed a residential neighborhood for a then-unbuilt section of Las Trancas Canyon at Malibu. His sister Mimi had begun studying at the University of Southern California in 1945, and his widowed mother followed her there. Two aunts lived in Los Angeles as well, and Charles worked on his thesis while staying with one of them in the summer of 1946.

After the 1939–43 schoolboy designs in his scrapbook, but before the unbuilt house Roger Bailey spoke of, there was another house, made out of a remodeled barn in upper Michigan, which Moore designed for Bailey's office in late 1946. "That was the first one I could actually walk into, and there it was." In the summer after his freshman year, he worked for architect Louis Sarvis on hospital projects around the state for the Kellogg Foundation. ("Should I go look at those?" I asked. "No!")

The more-or-less definitive "Chronology of Works" printed in a fat special issue of a Japanese magazine devoted to Moore begins with a Jones Cottage, Torch Lake, Michigan, designed in 1946 and constructed the following year. "The Joneses were neighbors of ours in Battle Creek. The mother was a friend of Dad's first wife and my older sister Lilla. Their son was Mimi's first boyfriend and also a close friend of mine. They had this property at Torch Lake in upper Michigan. Don't you know Torch Lake? It's supposed to be the fourth most beautiful lake in the world. I don't know what the other three are. Anyway, I designed a cabin for them there, very simple: sixteen feet wide, concrete block, shed roof. The next year they moved to Eugene, Oregon. I visited them with Mother and designed another house for them there. But they came back to Battle Creek, so it never got built."

After graduating in 1947, Moore was offered a teaching job at Michigan, but he decided he was fed up with school. Happy memories of California, and the fact that his family had now relocated there, drew him west. San Francisco had seemed appealing to him on two previous visits: he had come out with his family for the 1939 fair and on his own in 1945. He liked what he had seen in the architectural magazines of what later became known as the Bay Region school, one of the stubborn provincial holdouts against internationalist modernism in America, closely related in spirit to the work of Saarinen senior and Alvar Aalto in Finland. "I thought the city was wonderful. It *was* more wonderful then than it is now."

Typical of the "first" Bay Region school (Moore himself, according to one art historian, was later to found the "third") were the simple, wooden, elegantly casual houses built around the hills and bayshore, championed by *Sunset* magazine and the San Francisco Museum of Art. Those houses (plus churches, schools, and other buildings like them) seemed at once "modern" and vitally responsive to local settings and tradition. The leader of the Bay Region school—and, after 1951, dean of the college of architecture at Berkeley—was William Wilson Wurster, a courtly native Californian, then fifty-two, who had already designed more than two hundred houses of great clarity, civility, and finesse. It was to the office of Wurster Bernardi and Emmons that the twenty-two-year-old Moore first went in search of a job. Failing there, he tried three or four others. He ended up obtaining a position as designer with another noted Bay Regionalist, Mario Corbett.

For Corbett, Moore worked on (among other things) a radio station and a hillside house in Marin County that cantilevered out over a steep Sausalito ridge. After nine months, Corbett, trapped between bankruptcy and a divorce, declared a nervous breakdown and left Charles in charge—unfortunately, without funds. He looked elsewhere.

This time he tried thirty-one different architectural offices before landing a position with Joseph Allen Stein. (One top firm rejected him as "overqualified"—at twenty-three.) "In Stein's office I designed houses for neurotic clients in Marin and down the peninsula that never got built. They were all commissioning houses in lieu of psychoanalysis. Then Stein—whom I really liked—ran off for the weekend in his 1934 Packard and never came back: Mexico, Switzerland, Israel; I think he's working in Calcutta now. One house I did for him, the Claire Falkenstein house, got published. That would be my first 'publication'; but of course it was listed as Joe's.

"Even before Joe Stein skipped town, though, I was getting bored. So I started looking for fellowships to go away and see things. I took the state boards around Christmas of forty-eight, and passed—only two out of one hundred and ten were said to have passed first round that year. So now I was licensed. The very day I got my next job, at Clark and Buettler, I found out I had won a

Booth Traveling Fellowship from Michigan: twelve hundred dollars for a year's travel. It was regarded as *very* big stuff. I decided not to mention it to my new employers for a while."

For Hervey Clark, of Clark and Buettler, Moore worked on a number of projects: one Japanese house in Woodside, California, "with balconies hovering out everywhere," he still rather likes. The traveling fellowship that took him away from San Francisco for a year in 1949–50 came with a peculiar string attached. In January of 1949 Roger Bailey had left Michigan to start a new school of architecture—virtually out of nothing—at the University of Utah in Salt Lake City. So when his prize ex-student wrote and asked for help in obtaining a fellowship, Bailey made him a deal. "I told him how to write his letter of application. He was to go out and find how people had lived in other places and other centuries, what sorts of spoons they used in Cairo, look out for cultural realities and how they affected buildings. The whole idea was to discover a way of teaching architectural history without putting kids to sleep in dark lecture halls with those everlasting slides. I promised him a teaching spot at Utah when he got back, if he won the grant."

Which he did. Together with a Michigan classmate, Charles traveled through Egypt, Greece, Italy, and Austria; then met Dona Guimaraes in Rome with her friend Laura ("Mother said I was too young to travel alone with two men in Europe, so I had to bring along a female companion"). The foursome continued through Italy, then did Spain and France.

(Seven years ago, Charles and Dona picked up where they had left off traveling in 1950. Every summer since 1976, together with three other unmarried friends, they have chosen a spot in Britain as a base—if at all possible, a minor ruin or stately home—and gone architectural sightseeing for two weeks.)

"I knew exactly what I wanted to see from my architectural history courses," Moore told me. "I had this maddening 'total recall,' at least I had then. I knew the height of the apse at Beauvais, the length of the choir at Chartres." A photograph of Charles on the sands of the causeway to Mont Saint Michel shows a tall gangling young man in white shirt and brown trousers, short hair and glasses, already slouched into his current self-effacing stance: chin down, stomach forward.

Dona Guimaraes remembers one particularly dramatic architectural adventure during the trip. "At the Duomo in Florence, there were these signs all over, *Raparazione in corso* or something, Repairs in Progress. We went in anyway. I remember coming out of that brilliant light into this dark, smelly old cathedral. Inside, these rickety flying stairs had been erected for the workmen. They circled the entire dome, spiraling up snail-fashion, right to the top. Well, you know Charles's obsession with stairs. He gave a few lire to the workmen, babbling on about being *professore al'Universita di Utah* or whatever, and literally forced us to climb up that awful thing: floating wooden stairs, they were, ten feet away from the walls, nothing but air all around us, circling, circling; it shook and wobbled as we inched our way up.

"But after all, he said, who had been able to see it like this since Brunelleschi? I could tell he was ecstatic: his shoulders gave this great *heave* of satisfaction at the top."

One unusual feature of this journey was a series of five motion-picture films he made, walking through architectural monuments with a camera, so that his future students at Utah would be able to share the actual experience of Karnak, the Acropolis, the Piazza San Marco, the Alhambra, and Chenonceaux. He also began taking colored slides for his now-fabled collection. Except for Karnak ("I used this crappy French film, and it all turned purple"), the 1949–50 films are still intact and usable, if somewhat primitive.

So he came back to the Great Salt Desert with his movies and his slides, and the only Citroën in Utah, to start as an assistant professor at $4,000 a year.

Periods in the life of this compulsive twentieth-century American traveler are often identified by his cars even more than by his houses. He is, after all, more likely to be en route than at home. Friends are always referring, in their recollections and anecdotes, to "Charles's Citroën," "Charles's Mercedes 180," or "Charles's enormous Buick convertible," as if they were parts of him rather than possessions, as if he had seen most of the world from behind a windshield, as if the latecomer had missed something wonderful not knowing these celebrated vehicles.

He has, for the record, owned seriatim two Fords, a Citroën, a Studebaker, a Chevrolet, a Mercedes, a Buick convertible, a Mustang, a Chevrolet station wagon ("I rolled that in Vermont"), a Pinto, a Torino ("I rolled that two years ago"), and, since 1981, a beige Buick. He, or rather his firm, owned a Cessna 310 airplane in 1970; but that's another story.

The funny French car was not the only thing that set the new assistant professor apart from the Mormon locals. The first year he was at Salt Lake, the new school of architecture was housed in an ex-army mess hall in which the "classrooms" were partitioned off by bright orange parachute cloth. ("It gave our slides a curious glow.") Roger Bailey remembered overhearing Charles "doing his Parthenon bit" one day behind a red-orange curtain, when a student's voice interrupted: "'Mr. Moore, how can you say this is beautiful when it was done by pagans?' Chuck took him apart," Bailey says.

"It was that same student," Moore wrote to Bailey later, "who walked out of the class when I illustrated contemporary planning theory with a scheme for closing streets in the Salt Lake City gridiron to make superblocks. Brigham Young had laid out those streets, I was informed, after suitable divine inspiration, and it was not for Gentiles to muck around. . . . Teaching architectural history, in a time not especially devoted to it, and in a place where it was presumed that history had begun on July 24, 1848 (when Brigham Young saw it and announced, 'This is the Place'), was not always smooth."

Since college days—and especially since his year abroad—Charles Moore had been at least as interested in architectural history as in the practice of architecture. Almost everywhere he has taught, he has taught both; everything he writes is infused with his knowledge and love of places past. Every building he has designed seems to carry cultural memories of its own, from the Japanese pavilions and North Coast barns "remembered" by his earliest California houses, to the vivid Palladian dreams of recent villas in Long Island and western Massachusetts.

"The architectural history I was taught was strictly Bannister Fletcher." (Fletcher was a meticulous British cataloguer of the Edwardian era, whose *History of Architecture on the Comparative Method* has gone through eighteen editions.) "All chronologies and categories, stylistic details to memorize from celebrated buildings. But I got interested in geography and literature, in what it was like to *be* there and see those things. French history came to me not as a series of cathedrals, but as people's lives. I knew all the kings from St. Louis to Charles the Fifth, neatly in a row. I could recollect where they all fit when I saw the places they built, and it gave me a great sense of power and pleasure. In my courses at Utah, I tried to make *sense* out of history. I don't do that anymore. I haven't convinced myself that most people can tell what came before what. The whole idea of sequence is incompatible with the way most people's minds work. But I like it. The notion that something came before something else gives me enormous pleasure. It seems to put some sense into things.

"I got depressed one day and made up a little quiz for my students. I wrote out a list of important historical events—the landing of the Pilgrims, the Magna Carta, the Civil War. . . . All I asked them to do was to put the events in chronological order. I had given up asking for dates. When I graded the papers, I found to my dismay that more than half of them had put the Declaration of Independence *before* Plymouth Rock. I drank a lot of sherry that night."

Years later, Moore declared that his two years at Utah were the most exciting time he had ever spent teaching, whatever he may have thought of the university or his students. This he attributed in part to the high-powered energy exchange among a small, enthusiastic, like-minded faculty, in part to the freedom and sense of possibility that a new school affords. "My recollection is of the three of us rushing almost daily to school with massive curriculum revisions, as we discovered (the night before) some new fragment of Truth." The three design teachers taught, ate, drank, traveled, painted together, as Roger Bailey ran interference against the fanatic dean of fine arts. "He would come into [Bailey's] office," Moore recalled, "and engage in explosions of religious bigotry and artistic misinformation, based generally on our failure to resemble some macho Mormon Michelangelo he had created for our emulation."

In order to force bad habits out of students who thought they had already learned something from local hacks, Moore and his two colleagues, Jim Acland and Gordon Heck, kept exaggerating the design problems to elicit more thoughtful and less automatic responses. "There were endless buildings to design on hurricane-lashed tropical islands or Alpine pinnacles where the snows were always of incredible depth. At least that way they found out that the standard solutions didn't always work." Moore sat up nights drinking sherry and choosing recordings of appropriate music to accompany his history lectures—Gregorian chant for early Christian, Bartok for the Egyptians. He would argue the virtues of early versus late (Gothic Revival, German Renaissance, whatever) in an apartment filled with homemade Italianate modern furniture too fragile and chic for anyone to sit on or use. He designed a house in Ogden for a local architect's office ("They forgot to put my name on the credits") and, all traces of malaria gone, joined the U.S. Army Reserve Corps of Engineers.

Lieutenant Moore's unit, based at Camp Lewis, was called to active duty in the summer of 1952, midway through the long winding down of the war in Korea. A benevolent fate saw to it that he was stationed for most of the next year at Camp Roberts, California (the National Guard area of Fort Ord), just minutes down the Coast Highway from Monterey.

That same year, as a prize for making some training films for the navy, his brother-in-law Saul Weingarten (a World War II veteran and an attorney, recalled to duty) had been offered his choice of billets, and elected Monterey. When he and his wife arrived in Carmel, brother Charles was happily established as a company commander at Camp Roberts. Charles loved the area and found to his delight that he could talk easily to all the men under him. Best of all, he was finished work by five-thirty every day.

So in his free time he designed the Weingartens' $10,000 house in Pebble Beach, zipping up on weekends in his '47 Studebaker to supervise construction. The house earned Moore his first award, not mentioned in his Japanese publisher's list of credits: "Cal Vet Home of the Month," in the Cal Vet News Bulletin for December 1953. "Saul fell for the lot, then got this contractor and plan I didn't approve of. So I made a new plan, but we used the contractor's details in order to stay within their budget. Its great feature was that fireplace wall and the 'flowing space' between the living room and kitchen. That was thought to be very revolutionary in those days. It has my best-ever nineteen forties Bay Region–style wood-edged detailing, if anybody's interested. I keep telling Saul he'll be living in a museum piece soon."

The house also helped establish his brother-in-law's legal reputation, since through it he broke the anti-Semitic restrictions of heretofore exclusive Pebble Beach, then under the absolute control of Samuel Morse and the Del Monte Corporation. Until that time, no house in the "private" streets of Pebble Beach could be occupied by "descendants of any person from Africa, Asia, or the former Turkish Empire"—which included Palestine—"servants excepted." The house was designed to expand easily to accommodate a family of four. "When Chuck learned I was having a third child, he was furious," his sister says. A fourth son came later—all raised in the little house their uncle designed.

In August 1953, Charles was posted to Fort Belvoir in Virginia, where he first saw Stratford Hall, the great 1725 Lee family mansion he was later to honor by references in his lectures and books, and by a manor house he designed in New Jersey in conscious imitation of its forms. On leave at Christmas time, he escaped to the U.S. Virgin Islands. "I played Scrabble with Gloria Swanson in Charlotte Amalie." After that came ten months in postwar Korea.

Like many men for whom national service is more an interruption in life than a step forward, Charles Moore has said very little about this particular year overseas. "In the army, I got to design a lot of groovy stuff with Quonset huts, which the Koreans would then do over in 1870 Wilkes-Barre Gothic. One A-frame there *did* get built more or less according to my design." He was not to travel abroad again for five years, and then not until ten years after that. Observers have been impressed by the "Japanese" style of the first houses he designed in California after his return (he spent three weeks in Japan after his tour). His own account of this influence, in his review of David Gebhard's book on Rudolph Schindler, is revealing:

Reading the book, I kept being reminded of my first trip to Japan, when I was aspiring to be a Bay Region architect. I had been to Europe, and had been transported by the presence of Chartres and the Parthenon and the Alhambra and Batalha; but I wasn't threatened by them. They were made of beautiful alien stuff. Now here in Japan were people who had taken boards—just what I used, though theirs appeared to be of better quality—and had made with them things more wonderful than I had ever dreamed of. That was threatening. And, of course, it was moving too.[1]

When his army time was over, his sister was surprised at the change in Chuck. "He had been so inflexible and demanding before, so impatient of other people's stupidity. The war experience changed him. He had all these normal, uneducated fellows under him in the company, and he discovered to his astonishment both that they liked him—and that he liked them! He hated the idea of war, of course, of barracks life. But somehow he adapted to it, brilliant and fussy though he was. It was through the army experience that he became the warm, wonderful, humorous person he's been ever since. I remember this army sergeant of his from Camp Roberts who came to visit us and kept going on about 'Good Old Chuck.' I just couldn't believe it."

5 / PRINCETON DAYS

BUT of all the experiences of Charles Moore's apprenticeship, none seems to have mattered so much as the five years he spent at Princeton after his military service. For a time, he and the younger schoolmates who became his partners in California were called "the boys from Princeton," not always with admiration. They, and other like-minded graduates of the university's architecture program in the late 1950s, were written of as the "Princeton school," which was presumed to stand in active contrast to the "establishment" schools at such places as Harvard, Yale, Columbia, and MIT. For a while, the Princeton school of architecture (along with nearby Penn) seemed to dominate, or to be fighting for domination of, American architecture.

Whether or not this is true, Princeton was one of the few major design schools in the United States at the time that lay outside the modernist mainstream. When the so-called postmodernist movement was invented, or discerned, by the architectural press around 1970, the reputation of these two schools was immeasurably enhanced: how *wise* of Princeton and Penn not to have been taken in! Reminiscences of the extraordinary number of Princeton architecture students of those years who have gone on to become professional leaders are even more suffused with the gilded nostalgia of a privileged elite than those of the average Ivy League class.

When a cease-fire was called in the battle of styles, and the concrete dust had settled, the publicity victors, at least, did seem to be people like Hugh Hardy, Charles Moore, Robert Venturi, and a number of other sons of Old Nassau, all influenced by the thinking of design teachers like Jean Labatut, Enrico Peressutti, and Louis Kahn. Many of them then went on to teach at or administer other architecture schools, thereby spreading the gospel according to Penn and Princeton to another and larger generation.

Charles Moore decided, while in Korea, that he had had enough

117

of Utah. What he wanted now was to get a Ph.D. in architectural history on the GI Bill. He wrote to Harvard, Yale, Columbia, and Princeton.

"Harvard wrote me one of their long, confused letters, the same kind they send out now. Yale wrote a really snotty letter, advising me to forget about grad school and apply as a freshman. I forget what Columbia said—maybe they never answered.

"But Princeton told me I was *exactly* what they were looking for. Donald Drew Egbert, the art historian, and Robert McLaughlin, the dean, both signed the letter. They told me they were trying to 'build bridges' between history and practice. They proposed for me a one-man curriculum that included lots of art-history seminars and all the undergraduate architectural history I wanted to take; getting a professional master's degree in architecture along the way by doing design studies and a thesis; and then coming up with some grand dissertation idea that combined design, history, and theory.

"And so I did that. I spent what was left of the year designing Mother's house in Pebble Beach, and then packed up my Studebaker and drove out to Princeton, New Jersey."

"I REMEMBER Charles coming to Princeton." Hugh Hardy, a principal of Hardy Holzman and Pfeiffer Associates, and one of the brightest stars of the new generation, is talking in the conference room of his firm's office, on the sixteenth floor of a fine old building on Park Avenue South. Blue eyes spark in a ruddy, eager face; he crackles with all the New York energies and ambitions, the mordant wit and broad intelligence one misses in many westerners. Out the window one can count the steel gargoyles on the Chrysler Building's scorpion-tail spire.

"Tom Hoving was there studying art history, Frank Stella was doing art. No one ever saw Bob Venturi. Not a wave. Architecture and art history were in the same building, McCormick Hall—that was before they added that excremental new museum—locked in a bizarre embrace. Of which I totally approved. It's so rare for most architects even to be exposed to any history. The Beaux Arts was still very much alive. In watercolor classes, people like Jean Labatut actually taught us how to look and how to draw." (Hardy's firm has built a considerable part of its reputation by doing sensitive adaptations of fine nineteenth-century buildings.)

"It's just an accident, of course, that we were all there together. The one thing we shared was an emphatic disgust for all the architecture of the fifties, I suppose. No one was forcing the link-up of past and present in design classes: we just absorbed the sense of an enormously rich past. We *knew* what we loved and what we hated. Egbert and Smith in art history were full of great passion and catholicity.

"Not that everyone at Princeton was supercultural. Our new dean, McLaughlin, was a prefab-housing man. His job was to raise money, I suppose. He was the one who got some rich alumnus to subsidize our famous trip to Yucatán. Enrico Peressutti brought his girlfriend along. It was a giant lark.

"When I first met Charles in 1955, I had the sense that he was being mocked by the proper Princetonians as a tall, fat mid-westerner. In defense he'd cut up—indulge in lots of sophomoric nonsense: both as a person and on the drafting board."

"JOHN used to tell me about this brilliant, wonderful person he had met at the design studio." Sally Woodbridge, a lively architectural critic and historian, was at Princeton with her former husband in 1955. "I had this image of a dynamic, incisive, brilliant man. Then late one night at one of those Museum of Modern Art things in New York, I heard this soft, thin voice behind me asking, 'Aren't you Sally Woodbridge?' And there was this very ugly man, so mild-mannered and soft-spoken. Then I think he was just timid. Now he's very aware of that contradictory image; he *plays* the self-belittling style, makes a persona out of it. Alongside other architects, he always looks so rumpled and pudgy and helpless.

"He was Princeton's first Ph.D. in architecture, and I don't think they knew what to do with him. He does talk a lot about Peressutti; I'm sure *he* influenced his thinking. He was one of the few design teachers at Princeton then who had actually designed a building. Enrico came in with his Italian high-style ideas, trench coat over the shoulders like a European movie star, then flew them all off on the famous Yucatán expedition. Charles and Venturi were once very close, I think, until Denise came along. They've drifted apart since. And Lou Kahn was in his pantheon from the time he started coming to Princeton for juries.

"But no one at Princeton taught Charles very much. He came to a prestigious place to get his degree and work on his own ideas.

His later partners may see it differently, but I'm convinced that Charles, in his soft, mild-mannered way, was the one who molded their whole concept of architecture. He used to present ideas he was absolutely certain about as if he wasn't certain at all, as if he was really inviting their advice. Then they could all feel they were collaborating as equals.

"My husband never fell for Charles's architecture. He was too disciplined, too much a rationalist. Charles is a very sloppy detailer—you knew that, didn't you? When he climbed up on the Santa Barbara Faculty Club, John Beach was very surprised: all the windows leaked! Charles couldn't detail windows at all. If you leave the circle of his admirers, David, you'll find a lot of people who think Charles Moore couldn't design his way out of a paper bag."

RICHARD PETERS, now a San Francisco architect and a professor at Berkeley, arrived at Princeton as a graduate student from Georgia Tech in the fall of 1956. By then, "the celebrated Charles W. Moore," as Peters likes to call him, had become something of a local legend.

"He still lived in the graduate college then. Actually he lived in the drafting room, he spent day and night there, and only came to the college for dinner. We wore black robes to dinner in those days. Charles was the assistant house master: he could come in nude under his robes, he could do all the Latin graces. He was finishing his master's thesis on old Monterey—fifty million layers of Zip-a-tone, all context, no individual buildings—and he would help anyone around who needed help. Later he worked as course critic under Enrico Peressutti.

"My class's big project that year was to do a town square for Morristown, New Jersey. I turned the square back to old cow fields, with one theater or something linked to the old church. Peressutti made a great thing about new–old linkages. We took our sketching trip, two or three weeks, to the Delaware Valley, Williamsburg, Stratford Hall, Winterthur. It was very nice, but we felt a little cheated after hearing about Chichén Itzá.

"The next year Charles moved to an apartment on the top of a house on Washington Street, which became everyone's meeting place after studio hours. We'd go for beer at the Nassau Inn, or a

King's Inn pizza, then up to Charles's apartment. He always had what he called 'adequate' sherry, ninety-nine cents a bottle. We didn't drink hard liquor, although I remember somebody making purple popsicles with gin for the boat races. Hugh and Felix [Drury] brought various ladies. That was when I first met the famous Dona.

"Hugh had been in the Princeton Triangle Show; there were lots of Tom Lehrer songs around the piano, all very wild and outrageous. Charles knew the words to everything, of course. I remember him throwing someone else's radio out the drafting-room window, though, when the owner wouldn't turn it down.

"We all went on a lot of sketching weekends, looking at old buildings. The idea was never to bring a camera, so you were forced to *look* at the things as you drew them. In New York, we went dutifully to see Lever House and the Seagram Building; but more often things like Penn Station. The past-to-present relating was very big at Princeton.

"By fifty-seven we were becoming more aware of Bob Venturi. Don Lyndon got him to come up that fall and show slides of some house in his exquisite pencil drawings. Simultaneously Louis Kahn was coming onto the scene, the whole so-called Philadelphia school. Charles was a major design teacher by then, Billy and Don were the stars, and everyone trekked down to Trenton to see the Lou Kahn bathhouses.

"That was the year Charles presented his own Ph.D. project, 'Water in Architecture.' God, was that a performance! Everyone worked on it. It was a grand production. His mother came out from California to see him get his degree. I think that was when he first found out that she had cancer.

"By then he had already talked John and Sally Woodbridge into moving to California. Don Rice and I decided to move out in fifty-eight, when I was offered a job at Berkeley. Then Charles came out in the fall of fifty-nine, Billy a month or two later, Don the next year, after his trip to India. All of a sudden, everybody was on the Coast."

THE "famous trip to Yucatán" these people all talk about, with nostalgia (if they went) or envy (if they didn't), was a lavish Princetonian extravaganza led by Enrico Peressutti over the Christmas holidays of 1955–56, in which all first-year graduate students in architecture were flown via Havana to Chichén Itzá, the great

Mayan capital founded in the sixth century, abandoned, reoccupied five hundred years later, and abandoned permanently in 1194. The class project was not only to observe and learn from this matchless set of the ruins of two civilizations, but also, on their return to Princeton, to design a modern museum for the area that would somehow respect what was already there.

Charles Moore on the Yucatán trip: "I remember Enrico saying, about our doing this new building alongside the ruins, that it was like a young person meeting an old person on a train. It would be appalling if the young person weren't at least thoughtful, congenial, attentive to the older one. But it would be just as insulting to copy him, to ape his manners exactly. My own solution—I've still got it somewhere—was a folded-plate phenomenon with big holes in it, like Ronchamps, painted in funny colors, where they were supposed to display Mayan artifacts. It was well regarded, as I recall.

"One of my classmates did some huge megastructure that just slabbed across the ravine, and we all got screaming about what an idiot he was, how he'd done it all wrong. But he was a very strong designer. It *was* one of the most exciting things anyone in the class did.

"That sort of thing was not officially shunned—Princeton had no party line—it was just not heavily argued.

"Dean McLaughlin tried to run a countertrend to people like Labatut and Peressutti. He brought down people from New York to lecture to us, like Gordon Bunshaft." (Bunshaft, a partner in the New York office of Skidmore, Owings and Merrill, and chief designer of Lever House, was one of the most honored American-born representatives of the international style.) "He was perhaps the most unpleasant creep I ever met. Really awful. All these sharp New Yorkers wheeled in to instruct the young of Princeton."

Other reigning masters, like architects Edward Durrell Stone and Paul Rudolph, and the critic Siegfried Giedion, were (Moore insists) similarly rejected when they came to spread the word. "When the heroes of the modern movement came, we usually thought they were the prime idiots of all time. I remember Siegfried Giedion announcing (in a thick German accent, suitable only for Harvard) that the ideal size for a city was seven hundred thousand. And when questioned by us about that presumption—which, apparently, people at Harvard had simply accepted—he announced that Rotterdam was about seven hundred thousand, and Rotterdam was a nice city, and so seven hundred thousand was it.

"No: the models that were so strong elsewhere in the fifties were just not very strong at Princeton."

THE "models that were so strong elsewhere" in the years between Charles Moore's return from Europe in 1950 and the Sea Ranch breakthrough of 1965—as measured by major design awards given during those years—were mostly rectilinear boxes of various configurations, straight-sided, flat-roofed, and pure. They included mammoth projects for leveling hundreds of city-center acres and replacing them with machined slabs of housing. They included the gridded facades of modular office towers all across America and apartments that looked like ice-cube trays standing on end. The big-dollar design firms—Welton Becket; Pereira and Luckman; I. M. Pei—leagued with speculator-developers to erect new shopping center, office, and apartment complexes. By the early 1960s, the sleek boxes were alternating with concrete cage structures or enlivened by checkerboarded or asymmetrical fenestration. But still they looked like boxes made by machines.

The "models that were so strong" included candy-box school buildings, two or three of them punctured for rectangular inner courts and then connected by linear breezeways. They included floating shoeboxes perched on stilts or cantilevered over slopes. In these minimalist studies in skeletal structure and glass wall, chic people in New Canaan and Bloomfield Hills somehow contrived to live. They included the rigorous purity of blind-faced new art museums, factorylike colleges and collegelike new factories—all of them in the same unadorned cubist style. Prizes were won annually by multimillion-dollar corporate headquarters, or research-and-development villas, set amid Blenheim-sized parks and lakes—impeccably detailed boxes of concrete and glass riding low on the landscape, designed for General Motors and John Deere, Connecticut General and Emhart, Schlumberger and Corning Glass. Through the 1950s and beyond, the international-style prisms were very nearly ubiquitous.

Today, when the bloom has faded from the white modernist rose, most observers will agree that the period did have its masterpieces—boxes (usually by Eero Saarinen, Philip Johnson, or Skidmore, Owings and Merrill) of a purity and finesse so exquisite that they transcended the limitations of their minimalist geometry and their machine-made associations. A few daring masters ventured nonrectilinear shapes, to express things like flight, engineering dynamics, or otherworldly values. Religion, by and large, was the most acceptable excuse during these years for using curves or acute angles.

By the early 1960s, many celebrity architects in the United States were betraying some impatience with puritan norms. One faint gesture of revolt was the use of pierced screens cast in concrete (Edward Durrell Stone) or metal (Minoru Yamasaki), usually in conjunction with reflecting pools. Another was the emergence, especially after Paul Rudolph's Art and Architecture Building at Yale in 1964, of chunky, asymmetrical, fortresslike concrete structures of a style the British expressively labeled "new brutalist." Buildings of the first sort were found "romantic" and "humane"; those of the second were praised for their "boldness" and "character." Lesser variations were played with concrete roof forms: for about five years, they kept ballooning up into white barrel vaults or cracking into zigzag sections called folded plates. Walls sprouted eccentric sunshades or broke out with embossed panels. Canny populists played garish games with Las Vegasy shapes, and still managed to garner awards.

Through this (for Moore) frustrating decade and a half of modernist rule, there were occasional hints in the annual awards announcements of the strange directions American architecture was to take after 1965. On both coasts, a few architects were attempting "human-scaled" housing projects of varied two- and three-story house forms set casually under trees and around private garden walks. Charles Colbert, in 1960, seemed to be reaching for a new and more complex kind of order, one that split the formal integrity of the box, in a Louis Kahn–like house plan for New Orleans. A few years later, Colbert designed additions to a private school with steep-pitched roofs that visibly respected two Victorian mansions on the site. In the Northeast, Louis Sauer also broke with the right angle, putting shed roofs back on brick-and-cedar houses and adding old-fashioned projecting bays; one house he fitted into the ruins of a nineteenth-century mill.

But awards juries continued to argue over unorthodox or antimodern designs, even as they awarded them prizes. Earl Carlin's exciting New Haven fire station of 1961 outraged juror Edward Stone by its "capricious disorder," its "stage-set, expressionist, New Brutalist Yale approach." The model, design, and rendering of Moore's Orinda house, published in the P/A awards issue of January 1962, created a kind of surrealist shock. The MLTW Coronado Beach condominium plan, honored in 1963, was both praised and condemned for its efforts to "break down the spaces."

The defiantly independent northern California regionalists, in whose Bay Region idiom Moore had once worked, held their own through the heyday of the glass-and-concrete box. Some of the most handsome and humane designs honored during these years—comfortable, pitched-roof wooden houses that still looked like houses, residential developments and schools that sat easily among trees or on hillside slopes—were designed by the same Bay Area firms from whom Moore had sought work in 1947 and 1948, or others who had joined them since.[2] If their work was unadventurous and formally "loose" (by the standards Moore and others set in the early 1960s), and got clumsier as it got larger, it still tended to respect the past, people's emotional needs, and the natural landscape with more grace than most of the prize-winning work of large East Coast and Los Angeles firms.

With this one exception, architecture that attended to the past in any conscious way tended to be ignored by design-award juries between 1950 and 1965. At places like Harvard and Yale, modernist landmarks were plonked down unthinkingly alongside period-piece neighbors. Some minor essays in what is now called historicism or contextualism did sneak through: Colbert's girls' school additions of 1965; a neo-neoclassical brick pavilion house with sixteen interior columns (Robert Finkle, 1962); a lacy Victorian tennis pavilion for Princeton, designed by Ballard, Todd & Snibbe in 1962; and an impeccably joined extension to a 1903 San Francisco office building from the office of Clark and Buettler (AIA Award, 1965), whose chief designer, working between university duties at Berkeley, had been Charles W. Moore.

"I had started out thinking of myself as a 'Bay Region' architect," says Moore, "and then had been swept in turn by Europe and Japan. I had taught history at Utah, and I came to Princeton to do a degree in history. So Peressutti's concern with the past was wonderful. The idea behind each of his sketching trips was for us to take something old and full of context, and then to try to put new things *in* them—but new things that would not be like imposters, but like those congenial fellow travelers on the train.

"Jean Labatut, also—although I never got as excited about him as Don and Bill did; he didn't seem to be able to turn out buildings I could admire—he had been everywhere. He knew exactly what the Marques de Pombal had done after the earthquake of 1755, and how you could stand in some corner of the main square of Santo Antonio (which I subsequently tried, and he was right) and get all the black-and-white lines of the plaza to converge in some curious way, so that they appeared to diverge in some other curious way. He did the fountains at the 1939 New York World's Fair.

"I had never heard of Louis Kahn when I first went to Princeton, but he eventually came to seem more important than anyone else. In my last year there, during Labatut's sabbatical, I was teaching full time with him. We got very excited listening to him. The thesis class would go down to his office in Philadelphia one evening a week. Each one got to put his work on the table and then Kahn would talk about it, sometimes an hour on each one. It went on till two in the morning. Our minds just boggled; it was so marvelous. It went on all year. Kahn was much more magical than Peressutti; he made everything seem so wonderful. It was a whole new world. There was so much moral fervor to everything: it really *mattered* what color bricks you picked. That business of keeping rooms 'sanctified places': it was all very highly charged.

"In the end my big decision was whether to accept Bill Wurster's offer and come back to Berkeley, or go to work for Kahn. I guess I thought I was a little old for the apprentice role."

Charles Moore's own major design projects at Princeton were the Mayan museum; a model historic-preservation plan for Monterey, California; and his magnum opus, "Water in Architecture." He also began writing articles for *Architectural Record*, contributed a chapter to someone else's book on plaster, and did a hundred-dollar potboiler on architecture for *Encyclopedia Americana*. Each summer, back in California, he would design one more house— plus, in 1956, a small office building for his brother-in-law.

His own dissertation finished, Moore stayed on at Princeton two more years (1957–59) as a postdoctoral fellow and assistant professor, working with both Peressutti and Kahn. He went along on the first-year graduates' sketching trips—with Dick Peters's class to the Delaware Valley, Bill Turnbull's to Newport, Donlyn Lyndon's along the C & O canal from Washington to Hinkerstown. ("Hugh Hardy set up placards all along the canal to welcome us in.") He helped young Turnbull and Lyndon—soon to be his partners—to complete their own master's projects, improvements to Ellis Island and the Boston Museum of Fine Arts, respectively.

6/L, T, AND W

DONLYN LYNDON—the L of MLTW—has opted, since 1965, for the relatively tranquil but unspectacular career of a writer-critic-professor who sometimes designs buildings—as opposed to Charles Moore, an architect who writes and teaches and lectures (and tries to do all these at once). Like all the original partners except Whitaker, Lyndon has put on some weight since 1962. Like all of them, he signals the modified bohemianism of his profession by a trimmed display of facial hair. He has been married for twenty productive and mutually supportive years to Alice Wingwall, a sculptor and photographer. They have three grown or growing children. If the Lyndon family has been blessed by the stability of academic life, it has also been bedeviled by serious physical mishaps and the difficulty of sustaining a profitable, attention-getting practice while running a university department. Since they went their separate ways, Lyndon has designed far fewer buildings than Turnbull or Moore. But one of his projects (the Pembroke College dorms) won *Progressive Architecture*'s first design award in 1975. Several handsome houses across the country bear witness to his individual talent. Berkeley land and construction costs being what they are, he and his family now live in a remodeled bungalow south of campus. He, his current associates, and his wife share an office in a renovated industrial-district plant.

Like Bill Turnbull, Lyndon may be said to have "inherited" his profession. His father was a modernist architect of considerable reputation who practiced in southern California after World War II. ("I still remember Arthur Drexler's 1948 book, *Made in USA*. It was the first time I'd seen somebody writing about my father.")

Even so, Don Lyndon thought he was going to be a radio announcer or some kind of journalist until he got hooked on buildings during high school, mainly through a pile of old architectural magazines salvaged from a family friend's basement. "By the time I was eighteen, I could tell who had designed any important modern building just by looking at the photograph." Later, at Princeton—converted to the Italian Renaissance by Geoffrey Scott's *The Architecture of Humanism*—he mastered the same game with sixteenth- and seventeenth-century buildings. Like Moore, who arrived at Princeton as a doctoral candidate during his junior year, Lyndon became a lifelong devotee of the buildings of centuries and continents other than his own. Like Charles, too—with whom he later taught a highly unorthodox survey course at Berkeley on oriental architecture—he was seriously tempted to become an art historian rather than an architect. But, despite some agonizing uncertainty over his own design abilities, he persisted in wanting "to make things you could *be* in."

He presumed—again like Charles—that he would study architecture at the University of Michigan, his father's alma mater. But his stepmother insisted he go someplace "good," so he applied to Harvard and Princeton, hoping to get into Harvard. All Harvard offered in the way of financial aid was a dining-hall job. Princeton offered a full scholarship—"and Princeton let you start doing architecture in freshman year." Once there, he was shocked to learn that no one at Princeton had heard of his father. Despite his admiration for certain teachers and friends (including Charles, who was both), Lyndon remained insecure and unhappy for much of his five years there.

"You have to realize that the Princeton architectural school was a very small place. Every student, from first year through the grads, had his desk lined up in one room no bigger than Bill's office in San Francisco." (The Princeton drafting room was about 110 by 30 feet.) "Any student the least bit inquisitive walked around and looked at others' work. As a sophomore I went up and checked out the juniors, the seniors, and the grads. That's how I got to know Chuck. He arrived in my junior year.

"The first thing we really talked about was his master's thesis on historic Monterey. I went over and looked at it, then launched into a diatribe against it. *That* wasn't what architecture was supposed to be like! I was still playing out of the international style and my father's rationalist mode. I couldn't make any sense out of Chuck's California historical references.

"Through Chuck, I got to know Bill. We'd go over to Chuck's house and look at slides together, take trips together: trips to Philadelphia, New York. I remember Hugh Hardy sliding down museum bannisters, seeing *My Fair Lady* together right after it opened.

"Bill became a very close friend, but Chuck at that time was more of a mentor. He clearly knew and had done so much more. Even then he was recognized as someone different and amusing. 'You really ought to pay attention to him,' other grads told me. 'He knows what he's doing.' But the things he was designing then struck me as reactionary and evil. I didn't understand.

"I won some travel money in my fifth year and went to Europe for the summer and half of the fall. In Rome I met George Rolley, my art-history professor, and we taxied around looking at piazzas for a book he wanted to write. Back in Princeton later that fall, we'd meet for dinner once a week, Labatut, Rolley, Bill Shellman, Charles Moore, and I, to discuss the meaning of piazzas. Nothing much came of it, though, because we drank so much.

"Enrico Peressutti ended up as my fourth-year studio teacher. Chuck was his teaching assistant. The next year Bill was in that class, and Chuck was an instructor. By then he was designing these little houses in Monterey, where his mother and sister lived. That pavilion house for Duane Matterson, very Japanese, very Lou Kahn—we all had a hand in that.

"Labatut was on leave my last graduate year, so I had Louis Kahn for my thesis. Kahn means less to me now, but he was a very important influence on our group when we started. Chuck was his T.A. on *both* Bill's and my theses. Our common experience with him, I think, was a major factor in keeping us together. It helped to congeal a common language we all understood. It was easy for us later to create our own 'California' language on the Kahn basis— which Chuck knew so much better than the rest of us."

Back in California in 1961 ("It was either teach or go in the army"), all three—Moore, Lyndon, and Turnbull—shared a converted-garage office in a small south Berkeley apartment building. When they discovered that their below-grade drafting room flooded during heavy rains, they moved into a disused train station across from the Heinz cannery near to the bay. "Chuck and I, and later Dick Whitaker, were all teaching at Cal. Bill was working for SOM [Skidmore, Owings and Merrill] in the city. We'd all take our separate private projects to this little office and walk around criticizing each other's work. We entered a couple of competitions—a fountain in Seattle, the Boston City Hall (that one wasn't very good). The first major thing all three of us worked on was a condominium in Coronado. It didn't get built, but it did get published. The basic massing was Chuck's, but I did a lot on the final form—mainly because I happened to stay around later than anyone else that one night.

"That's how we worked all along. Someone would draw something; someone else would work it over; a third person would grab a pencil. There was a lot of this drawing together, a collective search for forms. We never partitioned up the work. But Chuck was usually the prime generator, the one who'd actually sit down and lay out a precise set of diagrams, the one who congealed ideas so they could generate *new* ideas.

"It wasn't always cheerful and fun. There were often real battles, bad feelings—never sustained bad feelings, but it got pretty heady sometimes. There was much greater emotional involvement than I've ever experienced in any other office. We all knew the stakes were high."

Donlyn Lyndon spent a year in India in 1960–61, a trip he feels was profoundly important both for him and the partnership. He sees the influence of the Hindu sense of "special places," of temple porches, bays, and layered walls in almost everything he did thereafter. Directly he returned, Charles—by then chairman of the department of architecture at Berkeley—concocted a new course that the two of them, a pair of passionate but unscholarly amateurs, would teach together on Asian architecture.

"We were trying to teach art history in terms of personal pleasure and meaning: a new way to look at and study the architecture of the past. It was more theory than history, really: all about platforms and markers and axes. It bore no resemblance to what real art historians were doing. We were trying to teach the students how to *look*. So we did that in the mornings, taught design classes in the afternoons, and did our own stuff in the evenings. In the process, we developed a common language for our classes and design work: the carryover was tremendously productive.

"Chuck, Bill, and I would eat together most of the time, then go back to work till one or two A.M. There were usually others on the scene, Berkeley students like Marvin Buchanan and Ed Allen who ended up as co-workers.

"One of the reasons we were able to do all the things we did is that we spent so much time together. Most of our designs started as drawings on napkins over dinner at Kitty's on College Avenue, and after dinner we'd go back and work till two in the morning. That was one of the reasons Dick Whitaker was never as much a part of the scene. He was married, then, and had a child; he couldn't operate on our crazy schedule.

"Once I got married [late in 1963], I could see that I wasn't going to be able to do that number much longer either. You can't go on living like graduate students forever."

While he was wondering what to do about that, a letter came from the dean at the University of Oregon asking him—at twenty-eight, after just four years of teaching—to become chairman of their department of architecture. After four years building up the program there, Lyndon went on to serve as chairman of the department of architecture at MIT, one of the power positions in American architectural education. (William Wurster had held it for seven years before taking over at Berkeley.) Both at Eugene and at Cambridge, Lyndon maintained his own practice and continued to collaborate from time to time with MLTW—on the Santa Barbara Faculty Club, for example, and the large recreation center at the Sea Ranch. The innovative dormitory village for Pembroke College in Providence, which began as a Moore Associates project, ended up as Lyndon's, and won him his first national attention as an independent designer, with a style distinctly his own.

He has come to be regarded, rightly or wrongly, as the group's theoretician, "the brains of the mob." He has written several important articles summing up the group's ideas, an architectural guide to Boston, and a share of *The Place of Houses* (with Moore and Gerald Allen); he has lectured around the world and generally helped spread the gospel according to Princeton '59. In 1975, after recovering from a serious automobile accident, he accepted an invitation to return to Berkeley as a professor of architecture. He now maintains an architectural office there in partnership with Marvin Buchanan, his former student and longtime associate, only four blocks north of the ex-train station they both worked in with Moore, Turnbull, and Whitaker twenty-two years ago. Except for one MLTW reunion house in Illinois, which all four partners worked on in 1979–80 for a client of Dick Whitaker's, Lyndon has not worked officially with Charles Moore since 1971, though he and Bill Turnbull do still get together for occasional jobs.

I asked Donlyn Lyndon about the different roles he and Charles played in the early 1960s, about the difficulty of building an independent career in the shadow of a more celebrated and flamboyant mentor-partner-friend.

"I guess I would defer to his . . . no, not defer; but I would admit that he has a kind of driving energy about *imagery* that I don't have. There wasn't necessarily any deference about that: but he initiates more than I do. I tend to want to look at all the possible alternatives. Chuck tends to initiate more.

"My role in those days was to follow out a rational line of argument, about why something was being done *this* way rather than another. It's part of my essential moralism, I suppose; something I inherited from my father.

"I think the condominium is in many ways the best thing any of us has ever done. And I think it is so because there was a tension between really trying to put it together for good *reasons*, and having the wit to make unreasonable moves. My perception is that Chuck's work *after* we worked together went crazier."

A handsome, fat folio of work was printed in Tokyo in 1980, entitled *Charles Moore & Company*. Four of Donlyn Lyndon's individual designs of the last ten years were included (along with thirty-five other works, by fifteen other architects) under the "& Company" rubric. How did it feel, having to exist professionally under those terms? Was the preeminent position inevitably given to Charles Moore a result of his greater freedom, his better contacts, his more ingenious self-promotion? Or did he really deserve it?

"I think the first part is unquestionably true," Donlyn Lyndon replied. "He's very good at generating publicity. He always had an eye for what counted, for the crucial relationship, in design as in promotion. You know the Coronado condominiums, the first of our collaborative design awards? I remember distinctly his absolute insistence on what mode of presentation that should be, exactly how many layers of Zip-a-tone [a transparent plastic overlay used to represent shadows] we had to use on the drawings.

"Yes: he's crafty about that stuff. Much craftier than I am. But to the second part of your question, does he *deserve* the number-one role, the 'Charles Moore and Company' spot—again I say absolutely yes. I don't think I'm particularly shy about my own abilities, but I'm not at all shy about saying that I think Chuck's are greater. There's a richness of imagination, and even a kind of . . . *discipline*, ultimately, that he has and I don't."

T—William Turnbull, Jr.—still manages to come across as boyish and cocky, despite his thinning black hair and thickening middle. A well-born easterner, now forty-five, he cultivates with engaging aggressiveness a gray-speckled beard and the style of an overworked farmhand who would far rather be wearing jeans than a suit, riding a horse on his brother's ranch in Colorado, or tending his vineyard in the Napa Valley: in fact, doing almost anything except designing and dealing in this goddam office in this goddam city. (Bill cusses a lot.)

Unlike M, L, and W, he has rarely published his ideas or flourished in an academic setting. When asked the reason why, he plays the uneducated hick: "I'ma no talka too much." (This is disputable.) "Uncle Chuck told me a long time ago that I couldn't write a decent sentence. Those guys [Moore and Lyndon] have always been writers and intellectuals. Why should I try to compete? Me, I'm just one o'them truckers."

But he lets one know the distinguished chairmanships he's been offered. He has his secretary distribute lists of his own honors and guest lectures. And he makes it clear that he did some of the partnership's most significant writing: the short blurbs, or explanations of each project, which accompany submissions for design awards or publication—and inevitably end up being quoted verbatim by lazy judges and editors (and then repeated in the histories and textbooks).

Less a prodigy than his more celebrated "uncle" (though his precision draftsmanship is a marvel), less blithely endowed with self-confidence, Turnbull speaks with disarming candor. He seems to be genuinely and totally engaged in the business of designing good buildings for real people in real places, free from either theoretical preconceptions or the urge to shock, to shine, or to make art. Charles Moore may communicate a sense of awesome insecurity in worldly terms (how on earth will his bills get paid, his jobs get done, his affairs ever come into balance?). But at the same time he imparts a corresponding sense of living sublimely above and apart from such boring details, secure in the treasure house of his ingenuity and wit, his historical and spatial recall, his wizardry at solving architectural problems. He accepts as his due the support of his entourage. Bill Turnbull is short-tempered and ambitious, but more of-the-earth earthly. He would like to love and keep a family; to sail and grow wine grapes; to teach, talk, travel, deal civilly with others. He would also like to design a few of the finest new buildings in the world. But he suspects that no one can do both—and that perhaps he *alone* couldn't achieve the latter, in any case.

He may be said to come naturally by his occasional cowboy or country-boy mannerisms and inflections, although the Turnbull dairy farm in Somerset County, New Jersey, wasn't exactly hicksville. "My grandfather moved out of the Oranges in the eighties and set up a farm in the eastern tradition of the country gentleman. But that didn't mean I didn't grow up with livestock. I claim my growing up in a rural environment as proudly as Chuck claims his peripatetic yearly travels to Los Angeles in the Dust Bowl. If my main contribution to the group was a land ethic—a sense that the land has a life of its own and deserves our respect—it comes from growing up in a valley farmed edge to edge, with three generations working it; a defined landscape, a four-season cycle, three and a half miles to play in. Whenever I got depressed at college, I'd quit and go home—it was only thirty miles from Princeton—and work the farm. The bigger problems and patterns there reduce yours to size."

For all his genteel agricultural background, it is not surprising that Bill Turnbull ended up studying architecture at Princeton. There have been architects in his family since 1865. One of his great-grandfathers (George B. Post) studied at the Ecole des Beaux Arts in Paris, worked with Henry Hobson Richardson in the seventies and eighties, served as president of the American Institute of Architects in 1893, and won the institute's gold medal in 1895. His father (Princeton '30) studied architecture at Yale under Eero Saarinen, although he never practiced. An instructor in mechanical drawing at his prep school (St. Mark's) recognized Bill Jr.'s genius for drafting and helped him on the path toward MLTW.

"It's hard to think of Chuck as a 'teacher,'" he says of the Princeton connection. "More a sort of wise friend. I got to know him best when he was running this course with Enrico, the fall of my second graduate year. We went off on two- or three-day sketching trips to Newport for that year's project, to drink and talk and sketch, walk along the cliffs at night.

"Back at Princeton we'd meet for coffee in the morning, meet for pizza and beer in the evening at the King's Inn, then work on in the drafting room till two; take weekend escapes. He was teaching all the time. He had ten more years of experience than we did. He spent *all* of his time in the studio, all day and half the night. I pity the poor kids now who can't catch him between planes and phone calls. Chuck was the pivot of our lives, even then."

In the traditional Ecole des Beaux Arts system, lower classmen at Princeton helped graduate students in architecture draw their thesis projects, rather like younger Boy Scouts helping a senior with his Eagle Scout project. Both Lyndon and Turnbull helped Moore with his "fabulous" Ph.D. presentation in 1957. He in turn served as a co-instructor, first with Enrico Peressutti, then with Louis Kahn, on their master's theses in 1958 and 1959. The three designed a house together in 1957, a mixture of Japanese forms, Louis Kahn ideas, and cheap factory components, finishing the working drawings in McCormick Hall over the weekend of the Yale–Princeton football game. ("Everyone else was down in the stadium," says Turnbull, "and there we were up drafting.") The house was built the following summer, for a schoolteacher-potter and his wife in Monterey. ("He paid us in pots.") The friendship among the three grew, deepened, and—most surprisingly—endured. "The friendship is the glue that's carried us through all the good and bad times." In fact, at the start Bill Turnbull thought of Charles Moore more as a good friend, and a man dedicated to excellence, than as a particularly great architect. "He was just great fun, as he's always been. I didn't think him a great designer till he did Orinda."

In 1957, Bill Turnbull (who led his class all six years at Princeton) got a summer job at the San Francisco office of Skidmore, Owings and Merrill, the largest architectural firm in the country. After finishing his master's thesis, and spending six wretched months in the army reserves, he came back to the Bay Area and was hired full time by Skidmore, where he remained as a designer for three and a half years.

He moonlighted with Moore and Lyndon in Berkeley almost all of that time, sometimes setting up appointments with private clients at six in the morning.

"When I first arrived in California in June 1960, Chuck had an extra pad in his apartment, so I slept on the window seat. And when Don arrived, he slept in the living room. We all slept under the same roof until we couldn't stand it anymore.

"I worked eight hours a day for Skidmore, five days a week; and I worked four hours a day and weekends for us." Didn't that bother Skidmore? "It bothered the hell out of some people."

When the Sea Ranch Condominium project came their way late in 1963, Turnbull took a leave of absence from SOM. When work on the project slowed down briefly a few weeks later, the partner in charge at SOM–San Francisco refused to take him back. "I can remember going into Skidmore in January sixty-four, because the job was on hold, and asking Chuck Bassett for my job back, and being told to stuff it in my ear. And I remember telling these other guys in the office that it didn't make any difference, because we really had a good one. We had as good a building as anything Skidmore was doing."

In an introduction to Yukio Futagawa's elegant photo album on their Sea Ranch work, Bill Turnbull wrote in 1970 of the specific program and process that led to the final siting and shapes of their most famous building. (Moore, Lyndon, and Halprin have all written on it as well.) Later, and privately, he tried to explain why it came out as well as it did.

"The way I see it is that the four of us had strengths that instead of exploding, imploded. I think of Don as a really outstanding theoretician, sort of a yardstick maker, verbalizing and setting out the ground rules. And I think of Chuck as being a marvelous free spirit, filled with whimsy and fantasy and a tremendous sense of scale in interiors. My own strength, I think the other three would agree, is basically in the landscape—how buildings work in the bigger picture. And Dick's . . . [laughter], Dick's I've never quite figured out.

"Dick was picked up originally at Berkeley hoping that his strength would be working drawings and production. We were weak in that area; we just needed another set of hands. And Dick turned out to be a very sensitive guy who had a good eye and who wanted to do the same kind of things *we* wanted to do. But he didn't go through the Princeton stuff with us, he wasn't exposed to the same people. Remember, Chuck and Don and I go back a *long*, long time. Dick came in at 1960 in Berkeley, and we'd already been working together for five years.

"Princeton didn't have a party line; I'm not saying that. But we liked some of the same things. We liked barns, crazy stick-style stuff, supergraphics, history, people like Frank Furness. . . ."

Turnbull agreed with Don Lyndon's judgment that the Sea

Ranch Condominium was still the best thing any one of them had ever done.

"There wasn't anything else, frankly. So you had three good minds hard on one building, on a super site with a client who did not tell you how to do it but only demanded excellence, and if you didn't give him excellence he kicked your ass. So you kept reaching, reaching, reaching; extending.

"We haven't had one job like that since. If we had one job and the three of us and time, open-ended time, we'd get you another good building. Christ, if I could just get rid of some of the work in here! Not because I don't want to do it, but because I want to put my mind one hundred ten percent on one project. And not have the telephone ringing, and not have to go out at six-thirty in the morning to put a skylight on somebody's house. The plate's too full.

"Anyway, the secret of that building's success for me was the magic of the site—damn it, that was a fantastic opportunity! Then, it was pioneering: there wasn't anything like it; there was no precedent. Well, in one way there was a lot of precedent—barns. Indigenous nonarchitect architecture, stuff we all liked.

"But I think basically it was time. The business of being able to devote the energy to one thing. It symbolizes what the hell we *could* have done if we'd held that together—if our personalities could have survived the stresses for thirty or forty years."

When Charles Moore left Berkeley for Yale in 1965, and the two other partners quit the firm, Bill Turnbull stayed behind just long enough to close up the California office. He planned to follow Charles east and reestablish the firm—now reduced to MLTW/Moore–Turnbull—with a Connecticut base. For a year, all work was sent out to New Haven, and Turnbull commuted back and forth, spending one week out of every month in the East. "But New Haven was hell. I just decided, 'Screw it.' February in New Haven is so grungy—especially when you've just left the acacias and the cherry trees for that mud and slush. It gets to you after a year."

Many of the plans Bill Turnbull carried back and forth during that transition year were for other buildings at the Sea Ranch: a new swimming and tennis club, private house commissions that had come to them from people impressed by or involved in the first condominium. These continued to win them awards and attention and to popularize the Sea Ranch idiom of fanciful spaces

inside rough-finished, odd-angled sheds. All these were still collaborative efforts, as were a number of other northern California
houses. Two major commissions from the University of California
came their way just as Moore was leaving: one for a residential
college at the new Santa Cruz campus; another for a faculty club at
Santa Barbara.

On both of these, Moore continued to participate actively in the
design, both from New Haven and during trips "home." ("Santa
Barbara was basically Chuck's job," Bill Turnbull says; but both he
and Don Lyndon contributed ideas.) After Turnbull decided New
Haven was hell and established a separate San Francisco branch of
the partnership, most of the work done in California became more
and more his, and less Moore's. "He had his houses in the East,
and I had mine at the ranch. His clients talked to him, mine talked
to me, but then we'd talk to each other, too. It was still Moore–
Turnbull, all that time."

On April Fool's Day 1967—his thirty-second birthday—William
Turnbull, Jr., married an active, attractive, and socially prominent
San Francisco woman. After that, Turnbull realized that he and
Moore would never again be able to work together with the same
symbiotic intensity. During a long night's conversation in Washington that year, they concluded that it was still worth the effort to
try to continue as partners. For two more years, they did.

Reading back from their independent work of the last ten years,
one tries to assign features of their collaborative efforts to this
man or the other; but one's guesses are very often wrong. Turnbull
picks up a cardboard model of a large house in Aspen, Colorado,
that he and Charles designed together recently. "Looking at this, I
bet you'd say, 'Well Jesus: the barn-ness and simplicity of that big
old gable, that's Turnbull, I can tell. 'Cause that's the kind of simple country thing he does. And the crazy kooky stuff on the inside,
all these splayed walls; that's obviously Moore.'

"In fact, it's absolutely the reverse.

"Chuck was involved in all these things of mine, and I was involved in a lot of the stuff that is credited to him. He was involved
in the Binker Barns at Sea Ranch. I was involved in his Klotz house
in Rhode Island. He complicated the chimney of the Rush house
for me.

"But it's an involvement of discussion, of ideas—not necessarily
even drawings. All those beginning stages are wrapped up among

the two, sometimes the three of us. It's very hard in that type of family to say which guy did what. Someone else's throwaway idea may be the trigger to your solving a problem."

In 1969, the Moore–Turnbull partnership was dissolved, legally and completely. Still loath to abandon the by-now-famous initials—and the only one left with a financial stake in the original firm—Turnbull now calls his office at Pier 1½ in San Francisco, just north of the Ferry Building, MLTW/Turnbull Associates. Under that umbrella, he and his new team have designed—independent of Uncle Chuck—more than fifty completed buildings, which have won them several prizes and frequent publication and gained them the reputation of one of the best architectural offices in northern California. Their most honored works, oddly, are houses in New Jersey, Virginia, and Tennessee. Unlike the globe-trotting Moore, Turnbull has no objection to the idea of a permanent local base.

"Chuck doesn't have a strong land ethic. He never attaches himself to a piece of ground and roots and makes things grow. Chuck is like a pioneer scout; he rides a lot of terrain, he *knows* a lot of terrain; and it's always a campfire and a bedroll. My problem is I'm land-oriented, land-poor. I've got too much land. When I was married and had two kids, I lived in the oldest house in Sausalito. I still own it. I've got a vineyard up in Napa, building a barn. I've got six marvelous acres out of Point Reyes. Now, Chuck builds and moves on, because the land underneath isn't that important to him.

"We've got a good tradition of building here in California, the so-called Bay Region style. That is something I still believe in. If I was going to take a day off and go look at buildings, I'd go look at Maybeck. He speaks to me more than anyone else. Maybeck, Wurster, Esherick—twice now I've lived in Joe Esherick buildings; he's my real competition, he's just *so* good—and after I think that it comes down to us. I feel a funny obligation to try to maintain the standards of excellence that those guys set up."

California roots or no, Turnbull crossed some sort of professional threshold in 1975, when he and a group of students won a nose-to-nose competition with "star" architects from New York, Chicago, and Santa Fe for the design of a library and cultural center in Biloxi, Mississippi. That same year, an ingenious lattice-wrapped house of his in Virginia won *Progressive Architecture*'s First Honor Award. In 1977, he was able to salvage parts of Charles's and

Dick Peters's old scheme for the California governor's mansion, and use them in a wonderful house in California's Central Valley. In 1980, he and Moore joined forces for a spectacular, $1.7 million vacation house in Aspen. Since then, they have been working together on the New Orleans World's Fair and two Houston commissions. A many-windowed Bavarian castle in the Rockies (actually a skiers' condominium) won him another P/A prize in 1981. A new house in Kauai (Hawaii) looks like something out of a Somerset Maugham dream. In a recent interview on the state of American architecture, Philip Johnson pointed out, "You see, Turnbull, we usually think, is with Moore; but he is independent. And very good." After twelve active years on his own, it was nice to have someone realize that.

"I wasn't really secure until Zimmerman" (the house in Virginia), he admits. "That house was as important to me as Orinda was to Chuck. 'Hey,' I thought. 'You can actually make a good building!' Don likes it very much. He thinks it's as *clear* as the condo, if not as rich. It's still very stiff inside, though; very straight. If only I'd had Chuck and Don in on it. Don's clarity of insight would have helped; and Chuck knows how to get the lightning bolts in."

Turnbull's response to Moore's work since the dissolution of their partnership is a guarded mixture of respect and dismay.

"Chuck is a brilliant, brilliant, brilliant designer, but there's nobody, it seems to me—in Essex, LA, LA twice, Perez—that says no to him. Nobody has told Chuck, 'No, no way,' in quite a while. I can still do it. Don can still do it. It's a question of weeding out the stuff that will seem like a joke, and wear in a year—and leaving in the things that will wear for a long, long time.

"Chuck is the strongest designer of any of us, but there are no checks and balances on him now. He's so bloody talented, it's so easy for him to design, that it runs away from him. The discipline of the *appropriateness* of the design doesn't enter in a lot—especially now, with everyone scared to death of the Great Charles Moore, Noted Architect.

"Now on my side, they can both say, 'Hey, you're too timid; risk, risk more!' I fought Chuck on the heavy framing of the Sea Ranch because I was afraid of what it would do to the budget. And I backed off. Thank God I backed off, and he carried the day, because it's one of the ingredients of the condominium that makes it magic. But we *were* one hundred percent over budget—or one hundred percent over what they wanted. And so I was right. But he was *more* right.

"There's an apocryphal description of designing the condominium, sort of everybody around the board with one pencil. And you could only hold the pencil as long as you made sense.

"It's pretty close to true. It wasn't one pencil. It was respect for the other guy.

"The stuff I do now is A, but if Chuck and Don were around it would be A-plus. He's reaching out, but I can't easily give him A-plus either. I never thought his triplex in LA was A-plus. Uncle Chuck and I, and Don—we can design so quickly when we're sitting like this, across this table, it's just a fucking magical process. Everyone gaming it, playing it, swirling it up into some new subtle answer. It's an incredible experience. When there were only the three of us, three heads going down on the issue at hand—discounting Dick, because Dick didn't really participate in that—it was a succinct, rapid, and delightful process, with a lot of Eastern cynicism and sarcasm thrown in on top of the pencil lines. We might bitch, about someone not being there sometimes, a little sand in the gears—but there was very little arguing, except of the sort, 'You can't do this, because then *we* can't do that.' Never negative. It was a happy, delightful time.

"Damn few of mine would want to hold up against Chuck's—because they don't cut it. Yet damn few of his nowadays can I really call great. There are superb arabesques and flamboyant, marvelous crescendos. But they don't really go to the heart of conceptually saying something. You look for the story line in there, and there isn't one. And that really bothers me."

What of *Charles Moore & Company*? Does that title bother him?

"That was a negotiated title. It was the best we could get out of them. But if you're trying to get me to say something about the whole credit-and-PR question, David, I'm not gonna rise to it. And the reason I'm not gonna rise to it is that someday somebody *else* is gonna have to unscramble all this, make sense out of this. I get pissed off at Chuck, and get mad at him, and get envious—get feeling second fiddle—but we have a very, very close friendship that goes back to school days.

"I'm gonna bitch about Chuck getting credit? No way. Chuck's always shared the credit, and the magazines don't understand, and the publication boys don't understand, and there's not a goddam thing I can do about it.

"He's got ten years on me, eleven years on Don, and four years on Dick. But he's also bloody damned good. And he's bloody good with a verve; he's got an *esprit* about him that makes people just love him. Sure, he's an actor, a salesman, a personality, all of that. But he also may be better than all of us."

"*May* be?"

"Hey. There's no way I can measure that."

"Even in the middle of a collaborative effort, you never felt that he had more to offer?"

"There are times when I tell him he's full of shit."

"Over the years, then? Putting everything together?"

"Ah, David. That's really hard. He's got all these wonderful qualities, imagination, self-renewal. But you as a critic have to measure, say, the piazza against the condominium. The question is, Does a brilliant man without checks and balances—respected checks and balances, not just restrictions; *good* critics—doesn't he do a better job with a little help from his friends? Is the sheer brilliance that you see in the Piazza d'Italia of really lasting quality? I'm afraid the New Orleans thing is too overt for me. But that may be my problem. It's one building I won't talk about in public lectures."

One crucial difference between Moore and his most professionally successful former partner is, perhaps, the totality of their commitment to architecture. This subject came up when I introduced the complicated question of Charles Moore's private life. In a year of interviews and conversations, I had heard rumors galore; but having assayed them all, I was nearly ready to conclude that Charles Moore had no private life whatsoever.

"I was in love with him for years," an attractive young woman had told me. "Totally, physically, the works. There was a twenty- or thirty-year difference between our ages, but everyone knew what was going on. He did ask me to marry him once, after a party—but of course he was totally drunk. So I said no."

Another woman friend of longer standing insisted, rather guardedly, on prior claims. "If he loves anybody, it's me; and if I love anybody, it's him." But I had heard rumors that she, too, had once rejected his proposal of marriage.

At least two female clients, Moore told me, have tried to seduce him. Like many older architects, he is frequently accompanied (or surrounded) by handsome and devoted young men—which may have led to the gossip that kept him from a full professorship in 1963. But one who has a better than usual claim to know him intimately declared, "He has zero human passions, and absolutely no really close relationships." "None of his friends is as close to him as they pretend—or as they would like to be," said another "close" friend, a woman. "He's not threatened by *any* relationship—man or woman, young or old, close or distant. He needs and uses us all."

"I wish he loved somebody closely in his heart," was the comment of a sympathetic young associate. "And I wish there was somebody who really loved him."

Bill Turnbull waited an uncomfortably long time before risking a remark on my uncomfortable conclusion.

"Chuck's thought—although I've never heard him say it in so many words—is that if you're going to be top, you can only have one set of commitments."

"You can't work as well as you ought to, and have a wife and children too?"

"No."

"You mean, if what you're doing is as important as it ought to be, then the person you're married to isn't?"

"That's right. You're dead. I lost a super woman. I couldn't hold it together. And I worked like hell at it. But I was here seven days a week. I was never home."

W—Richard Whitaker—is now head of the architecture program at the University of Illinois' Chicago Circle campus, which he began in 1966. He lives with his wife and two boys in half of a spacious, handsome 1895 prairie-style house in Evanston. He is a tall, thin, ingratiating fellow with bushy sideburns and a thick gray mustache. Deep-set eyes, a prominent nose in a long, sharp-boned face, gray hair worn long behind a bald dome: his voice has the dry, homey drone of a Rotarian from the wheatfields, although he was born and raised in California. He has a good word for almost everything.

After Donlyn Lyndon left for Oregon and precipitated the MLTW split, Dick Whitaker spent two and a half years as director of education for the American Institute of Architects in Washington, D.C.;

then ran the design program for four years at the University of Colorado. He continues to practice as an architect in Chicago.

Despite this very respectable career, Whitaker's notoriety today depends very much on the two years he spent as an unequal partner of Charles Moore's twenty years ago, which he reminisces about with practiced and jovial ease. According to the other three, his was distinctly the lesser role in the original collaboration. He remains a more distant friend of Charles Moore's than either Lyndon or Turnbull. He missed the crucial common experience of Princeton in the fifties, of Peressutti and Kahn. Midway in age between Moore and his two closer associates, he had neither the learning, authority, and magnetic presence of the senior partner, nor the opportunity to experience the highly charged mentor relationship the younger men enjoyed—a relationship that permits Bill Turnbull, for example, still to refer to Moore as Uncle Chuck (actually an imitation of Moore's own four nephews). A mature student at Berkeley in the late fifties, Whitaker was beginning a second career. Returning, after graduation, from a year in Europe in the fall of 1962, he chanced to pass Moore on Euclid Avenue in Berkeley. The new chairman invited him on the spot to teach first-year design and to drop by the office on Alcatraz Avenue to see what he and the boys were up to.

"It was just that casual. A total fluke. It just all fell together."

He served as supervising architect (a role different from that of chief designer) on two important MLTW houses, and contributed to the virtually inseparable communal design of the Sea Ranch Condominium.

"But there was no job we all weren't involved in," he insists—"at least on preliminary design. It was a total atelier—with always a couple of students and friends. We were forever poking pencils in, bouncing ideas off one another. Someone would come up with a theme, like How to Deal with Openings. 'O.K., let's make it super-special,' someone else would say, 'and make every opening a different shape.' 'Gee, that looks *awful!*' So we'd try to superimpose some order, drag in ideas from Mexico or Morocco. Or let the overall order of the roof plan allow some wild play with bays and balconies. We *shared* lots of these images; no one felt the need to go off in a corner and be different. What mattered was subtle variety. Order didn't have to mean lining things up in a row.

"All of us deferred to Chuck. Most of the time he was right. It'd be three A.M., very tense, tempers ruffled, people stomping around the room after six hours together, total fatigue, Charles is disagreeing with everybody else, bound and determined to have it his way. He was obviously totally nuts. So he'd draw it up and damned if he wasn't right.

"We started entering design competitions for the publicity. *Look*, we wanted to say: we're *doing* something! We were really pleased with the way things were going. That's where Morley Baer came in. The trick of getting things published is to have a good photographer who knows the editor of a magazine. He knew what editors liked. He'd do one set of shots for *House Beautiful*, one for *House and Home*, another for *Progressive Architecture* or *Sunset*. We'd refurnish people's houses just to get them published. Morley always brought along the shawls and pillows. It was Morley who built up our notoriety. The editors would call him up and ask what he had that was good, and then he'd call *us*. He'd charge us nothing, or maybe a hundred dollars. But he'd charge the magazines plenty.

"We never made any money. The three of us depended on our teaching, Bill on his job at Skidmore. There's no way to make an office pay doing six- to nine-thousand-dollar sheds, one twenty-five-thousand-dollar house. We'd spend hours and hours and hours, do three, four, five plans. Even Sea Ranch only came in at two hundred fifty thousand dollars. You can't make money with all four principals sitting around designing the same little building. And any profit we made we'd feed back into photographs and presentation drawings to try to get publicity.

"One thing wrong with those guys, they were all bachelors then. They were always scrimping on bathrooms and kitchens something awful. I remember sneaking back one night to make a bathroom larger. Then when Don got married, more doors started appearing on bedrooms, more walls went up to the ceiling.

"But Charles was always the strongest. Did you know he has a virtually photographic memory? It's unnerving. He can give a one-hour lecture on architectural history without notes, and get all the names and dates right. I've never known anyone with his command of space, his three-dimensional abstract space sense. Since then, he's gone on to explore many more things. When natural materials got too expensive, he turned to Sheetrock, painted walls, cut-out planes, illusionary space, the whole metaphor thing. He's just incredibly prolific. I don't know how he does it."

7 / PROFESSOR MOORE

C HARLES MOORE was invited to Berkeley as an associate professor with tenure, since he had already served as an assistant professor for two years at Utah and two years at Princeton. Shortly after he arrived, the youngest tenured member, he was offered the position of chairman of the department of architecture by Dean William Wurster.

"Why?"

"I wanted it. Joe [Esherick] got it for me. Bill and Vernon had a falling out about something, and Bill decided it was time for a new chairman." (Vernon De Mars's version is that he had simply grown tired of administration, and that he recommended Moore to Wurster as his replacement.) "Wurster's concept," says Moore, "was one of organized chaos. His idea was to encourage polarization, make the different camps dramatically different. His own choice for a new chairman had been one of the senior men. When Joe Esherick heard that, he blew up. He told Bill we needed someone young and exuberant.

"I tried to hire new people to foster and extend the Wurster ideal: people like Chris Alexander, Sim van der Ryn, Horst Rittel. We had others on our team, like Don Lyndon and Dick Peters from Princeton, Ezra Ehrenkrantz, eventually Gerry McCue. When our historians, Ackerman and Jacobs, left for Harvard and Cornell, I got John Jacobus from Princeton and Norma Evenson and Spiro Kostof from Yale. My idea of the way to run a school was never to call a faculty meeting until I'd counted the votes in advance and knew I could get what I wanted.

"Those were very optimistic years. We thought that if we could catch the subtleties of new academic fields and technologies, then we could get students to do work as fresh and new and good as what Joe Esherick was turning out at the time. I was terrifically excited by Joe's Cary house of 1960 and by George Homsey's Rubin house on Albany Hill—as perhaps my own later work shows. Catherine Wurster (whom I idolized) helped a great deal. She and I, and Mel Weber and Martin Myerson in the planning department, used to get together and talk about this a lot. We decided that places like Penn and Princeton and Harvard, where we had all come from, were the old guard; their day was over. We were the new guard.

"It was all very Brave New World. We thought that if we could just get it all together, we would improve architectural education, which would lead to better architecture. And we felt that Berkeley was the place to make it happen."

Berkeley came to stand for other things than improved architectural education in the years (1961–65) of Moore's tenure as chairman. In the fall of 1964, after a long hot summer of civil-rights battles in the South (in which many Berkeley students had participated), Chancellor Edward Strong decided to begin enforcing more strictly rules regarding on-campus political advocacy. In September, a police car which was taking away one of the students who had defied the chancellor's orders was surrounded by hundreds of other students and immobilized for thirty hours. From the roof of the car, a former philosophy student named Mario Savio made passionate speeches about bringing the unresponsive university bureaucracy to a "grinding halt." Overnight, the Berkeley Free Speech Movement was born—and a decade of U.S. campus protest movements had begun.

In December, Savio and 813 other students sat in the campus administration building until they were carried out by police and arrested one by one. A week later, after a campus-wide assembly in the Greek Theater, the academic senate voted to support the students' position. Chancellor Strong resigned, to be replaced (temporarily) by city planner Martin Myerson, who had replaced Wurster as dean of the college of environmental design in 1963 and was Charles Moore's immediate supervisor.

"I was pro-Savio, of course," Moore recalls. "Ed Strong was such an ass. Some departments were one hundred percent hostile to the demonstrators. Others, like architecture, were one hundred percent pro. I think architecture students are more disposed to be revolutionaries. It's related to the way they're selected and trained. They're always thinking about what it would be like to *change* things. And in those days the department at Cal was more or less committed to indiscipline. It was populist with a vengeance. Of course, some people, like Jesse Reichek and Sim van der Ryn, declared themselves revolutionaries at once and stopped holding classes.

"My own involvement was pretty much limited to strategy meetings with other department chairmen. That's when I first realized that the newspapers printed lies. I remember borrowing a loudspeaker from the student radicals once, when the administration ran out of them."

Was that why he left Berkeley—the storm and stress of the early sixties?

"Oh no. The FSM was no threat. I still thought Berkeley was wonderful, that we were on the way to doing something of great import and interest. But the top administration were all such fools. At Berkeley, one set of faculty runs the university, and the others get Nobel Prizes. At Yale the same people do both."

Although chairman of a major department, Moore was never promoted to full professor. He was never told the precise reason, but he was not pleased. He presumed, however, that since first Dean Wurster and then Dean Myerson appeared to be on his side, this would have been rectified sooner or later. "I was annoyed, but not crushed," he says. "That wouldn't have sent me running away."

(The full story is not one that reveals the academic world at its most enlightened. Dean Wurster had indeed proposed Moore for promotion, but two members of the three-man faculty committee appointed to review his case—the Berkeley faculty maintains review power over appointments and promotions within its own ranks—were set intransigently against him. The chairman of this committee devised various stalling tactics, then stopped calling meetings altogether; in the end he refused to submit any report at all. The third member, who was favorably disposed toward Moore, protested to the chancellor, to no avail. He finally demanded that the committee chairman tell him what he had against Moore. He was told that "there were rumors around that he was gay," this professor recently told me. "They kept coming back to that. They simply didn't want him here. Naturally, I could never say anything about it to Chuck. Wurster didn't know; Vernon De Mars didn't know. And so when he left for Yale, I couldn't blame him.")

Then there was the business of the university art museum. Dean Wurster had proposed that the university offer the design commission for its new $5 million art museum to MLTW, partly as a way to keep Charles Moore in California, and Charles was led to believe that the job was theirs. "I would have stayed for that," he says. "If I'd had as important a job as the museum, I would have been much more reluctant to go." But in the end it was decided to hold an open national competition, and the MLTW scheme was not among the finalists.

A more important factor in prompting his decision to leave, and one more revealing of Moore's personal priorities, was the difference in the way he felt himself esteemed by the heads of the two universities. "I only remember having one contact with Clark Kerr [the University of California president] the whole time I was at Berkeley. That was when some people who lived uphill from the Talbert house called his office to complain that one of his faculty members was designing a house that was going to block their view of the bay! I got this offensive call from one of his secretaries about it, and I told her to buzz off. Other than that, I think Kerr only discovered that I existed when he read in Herb Caen's column that I was going to Yale." To this day Moore remains outraged over the incident. "I was so pissed off at Kerr I was delighted to go away from his stupid university." ("I bear grudges forever," he confesses.)

Kingman Brewster, on the other hand, was all diplomatic grace and polish, and he suavely stroked Moore's sense of self-esteem. "He was a supercharmer. He had done his homework. He knew all about me. *That* impressed me. No one in the Berkeley administration knew or cared anything about me. I saw more of Brewster in two weeks than I'd seen of Kerr in two years." Paul Rudolph, who got along less well with Brewster than with his predecessor Whitney Griswold, had recently decided to resign as dean of art and architecture at Yale. Vincent Scully, the Yale architectural historian, was promoting Robert Venturi, whom he had adopted as a protégé. But both Venturi and Scully had their enemies on the faculty, and in any case Brewster wanted (he told the press) "an active designer of international reputation." Gia Pisanella, with whom Charles had worked on a project in Lexington, Kentucky, mentioned his name to Edward Larabee Barnes, who was Yale's planning consultant at the time; and Barnes suggested him to Brewster. Charles was invited out to New Haven, put up at the president's house, introduced to Mrs. Brewster and the faculty.

The result was announced in the *New York Times* on May 14, 1965: "Coast Architect to Head School at Yale." The newspaper photograph showed a big egg-shaped head, face and jowl and forehead forming one large oval, with drooping worried eyes behind owllike spectacles. At thirty-nine, Moore wore a little mustache (the great whiskers were still to come) and a shaven crew cut that edged the very top of his nearly bald dome.

But the academic big time had its drawbacks. For one thing, Moore came to agree with Bill Turnbull about New Haven. "It's the pits. It's the awfulest, ugliest town in the United States."

"What didn't you like about it? That it was ugly?"

"Yes."

"Cold?"

"Yes."

"Narrow minded?"

"Yes."

"Filthy?"

"Yes. All of those. It's also the most corrupt city in the United States. The Mafia totally run the town. New Orleans is benign by comparison." Charles Moore told some off-the-record tales of the ways in which architects and builders were obliged to come to terms with the extralegal powers of New Haven. But when I asked him what he thought the best architectural school in the country *today*, he replied, "Oh, Yale, of course. It may not be as good as it used to be, but it's still number one. Nothing can compare for excitement with a new school, when it's just starting up—a school like Utah under Roger Bailey, or Mississippi State under Bill McMinn, or Maryland under John Hill. But that first excitement can't last very long. No, I'd have to say Yale."

Finding himself once again the junior tenured member of a divided department of which he was also chairman, Moore tried to adapt his willfully chaotic style of governance to Yale. "I made no attempt to adopt the life-and-death imperial style of my predecessors," he claims. "People thought I was afraid to hold faculty meetings. But I made a point of being smarter than I seemed."

("He landed with no game plan at all," remarked a former associate. "He just planned to wing it, the way he had at Berkeley. But he was eaten alive by the factions.")

Moore's version is at once more complex and more flattering to himself. "It was harder to hire good people at Yale than it had been

at Berkeley, for some reason. I got Kent Bloomer in sixty-six, Felix
Drury in sixty-seven, both from Carnegie Tech. Felix had master
minded my own Ph.D. at Princeton. Kent and I taught the first-year
graduate course together from the time he came. That first class of
ours, Jim Righter's and Peter Rose's class in sixty-six, they adored
Felix. But when the Yale revolution started, student hatred seemed
to pour in on him rather than me."

New Haven got in on the student protest movement during the
second big wave (minority admissions, student power, Vietnam
and Cambodia) of 1968–70. As chairman for four years, and unwill-
ing dean of a reorganized school of architecture and planning for a
year and a half, Moore saw enough of Yale radical activists, black
and white, to decide they needn't be taken too seriously.

"The white radicals were far more to the right than I was. It was a
lot of New Haven radical chic. Half my time was wasted on pam-
pered aristocratic Marxist Yalies who are now all three-piece-suit
men working for Philip Johnson. It wasn't what I would call exhilarating. These so-called revolutionaries—people like Ed Cox (who
later married Tricia Nixon), Bob Knight, Doug Michaels, Gyorgy
Kepes's son, some Finnish baron's son—would keep threatening
to present me with their nonnegotiable demands for a student-run
school: by which they always meant, 'Would you be able to meet
with us and talk about this?'

"But they were never able to come up with a proposal. In the
end, I wrote their manifesto for them and gave it to the revolutionary leaders. Kingman Brewster knew I had written it and was not at
all pleased.

"About 1969, Topper Carew [a black architect and activist from
Washington] had come in to teach a course on 'How to Make a
Revolution' or something, in which he attacked President Brewster
right and left. The chairman of city planning had simply caved in to
student demands and admitted double his 1969 quota to get in
lots of blacks. Then when they burned out the building, and the
bomb threats started coming, Brewster just shut down planning
altogether.

"For a while it seemed as if the university was trying to get rid of
all the noisy, artsy-craftsy departments full of trouble-making students, especially those that didn't have rich and powerful alumni:
art and architecture, music, the drama school. I would have *loved*
some rich alumni, but unfortunately very few architects ever get

rich. I was even prepared to accept [he named a rich architect]'s son, who had about a C-minus average. People like Bob Brustein in the drama school and I were leading the fight to save these departments. We had a meeting on the future of art and architecture with a very high-powered committee of Yale trustees—Irwin Miller, Jock Whitney, Mayor Lindsay, Governor Scranton. I was prepared to reduce the size of the school to keep to any budget they would propose. In the end, I think, I *did* save the school.

"When Brewster decided to split art and architecture and reorganize it under two separate deans, I agreed to take the architecture and planning job only under three conditions: one, that I reported directly to him; two, that I had no chairmen under me; and three, that I could trade my two remaining years as chairman for one year as dean.

"In the end he kept on pushing, so I stayed on for a year and a half. But it was not what I was cut out for. I felt I had done my duty, damn it, saved the school, seen it through its difficult years. But Brewster is still mad at me for quitting.

"I was still seen as a fascist pig by some of the students, of course, but I wasn't as bad as Brewster or the art school dean, so I emerged relatively unscathed. I hadn't said or done anything more than usually offensive. I had been against the war from the start, of course, in favor of student responsibility."

Even so, Charles Moore had his own frightening confrontation with Third World representatives. During Yale's first, ill-planned affirmative action campaign, the architecture department had admitted a number of below-standard black students from the South. When one of the group stopped attending classes, Charles suspended him. A delegation of blacks showed up in his office to present "their usual nonnegotiable demands," and specifically an order that this brother be reinstated. As the leader of the delegation spoke, he kept lighting matches with his fingernail (this was shortly after a fire "of undetermined origin" had laid waste two floors of the art and architecture building) and flipping them onto the chairman's desk.

"I can see gold teeth in black faces, gleaming in the light of these little fires they kept lighting in my underground office. It was—God!—it was like some weird Asian movie."

Although he never felt the condescension or rivalry one might expect from the prestigious crew of Yale art historians ("after all, I was one myself"), he never taught architectural-history courses, as he had at Utah and California. "Scully had those sewed up." Instead, he concentrated his teaching efforts on the graduate-thesis studio and a highly imaginative first-year graduate course he taught with sculptor and friend Kent Bloomer, which few students who took are likely to forget. Many of the wide-ranging, humanistic, anti-Cartesian ideas of the course—a kind of subversive apologia for nonmodern architecture—are included in their book, *Body, Memory, and Architecture*, published by Yale in 1977. The method, and its effect, were later described in an article by Andy Burr, one of the students in Moore's and Bloomer's "miracle class" that arrived in 1966:

The class of 1970 became increasingly aware that they were being treated in a different manner from the classes ahead of them. Older students were often envious that Charles Moore spent nearly all his teaching time with *first year*. [One of Burr's classmates thought this was the result of Charles's desire to work with fresh and open-minded students, untainted by any of his predecessors' ideas.]

In the second semester of first year, Moore and Bloomer introduced a startling idea. The class would design and construct a real building. Through Tom Carey, who had been a VISTA volunteer, a project was found. First year would design and build a community center for New Zion, Kentucky, a tiny town in the Appalachian Mountains. . . .

The class arrived in Kentucky with a vague design and many uncertainties. New Zion was a genuine backwoods town with no local government and not one flush toilet among two hundred inhabitants. The extreme rural conditions meant that there were no subcontractors available, and so the Yalies had to do all the work themselves, hand-digging the foundations and the septic field, installing the plumbing and wiring as well as building the structure. Stimulated by adversity, many talents emerged. . . . Charles Moore, on a weekend visit, did his part as a member of Turner Brooks' team digging the septic field.

After eight delirious weeks first year had a building, not to mention a pleasant feeling of satisfaction and self-confidence—a feeling not at all diminished when the September issue of *Progressive Architecture* featured the New Zion Community Center on its cover. . . .

It was an exciting, highly charged atmosphere. The curriculum was very loose, and everyone was involved in making very real architecture. In this climate it was easy to overlook rules and regulations—they seemed so trivial. . . .

The class had few heroes in the modern movement—all those white boxes and glass towers were lifeless and boring. It was an easy step to take; condemning Nixon and Agnew one moment, Pevsner and Giedion the next. They felt it was time for a new kind of architecture. They had no name for it, but they knew it wasn't modern.[3]

Actually, this novel hands-on approach to the study of architecture at Yale began with a class of Felix Drury's the year before Moore's project at New Zion. That year, Bill Hersey's design for an eight-bunk summer-camp shelter was chosen by the jury and built by the class, on a budget of $1,200. The Appalachian project was larger in scope ($4,000 budget, plus donated material); it involved more people (a design team of eight, a building crew of thirty); and it was more specifically intended as an act of social reform. "They had all wanted to do something in Harlem or the Deep South," Moore recalls. "But I thought all those blond Anglo-Saxons from Yale might get a slightly warmer welcome in the hills of Kentucky."

There are now a dozen or fifteen buildings designed and hand-made by Moore's and Bloomer's first-year Yale design students scattered around the East: a community center, a beach pavilion, outbuildings at a day camp. Robert (Buzz) Yudell, a former Yale student, now a partner of Moore's in southern California, recently redesigned a little house not far from the Pacific Ocean for himself and Tina Beebe. Given the intricacy of the remodeling job—thick, curved interior walls punched through with openings, a mirrored wall, a door hidden in a bookcase, the whole facade remade of found windows—I was astonished to learn they had done virtually all the work themselves. "Remember, I did all this stuff at Yale," he pointed out. "Charles's approach completely demystified the building process for me."

James Volney Righter, a more than usually successful member of the 1966 group, agrees. "It gave people enormous confidence to learn that there was no magic to it. You just put up a whole bunch of studs and cover them with Sheetrock. The only trap was that it had led a lot of callow Yale youths into thinking, 'Aha, I can do it!'—and then sprinkling the Vermont woods with woodbutchered cabins."

CHARLES MOORE'S specific teaching methods—beyond setting out problems and projects that contain within themselves such worlds of possibility—are harder to define. Like most famous

American architects, Moore lectures frequently before students and professional groups, both in this country and abroad. This is teaching on a grander scale than any one campus permits—as well as a legitimate form of self-promotion. Many name architects' traveling lectures, in fact, are little more than slide shows of their recent work, with a sentence or two of commentary per slide.

Moore's lectures do depend heavily on his fabulous slide collection, but as a rule he saves his own work for last—if he chooses to discuss it at all. ("It is the speaker's prerogative to conclude with his own work," he declared at one lecture, "as if it were the culmination of everything that has gone before.") Since his first trip abroad in 1949–50, he has taken and assembled more than fifty thousand slides of built and unbuilt places. From this collection, he is able to draw materials to illustrate almost any topic related to landscape or architecture.

Audiences who know him only by reputation are inevitably dismayed at the outset of his lectures. He ambles to the lectern, stooping as if to hide his size, looking like a tall, awkward, slightly scruffy banker. He usually talks without notes—perhaps a few scribbles on an envelope, written on the airplane coming in. Once he is under way, he seems to let the slides direct his remarks. The treble, halting voice is distinctly nondynamic. In some lectures he seems altogether lost. He rambles aimlessly about, leaving his fans baffled and disappointed, with nothing more than a slide show and a string of one-liners.

But in his better public performances, he matches wild and wonderful images to great spinning wheels of thought. He cannot (or will not) assert or declaim, so his presentations inevitably start out seeming oblique, indirect, even mock-apologetic. Because he *appears* to be such a hapless public performer, the sharp jabs and radical enthusiasms come with all the more force.

As a rule, he is promoting a liberating, rule-defiant openness of vision, which he defends and demonstrates by slides and analyses of his favorite eccentric places, Arcadias and Edens of every shape and size. Beverly Hills and Bomarzo and the Brighton Pavilion; Stourhead and Shalimar; his faculty club at Santa Barbara; Hadrian's Villa, mansard-roofed trailers, Disneyland, the Villa d'Este. He flashes on fairylands and troll lands, toy towns, ruins, follies, Texas breweries and Cape Cod barns, neon-lit streets, the water gardens of the Moghul emperors, trying to seduce his listeners out of the fashionable idioms and accepted canons of good taste, out of a blind acceptance of parking lots and Savings and Loans and back to the open spaces of the free imagination—"the distant, fantastic realm of things where breezes blow from the Infinite."

He loves hidden courtyards, pinnacled towers, island gardens, stage sets, weathered old farmhouses. He tries to persuade his listeners—by his slides, his wit, and his tangible enthusiasm—that they should like them too. Franco-Swiss chateau-style bunga-lows are O.K., "whatever the architectural textbooks may say." Isola Bella—an astonishing seventeenth-century terraced island garden in Lake Maggiore—is "awful eclectic Beaux Arty gaga, ugly and ambiguous, inaccessible and uninhabitable, and filled with dis-gusting statues"; by which I think he means he loves it and expects us to love it too.

In a good Charles Moore lecture, the image of the giant, stutter-ing clown melts in the heat of his eloquence and convictions. Then the wit and the foolery, the apparent aimlessness and outra-geousness all contribute to make his case for a more humane and imaginative world.

In the design studio, Moore never redraws a student's work, and usually finds something to praise in the clumsiest sketch—even if it's only the way one draws leaves on a tree. "I once spent *days* on a project," said one of his UCLA students, "and he raved about some dumb *cows* I had drawn in the distance." Just as he will accept al-most any idea of a client's, however bizarre or apparently unwork-able, so will he find a place for the strangest of a student's authentic intuitions. As a teacher-critic, he works with word pic-tures, open-ended images—which can comprehend so much more possibility than lines. Jim Righter regards Moore as a "nonlinear" thinker who dislikes anything closed and determined. He sees him as favoring vague, stratified images and indeterminate processes that may trigger the unexpected, and perhaps wonderful, result.

The freewheeling (but very serious) fantasy making of the New Orleans fair project reminded Moore of a design problem he first dreamed up at Yale around 1974. He assigned it twice to students there, and once since at UCLA. "I use it as a last resort," he said, "when they're all getting bored and surly."

Moore distributes to the class an elaborate contour map, full of isthmuses and swan bays, Merlin's groves and Venus's vales. It is the land of Broceliande, legendary home of Merlin the magician. The map becomes, in Professor Moore's sketch problem, an island west of Oregon—"but even more ecologically concerned than Oregon." The Brocelianders, he informs the students in a descriptive handout, live in great peace and happiness: they know not war, poverty, or deprivation. They possess all the natural building materials that we do, plus a wonderful pink alabaster that cuts easily into four-by-eight-foot slabs, two inches thick. They scorn to use any petroleum by-products, however, except for the plastic wheels of their skateboards, for which they trade a bit of their precious alabaster. (All Brocelianders travel by skateboard, which they handle with grace and dexterity.)

They led their even-tenored lives for many centuries, until exactly five hundred years ago, when a creature called the Light Giver arrived on a swan boat to show them the beauty of their ways. He brought them joy. They adored him. Then he disappeared.

After he left, eight holy holograms washed up on shore, each twenty-four inches ("or sixty centimeters; Yale was going metric then") in diameter. Inside each was a figure who spoke wisdom to all who consulted it, like a sibyl. The hologramic face inside the sphere would tell you the future, tell you what you needed to know.

One was silver, and represented communication. One was peachy pink, and dealt with love. The green sphere was Merlin's and stood for truth and the earth and real things. The red hologram was supposed to tell of war, but since the islanders knew nothing of war, it told of business instead. The fifth hologram, alas, was left out in the sun and broke into many pieces. The islanders gathered up the pieces and kept them in a bag, as a warning never to leave the holy holograms out in the sun again. The white sphere represented earthly power, human reason; the black, magic; the blue, Neptune's sphere, the sea.

To celebrate the five-hundredth anniversary of the coming of the Light Giver, the Brocelianders have decided to commission a new and wonderful monument to hold these holograms (out of the sun, of course—and at the latitude of Oregon). The students are to decide where best to locate this monument on the island, then design it in such a way that all the remaining holograms can be circumskated (counterclockwise)—a necessary ritual in the consultation of these oracles—with all the pitches and dips required for graceful skateboarding. In addition to their regular consultations, on Midsummer Night's Eve the islanders hold a great celebration in which thousands of them circumskate all the holy holograms, like Stations of the Cross, then skate up a path (this too the students must design) that winds gracefully up to a broad beach of hard-packed, Daytona-type sand ("very good for skateboards") for an elaborate rolling dance under the moon.

After a week, the students submit their designs and models for the temple. "It's worked very well every time," says Moore. "One group at Yale the first time went far beyond the assignment. They worked out all sorts of numerological details for the rituals—a sort of C. S. Lewis or C. K. Williams world. I was delighted."

WHY did Moore leave Yale for UCLA? "Oh, you know—the palm trees . . . happy memories of childhood. Actually, I was asked to come by Tim Vreeland [a Princeton classmate], for whom I had considerable respect—perhaps more than I have now. And by Bill Mitchell, who was chairman and whom I'm fond of and listen to. He made it seem reasonable."

One impulse that may have led to the move in 1975 was his growing fatigue, even boredom with the Essex–New Haven scene, in which he felt increasingly out of place. To this was added the pull of his growing clientele and reputation in southern California. He had friends there, roots of a sort, and had done three very successful buildings (including the Burns house) in something like the local style.

"I stayed on for that extra half-year as dean, and then took off for a sabbatical in Mexico. That was the spring of seventy-one, which of course was the semester the office fell apart. What an awful year! When I came back, the sheriff was at the door, and Brewster was still mad at me for leaving. There was the usual 'ex-dean' scene at Yale, with the new dean going around telling everyone they were having a renaissance—by which I presumed he meant that my term must have been the dark ages.

"I was still teaching first year, which is what I'd been doing all along, and that was all right—well, not *very* all right. And I was living in Essex and trying to pay off the bills for the debacle. I was working very hard and not really liking it, not feeling any particular connection with it. I was less central. We had interesting work, which was gradually increasing. (There was absolutely none for a while after everything fell apart, but gradually good things came.)

"I would spend the morning at the office, then drive the frantic forty minutes into New Haven and deal with my class or whatever, and then jump in my car and grab some dinner on the way, and go back to the office at the end of the evening, and finally go to bed. Grover and Harper and the others could all go off for a pleasant lunch somewhere, while I was in the car running off to my afternoon class. And I was just getting bored."

Some days stretched even longer. Jim Righter recalls a period when he drove out from New Haven each dawn, woke Charles at six, then spent two and a half hours working alone with him on a Florida project at the house with the funny green pyramid before Charles went next door to his office to start the day's work.

"The others were all caught up in the spirit of the town," Moore recalls, with a hint of envy, or perhaps self-pity: "their kids in school, their wives in the PTA, going to picnics together. And that was fine. But I didn't feel any connection to that at all.

"I was still very fond of California, and I often thought it would be very nice to get out of there and get back here. Berkeley had asked if I would like to come back, but I decided that would be just retracing my steps, to come back and pick up where I'd left off ten years before. UCLA started asking. My mother had lived there, and I had connections with it. And I thought it would be more pleasing. And so I did it."

He has mixed feelings now about his decision. Los Angeles offered more creature comforts than New Haven, but its university lacked Yale's age and respectability and some of its finesse. One night when he was working late in the office, UCLA security guards stopped him and frisked him for weapons, refusing to believe he was the professor he pretended to be. His teaching assistant, they insisted, was dealing in drugs. "Yale did everything right; UCLA does everything wrong. When I told Kingman Brewster of my decision, he said, 'You made a *terrible* choice!'

"But I've never done it right. I thought then, as I've thought numerous times, that I could get out of a too-frenzied situation and into another, pleasanter one, by making some switch in where I was and what I was doing. Each of these moves was intended to be calming. But each time it's only gotten worse.

"I didn't have either the money or the stomach to set up a new office. We had just got the one in Connecticut to the point of breaking even, after months and months. And UCLA offered me this ready-made commercial office in UIG [the Urban Innovations Group]. If that hadn't been part of the package, I couldn't have afforded to do it."

Very soon, though, he realized that the UCLA–UIG setup didn't allow him the freedom or potential income he needed as an architect or the office help he required for his other work. So he invited Robert (Buzz) Yudell, a former Yale student who had worked in his Connecticut office, to come out to California as his assistant, to sort slides and help prepare lectures and do research for the books he had promised to write. Soon Buzz was working on independent design commissions Moore managed to get apart from UIG, in order to provide them both with a bit more income.

"But that ended up costing more to do than we were getting. And so when Buzz proposed forming a new partnership, and doing some of the stuff himself and taking part of the money from it, I was relieved and said, 'Yes, that'll be lovely!'"

Thus was born Moore's second Los Angeles office, Moore Ruble Yudell. "Unfortunately, what I didn't realize was that the UIG people were going to be flaming jealous, simply furious about it. They spent hours burning my ears telling me what a horrible mistake it all was." (Having engendered such passionate feeling at its inception, the split still fosters occasional ill will. Both offices, for example, bid on the same Pacific Palisades church project, each using Charles's name up front. When it went to Moore Ruble Yudell— which the parish building committee thought of as his "real" office—the UIG staff was livid.)

"Of course, I'd prefer that Charles worked exclusively at UIG," says Harvey Perloff, dean of the UCLA school of architecture and urban planning. "It's an invaluable extension of our teaching program, like internships at a university teaching hospital. Students love it. But I realize Charles works best in what he thinks is the right context for each particular job. He brings us his reputation and his skill and his charm, and we settle for as much of him as we can get." Joint Moore–UIG credits so far include the Piazza d'Italia and Gulfport Plaza (both in conjunction with Perez Associates of New Orleans); seven completed houses in California; and a prize-winning cluster of housing for old people. Among their unbuilt projects were a fantastic theme park for Indianapolis, a facade for Best Products Company, a condominium in Hawaii, and a new wing for the Huntington Library. Early in 1983, there were six major

Moore–UIG projects in progress: the Beverly Hills civic center; a country club for Steamboat Springs, Colorado; a seventy-two-story tower next to Carnegie Hall; a park remodeling for Houston; 120 luxury condominiums for Dallas; and some new buildings for the University of California at Irvine.

Not long ago, I was told, a student protest demonstration was mounted against Professor Moore at UCLA. During the 1981–82 academic year, according to his own secretary's records, he made three trips to Minneapolis, three to Aspen, five to Indianapolis, nine to San Francisco, seven to New York, three to Chicago, three to Hartford, four to Houston, five to New Orleans, three to Berlin, three to Monterey, and one each to Rome, Pittsburgh, Buenos Aires, Columbus (Mississippi), Lexington (Kentucky), Stuttgart, Washington, D.C., Palm Springs, Copenhagen, and Vienna. He was at home during these nine months—insofar as he has a home, other than airports and hotels—for a total of fourteen weeks, the longest a stretch of twenty-four days. Some unhappy architecture students, including men and women who had come from Australia, Japan, and France to study under the great man they rarely saw, were said to have made a poster for this demonstration bearing the words, Charles WHO?

In fact, Moore was officially on leave from his university duties in the fall of 1980—part of which he spent guiding a group of UCLA students about Rome. In spring term he tried to catch up by teaching two design classes and guaranteed the university thirty of his afternoons. One of the classes was in landscape, with forty students and three instructors. The other was a master class for eighteen called LA Spectacular. After exploring the city thoroughly, the students divided into teams to study and design six locations for subway stations on an imaginary line running from Wilshire Boulevard into San Fernando Valley.

In May Moore drove with this group to the Sea Ranch. Some made stops en route at two of his favorite classic California follies—the Madonna Inn in San Luis Obispo and the Hearst Castle in San Simeon. He fed and bedded the class at his condominium, led them through several MLTW buildings, and then turned them over to Larry Halprin for a couple of days of his mellowing-out rituals.

"The secret is to get very good people to work *with* him," said Dean Perloff, "and to try to schedule his appearances in advance."

Charles has co-taught design with the Spanish architect Elias Torres, his partner (and former student) Buzz Yudell, psychologist George Rand, and anthropologist David Stea. With Stea, he devised quarter-long projects on housing for Navajo Indians and for deaf, dumb, and blind people, both of which proved fruitful.

"But there's going to be a certain amount of student dissatisfaction, nevertheless," says Perloff. "Architecture students are always dissatisfied. They want you twenty-four hours a day. Still, most of them here learn very soon that they get more from Charles in less time. What he gives them is quality time. I've seen it happen. He's just off the plane from Berlin, he takes a cab to the campus from LA International, grabs a salad, and walks into the studio and starts in where he left off with the greatest enthusiasm, throws himself right back in. Zero jet lag. There's no one else like him."

Bill Mitchell, Moore's closest colleague at UCLA (and now his department head), still consults with him regularly on courses and curricula, and insists that his influence on the program is very strong. "It's up to Harvey and me to keep students happy in his absence. They're always jealous of any work he does elsewhere. Of course, he's very scrupulous about taking unpaid leaves or percentage pay cuts whenever he's overengaged somewhere else. But he's hopeless without a co-teacher in design." And dealing with his hard-working, stay-at-home colleagues, Mitchell admits—who don't rate these special attentions and are wary of being "used" or "exploited" while covering for Charles—can be a sensitive business.

In 1982, Charles took two more quarters of leave and taught four weeks each at Harvard and the University of Houston. In 1982–83, he coordinated the architecture portion of a multicraft, multi-museum exhibition planned for Los Angeles on "American Vernacular," and spent a fair amount of his time at the University of Houston traveling about the small towns of the state with his students in search of good examples. (Favored spots: Waxahachie, Fredericksburg, Castroville.) He also added the catalogue of the exhibition to his backlog of unfinished books.[4] That academic year he taught two advanced design studios at UCLA, with an American Vernacular seminar attached to each one. Class members accompanied him on old-building hunts in New Mexico.

He and Bill Mitchell (who traveled to India together in 1978 and are collaborating on a book on gardens) regularly offer a course in the history of landscape. He has also taught seminars in modern architectural history (with Charles Jencks), the architectural history of Japan, and architectural writing.

In the spring of 1983, Mitchell and Moore had planned to take a group of UCLA students on a study trip to Indonesia, to measure Balinese temples. "It's my version of an old architectural tradition," says Mitchell, "like Robert Wood's eighteenth-century trips to Baalbek or Palmyra: you go there, measure what you see, draw it up, and bring it back." Despite the urgent demands of all his professional offices, Moore found the proposal irresistible. But when the required funds failed to materialize, he settled for a short vacation in Japan with Dmitri Vedensky.

8/THE VIEW FROM 1982

I T isn't easy to define the current stance of so volatile and unsettled a performer, a world-traveling architect-lecturer-writer who still, at fifty-eight, with five books and more than a hundred buildings to his credit, works more or less free-lance. His situation in 1981–83 (when we talked) was quite different from his situation in 1980; his situation in 1984 is likely to be different from both. Through a spring afternoon near the beach at Monterey, he reflected on his tangle of professional relationships, while seagulls flew circles over the surf, and his forehead burned red in the sun.

We gossiped for a while about good and bad clients, moved on to good and bad partners, then to his financial problems, then to his future. I started out by mentioning some southern California clients of his whose buildings I had recently visited and whose motives and attitudes left me puzzled. In particular, I wasn't at all sure I liked David Rodes's "neo-Palladian" house, recently featured in *Life*.

"I'm not at all sure that I like it either," Charles admitted. He drew some sketches for me of what he had originally wanted the house to look like. "I was enamored of a scheme for the living room—as David doubtless told you—rather like my own floor in Los Angeles, very cheapo-looking, marble squares and particle board. And I think that, in its slight goofiness, its sweet-and-sour cheapness, would have been just the ticket to reduce that room from being so stuffy. But one of his rich friends got to him and said he couldn't *possibly* have a cheap particle-board floor (actually it would have been very expensive by the time it was done, because of the cutting of all the pieces), but that he had to have seven-inch-wide white-oak planks, which were notoriously expensive.

"The clients I get along with best, feel the happiest about, are the ones who have very much their own sense of what they want, and maintain their own veto power, and tell me no when they don't like something or want something different. With David, I admit part of the problem may have been that as it went on, I was getting increasingly busy, running around to various faraway places."

We talked of people and projects he was happier about—like Leland Burns's rose-colored villa on its Pacific Palisades hill.

"One of the nice things about Lee's job is that Lee is so nice. Although he harbors secret grudges against people like the electrician on his house—who was a real creep—still he was so charming to everybody that everyone on that job outdid himself. Every subcontractor (with that one exception) went out of his way to do everything just right. Lee was there a lot, but not fussing, *helping*, making sandwiches, pots of coffee. It makes the whole job a beautiful thing. And of course Miriam Licht [another favored client, owner of a Charles Moore house on a Marin County hill] had this dream of a Danish contractor: a charming, beautiful guy. And he'd never even done a house before! It was like being in some really nice movie. Everybody was so well mannered and handsome and smart and interested.

"I have had my losers. Oh, have I had my losers! Evil people. Crazy people." We talked about a few. He told me the story of an office building in Los Angeles he had designed for twenty-one psychoanalysts, in which the nervous fretfulness and suspicions of one difficult client were raised to the twenty-first power.

"But I don't like unpleasantness. I'm not very good with it. It doesn't get my adrenaline up in ways that are exciting or important to me. I tend to leave that to the people I work with"—a remark that was confirmed to me by two of his Los Angeles associates, who were left to deal with, respectively, the twenty-one psychoanalysts and the owner of the neo-Palladian house in Brentwood.

"Some of the people I've worked with, like Mark Simon, have a capacity to do all the day-to-day stuff with the clients after I've done my work, stroke them or fight with them or whatever, and to call me, not all the time, but regularly, to keep close touch with the job. So I can continue to think of those places as 'mine.' They know when to ask me to redesign the dining-room ceiling or pick out some hardware or do something that seems to be the critical touch at that moment. Others don't operate that way. They're aggressive and very fast, and they just don't include me in the discussions after the initial scheme. I'm very fond of them and happy to back them up—but in cases like that the building isn't really *mine*, doesn't give me any pride of accomplishment." He described the embarrassment of showing a writer from a posh decorators' magazine through one of "his" Los Angeles houses and recognizing very little of what he saw.

The conversation shifted to some snags in a recent experiment which he and his young Santa Monica partners had tried with the members of an Episcopal parish, who wanted (under Moore Ruble Yudell's guidance) to design their own new church, replacing a woodsy, Bay Region–style landmark that had recently burned down. "They waited until everyone was furious, then *ordered* me to come down, in a kind of last-ditch ultimatum. My surprise was that I thought we were doing what we said we were doing all along; which was this 'participatory' business; which featured me not as the form giver—that's ruled out by the very process—but as the avuncular 'facilitator,' who would make people happy and get everybody's ideas and remove whatever impediments there were in the way of people saying what they were up to. And I thought that, having done that, I could go away and let the working-drawings people do the working drawings."

He professed himself depressed by what he felt was his young colleagues' own lack of excitement in the Halprin-esque experiment. "I think part of the expectation was that, in some way, Buzz and John and the parishioners were going to do this participatory-process act, and then by some magic laying on of hands on my part they were going to get a brilliant, 'arky-tect' design out of it."

In fact, this is almost exactly what I had been told, a few days earlier, by the vice-chairman of the parish building committee. He was less than enthusiastic about the way the church design was evolving (in the end, I think, it turned out quite well), but he kept his faith in the magician from Battle Creek.

"I have great hope, even faith in Charles Moore," John Davis told me. "He's a master; I told everybody that. He *understood* the parish-participation idea. He could tell us how to proceed.

"I have hope and faith still. I'm overwhelmed by one fact: Charles Moore is a master. He listens. The genius part is his ability to see the infinite number of solutions proposed and still be creative. There were all these people screaming for more glass, and the incumbent vicar telling us it had to be low and cozy and wooden, and Father Fenton's faction insisting on something grand, something sublime and ritualistic.

"What the architects have come up with so far is handsome, oh, I'll grant you that," said John Davis. "But I'm still hoping for something magic. I want to say to him, 'Go, Charles Moore, give us something great!' One solid month here and he could do it. He has the chance. But he's never here! We hired Charles and we haven't seen him. We love John and Buzz, of course; but a church is a public building. It may last two hundred years. He should care more."

When I report this conversation, Charles Moore grows testy. He thinks he's already given St. Matthew's more of himself than he bargained for. He sighs and speaks with a mixture of chagrin and self-assurance.

"Part of my trouble is that I vaguely presume I *can* still wave some magic wand and give them what they want. If I get pissy with John and Buzz, it's because they don't show any signs of picking up any adjacent sticks to wave around in the air themselves, just to see what might work. I guess I've been spoiled by working with people like Bill Turnbull and Don Lyndon and Marvin Buchanan and various others along the way. I had supposed that the boys in LA would also, in a much-reduced portion, be contributing some kind of enthusiasm and energy and 'magic' to it too. But they don't show any signs of knowing what that process includes. Which means I'm supposed to put in *all* the magic." He moaned over other projects in progress at both his Los Angeles offices. "This whole business is causing me considerable worry."

Could his current junior partners sustain the quality of work expected of a Charles Moore project?

"The answer to that at this point, unfortunately, is no."

"ISN'T that just like him?" exploded one old friend, when I passed on the assessment. "He loves to play one of his regional offices against another. He bad-mouths all of them behind their backs." Another ex-associate suggested that the problem lay in the fact that "the people around Charles Moore—the sort who will put up with the difficulties of working with him—aren't always the best designers." "He does sometimes choose second raters," said another. This "bad-mouthing"—a favorite Charles Moore & Company phrase—seems to go on at all levels of his entourage.

"Many people get very dependent on him," said Tina Beebe, in an attempt to analyze the discontent that sometimes poisons the air between Charles Moore and his junior associates. "They desperately want his approval. He's basically very sweet, but the things he says and does to people can be terribly destructive and cruel. He squashes people. It's frightening the way he goes through people, destroys them.

"He meets a young, intelligent student—usually somebody cute—and decides he's brilliant. He used to hire these guys while they were still in school and set them up as job captains, turn them loose on barracuda clients, before they knew *anything* about schedules or budgets. They were all talented guys. But he sets them up with these unrealistic expectations. Then he goes away. And if they fail, he bad-mouths them. It's so demoralizing. He may praise Bill Grover now, but ten years ago he was telling people Bill Grover couldn't design his way out of an outhouse."

"He sees the 'medieval apprenticeship' thing as essential to architectural training," is Dona Guimaraes's explanation. "Just like Wright. But one goes, gets replaced, another comes. The problem with these acolytes is they don't always know when their time is up."

Ron Filson was once a student-apprentice of Moore's, then a colleague. He is now dean of the school of architecture at Tulane. "Charles has never been able to get together a working machine in which others can interpret his ideas. Instead, inexperienced students and others scramble to finish the job. It's all very exhilarating, very educational—but also very frustrating."

Still, *he* escaped intact: how did he manage that?

"I'm beyond being charmed by Charles Moore," Filson replied. "The trick is to know when he's kicking you on the ass, *telling* you to go out and make it on your own. A lot of people can't understand that, and it totally screws them up." Most young architects I talked to who have worked with Charles Moore admitted the difficulty— and yet the importance—of trying to break free of him and strike out on their own.

In an article he wrote about the late-nineteenth-century Boston architect Henry Hobson Richardson, Charles Moore may have been revealing some of his own feelings about architectural teamwork. "I wonder," he wrote, "if [the] problem of parlaying a limited amount of energy into a large and influential body of work is not really the central problem of the professional practitioner. . . . The wonder is how a set of tiny Richardson sketches had the power to summon from his associates contract drawings which produced . . . the 'massive and simple' buildings that have provided the image for a whole age. . . . I confess I still don't see how he did it." He concluded by praising Richardson (perhaps with a trace of envy) as "the quintessential full-time architectural professional, the un-disputed leader of a complicated team that accomplishes things (the building of buildings of lasting power) with a beautiful econ-omy of effort and a knowledge of how to be effective." [5]

IF he felt that his name and reputation were being tainted or cheapened by the less-than-magical work of his associates, why not retire into the honored but nominal role of a silent senior partner, a gray eminence—like Nathaniel Owings, say, of Skid-more, Owings and Merrill—who for years no one actually expected to take up a pencil and draw? One client, in fact, told me that he thought that Charles Moore was already being used by his firms as a kind of Colonel Sanders, wheeled around the world as a flashy front man for the people who did the actual work.

"That doesn't strike me as a very satisfactory way to practice architecture," Moore replied. "The only reason to do that is be-cause it pays you a lot of money. Which it does for Nat Owings."

One of the major complaints I had heard from junior partners and associates in Charles Moore firms was not unlike that of the UCLA students. They claimed that he took on gigantic projects, did a few cryptic sketches, and then left them to sort things out. "He leaves people in the lurch, gives them those incredible projects, and then flies off to Peru," I was told. "Life with him is very difficult, and working with him is impossible. He's not around enough. It's become manic, all this running around."

Charles Moore took forty-one separate plane flights around and out of the country in the first six months of 1982. "My traveling has become a vicious cycle," he conceded. "I like to travel, obviously. But it's becoming self-perpetuating; I feel I can't stop." It began, he thinks, as a rational necessity—cultivating enough clients na-tionally and internationally to keep the practice going, making public appearances to help build its reputation, teaching in be-tween to pay the bills. But lately, he admits, he sees his traveling more and more as sliding into an irrational obsession.

"Sometimes I don't even remember where I am when I'm there. The worst times are like Vienna last week. My hosts had driven me around showing me lots of Otto Wagner stuff. I was staying in the old Hotel Bristol, nineteen hundred or so, across the street from the Staatsoper, and that was wonderful. They had bought a single ticket to the opera for me, a front-row seat to *The Barber of Seville*. I sat down, waiting for the overture—and reached down to buckle my seat belt!"

Some friends worry about what this unreal travel schedule may be doing to his health. "All this globe-trotting of his is really frightening," says Bill Hersey. "He eats garbage; he doesn't care for his body; he lives in airports. I'm always afraid he'll go down like a stone in some airlines terminal. He had this nosebleed one night in LA from his high blood pressure and was terrified out of his wick."

But tales of his heroic constitution are equally common. "I've just got twenty minutes," he will insist, and then settle into a three-hour restaurant feast. Up till 3:00 A.M. on one project, he will schedule a 6:00 A.M. meeting on another. "Don't worry about Charles," I was told. "He's in control. He knows what he's doing."

Lately gout has been added to high blood pressure, and the consumption and variety of his pills have increased. He makes use of fat farms in southern California and Mexico in his struggle to keep his weight around two hundred pounds. But at his best, his stamina is astonishing. "He will race down the freeway at ninety," admits Hersey, "drop off his rental car, then *run* down the airport corridor with a hastily packed thirty- or forty-pound suitcase—and be on his flight with seconds to spare."

Whether or not all this traveling is good for him, Charles grows impatient with colleagues who complain about his absences—just as they grow impatient with his peripatetic ways.

"If they don't like it, they can always do something else," he remarks grumpily. Then he reflects some more on the Richardson case—the erratic genius-architect with a team of assistants so willing and alert that they could translate his merest sketches into good buildings. He *did* envy Richardson his atelier, he admitted. He had once hoped to build something like it himself.

"At twenty-eight, or however old I was, it seemed to me perfectly reasonable that one could do all that, that it was a totally plausible way to go about the business of architecture. And it gradually appears, year after year, less and less plausible.

"I had lunch with Wes Peters at Taliesin last fall, and we got to talking about George Shepley, Richardson's son-in-law and successor. The amazing thing was that Shepley and his partners had taken over Richardson's very personal-style office after he died and totally changed it, from a genuine artist's atelier to a large professional firm—which is much harder to pull off successfully.

"You say these young associates of mine feel that the great problem of their lives is to get clear of *me*, to get quit of the erratic genius. Well it seems to me—if I may say so, speaking from the other side—that there are only three things you can do when you get quit of the erratic genius. One, you can take up selling shoes or something. Two, you can go and become an erratic genius yourself (which has not worked out very well for most people most times). Or three, you can do Mr. Shepley's number and try to pull from the energies involved in the erratic genius a *system* that will allow you to produce something worthwhile."

William Wesley Peters, for many years a student and associate of Frank Lloyd Wright's, became chief architect of Wright's successor firm, the Taliesin Associated Architects, after the master's death in 1959. Most architectural practices that grow up around one or more geniuses, erratic or otherwise, either dissolve or transmute into practices surrounding someone else, when the genius retires or dies. Thus the Taliesin Architects "carry on" for Wright; Roche and Dinkeloo are regarded by some people as the heirs of Eero Saarinen. A few firms retain the name of the founding fathers (Holabird and Roche, Skidmore, Owings and Merrill, Wurster Bernardi and Emmons) even after the founders have ceased to participate actively, and their particular style and inspiration have disappeared. This is markedly the case of the large successor firms to H. H. Richardson—first Shepley, Rutan and Coolidge, then Shepley, Bulfinch, Richardson and Abbott, which has nothing to do with Richardson *or* Bulfinch, except legal continuity, and the right to continue using their honored names.

"When [Richardson] died, the office lost more than an executive; it lost all possibility of personal or even of consistent creation. The executive became a general staff; and the commissions, which still came in almost as great numbers as in the last few years of Richardson's life, were handled by committees. . . . But with Richardson gone, there was no one individual to maintain the old standard, nor anyone apparently with a sufficiently strong artistic personality to set a new one. The leadership of American architecture passed away from the firm."[6]

Moore's happiest current collaborators are those who can accommodate their work to his nervous, globe-trotting style. "He can come in once every three or four months," said a partner in the August Perez office in New Orleans, "and bring in enough excitement to carry you for three or four more. Whenever he comes it's festive, it's an event. You get this *rush* when he's around—it's almost like you were doing drugs.

"But we've learned not to expect anything. 'Back in six months, Charles? Fine. That's O.K.' This place isn't struggling. We're full of jobs. But he knows, and we know, that he can roll in and make something better. When all of us are checkmated, he can find a way."

Bill Hersey, who often follows Charles around to different jobs to sit at his elbow and draw up his ideas, feels that his crazy schedule is justified. "He creates chaos, that's for sure. He knows he's doing it. He *likes* to do it, that's all. But when Charles Moore flies in with a bunch of people and designing starts, it's so electric, so fantastic: *sparks* of electricity go off.

"Working on the world's fair in New Orleans, Charles was flying through the air, he and a bunch of us. He has this huge range and scale of architectural visions, it's so extraordinary—all these images and devices are at his disposal. It's based on all the architecture he's seen around the world. It's so *available* to him."

The awe and admiration (and some of the complaints) were echoed by the resident partners at Moore Grover Harper in Essex, Connecticut—which, like Bill Turnbull's San Francisco office, has established a solid reputation of its own. In early 1983, they had forty projects under way—only three of them involving Charles Moore. Still, their most newsworthy work does tend to be at least ostensibly "his," because it is his reputation and personality that attract clients like Nobel laureate James D. Watson (for the Cold Spring Harbor projects) and the trustees of Dartmouth College.

"He's the fastest designer in the world, no question," Bill Grover said. "Unfortunately, he expects everyone else to be equally fast, and gets impatient if you're not. Of course, one source of his speed is that he depends entirely on himself. He leaves us to agonize over clients. He never works beyond sketches on yellow tracing paper anymore. He does his bit, hands it over to one of us, then flies off to Buenos Aires. The client says no, and the junior panics. 'Call Charles.' 'But he's in Buenos Aires.' 'Call Buenos Aires.' Charles flies back, arrives at eleven P.M., has just an hour to spare. And then what you've been struggling over for two weeks he solves in fifteen minutes. It can be very deflating. You've got some impossible problem in nine variables, you've got to fit a stairway into a corner of the living room under some vital structural beam and make it all work out handsomely and naturally. He comes in and in five minutes he figures it out. Probably out of something he remembers seeing Borromini do somewhere. Or Aalto. Or a combination of both."

"What he does," said another Essex partner—we are sitting around a flawless French lunch at a restaurant across the street from their office—"isn't really magic. He just brings a fresh look. He can unscramble what's screwed up. Something he saw on his last trip, something from Knole House or Helsinki."

"But you can't count on him," said another. "We learned to let him go his own way years ago. Dartmouth wanted him to come up there personally to talk about the museum, but it was hell finding a day when he could fit them into his schedule."

In the end, Dartmouth got far more of Charles Moore than most recent clients have. After an interview in the summer of 1981, his firm was chosen by the trustees from a short list that included Robert Meier, Hugh Hardy, and Charles Gwathmey. In the fall of 1981, he spent three weeks in Hanover presiding over an elaborate series of client-architect workshops, based in part on his similar adventures in Santa Cruz, Seal Beach, Pacific Palisades, and Dayton. Chadwick Floyd and Glenn Arbonies, two of the Moore Grover Harper partners experienced in this kind of design diplomacy, were also on the team, along with a few youngsters able to draft double-quick and stay up all night building cardboard models. On the clients' team were David McLaughlin, the provost (later president) of Dartmouth College, and a committee that included trustees, top administrators, and representatives of the museum's donors.

"Rather than telling them which site on the campus to choose" (this is Moore talking again), "we gave them their choice of six. They protested. 'You're the architect, you pick it.' 'No no no,' I said.

'They're all fine with me.' Then we designed—or rather I designed—a different building for each of the six sites. They were all
very tight, very difficult to fit. Our boys then worked like absolute
fiends and built a model for each of the six designs. They were all
very different.

"We held six meetings with the whole college committee in the
space of three weeks. We showed them our six models, and they
turned down four." ("It was a kind of beauty contest," he said later.)
"We then designed five *new* ones. In all, we designed seventeen.
different buildings—me, Chad Floyd, Glenn Arbonies, and two
kids, plus a couple of others who came up to help under pressure.

"We went away for two weeks after that to let them mull it over.
When we came back, they had narrowed it to three sites. Two were
simply different versions of the same design; both faced the
Dartmouth Green, where every other architect had told them to put
it all along. Number three, the dark horse, was behind the green,
connected by a courtyard to this huge nineteen-sixty-two barrel-
vaulted auditorium by Wallace Harrison, to which we had somehow to 'relate.' As it turned out, the two leaders wiped each other
out: people who loved A hated B, and vice versa. In October they
voted for C. We then spent a month in Connecticut actually designing the building. We made a nice model, and with the help of this
wonderful provost—who liked us *and* the building—we showed
the schematics to the trustees in mid-November. They loved it.

"Later I decided that the design we showed them was a little too
hot—all those cute English-villagey dormers next to that barrel-
vaulted monster were a bit much. Fortunately we were over budget,
which gave me a chance to simplify it."

IN 1970, Charles Moore's Connecticut firm—the predecessors of
Moore Grover Harper—came within inches of having to declare
bankruptcy. Under the exuberant direction of an office manager
with grand ideas, the partners had overextended themselves out-
rageously on speculative projects, get-rich-quick schemes for development. They bought a company plane to whisk Charles and
others from prospective client to prospective client, commissioned
engineers and consultants, feasted on expense-account meals,
and spent hundreds of costly hours designing dream projects all
over the East. "Since we couldn't make it in architecture," said one

of the survivors, "the idea was, let's do other things to support our architecture habit. The development consultant here was earning twice as much as any architect."

They were being harassed by bureaucrats over a large, showcase public housing project in New Haven. It dragged on for years, hemorrhaging money out of the firm. When the recession hit, firm contracts for many projects they had invested time and money in failed to materialize. Charles Moore Associates found themselves $250,000 in debt and about to lose the wonderful old building they worked in.

A $60,000 loan from Charles Moore's attorney brother-in-law (who also worked out a consolidation of their fifty creditors) helped them save the building. But it took the partners four years of dogged effort to get their heads back above water and regain the respect of their bankers. There are people who believe that a great deal of Moore's refusal since then to establish or settle permanently into the sort of sizable office that might permit him to win more major commissions, and see them through to completion, derives from the trauma of 1970. ("He was terrified of the thought of being sued and actually having to go to jail.") He is determined, they believe, never again to find himself locked in a position of such terrifying responsibility. Given the epic scope of projects like the Tegeler Hafen redevelopment for Berlin (over $100 million), and the limited resources of the office undertaking it, I wondered whether he might be setting himself up for another 1970.

"I'm afraid that's a very real possibility. I've been trying to get some accounting of the way the Berlin moneys have gone, and I haven't succeeded. Yet. So I *do* have some of the same vibes I had in 1970."

("That's nonsense!" said a close friend of the partners involved. "The firm only started making money when Charles stopped negotiating contracts. He's *terrible*! He only bills for a percentage of the estimate, no matter how much the project runs over. And then he blames his assistants. David Rodes asked for a sixty-thousand-dollar house. It came in at one-twenty, but we were still only paid on a sixty-thousand-dollar basis. Buzz put in sixty-hour weeks on that house, went without salary . . . and Charles has the nerve to blame *them* when they don't make any money!")

A year later, it looked as if at least half the Berlin project was likely to go forward. Moore Ruble Yudell will probably collaborate with a Berlin-based project supervisor, whose office could supplement their small team of craftsmen. They had just won a $20 million hotel project in San Juan Capistrano. But on that particular afternoon in Monterey, in March 1981, Charles Moore was still feeling insecure about his southern California operations. "The Connecticut office I don't worry about. Bill Grover runs that now, very carefully, very conservatively."

Anxious friends wish that Charles would settle down with an established and well-organized firm, so that he could stop fretting about profits and commissions. His brother-in-law Saul is among them.

"Well, he's right."

But wouldn't that reduce his independence, narrow his opportunities for innovative design?

"I don't think so. Some of the best things I'm doing are with the big bad Perez office in New Orleans. It may not work forever, but that does seem to be one route for the future. To stick with organized firms, where they put together the bookkeeping, and I roll in and out and design things. I'm obviously operating on their sufferance then, for just as long as I'm valuable to them. I have to depend on their capacity to deal with the clients—which in the case of Allen Eskew is a pleasure, because he deals with them beautifully.

"What happens in LA is that I never get any money anyway. One of my firms owes me five thousand bucks at this point—out-of-pocket money on plane tickets and stuff. I got money out of the Indianapolis project, eighty bucks an hour, and that's just lovely. But the teaching and lecturing are essential. I suppose that the amount it's cost me to have an office over the last twenty years is maybe a hundred thousand bucks. Some years there's been a profit; some years there hasn't. But putting it all together there has *not* been a profit. So the main gift to me from all that has been some satisfaction about jobs that I've liked. I would rather do them the way I want and not make any money, than be boxed into something, and *still* not make any money."

("He plays his money cards very close to his vest," says Bill Hersey. "He will wipe himself out over and over—cut very close to the bone, end up all but penniless, and still not seem to mind. He knows all the stories of Lou Kahn's debts, Frank Lloyd Wright's debts, tells them all the time.

"He 'uses' us all, but he's not unscrupulous. He was in a terrible bind once, had to have two or three thousand dollars at once. He was near tears. I couldn't stand it. 'Look, Charles Moore,' I said. 'I'll get the money for you.' And I did, by that night. I never expected to see it again, but he paid me back.")

Two years later, with well over $100 million in confirmed bookings, things were definitely looking up for Charles Moore, Struggling Architect. But his apprehensions of 1981 (and of 1971) had still not entirely disappeared.

At UCLA, as a "Professor VI" with an off-scale salary, Moore is now paid more than $50,000 for each academic (i.e., nine-month) year he works full time. He accepts unpaid leave, or part-time status, when the pressure of other work keeps him away from the university overmuch. ("He could make more money if he quit teaching," one of the Connecticut partners insists. "He could do buildings all the time.") The balance of his income comes from his share of the two partnerships, hourly stipends on other design jobs, lecture fees, and royalties.

"People were joking in New Orleans about my getting so frantic, because I had so many things going and I wasn't getting them done. And then Ron [Filson] made a date with some woman who was about to get a grant and wanted me to do a float for next year's Mardi Gras. And so I said, 'How wonderful! I can do a float for next year's Mardi Gras!' And so I dropped everything and went out and talked to this woman and said I'd do it.

"It later came over me—or over Allen, or somebody—that the only reason I had said yes was that I was so far behind in everything *else* that if I took on something new, a brand new job, then at least for a little while there would be this one thing that I *wasn't* behind on." (For better or worse, the Mardi Gras float never came off.)

Lately Charles Moore, in what might look like a willful rejection of the sound and profitable career that has eluded him for so long, has been doing more and more things like Mardi Gras floats: conceptual or theoretical models, toys, fantasies, and follies that are never intended or expected to get turned into buildings. There was an antimodernist model for a 1980 meeting in Stuttgart; a doll's house designed on the invitation of a British architectural magazine; a make-believe house for Karl Friedrich Schinkel; a "late entry" for the Chicago *Tribune* Tower Competition, restaged sixty years after the original. He has done art-architect exhibition designs for the 1980 Venice Biennale, the Museum of Modern Art, the New York Architectural League, and the Castelli Gallery; travel sketches and fantasy islands for the Max Protech Gallery in New York and for Pierre Bonnafont's in San Francisco. What good was all this time-consuming, nonarchitectural work doing for his career?

"I used to worry about Louis Kahn on those very grounds. Why is this man doing the Venice auditorium project? I would ask. Everybody knows that's a piece of PR fluff that's never going to get built by anybody. Why is Louis Kahn spending all his time on this?

"He had no answer. I have no answer.

"Some of them do pay. The Best Products Company thing at the Museum of Modern Art was ten thousand dollars—first thing I ever made fifty percent on. And now we may be able to use part of it for a park in Houston. That thing at the Architects' League with Alice Lyndon was for two thousand bucks each. I probably didn't lose more than a thousand on it. Formica paid me five thousand dollars for that foldup armoire. There's always the chance to experiment. And the publicity. And they're usually fun to do.

"But they do serve a professional purpose too. I used to say that one of the great things about doing houses was that you could get them up and see them, have the people move into them, take their pictures while you could still remember why you started. The big stuff takes years and years. Kresge College took almost ten years. It's very hard for me to maintain a consistent attitude toward anything for ten years. So these little things, like the houses, are diversions that come to their logical ends."

One of his most recent protégés quoted Charles as insisting, apropos of these unbuildable commissions, that " 'to say no to anyone, even if you have no money, no time, is to cut yourself off.' He sees the day just around the corner when he'll have nothing to do, feels the day of collapse is at hand. He knows he loses out on big jobs because he doesn't have one responsible organization behind him, the way Cesar Pelli and Hugh Hardy do. But Charles tires quickly of people and places. He needs to go off. One office would kill him."

"He's definitely, definitely, definitely moving into fantasy architecture," insists Bill Hersey, his wizard draftsman. "Not only these little follies, but these giant theme parks and world's fairs. The big glass greenhouse full of palm trees in Minneapolis or Berlin or somewhere. He wants to do a lake with a huge man-made turtle in it and a little temple on the turtle's back. Like taking one of those fantasy drawings of his and *building* it. I think he'd like to go beyond architecture and style and just float.

"I still imagine the perfect client waiting for him in the wings with millions and millions of dollars, and saying, '*Here*, Charles Moore: do what you want!'"

A MOORE TOUR

TOP LEFT: Charles Moore at five (Courtesy Mimi Weingarten)

TOP RIGHT: Charles Moore at twenty-one (Courtesy Mimi Weingarten)

LEFT: Dean Moore at home in New Haven, 1970 (Courtesy Mimi Weingarten)

Moore–Heady house, Orinda,
California (1962) (Morley Baer)

FACING PAGE:

TOP: Professor Moore (*center*) with Yale
students at New Zion, Kentucky, 1967 (James
V. Righter)

BOTTOM: Charles Moore, Donlyn Lyndon, and
William Turnbull, Jr., at Cuernevaca, Mexico,
1972 (Hugh Hardy)

Moore–Heady house, Orinda, California
(1962), interior: living area with columns
(Morley Baer)

Moore house, New Haven, Connecticut (1966),
interior: window (John T. Hill)

Moore house, New Haven, Connecticut (1966),
interior: Tower "Howard" with Willard family
portraits and living room (John T. Hill)

Moore house, New Haven, Connecticut (1966),
interior: Tower "Ethel" and kitchen (John T. Hill)

Bonham—Cahill cabin, Boulder Creek,
California (1962), exterior by night
(Morley Baer)

Bonham–Cahill cabin, Boulder Creek, California
(1962), interior (Morley Baer)

Talbert–Halvonik house, Oakland,
California (1964), exterior from
below (Morley Baer); and
axonometric drawing (William
Turnbull)

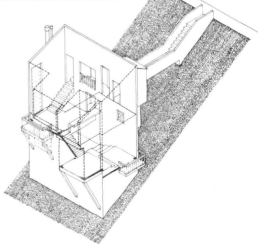

FACING PAGE:
Citizens Federal Building (1903)
and addition (1963) (Morley Baer)

FACING PAGE:
Condominium I, the Sea Ranch,
California (1965), exterior from west, up bluff
(Morley Baer)

Condominium I, the Sea Ranch,
California (1965), interior of Unit 9
(Morley Baer)

Johnson house, the Sea Ranch, California
(1966), interior (Morley Baer)

Typical "Binker barn" (Spec House II), the Sea
Ranch, California (1967–69) (A. Youngmeister)

Condominium I, the Sea Ranch, California
(1965), exterior (Morley Baer)

Kresge College,
University of California,
Santa Cruz, California
(1974) (Morley Baer)

Faculty Club, University of California, Santa
Barbara, California (1968), central court
(Morley Baer)

Faculty Club, University of California, Santa
Barbara, California (1968), dining room
(Morley Baer)

Koizim house, Westport, Connecticut (1971),
living room (Ezra Stoller, © ESTO)

Koizim house, Westport, Connecticut (1971), exterior (Ezra Stoller, © ESTO)

"House near New York" (1976), central hall
(Norman McGrath)

Piazza d'Italia, New Orleans, Louisiana (1978),
fountain with Lykes Building (© Alan Karchmer)

Piazza d'Italia, New Orleans, Louisiana (1978),
children playing (© Alan Karchmer)

Sammis Hall, Cold Spring Harbor
Laboratories, Long Island, New York (1981),
interior of central hall (Balthazar Korab, Ltd.)

Wonderwall (under construction), Louisiana
World Exposition, New Orleans, Louisiana
(© Alan Karchmer)

St. Matthew's Church, Pacific Palisades,
California (1983), nave under construction
(© Raymond St. Francis)

Tegel Harbor Project, Berlin (designed 1980),
sketch of waterfront promenade (Bill Hersey
for Moore Ruble Yudell, Architects and
Planners)

ABOVE: Beverly Hills Civic Center, California (designed 1982), model (Philip J. Kirkley, Jr.)

LEFT: The Parador (resort hotel), San Juan Capistrano, California (designed 1982), model (© Raymond St. Francis)

OVERLEAF: Charles Moore medallion, Piazza d'Italia fountain, New Orleans, Louisiana (1978) (David Littlejohn)

Part Two THE WORKS

9 / AROUND MONTEREY BAY

I MEAN it as no criticism of the architect or his clients—most of the latter family or friends of his family—when I say that none of Charles Moore's work before 1960 is of great novelty or distinction. He solved problems well, gave his clients what they asked for and more, and demonstrated an adroit handling of forms, spaces, and light. The buildings look like other good California work of the time. The Japanese influence I have referred to is clear in two or three cases. The alert student of Moore's later work can begin to trace buds of ideas that were to burst into more exotic bloom. But had he not gone on to (and beyond) the phenomenal buildings of 1961–63, no one would be driving around Monterey today trying to find these surprisingly unsurprising examples of early Charles Moore.

I described, in chapter 2, the houses he designed for his mother and his sister in Pebble Beach. Mother's (1954), as we have seen, has a few ingenious and distinctive features. But the Weingartens' (1953, enlarged in 1963)—green-painted wood, simple pitched roof and carport, the usual rooms—should satisfy even Robert Venturi, who professes to admire very ordinary-looking buildings.

Saul Weingarten, Charles's brother-in-law, got him most of his other early commissions. First came a small two-story office building in Seaside, a racially mixed young community north of Monterey, where Saul Weingarten has his law office; then a twenty-four-unit apartment building on a Monterey hillside in which he had invested. He asked Charles to enlarge it by adding seventeen more bay-view townhouse units over the garage at the top of the hill.

Although Saul Weingarten is very proud of his office ("It's the only earthquake-resistant building in town"), the Seaside Professional Building (1956+) looked to me like any ugly and ordinary commercial-strip cube. I circled it three times before I spotted Saul's shingle. Only then was I convinced that this unremarkable building really had been designed by the hero of the international architectural press.

The Monte Vista Apartment addition (1963)—which Saul calls his "favorite" among Charles's designs—looks very suburban California modern from the street. It's an ingenious, thrifty, habitable solution, which allowed the owners to leave most of their property green and unbuilt on, and still almost double their income. By building up rather than out—a favorite MLTW solution in years to come—Charles was able to give each unit a two-story section of living room, overlooked by a bedroom opening, and to play a few games with view-catching balconies and bays. But I was surprised that it gained national publication.

Two later housing commissions in Seaside also came to Charles via Saul Weingarten, a liberal activist lawyer then serving as counsel to the local redevelopment agency. Saul got together a league of civic groups and persuaded them to undertake an eighty-unit park of little houses for old people. Then he persuaded Charles to donate a plan. The result (called Villa del Monte, only completed in 1967) is a quaint but agreeable village of very small, Charles Moore–looking duplexes. The white stucco blocks have reverse-pitching shed roofs, which yield one very high living-room window wall per unit, facing a little court. These toy blocks are disposed about a central lawn, miniature gardens, and winding paths, all now gone a bit to seed. The second project, Del Rey Oaks, a condominium subdivision of thirty-six units on eighteen acres, has endured many years of planning-commission delays and was still awaiting financial approval when last I heard.

Saul Weingarten also led Charles to the job of designing a house in Monterey for his former law partner in 1956—a woodsy, pseudo-Japanese place now half hidden in trees, with intersecting, normally pitched and eaved roofs over a cross-shaped plan. A driveway dips under the living-room/balcony wing. For Roy Hubbard—the local contractor who built Moore #1, and a student of Saul's in Naval ROTC School—Charles designed in 1957 an almost classic Japanese-style house in Pacific Grove. This pure, clearly framed rectangular redwood box is set in the middle of a traylike deck that floats on stilts over the landscape. A widely overhanging, low-pitched shingle roof with projecting gables completes the illusion of an Asian island pavilion, now extended at the rear into a trel-lised shelter under the trees. The house is now owned by a Japanese-American family. Weary of Moore tourists, they no longer allow strangers inside. They have landscaped it with appropriate austerity and hung a bright yellow calligraphed banner at the door.

Two years later, in collaboration with his Princeton friend Richard C. Peters, Moore designed for Mr. Hubbard an elegant house intended to help the builder sell property in Corral del Tierra Estates—an upper-income tract overlooking a new golf course near Salinas, a few miles inland from Monterey.

Hubbard #2 of 1959–60 (now the Hubbard-Phillips house) is an impeccably handsome, white-plywood-sided California modern house. It floats low and easy over a graveled car court in front and a wooden deck behind. From the deck, one faces golf-course lawns that dip toward a spectacular mountain view. I have no quarrel with the publicity and prizes it won. But it is certainly the most conservative large house Charles Moore ever had a hand in. The only signs of Moore's later tastes come in a glass-walled niche, like a shrine, at the door, and a provocative hint of overhead light. This enters through clerestory windows in a high central light box, which rises like a square flat hat out of the low-sloping, pyramidal roof. Rooftop light boxes like this were soon to take on a more exciting role in Moore's work.

Had he gone on in the direction suggested by these early houses, Charles Moore might have become one of the large number of highly skilled and sensitive Bay Region–style architects—a group he worked with in the late 1940s, planned to join in the 1950s, and has always admired. (He paid respectful homage to the school in a thoughtful critical essay of 1976,[1] well after he had moved off in directions of his own.)

To me the most interesting of all these early Monterey-area buildings is Duane Matterson's house (1957–59) in Pacific Grove. This is the "mixture of Japanese forms, Lou Kahn ideas, and cheap factory components" to which Bill Turnbull and Don Lyndon—who worked with Charles on the design in the fall of 1957—have already referred.

I love this little house in the trees, formed of three off-centered, sixteen-foot-square pavilions. (Modular halls, decks, and service areas fill the spaces in between.) Since it had to be built very cheaply, the walls were made of an asbestos fiber-board sandwich braced by vertical studs every four feet, all of this exposed. The roof of each square pavilion-room is framed by an intricate open pyramid of trusses. The timbers meet at eighteen-inch-square bubble skylights in the middle of each ceiling. "I wish we had used four-by-four skylights," Duane Matterson told me. "Those little ones cost twenty-five dollars each. But even that seemed a lot, then." A schoolteacher-potter with bright blue eyes and a red beard, he, his pots, his three youngest boys, and all their well-used possessions fit the house like a calloused hand in a beloved old mitt.

The house does not so much add together its different design sources as it fuses them into a novel and wonderful whole. One does not feel it as Japanese or low-tech or modular-formal, but as a private and very livable place hovering high in the oaks, through whose branches light filters in from the sun as it circles behind them. "The boys have to keep pruning those branches back if we want to see the mountain."

Delicate trellises built over the deck carry the branches on in and extend the ceiling trusses on out. I admire a pattern of four parallel ceiling studs, only to learn that they were added by the carpenter, to block some rafter ends that didn't quite meet the walls. Charles insisted that some intricate knee braces were needed for support. "But I think he just liked the shapes," Mr. Matterson says. Handsome wood light boxes mark the corners of the deck.

This blend of readable, sunlit spaces, with their ingenious wood detailing and indoor-outdoor flow, resulted in a sort of inelegant, handmade version of a Frank Lloyd Wright house. Playing with ideas, the three student-architects came up with a one-of-a-kind prize: an interesting, early Moore & Company house still used by the good people for whom it was built.

10 / THE BREAKTHROUGH

EVERY house Charles Moore had worked on before 1960, however "Japanese" or "Californian," fit comfortably into the American domestic norm, evolved over three hundred years. Their roofs were all symmetrically pitched at low angles and overhung the exterior walls. Floors stayed on the same level. Rooms—despite a few open-plan freedoms—were definable boxes, rectangular in plan, with ceilings either furred flat or following the roofslope, a few feet over one's head. He took a few liberties with windows and seemed to have a special fondness for skylights. But in nothing did he go beyond what other Bay Region architects were already doing. These low-lying, horizontal houses looked like what most Californians thought houses *should* look like, and conveyed a desirable sense of property, security, and comfort.

Although Moore sometimes pretends they were just matter-of-fact solutions to everyday problems, the radically novel houses of the next four years (Jobson, Bonham, Moore–Orinda, Talbert) didn't look or function at all like what most of us think of as *house*. To many people, then and later, they looked like jokes. On the outside, they were very funny-shaped. They seemed to be squeezed in and up, almost by hand, with none of the horizontal of-the-earth easiness of most postwar ranch-style homes, or the solid, bricklike stability of traditional eastern dwellings. Their roofs pitched in odd directions, unevenly and steeply. They stopped at the wall line without overhangs, like the roofs of cheap rural sheds. Windows popped out all over, in different shapes and sizes, without mullions, moldings, or shutters, as if they had just been sawn or punched out of the wall surface. Exterior walls were of unplastered (often unpainted) cheap wood siding, even of sliding barn doors. Interior walls either laid bare their framing or covered it with gypsum-board sheets. Roofs might be of tar paper; chimneys of plain metal pipes. Sometimes these shed houses grew their own lesser sheds, little dependencies that sprouted from their sides like cubic mushrooms.

Inside, there were virtually no rooms at all, in the traditional sense. The interior spaces of these odd-looking structures (bar the occasional toilet) tended to be left completely open. This space might run through several different levels, soar for yards over your head, and be dominated by a staircase that filled up a major part of your house's insides.

These were not simply variations on the Idea of a House. They were total rethinkings of what domestic space might be, contrived by people suddenly liberated (between 1959 and 1960) from a great deal of their immediate cultural past. Circulation could be vertical, rather than horizontal. Beds could be placed on open lofts instead of in darkened private rooms. Stairs could be turned into seats, tables, stages. All one's furniture could be a part of one's spiraling, ascending or descending Alice-in-Wonderland house. Rooms—enclosable private places, each intended for its own discrete function or occupant—could be dispensed with entirely, in a kind of atavistic return to the Indian hogan or pioneer log cabin or Germanic timbered hearth-and-hall concept of a dwelling. One could bathe in the open or bathe in the trees; live like kings and princes in tiny cabins designed around ten-foot columns and twenty-foot windows. Sunlight could hit you from every angle, winking up, showering down. Glass and opened walls could let in as much of the outside world as you could stand.

Summing up, I would reduce the major innovations of these breakthrough buildings to these four:

1. They abandoned traditional roofs for whatever tops seemed appropriate to primal shape and shelter needs.
2. They abandoned the usual limiting notion of ceiling (lowered and flat, or the underside of a simple roof pitch) for the almost infinite range of psychic and spatial possibilities one obtains once that notion is dispensed with. Suddenly a whole new vertical world over one's head was rendered emotionally accessible.
3. They abandoned the constriction of rooms as such in favor of "total places"—specifically the idea of one large space modulated by mezzanines and perches, aedicules and nooks, decks and balconies; then unified by voluptuous ceilings and celebratory stairs (which themselves might become additional living spaces—or works of art).
4. They rethought the idea of window from zero, casting out all inherited

notions of what windows ought to look like or where they ought to go. This freed them to decide, first, where they *wanted* light or a view (of a cloud or the moon or tree branches or the earth), and only then and there to cut open the wall.

No one has ever explained to my satisfaction what led to this liberation, to this radical reconsideration of what a house could be. Sources have been mentioned—Louis Kahn's theory of "served and servant spaces," John Summerson's 1949 essay on aedicules—but I don't think that gets us very far. "I'm not even sure I had read Summerson yet," Moore admits. "Lyndon had, certainly. And that *is* our official lecture version of how it all began."

Proper apportionment of credit soon becomes complicated, but the first three of these houses—Bonham, Jobson, and Moore–Orinda—were essentially solo Charles Moore efforts. The other partners in the newborn firm did participate in the Talbert house design, although the original client talks only about Moore in discussing the process of design.

OVER two bottles of after-dinner champagne at his Sea Ranch home in early 1983, Charles Moore endeavors, on my behalf, to make sense out of what had happened more than twenty years before.

"It's very hard to say. *Something* was happening; I was aware that something was happening. And it never happens to any of us more than once."

He thought it derived mainly from Joe Esherick and the revolutionary feeling Joe was trying to impart to his colleagues on the Berkeley faculty around 1960. "It was a very short, magic time. I was doing something different from Joe, and George Homsey (who worked for Esherick), and Chris Alexander, and the others. But it couldn't have happened independently. There was never any heavy competitive sense among us, none of this Eisenmaniacal I've-got-my-ideas-and-you-keep-your-hands-off. We traded ideas all the time."

John Echlin, one of Moore's young designers who is seated at the table, asks if he hadn't felt at the time any desire to "do it different."

"No," Charles replies. "It wasn't a matter of trying to do it different. In fact, I wanted to do it like *they* were doing it. George

Homsey's Rubin house, Joe Esherick's McIntyre house, I just thought they were wonderful, and I wanted to do something like that. Each of us was doing his own version of the same thing. No one felt 'ahead' of anyone else."

When I press, he tries a little harder to understand what pushed him down his particular path in 1960. Perhaps what set his work of the time apart from that of the other Bay Regionalists, he speculates, was the fact that he was able to make these small, one-shot jobs more *conceptual* than theirs, build them around one simple, formal idea—whether the idea came from Kahn or Summerson or somewhere else.

"And what I remember about George's and Joe's houses was that there was *not* one single conceptual '*whammy!*' but rather a *set* of wonderful things happening. I don't want to call them 'fragments,' because they were more than that—the way light slipped between volumes, the way windows revealed different aspects of the exterior. But they did seem like separate pieces."

I toss in my "unifying-concept" theory, which had seemed to me crucial in all of Moore's successful works I had seen since 1980. Dmitri Vedensky (who is also sharing the champagne) spent eight years working with Esherick before he met Moore. He takes the position that Wurster and Esherick were far more committed to *restraint* than Moore was, far more opposed to anything "showy"; and that no one on the West Coast before Moore had thought of unifying concepts as important. "We didn't work that way out here. It was Charles who introduced the 'unifying concept' into our loose and particularized West Coast style."

"That may be it," Moore considers. "After all, I was always screaming against Wurster's idea of 'organized chaos.' I was all for disagreement, but I thought we should have something to disagree *about*."

John Echlin, who was trained as a painter as well as an architect, wonders if the change had something to do with Moore's re-introducing "figurative space" into the existing abstract spaces of architecture.

"No, what Charles did," Vedensky counters (all three of us are eager to answer Moore's questions for him), "was to take Bay Area figurative space and pull it *into* an abstract order—which we on the West Coast didn't have any feeling for or even think we needed."

"That sounds about right," Charles concedes—which is as close as I may ever get to my answer. He recalls the very strict attitudes of Bay Region architects he knew in the forties and fifties toward details, their rigorous sense of right and wrong regarding the *pieces* inside their loose and easy formats. "There was an enormous Lou Kahn–like moral significance to the way a door frame went onto a door, for example. And what I think I was doing in these two or three houses here, and later in the larger New England houses, was to try to pull those attitudes and that sensibility back into some formal sense (which I'm sure Kahn had something to do with) of how a *whole thing* ought to be."

WHATEVER the ultimate source of the breakthrough, there was no doubt something in the pressure of collaborative work among three like-minded and similarly educated architects, all brilliant designers in their own right, that pushed Charles Moore into the extraordinary risks and freedoms of 1960–63 and refined the results into buildings charged with the force of *all* their ideas. These were buildings as right as they were novel, full of usable suggestions for a way out of the modernist impasse.

Moore's three ex-partners have already described the spirit of the Heinz Avenue studio, which seems to have had something of the intoxicating air of a revolutionary conspiracy. It may have been this atmosphere which allowed Moore to break the residual membrane of propriety that had kept his work, until 1960, essentially similar to that of other men. Pushed, challenged, and supported by his partners-to-be, living in the fresh air of Berkeley 1960, he felt free to forget what other people were doing and to return—in the manner preached by Lou Kahn—to first principles. He could allow his fantasies greater range, let his primal space-and-light urges, his enriched imagination, and his sense of metaphor play major parts in determining the shape their buildings might take. Given a few tolerant clients, he could now begin to play with some of his favorite ideas: the single great tentlike roof, draped from a peak to form high and low spaces; little houses inside big houses (aedicule tabernacles, saddlebag bays); large, light-trapping boxes on the roof. He and his partners were even free to experiment with ideas (like the eaten-away roof of the governor's mansion project or the open-to-the-air center of the first Jenkins scheme) that were not to be realized in actual buildings for years.

The right clients, of course, were indispensable. Moore was his own client in Orinda. But in Cyril Jobson, Marilyn Bonham, and Wilkie Talbert he got precisely the people and programs he needed to set him free.

CYRIL (CY) JOBSON, the first of Moore's three essential early clients, bought two and a half acres in Palo Colorado canyon, a heavily wooded gully two miles inland from the Pacific Ocean, between Carmel and Big Sur. When the time came to build a family vacation cabin on the property, he inquired among some of the better-known architects in the area. "But they only wanted to design for Pebble Beach millionaires." So he asked Donald Canty, then a Bay Area architectural editor, to recommend someone else. Canty, who had known Moore at Berkeley, suggested his imaginative friend.

"All I told Chuck," Cy Jobson recalls, "was that I didn't want a miniature city house, a place with lots of rooms. I wanted one big space, one big room with a sleeping deck looking down. Otherwise I gave him a free hand." Jobson also asked for maximum sleeping capacity, minimum upkeep, and a total cost of under $10,000.

This freedom allowed Moore to design a nine-hundred-square-foot, all-wood cabin enclosing the one big space Jobson had asked for—a space thirty-two feet wide and twenty-three feet high at its peak.

Imagine a square central tower of space rising to a light box on the roof, where a large, southwest-facing window pulls in sunlight from above the tops of surrounding trees. From this high central "tower," four hipped roofs slide dramatically down at identical angles, but to different lengths. Intersecting the outer walls at different heights, they look at once logical and odd. Since the north and west roofs stop fairly short, the north and west walls remain high. The south and east roofs reach out much further, and end up sheltering a low-ceilinged deck and a cozy seating corner. Modular dimensions impose a covert order on the apparent eccentricity. A detached shed of the same slope as the main roof looks like a piece of the house that someone sliced off and slid away.

This formalist logic is no doubt responsible for many of the cabin's secret satisfactions. (Charles Moore personally drew up twenty-four pages of plans.) But it also *works*, functionally and visibly. A steep, open-riser stairway placed under the central space tower conducts one to a U-shaped mezzanine that embraces the high walls north, east, and west, and looks down on the big open room. The sides of this loft accommodate six beds. Underneath it are fitted a snug kitchen, bathroom, closets, and two back-to-back double beds, now closed off in a pullman-sized alcove. The big room has plenty of comfortable seats (including two window-seat couches at the low southwest corner, which bring the maximum sleeping capacity to twelve); a Swedish metal fireplace; a dining area; and plenty of high and low windows, carefully aimed into the redwoods or down to the creek. Three separate decks extend life into the trees and complete the modular pattern.

The odd (but oddly pleasing) exterior shape—later to become an emblem of MLTW houses—is now mostly hidden by second-growth timber. The interior is so comfortable it's possible to over-look that astonishing light box so far over one's head, the vividly framed roof tent sloping in four directions, the free-floating stairs and sleeping deck; the lower windows placed like frames around their views. But one cannot ignore the great variety of interior spaces and light all these together create. The structure (built by Roy Hubbard) was kept consciously barnlike and exposed, so one could "share vicariously in the act of building." Moore made the light fixtures himself out of discount-mart baskets. He drove down a truckload of Berkeley students who nailed in the interior siding, and repainted the walls himself, so it would be ready in time for the photographer from *Life*.

Some of the Jobson family balked at living so out in the open, at the minuscule kitchen. The local water was so bad (and the morning cold so intense) that the family never stayed longer than a few days at a time. Some wood rotted and got replaced. Chuck personally helped Cy rebuild one concrete footing. After Mrs. Jobson's illness in 1963, the family never used the cabin as much as they had hoped to.

His children are now grown, but Mr. Jobson (now a widower) still loves to drive down and work here whenever he can. "I never expected it to become historic," he told me. "I've willed it to my children *and* my grandchildren, so it will stay intact for at least three generations. This place has made my life."

THE Bonham cabin in Boulder Creek, California, is also still lived in and loved, but not by its original owner or in its original state. Marilyn Bonham Campbell married and moved out of California only four years after it was finished. Her parents kept the place up for her until 1974, when they too moved away and sold it to its present owner.

In 1960, the senior Bonhams had bought six hillside acres in the Santa Cruz mountains and offered each of their three children the chance to pick a building site. Marilyn Bonham, a schoolteacher in Berkeley, chose for herself a steep wooded slope. Then she asked the husband of a fellow teacher (Warren Fuller, an architecture student at the university) to recommend an architect. Fuller proposed Professor Moore and ended up working with him on the design.

"I had no preconceived feelings as to how it should look," Mrs. Campbell recalled, more than twenty years later. "It may have ended up strange, but then I was pretty strange in those days myself. I only specified two things. I had spent many summers in little cabins in the Santa Cruz mountains that were all dark and damp and spidery, with little tiny windows, and I knew I didn't want that. I wanted it to be open and airy. And second, I wanted to enjoy the redwoods, have them inside with me, even if it was raining and windy outside. I was very antibulldozer then. I wanted to save all the trees. But it was Chuck's and Bill's idea to build *up*, more than mine. I was very young at the time; I suspect that a lot of their design concepts were over my head.

"I knew they planned to enter it in competitions and publish it in magazines, so they worked extra hard. They all came down and helped paint the place themselves, those special oranges and blues that Chuck wanted. He took me to San Francisco and helped pick out fabrics for the mats and pillows. He wanted to hang these Mexican clay pots he had got from Oaxaca for lamps, but the building inspectors said no.

"We had lots of trouble with the inspectors. This was a very conservative little valley at the time. Their original design had sleeping space on top of four telephone poles or something, and the inspectors absolutely rejected that. Our little local weekly paper was shocked by all the glass. They imagined people staring in at me in my underwear. People couldn't even *find* the place for the trees!

"I got a superexciting place to live—*and* a good deal." (The total cost was $7,800.) "I'd be a lot fussier over any house I built now, but it accommodated my life style perfectly at the time. I had no great need for privacy." (Her bed was on a tiny open deck halfway up the stairs, in full view of a huge wall of glass.) "The friends I asked down on weekends or in the summer would just spread out sleeping bags around the fire pit or along the window seats."

The Bonham–Cahill cabin is a living place even more radically novel than Cyril Jobson's. "It looks like an outsized outhouse," said one offended awards juror; and from some angles it does. Never were forms less imposed, more allowed to grow out of a client's (and an architect's) rational and irrational needs. In the end, the Bonham cabin created and validated its own aesthetic. It contained within its tiny (567 square feet) floor plan—and more especially in the spaces above it—ideas that helped to shape a great deal of Charles Moore's revolutionary future work.

To save all the trees, and because he *wanted* to build up, Moore started with a dinky living platform about nineteen feet by fourteen. This obviously wasn't big enough even for Miss Bonham's spartan needs, so he hung on a small kitchen shed (plus entrance porch) to the south; then a screened dining porch, with its shed roof, to the north, where it stops just inches from the nearest redwood; and a window-seat projection along the west wall. This business of hanging on extra spaces and sheds to the outside of a basic shape is what MLTW called their *saddlebag* approach.

That still provided no space for a bedroom or bathroom, and let in neither trees nor light. So he raised the main space up wonderfully high, filled the whole west wall with 250 square feet of industrial sash window, tilting in toward the top; fitted in more high windows to the east, plus a skylight in the roof. Then he built one of his narrow, free-floating staircases, which angled up to a sleeping perch halfway toward the roof, then bent back and up to a little bathroom fitted in over the kitchen. Underneath the stairs the floor sank for a cozy conversation pit, facing another Swedish metal fireplace. The architect arranged the rest of the floor on a series of ingeniously varied levels that kept turning into places to sit.

All this free-form designing engendered some very surprising geometry. All this height and light gave astonishing grandeur to a tiny upended box.

Described in this way, the design process may sound logical enough. The defiantly low-tech materials (which offended certain critics)—metal pipe chimney, plywood siding, tar-paper roof, industrial sash—could be regarded as the natural result of Miss Bonham's very tight budget. The architect could claim to be doing nothing more than solving her problems and meeting her needs.

But this was obviously more the work of a liberated and free-wheeling imagination than of practical reason taking step after step. Someone was imposing a whole new sense of order on the romantic (and fun-house) potentials of a place to live. The look, feel, and shape of the room were totally new, sometimes quite disorienting. The height of the ceiling and the size of the west window were outrageous. The idea of a bedroom perched on the landing of a flying staircase was next to absurd. According to the architect, what he was after was a kind of "dream grandeur," derived from "the constant juxtaposition of the spacious and the close: oversized windows and undersized stairs, a tight sleeping balcony floating in space, the central room clasped at its sides by roughly built shacks, all of it set among the redwoods on a diminutive foundation and a curious array of posts."[2]

Many of the effects he worked so hard to achieve are no longer there. The present owner—who lives in the cabin full time, not just weekends—added a large deck to the north (with a carport underneath) on which she spends most of her free sunny days. She replaced the Swedish fireplace with a Franklin stove, and repainted the gray exterior a chocolate-milk brown. She opened up the screened porch and replaced its leaky doors. She added a couple of storage sheds ("They didn't care much about storage, did they?"), and filled the house with her own special plants and *objets*.

Then, in 1980, she extended the floor of the sleeping deck the full width of the cabin, to provide herself with a more practical bed–dressing room. As a result, the "soaring space" from floor to roof peak is now completely lost and the great west window is divided in two. ("At least now I can wash the upper half.")

"It's more livable now, don't you think?" Hope Cahill asked me. "After all, it is my house. I'm sure the architects would approve. But when I called *Sunset* magazine and told them what I'd done, to see if they wanted to come back and take some more pictures, they were shocked. 'You can't do that!' they said. 'That's a historic house. You can't change it!' Isn't that silly?"

THE Talbert (now Talbert–Halvonik) house of 1963–64, in the Oakland hills just south of Berkeley, is a variation on the Bonham–Cahill idea. Here the square-turning staircase runs *down* from the entrance instead of up and clings to the outer walls of its vertical box as it winds around the high central space.

Beginning with a nearly impossible lot (it slopes downhill from the street at a rate just short of 60 percent), the architects opted for what they called a "slim tower" rather than one more ranch house on stilts. All the houses on this street gaze into miles and miles of San Francisco Bay, encompassing both the city and Marin. Wilkie Talbert got his share of the million-dollar view for $6,000, probably because of the unbuildable slope.

Designing the house as a tower allowed the architects both to minimize foundation pouring (which had to be done by workmen let down by ropes, like mountaineers) and somehow to capture inside some of the kinetic excitement of the site. Seen from outside (particularly from the street below), the Talbert–Halvonik house is strikingly dramatic: a gray-painted, vertically scored wooden-box tower that rises sharply up the cliff, accented by hung-on balconies, saddlebag bays, very tall windows, and the double black pipes of the fireplace flue; all this framed by tall eucalyptus.

One enters over a long stepped footbridge or gangplank that leads directly from the street, through the front door, to the master bedroom. (The bedroom *does* have a door, but it's usually left open; its north side is unwalled, forming a balcony over the stairs.) West off the bedroom a tiny deck, later closed in to form a study, and a bathroom with its own view take up two of the four saddlebag extrusions on the exterior. Over the bedroom railing twists a thick, hairy indoor plant, which spills green leaves down for yards and yards.

If you aren't heading directly for bed, you can turn right and start down the stairs. After their first ninety-degree turn, these stairs— the real heroes of this house—carry you halfway down a slim north window twenty feet high, which reads like an interior version of the trees outside.

The stairs break for a dining balcony midway in their descent. From here one's line of sight can travel freely up or down, following either the dark wood stairs, the white gypsum board walls, or the outward-drawing windows. A snug, straight-line kitchen is fitted in off the dining mezzanine.

Another right turn and seven more steps carry you down to a spacious projecting bay, opened up on three sides with standard aluminum factory windows. This light-filled "sitting room" affords a unique combination of openness and enclosure: you feel yourself hanging in a glass cage over the trees, and at the same time safe in your own cozy niche.

Yet another right turn, and three broad seating stairs descend to an upper level of the "living room," where the current owners keep a baby grand piano. The fifth and last leg of the stairs—all wide as benches now—leads to a low-ceilinged snug under the dining deck and a metal fireplace whence begin the tall chimney pipes we admired outside.

This design quickly became a classic: outside, a vertical shoebox breaking into bays and appendages; inside, a plunging spiral stairway giving off onto little living platforms, from which one could enjoy monumental-feeling spaces and floods of light. Moore and Lyndon (in The Place of Houses) wrote of the house in theatrical metaphors, as if it were a many-staged setting for the play of daily life.

After buying this precipitous lot in 1962, Wilkie Talbert narrowed a list of Bay Area's best architects down to six and went to talk to them all. "I wanted someone I could work comfortably with, someone who was really interested, who would supervise construction—preferably someone a little on the crazy side. I liked feeling on the cutting edge of technology in my own work [Talbert was an engineer at the Space Sciences Lab in Berkeley] and got very excited at Charles's new ideas.

"But most of the other architects I talked to simply weren't interested—or else they totally ignored my budget" ($20,000). "They came up with things that would have cost fifty thousand to build—and with none of the excitement I got from Charles. He was a pleasure to work with, from the first interviews on."

Charles's original idea called for something even more radical than what's there now: structural members arranged in diagonal lattices so as to form "Swedish trusses" for the walls. Talbert was every excited about that, but it turned out to be too costly and difficult to build and of dubious structural integrity. Moore next moved to the concept of a central core with stairs coiling around it. From that evolved the present solution: a rectangular box with the stairs wrapped around the inside walls, circling downward in helical fashion.

"I loved it," says Talbert. "It was life-enhancing, a pleasure to come home to. It was small, but it wasn't just a bachelor pad. It was imaginative and fun to live in. You felt *lighter* with all that vertical space, like you were soaring up high."

Why did he move?

"I just decided I'd had this particular experience long enough. I was ready for something else. And I did get a little tired of having to go up and down all those stairs all the time." Getting married may also have had something to do with it. "But it was a satisfying place to be in."

I first saw the inside of the house seven years after Mr. Talbert had moved out. The whole midsection of the million-dollar view—Treasure Island, the Golden Gate, Mount Tamalpais—was now blotted out by tall trees, preserved to protect the habitat of an endangered species of hawk. The gray plywood exterior was sorely in need of repainting, but the interior seemed as visually rich as what I had imagined—and unusually spacious, after some of the ship's-ladder stairways I'd been climbing up and down. The space and light inside outdid anything I had seen south of the Sea Ranch and north of Monterey.

After she had finished law school, Deborah Hinkel (Halvonik) looked all over the Bay Area for a house. As soon as she walked in the front door of this one, which Talbert had put up for sale, she had to have it. "Now I wonder how I ever lived anywhere else. It's a continuous joy. The only problem was getting married. Two people can't make noise at the same time. It's obviously a one-person house. But so far we're coping."

11 / THE SEA RANCH,
CONTINUED

THE climax of MLTW's breakthrough style was the Sea Ranch Condominium, which I described in chapter 2. Charles Moore, Donlyn Lyndon, and Richard Whitaker all left California soon after that building was completed. But its phenomenal success led to a number of other Sea Ranch commissions for what was left of the firm. At first they were undertaken jointly by Moore and Turnbull, commuting between California and Connecticut; then, after 1967, primarily by Turnbull alone. Since the Moore–Turnbull partnership was dissolved in 1970, William Turnbull, Jr., has designed several additional houses at the Sea Ranch.

A popular guide to northern California architecture includes a map to guide the tourist past the various landmarks scattered about these five thousand acres. Such a map, or a good set of directions, is not only helpful, it's essential; most houses at the Sea Ranch post no street numbers, and every other one looks like an MLTW imitation. The hills and meadows are sprinkled with high-style barns sliced into odd shapes, with weathered rough-wood siding punctured by large rectangles of glass.

Two authentic MLTW masterpieces at the Sea Ranch, built after the 1963–65 condominium, are the Johnson house of 1965–66 (later enlarged by Bill Turnbull) and the Northern Recreation Center of 1968–71, to which Donlyn Lyndon also contributed.

For Reverdy Johnson, a young attorney working for the Sea Ranch developers, MLTW nestled a tiny (585 square feet) house between two stands of trees, facing some splendid downhill ocean views. Approached across a grassy clearing inside a stockade fence, the house appears a simple, flawless object, like Moore's own house in Orinda. A steep pyramidal roof is pulled out over the entry vestibule of what appears to be a simple, rectangular red-wood cabin. Large front windows look through to other windows on the ocean side of the house, making it transparent to the blue sea and sky.

Inside the real excitement occurs. To create a sense of one great central space, to enrich the light and views with an extra layer of frames, and to coordinate the functional spaces that surround it, Moore and Turnbull inserted an octagonal structure *inside* the peak-roofed box, supported on eight ten-foot columns. (These columns are made of peeler poles—the thick cores left when plywood layers have been peeled off logs. The architects bought them from a local mill for ninety cents each.) Atop these poles the architects set an eight-sided, freestanding fascia wall about five feet high, some distance away from the real walls of the house. This they painted yellow, then punctured every other facet of it with a large rectangular hole. Two of these holes frame nothing but a section of the wall. Two others line up in front of high windows looking out at the sky.

Into the corners and spaces of the "real room," which stand outside of and between the poles of the octagon, the architects fitted minuscule versions of ordinary rooms. Opposite the front door, facing the ocean, a wide window seat between two poles is piled high with bright cushions. Throw the cushions on the floor and you have a double bed. An efficient L-shaped kitchen occupies the niche to the right of the entry. The corner on the other side of the door was turned into a dining space, filled by day with sunlight from two windows, lighted at night by a junk chandelier Charles made out of old wine bottles. One pair of poles, facing the ocean view northwest, frames a floor-to-ceiling sheet of glass. A metal fireplace stands altarlike between two poles next to the window-seat/bed, its tall black chimney pipe rising between them. The space alongside it leads to a closet and bathroom tucked behind and slightly outside of the basic house shape. Add those up—not forgetting the entry vestibule—and you get eight, like eight side altars in an octagonal church.

Four skylights outside the octagon multiply the angles and interest of the daylight let in by seven large windows and the glass front doors. Large, clear rheostated "Broadway bulbs" and ceiling spots allow a rich play of artificial light at night over the bright white, yellow, blue, and green colors of the furnishings and walls.

This extraordinary space *lifts* one like a cathedral, reveals more of its magic the more time one spends in it. The alternatively wider and narrower spacing of the side-altar niches, the careful positioning of glazed openings, read like a subtle musical score. The eye is constantly drawn up as well as out by the mystical circle of poles, the yellow band, the high windows, the converging planked planes of the ceiling, the central star.

For Mr. Johnson's second family, Bill Turnbull added a dramatic and comparatively luxurious extension in 1973. (As they prospered in their separate ways, the two men stayed good friends; they are now co-owners of the Johnson–Turnbull Winery in Napa Valley.) The Turnbull additions are elegant and eccentric, if possibly a bit too precious to meet the original house. They enabled a pioneer owner to keep on using his now-historic cabin, by adapting it to changing family needs. But having slept in the handsome new wing, I can attest that the great treat of Reverdy Johnson's house at the Sea Ranch is still waking up of a morning and returning to that original little heaven-sized room.

THE Northern Recreation Center, begun in 1968 and finished in 1971, added three tennis courts and a twenty-five-meter pool (among other amenities) to accommodate a growing vacation population at the ranch. It is sunk beneath the surrounding land, completely hidden from view behind the old Ohlson Ranch stables. The area is wind-protected not only by its sunken site, but also by a cypress hedgerow to the north and the long wooden wall of the bathers' building to the south. To the west, paths lead directly to the beach. One can see the ocean from the pool and its sundecks and still feel warm and protected.

It remains one of my favorite Charles Moore designs, but this is partly because of the nonarchitectural pleasure I take in using it— pleasure not so freely available in a housing project, say, or someone else's private home. It is dedicated with consummate ingenuity to the pursuit of physical joy. Outside and in, it is an immensely satisfying arrangement of shapes, colors, materials, and unanticipated sensual delights.

The heightened turquoise color of the pool is enhanced by the ocean's proximity—as if the whole Pacific shore were there just to serve as a backdrop for your swim—and by the fading redwood of the locker-room building and pool slide. The shape of this long wall of a building, with its high sunning towers at either end, is deeply satisfying. The monumental pool-slide tower is also a free-standing wood sculpture, twenty-five feet high, silhouetted against sea and sky. (In fact, it is pure sculpture now; safety precautions bar its use as a slide.)

The color and space experiences inside the men's locker and shower rooms are as seductive as anything Moore has designed. Before a swim or a tennis game, you enter a bright, sun-filled changing room. Glossy red-purple and blue-violet walls are set at odd angles against white walls, mirrors, and the wood decking of a bench-become-floor. After your exercise, you reenter the building at pool level to the sauna and showers (safety nuts have drained the icy plunge), then climb a tomato-red flight of inside stairs under a skylight, to return to the locker-room level—or climb another half flight to the sunbathing deck in the tower.

The women's quarters are painted green and yellow, provide private places to change and shower, and once boasted a curving slide from sauna to plunge. Because they're less open, and less flamingly colored, they seem slightly less exciting than the men's.

Moore once tried to explain all these erotic space manipulations. "The skylit shower is a few steps below the dressing bench, and the sauna and plunge below that, to take advantage of one's special sense of self without clothes, and the pleasure of moving on stairs in the light." For whatever reason, I find the required ritual to be agreeably blood warming and contrived for quiet ecstasy. The spaces and colors surprise and delight every time.

THE other Sea Ranch buildings for which Charles Moore has claimed partial design credit are the first (or Moonraker) Recreation Center, of 1964–66; the builder's corporation yard of 1966; the speculative "barn-house" design, of which seventeen have been completed; and three more individual houses.

Although it includes little of the visual or spatial splendor of the second recreation center, the earlier swim-and-tennis club won considerable attention (and two major national awards) for the ingenuity of its design and the inventiveness of its interior. To preserve the apparent sweep of open meadow (and to protect users from north-coast winds), the whole complex was "buried" behind berms of earth dug out of the site and turned back into grassy hills. A twelve-foot swell of bulldozed, natural-looking earth hides the entire center from Moonraker Road; a row of pines screens it from Highway 1. From the top of the protective entry slope, you descend fourteen feet to the pool terrace, then climb up and down another man-made hill to the tennis court.

More unusual than all the heavy earthworks was the changing building itself. Until its big brother went up six miles to the north, this was the wildest of Moore–Turnbull's geode-type inventions: rough as a ruin on the outside, colored on the inside like a Las Vegas dream. The building is basically a high board fence 120 feet long, which serves as a windbreak and sun reflector along the north side of their man-carved bowl. Wood buttresses stiffen it on both sides, sloping up to the top of the fence at the same angle as the roofs of several shedlike buildings that prop up the middle section, rising to various interesting heights. A black metal flue and two high windows afford visual relief.

The interior spaces—men's and women's changing rooms, showers, toilets, a sauna up above (Moore is big on saunas)—are tight and complex, to fit into this series of essentially linear sheds and a $40,000 budget. Stairways bend acutely; decks turn into sitting platforms. A line of heat lamps over a row of rural mailboxes (low-cost "lockers") gives it a funky, low-tech look that was quickly picked up by the fashionable magazines. The giant windows one sees from the outside (and a translucent plastic roof) pour in quantities of light onto white walls and undressed people.

But the major difference here occurred when the architects, depressed by the austerity to which budget cuts had reduced them, hired a free-spirited graphic designer to "infuse the project with some of its original zest." Designing and painting on the spot, Barbara Stauffacher added red, blue, and yellow stripes, arrows, circles, and letters, all in gargantuan scale, which climbed stairs and bent around corners. They enlarged the rooms, reinforced the angles, accentuated one's movements up, down, and around, and greatly livened up the experiences of undressing and getting clean. Within weeks, her supergraphics had become a national craze. The first recreation center, wrote one critic, like the condominium before it, "captured the fancies of a whole generation of architects."

THE "Binker barns" were a set of speculative house designs devised for builder Matthew Sylvia and nicknamed for the real estate salesman who came up with the idea. In Sea Ranch legend, they tend to get credited more to Turnbull than to Moore. But both men are listed as the inventors of this engaging and popular concept.

There are seventeen of them, scattered over the hills and meadows of the Sea Ranch. Each looks private and unique, totally at home on its individual site, while obviously related to all the others. People who would have waking nightmares in farther-out Moore–Turnbull houses can rest easily here. The barn houses are as easy to love as old teddy bears.

Imagine a gable-roofed block about the proportions of a "Monopoly" hotel, enlarged to twenty-four by forty-eight feet on the ground, and reaching up twenty-four feet to the peak. Frame it with a cage of rough eight-by-eight posts, foot-deep ceiling beams, and diagonal bracers, to form a grid of twelve rectangles, each about eight by twelve feet. These reach up two levels at the sides, three at the peak. Leave all this framing exposed. Lay rough-sawn planking behind and on top of it for walls and floors. Add a couple of sheds for porches or window-seat bays (or storage, or a garage, or a spare bedroom—whatever you want).

Then close off one bedroom and bath. This will use up three end rectangles of the downstairs floor—and please a lot of conservative clients, who aren't quite ready for floating open bedrooms. Next build a kitchen and a stairway in the two central bays. Leave the rest of the main floor open around them—for a living-dining room or whatever you need—with a real brick fireplace at one end and sufficient glass for the views.

On the second level of this jungle gym of timbers, lay in two more bedrooms and a bath, with an open bridge between them, in such a way that you leave almost half the downstairs regions open all the way up to the sloping, skylighted roof. Above *these* rooms, just under the roof peak, fit in two sleeping or storage lofts, accessible only by ladders. Provide all these upper rooms with sliding barn-door windows, so people can look down on the spaces below. Add skylights and high windows wherever they make sense.

Although structurally stepchildren of the Sea Ranch Condominium, the Binker barns *look* like traditional gabled houses, which makes the pleasure of their high spaces, floating rooms, generous light, and exposed heavy timbers an unexpected plus.

ELLA LAWRENCE'S prize-winning house (1966) had as its major design feature a high-ceilinged, four-level living room built around amphitheater seats, angling around inside a marvelous series of view-framing windows—"for lounging" (wrote the architects), "ocean-viewing, sunset-admiring, or storm-watching." The windows are still there, but the seating terraces were torn out by subsequent owners. A six-bunk children's room below and a master bedroom on a balcony above the adjacent kitchen and dining area (all this fit snugly between the trees, under one great sloping roof) have also been converted almost out of recognition.

"It was totally unlivable, the dog of the neighborhood," explained the current owner, a management consultant who had done some of the remodeling himself. "The real estate man had shown it to thirty people before us. We got it for ninety thousand, spent a hundred more fixing it up. Plus forty for the new addition. We took out the wall along the stairs, pulled out the mezzanine, punched out the dining-room wall, gutted the upstairs, and added that big new master bedroom north of the stair. Plus the new guest house. Bill Turnbull came to a party I gave here for Matty Sylvia once. But he never said what he thought of the remodeling."

THE Shinefields' house at the Sea Ranch has (like their San Francisco remodel) been so long abuilding that construction outlasted their marriage. It's not altogether clear where the house will end. In both cases, Charles Moore left a great deal of the ongoing work of design and supervision to Dmitri Vedensky; Carol Shinefield seems to have taken a major part herself. To the original bluffside house, half hidden in the tall grass, have been added comparatively uninspired wings north and south, though a new bedroom has possibilities. The original core was sunk into the meadow to merge with the land, intrude minimally on the coastline view, and ward off winds from the terrace. It was then partially roofed with sod. Ingeniously contrived, it is still a joy to be in. Six rooms and two baths are fitted together in an interlocking three-dimensional puzzle of forty-five-degree and ninety-degree angles. The levels are connected by some very happy stairs, built around a white, triangular-section chimney core and a matchless window-seat prow hanging over the ocean view. Surfaces of pale brown tile and light-toned woods provide a background not only for miles of visible grassland, ocean, and sky, but also for Carol Shinefield's joyfully gaudy furnishings and way of life.

THE Halprins' house was originally intended to be no more than a sheltering shed. They like to live and work outdoors at the Sea Ranch as often as the weather permits. They own a site so envia-ble—acres of grass and woodland, a little natural amphitheater, a steep path down to their own rocky cove—that one understands their preference. But as they grew older, their wooden tent grew more permanent and more comfortable. To the usual Sea Ranch "barn with outbuildings" of rough redwood, they added a glassed-in eating area and a splendid Turnbull-designed living room and unrailed deck hovering over the cove. Larry Halprin closed in an upstairs sleeping porch and built himself a separate, nearly cubic wood-and-glass studio some distance from the house. Bright flow-ers and a wild, high, altarlike pantry (Charles's gift) add a domestic touch rare at the ranch. Every room is filled with their own special things. The result is a bit of a jumble, but it fits, and it's obviously theirs. At first, the architects' job here was to design as little as possible, to provide at most a backdrop for the natural, open-air experiences around which the owners' lives were built. But as they mellowed into grandparenthood, the Halprins have come to toler-ate a few more man-made comforts.

CHARLES MOORE no doubt had suggestions to make for the other seven private-family houses (and a second "spec-house" prototype) at the Sea Ranch built as MLTW/Moore–Turnbull proj-ects between 1968 and 1970. But he chose not to include them in his 1978 chronology of works and usually refers to them as "Bill's." A number of these—notably Dr. Don Carlos Hines's house of 1967–68—are stunning successes in their own right, both formally and functionally. Turnbull's more recent solo work at the Sea Ranch (like the Moss house of 1978) continues to demonstrate his extraordinary sensitivity to the site and his ability to keep expand-ing and enriching the vocabulary of the Sea Ranch idiom he and his partners invented twenty years ago. If the area has been devel-oped less gently and genially than Boeke, Halprin, Esherick, and the original MLTW partners had hoped in the early sixties, it re-

mains one of the most impressive images of recent American architecture resting in peace with its landscape. Living at or visiting
the Sea Ranch, one is still most aware of, and impressed by, the
sea, the land, and the sky—which is as it should be. But out of
MLTW's (and, later, Moore's and Turnbull's) struggles to discover
built forms that respected and responded happily to this setting
have come some of the most handsome and original designs of
the postmodern era—an era which they virtually introduced.

12 / OTHER NORTHERN CALIFORNIA HOUSES

I WOULD like to describe six other private residences in northern California (there are more) in whose design Charles Moore participated: three substantial vacation houses, two full-time residences, and one long-in-progress remodeling job on a shingled, three-story 1910 San Francisco home.

Seadrift is a narrow sand spit pointing westward off the north end of Stinson Beach, California. The town itself is your standard middle-class vacation community of family cabins, village stores, and sunburned teenagers, about half an hour north of the Golden Gate. But Seadrift is now a closed-off world for the wealthy and social, a single private road (with a guarded entry gate) lined with expensive if generally unpretentious looking beach houses, facing their own private ocean beach.

The sand spit was less pricey and prestigious in the 1950s and early 1960s, when the first simple cabins were put up on inexpensive sixty-foot lots. Today you're talking high six figures in Malibu north. Simple cabins are fast being outnumbered by loud architectural statements.

The Slaters' house there (now Mrs. Slater's; for some reason, Charles Moore's married house clients tend to get unmarried more frequently than other people) was built in 1964 to a simple and apt design that yields a sequence of very satisfying spatial experiences.

The basic scheme is one that MLTW toyed with for several buildings, notably the unbuilt first scheme for the Jenkins house near St. Helena: four roofs slope steeply up from four wings, pyramid fashion. But before they reach a peak, all four stop and enclose instead a central court open to the sky.

At Seadrift, this was not simply an aesthetic conceit. It made totally practical sense. It created a large, wooden-decked outdoor living space where one could bask much of the year completely sheltered from high winds and beach walkers' view.

One enters the central court up broad steps, through a forty-five-degree cut in the northeast corner, which gives deck loungers a view back to the Marin County hills. At the opposite end, a large opening, closable by a sliding barn door, provides a direct path to the beach. "We wanted our kids to be able to go to and from the beach without getting sand all over everything." A high cut-out rectangle over this "gate"—actually, just a beam across open space—lets in the southern sun. A flapping flag over it reveals the stiff winds from which you're protected.

This deck is the heart and center of daytime life in the house. But emotionally and visually, the greatest thing about the house is the roof. A row of large square windows high up in the courtside walls—built as high as Seadrift regulations permitted—reveals on three sides the close-set lines of deep ceiling rafters that run parallel to the roof slopes. (Their eight-inch-apart spacing provides far more rafters than the roof requires. But the visual effect is worth the surplus lumber.) From the open inner deck, these rafters graphically display the steep, converging rooflines all around you. From inside the house, they delineate the space that rises from all sides toward the great sunlit heart of the house. Inside or out, the roof plan—as well as the windows, deck, openings, and details that accompany it—creates a profound sense of unity, satisfying logically and psychologically at once.

Although fairly snug in plan, all the interior spaces are made special, even grand, by the great rafter-etched tent of the roof. One could fly, soar, levitate along the lines of these rafters into the light of the high inner windows—at which point the central core breaks free of roof and walls altogether and becomes the open sky. The walls of master bedroom and bath are washed with brilliant yellow light from *their* high clerestory row. In a separate children's wing to the north, the dramatic roofslope accommodates triple bunks at its high end, double bunks toward the street, their height enhanced by rough ladders and poles. A projecting window box bathes this room with muted northern light.

Sink, kitchen storage, preparation space, and an eating counter are contained in one high freestanding cabinet which stops short of the roof, allowing the eye to run around and over it unimpeded.

Rooms facing the south (sea) view are purposely kept darker.

South ceilings are low, south windows spare. The sunken living room, with its pebble-aggregate floor and intimate dining corner, comes into its own only after dark, when a fire is glowing and beach and deck are abandoned.

On the outside this house (like the Shinefield–Sea Ranch) was meant to disappear into the land, and it nearly does. The ocean front—plywood siding painted a pale green, like the wild grasses that surround it—is so nondescript looking one could easily miss it among the showier Seadrift neighbors with their big beachside decks. ("It was so shacky it bothered the neighbors at first," says Bea Slater. "Now of course everyone has a shed roof.") White-fir floors and stained walls are light beige or tan, meant to feel like (and to hide) the sand.

JUST up the road, fronting the same beach and view, the Boases' house of three years later is less coherent but more splendid than the Slaters'; more conceptually complex, richer because of accidents and challenges that were transformed into felicitous design solutions.

Nancy Boas was particularly impressed with Moore's way of listening, picking up clues from almost anything her family said. "We had three little kids then, and saw ourselves using the front beach as a kind of sandbox. As soon as I said that, he picked up on the idea and began imagining the house as a giant scoop pointing toward this sandbox. From that, he came up with the idea of the angled cut of the wall and windows toward the sea. Then he ran the house diagonally back from there, and cut a similar scoop on the other side.

"And there we were. I still have the model he made somewhere. But that's what he does. He *listens* to you, then responds with a visual idea."

The point of all these angles, scoops, and cuts was to maximize the views, while shoehorning a fairly spacious house onto a sixty-foot lot (minus setbacks), between oppressively near neighbors. Unlike the Slaters, the Boases opted for a seaside deck (protected by a raised ring of sand and high grasses) and focused many of their windows toward the ocean view. (Since Seadrift points west, the ocean view is in fact south.) But Charles also gave them forty-five-degree faceted walls and neatly framed side-window compositions, which point east to San Francisco and west along the bluffs.

Apart from the sandbox scoop, and perhaps a shiplike motif, this house is not so much determined by a central metaphor as other houses are: richness prevails over unity. Here one senses more the architect's willingness to listen to, to accept, and then to transform the ideas of clients he found congenial, as well as emerging needs and construction-stage discoveries. (Several changes were made while the house was being built.) Like Reverdy Johnson's house at the Sea Ranch, which the Boases admired, it's another geode design: outside, dark weathered siding punctured by glass, tar-and-gravel roof, unreadable bumpy-angled shapes; inside all joyful and uplifting, golden and bright. The psychological distance between is shortened by a garden of bright native flowers.

For some structural reason, the house had to be stiffened inside by three huge flying beams, which converge in a corner of the living room like parts of a giant carousel roof. Rather than trying to hide them in the ceiling, Charles Moore decorated them with large white light bulbs, made them a part of the interior drama. They're connected to the ceiling beams above—which run at different angles—by posts carved so as to twist gently as they rise and meet each beam square. Originally, the roof was to rise in one giant slope up from the beach side, then descend to the north for a lower children's wing. But this pushed its peak higher than the Seadrift Association permitted. So instead it starts to bend back down before reaching the entrance wall—another unsought complication that enhances the overhead space.

Everywhere the placing and shaping of windows was done with manic delicacy, at once sensitive and daring. The faceted set of view windows in the master bedroom is complemented by a double-height light trap over a loft to the north. High windows pour light into the kitchen from over the roofs of near neighbors. Spectacular double-height, double-width windows, perhaps twenty feet high, divided into four giant "panes" by elegantly simple moldings, open onto the front garden from the dining-table corner of the great central space. (They reminded me of the big window in the 1943 House in the Sun, in Moore's high-school scrapbook.) Over the table floats a segmented Japanese dragon kite. Moore houses seem to invite things hanging in space—fabric banners, bowl lamps on long cords, vines, kites—more than paintings hung flat against the walls. "The art is in the arrangement of space and light," says Mrs. Boas, herself an art historian and dealer, "not in finishes of luxury materials. We hardly have any art on the walls here at all. The house itself is the art."

The central excitement comes (as so often) from the overhead space play and the influx of light. But other details contribute. The walls are sheathed in suave, golden brown hemlock, because "we fell in love with hemlock. But this is three grades better than we specified," Nancy Boas admitted. "The knots kept popping out when they tried to dry out cheaper-grade wood."

It *is* a bit overelegant for early Moore—closer to Wright, perhaps, or late Turnbull. But as at Shinefield–Sea Ranch (or the much later Hines house), I found the high-quality wood a source of sensual joy. As if to compensate, the floors are concrete, tinted before pouring to match the color of the sand. Mrs. Boas demanded, and got, a spacious, high-ceilinged kitchen, with a ten-foot-high sliding door to the living room. To enliven a blank space of wall alongside it, Moore designed a cut-out moongate "shrine" (actually a bar), and then painted it deep blue to match a sweater Mrs. Boas was wearing. "It's very Charles, don't you think?" A segment of the cut-out circle was glued to the kitchen door. A piece of their bed head-board is similarly sliced. These tricks reminded me of even wilder things Charles Moore was doing about the same time to his own houses in Connecticut.

After the Boases moved in, Moore decided that the central, or children's, part of the living room was too unadventurous, so he designed a high podium, a house within a house, to lift people above the rest of the action and serve as both an ocean- and a TV-viewing platform. (The television swings on a wall tray "to hide its ugly eye.") The lower, south-projecting adults' living room is warm and full-fireplaced, yet has picture-framed views toward three points of the compass—plus its own views back into all the light, space, air, and wood of the rest of the house.

For the three (now four) Boas children and their guests, Moore contrived an intricate set of bunks overlapping at right angles in tiny, shiplike dorms that face a common playroom. He also built them a half-scale MLTW playhouse—since demolished to accommodate a Marin County hot tub.

OTHER work Moore has done on his own, and the recollections of the first owners, lead me to think of the Budge (later Budge–Lilienthal) house of 1967 as more reflective of Bill Turnbull's ideas than Charles Moore's. It no longer exists, and I have never seen it. But it appears to have been a nearly perfect design, one that satisfied equally the two families who owned it.

The original clients, a San Francisco lawyer and his wife, wanted to build a vacation house on a corner of a large family ranch near Healdsburg: hot and dry in the summer, shaded by great oaks, in the region between the Napa and Russian River valleys. They camped out on the site with Bill Turnbull in order to choose the ideal place to build. ("Do you recall any of the design process?" I asked Elaine Budge. "No," she said. "I recall drinking a lot of gin.")

What Turnbull and Moore gave them was a house serene in its temper, Japanese in its simplicity, and able to catch the heart (of a northern California native, in any case) by means of nostalgia precise and poetic. It is the first Moore–Turnbull project to make such a direct and pointed reference to buildings of earlier times.

This house is, in plan, a broad rectangle sheltered under a double-pitched, cedar-shingled ranch-house roof. Two-thirds of its perimeter is walled by screens. Shaded by oaks, on a dry patch of land overlooking a pond and a river valley, its image is that of a thousand old California ranch houses, in the valleys and foothills where long, dry ninety-degree summers were lazed away in rocking chairs and camp cots set out on the screened porches that had been added over the years to simple, homely cabins.

The exterior detailing was neater, more cleanly disposed than that of most of its anonymous ancestors. So it looked like a slightly *better* old California ranch house, a Platonic idea of one—at once strikingly original and dreamlike in its power.

Inside, ingenuity melted into simplicity. Bedrooms and kitchen, symmetrically disposed in opposing corners, were fitted into an inner rectangle with solid walls, inside the rectangle of screen. These solid walls were hinged in such a way that they could be folded up into the ceiling in the summer, thereby opening these parts of the house all the way to the exterior screens. The remaining fourth corner (the living room) was the only part of the house for which screen wall gave way to glass. That allowed this one room, heated by a fireplace, to be kept open to the out-of-doors even in winter, when the rest of the building was cozily shut in.

The central hall was left unceiled all the way to the skylit roof peak. On either side of it, up top, were two sleeping lofts, as in the

Binker barns—one reached by a staircase, the other by a wooden drawbridge let down by ropes over the central hall.

Unfortunately, the house was burned to the ground in 1978—probably by the same vandals who had already burglarized it several times. The determined tormenting of these thieves drove the Budges to sell it in 1976. After the fire, the new owners decided to have Bill Turnbull recreate exactly this classic California house. But thefts and harassment continued. So they too abandoned the place, and sold the land to a neighboring vineyard.

THE Karas–Fabrizio house in Monterey (1966) is a box thirty feet square and two stories high, built on a steep hillside lot. A solid nine-by-ten-foot core in the center of the lower floor contains a bathroom, a cast-in-place stone fireplace, and an eight-foot row of kitchen appliances. Alongside it is the staircase up. Around this core flows an unbroken sequence of public places: entry, living room, study corner, dining area.

On the level above—again, as in the Binker barns—two big rectangles of floor were left out at opposite corners: one over the entry (about seven by twenty feet) and the other over the study (about ten by eighteen). This gives these two corners very high ceilings. Upstairs, two bedrooms (and a bath) fill the corners adjacent to the high holes of space. Each bedroom has (in addition to normal windows) a sliding panel that allows it to share the inner air. The two bedrooms are connected by an open, railed deck built over the downstairs central core, which keeps a great deal of the upper reaches of the high box always open to view. A ladder from the deck leads to a hideaway loft.

Outside, the house is as abrupt and undecorated as a wooden box can be, with zero concessions to any traditional notions of "house." Neighbors on Dry Creek Road drew up a petition in 1965 trying to stop the intrusion of this alien shack—blank, faceless, hatless—into their traditional middle-class street.

From the front, it *is* simply a tall, flat-faced, silvery-shingled box rising out of its hillside slope, with an eaveless shed roof that cuts up at a low angle from the left, rises abruptly another ten feet, then dips down at a steep angle to the right. Five windows, without shutters, moldings, or panes, all of different sizes, appear to have been cut almost randomly in the facade, adding more dissonance to the unsettling shape. (The other facades are equally odd, but they are hidden in the trees.) The satisfying symmetry, the period reference, the "human-face" image most housefronts provide were all rejected in favor of a simple sheath designed to enclose spaces (and provide light and view holes) which were determined by interior needs, and to hell with the neighbors. "Friends tell me politely, 'Actually from the inside it's rather nice,'" said Ray Fabrizio, the current owner, "which is their way of saying they hate the outside."

It may be perverse of me, or the result of overexposure to buildings of this sort, but I find the "blank" exterior of the Karas–Fabrizio house as exciting as a trumpet voluntary, filled with the promise of great things to come. The total rejection of surface detail is definitely jarring. But the very oddity of the window and roof shapes has become a signal to me of spatial and visual excitement within.

And the promise is fulfilled. This is one of Moore's simplest and most logical designs, more livable and less radical than the stair-determined Bonham and Talbert houses. Basically a variant of the Sea Ranch Condominium idea (an apparently freestanding sleeping perch built inside a high living box), one can still go to bed inside normal rooms, rooms with walls and even doors. But the sequence of space and light experiences is unusually rich.

It begins with the entry space. At the "front" door (tucked around the side of the house), one turns and faces a twelve-foot-high window, which guides the eye past a tall pine tree out in front, then downhill to the half moon of Monterey Bay. Next one crawls (figuratively) into the low-ceilinged area, in front of a cavelike cast-stone sculpture that serves as a fireplace. Turn another corner, and bookshelves shoot up twenty-five feet, far out of useful reach. ("We knocked books we needed down with a pole," the first owners claimed.) One window on this high wall faces a fake yellow sun painted on a white screen, designed to bounce extra light and heat out of the treetops and fog. ("It really works," says Mr. Fabrizio.) From the stairs, the upper deck, and the interior bedroom windows this array of excess space is available from still other aspects and angles. The double roofslopes visible from the street (Moore seems irresistibly drawn to truncated prisms, reverse-pitching shed roofs that never meet) add to the excitement. The stretch of high wall separating the two roofslopes contains large windows that pour in more southern light.

A house like this is obviously not for everyone. Most people would want more of a kitchen, perhaps even a kitchen with doors and walls. (The Karases finally punched a very Moore-ish saddle-bag out of the rear wall to accommodate refrigerator and pantry. But still there are no counters.) Rough-sawn, unpainted structural timbers and black fireplace pipes running up through the center of a house clash with some visitors' notions of comfort and finesse. Twenty-five-foot-high bookshelves (Moore liked the way they "emphasize the height") have their limitations, as do open deck passages and small bedrooms close together. Ray Fabrizio, a professional musician and music teacher who now lives there alone (or at most as one of two) wonders how the Karases—who have retired to a big old house in England—ever managed with two daughters.

But the Karases found the experience of the house a constant pleasure—like their experience of working with Moore. Ready to move from a traditional family house into something more like a vacation place, they specifically asked him for a thirty-foot-square, two-story house with a balcony-bedroom, two-story bookcases, and no real kitchen. The first plans they saw—mostly by Turnbull, Mrs. Karas recalls—weren't quite what they wanted, so they all sat down together. Charles sketched and erased as they talked and soon came up with the idea of the central core, the platform above it, and the fireplace flue going up the inside. "It was marvelous to see his mind going and a plan taking shape before our eyes. A couple of weeks later, he came back with the news that we could also have a loft and a sun catcher (although I think that was Bill's idea). And *three*-story bookcases. It got better all the time."

THE Shinefield remodeling in San Francisco—of a shingled, three-story 1910 house with a turreted corner bay—began in 1968 (eight years after a first remodeling by Wurster). It still wasn't finished in 1981, when the owners' marriage broke up. This was an intense and frequently revised three-part collaboration among Charles Moore, Carol Shinefield, and Dmitri Vedensky, who took over as Charles's on-site partner when Mrs. Shinefield decided she could not get along with Bill Turnbull. Large new rooms were carefully made out of small old rooms, retaining many of the interesting original shapes—a vaulted ceiling, half-octagon bays, the bulging corner tower. The house inside is now mostly bright white—white walls and ceilings, white tile floors—set off by huge plants, mirrored surfaces, violently bright colors, and big antique pieces. It's hard to know when to stop thinking of it as architecture (whether Moore's or Vedensky's) and start thinking of it as Carol Shinefield's own job of fashionably eccentric interior design.

Downstairs, a superextravagant children's suite was carved out of former working quarters. From there, one of Moore's more dazzling staircases leads to a genuine *piano nobile*, all gleaming white and surrounded by views. Behind a mirror-faced bar (which doubles the view) stands a Finnish-designed kitchen in eye-popping primary colors. Potted trees reach up to vaults, beams, and high arches salvaged from 1910. Down the white hall is a master bedroom full of more exciting space-invader games: an orange-painted angled I-beam crashes through the white space; an unexpected mirror covers one side of a trapezoidal cupboard; the windowed bay of the old tower curves out of one corner of the wall. A long, thin window was slipped in for the prize of its light. Twin pipes rise proudly out of the fireplace. From another corner of the room, a miraculously sculpted spiral staircase rises to an eagle's-nest study, added to catch yet another dream San Francisco view.

The job has taken years and cost a fortune. The owners could afford to be fussy and were willing to work and rework to get the effects they wanted. It was deliberately intended as an ad hoc, change-as-you-go design, without detailed plans or models. From photographs and descriptions, I had expected an unbreathable surfeit of decorator chic. But in fact, the result (as of 1981) seemed coherent and livable, as well as the freest playground for fancy Moore has worked on (however much of it is his) since his own two live-in design labs in Connecticut.

MORE recently, Charles Moore (with Nicholas Pyle and the Urban Innovations Group) designed a hilltop house in Mill Valley for a retired Los Angeles lawyer and his wife, an active and successful potter. Louis and Miriam Licht had lived for twenty years in a large Los Angeles ranch house (on an actual Sunset Boulevard ranch) designed in 1939 by Cliff May—the man who virtually invented the California ranch style. Their children grown, they decided to move to a smaller house in Marin County, one that perfectly suited both them and their site. Like several other clients of the seventies, they learned of Charles Moore when they visited Lee Burns's house on a Los Angeles house tour. "We had talked to five other architects, both here and in Los Angeles," Mrs. Licht told me. "But—what can I say?—all their egos were so big, all their houses were such 'statements.' It was a kind of macho thing, big beams inside and outside. They never *listened* to us. I knew the feeling I wanted, although I certainly didn't know how to get it.

"But Charles was the most delightful man. He listened to all my fantasies. It was an intuitive decision, really. We just liked him and thought he'd be nice to work with. I knew whatever he did would have the Charles Moore stamp—but that we'd get the house we wanted.

"He'd sit there across the kitchen table and keep fiddling with his model. He'd listen to my suggestions, say 'That's a good idea,' and start cutting or pasting whatever I suggested! It made you feel so clever." When the work was done, Charles designed and Tina Beebe made (as a housewarming present) Japanese "lanterns" of white silk that hang in the hall-stairway and flutter gently in the air currents, like delicate Loïe Fuller veils.

The outside walls are board and batten, painted gray to match the oak trunks, under a conventional shingled roof. An angle-cut entrance arcade gives the forecourt a hint of Mexican hacienda. Defying Marin County conventions, Mrs. Licht asked that *all* the interior redwood and adobe be painted white. Then she chose a bright, black-flecked Alaskan yellow cedar for the floors. Beautifully selected and laid, it flows from room to room, enlivening the white spaces and providing a major clue to the house's success.

The house's sublime feature, though, is a wide stepped entrance and circulation hall that connects the bedroom (at the top landing), the entrance (in the middle), and the living areas and deck (at the bottom), all precisely fitted to their hillside slope. The breadth and grandeur of the hall grew out of the owners' desire to obtain a proper place for a great seventeeth-century Spanish chest (which they got from Hearst Castle surplus), as well as a few smaller pieces. Although they had rejected a preliminary design with a high view-catching tower, they liked the idea of high windows. So Moore turned this wide, processional stair space into a mammoth dormer, with a gabled roof of its own and six-by-ten-foot windows pouring in light fore and aft.

This singular inspiration provides the unique unifying concept all his best buildings possess. Since the design had to be contrived to fit between a large pine tree at the top of the hill and a fine stand of oaks halfway down, the rear dormer window looks bang on to the pine, the front one gazes over the branches of the oaks. The rest of the house spreads in two wings on either side of this dormer—hall, under a wide roof that slopes dramatically downhill in a way that can be felt from every room of the house.

The kitchen (the best I have seen in any Moore house) is huge: white and wood and flooded with light from a band of five double-casement windows over the deck, two skylights, and *thirteen* of Dick Peters's spotlights. The natural light on white changes from rose-colored in the morning to blue in midevening, and is dappled by the oaks and wisteria. One whole wall is made out of cabinets of painted wood planks, built by Stein Moeller, the Danish master craftsman who turned Moore's scribbles and Mrs. Licht's fantasies into this real and perfect place.

After four years ("You can't rush Charles"), the house ended up costing $400,000, almost twice what the Lichts thought they could afford. They decided to trust God and their builder, and both came through—the builder with an impeccable job; God with some luck on their investments. I think it Moore's most totally successful recent house (it was completed in 1979), a handsome reentry into the Bay Region tradition, and proof that he can do a splendid job without the challenge of impossibly cramped sites and budgets. It seems satisfied to look, in general, like most other houses, only better, and is totally devoid of spatial gimmicks and gaga effects. The California-ranch echoes the Lichts wanted—board and batten, adobe, the arcaded court and shady deck—may be muted and transformed, but they're unmistakable. At the same time, this house is unique, unified and made exceptional by the ceremonial central hall, the joy of its light, its roofslope, its materials. It nestles comfortably on its site, and was obviously designed for (and in part by) the civilized people who inhabit it.

13 / SANTA BARBARA AND SANTA CRUZ

THE two major California commissions the Moore–Turnbull survivors of MLTW won after the Sea Ranch were both from the University of California. Both were well publicized and controversial. In both cases, the original publicity (and the controversy) grew out of the defiant way these buildings broke most people's notions of what university buildings (a residential college for the Santa Cruz campus, a faculty club for Santa Barbara) ought to look and feel like, and out of their very determined theoretical "coding." Each set of buildings was shaped by a complex scheme of cultural communication and was meant to be "read" in a certain intricate way. This aspect of Kresge College and the Santa Barbara Faculty Club has continued to fascinate architectural critics, historians, and tourists somewhat more than it has fascinated most of the buildings' day-to-day inhabitants and users.

Moore and Turnbull got the commission for the faculty club through a cabal of their fans on the club's building committee and a mistaken presumption on the part of some club members that a Berkeley-based architect would give them something like the faculty club on the university's senior campus: a lovable, pseudo-baronial, redwood-walled and tile-roofed landmark begun by Bernard Maybeck in 1906. In point of fact, Moore (plus Turnbull, Lyndon, Marvin Buchanan, and Bruce Beebe, although nowadays everyone concedes it's "mostly Charles's") used the commission to experiment with some of his farther-out 1966 notions.

Much of the publicity, generated both by the architects and by their chief advocate on the Santa Barbara campus, art historian David Gebhard, dealt with the way in which they tried to revive and reinterpret a local architectural idiom. Santa Barbara was rebuilt after a 1925 earthquake in a romantic-fantastic Spanish colonial style. Much of this wealthy, conservative, blissfully sunny seacoast city, one hundred miles north of the malign influences of Los Angeles, maintains a homogeneity created by white-walled court-yards, arcades and fountains, mission-style tile roofs, Spanishy grilles and details, and semitropical flora. Charles Moore has written with enthusiasm of the city's "exuberant civic recreation of a past that never really existed"—a triumph of stage-set nostalgia over history—and admitted that he was trying to evoke something of that same spirit in his faculty club, forty years later.

The veneer of Hollywood Spanish is clear enough. But far more assertive are the architect's wild and crazy space games, carried further here than in any building he had designed up to the time, and his pop-eclectic blending of intentionally clashing styles.

You approach the club—as you approach almost everything on the Santa Barbara campus—from the huge circumferential parking lot; then climb a ramp, past the cactus, under the palms, into what looks like a mad little Moorish village of off-white plastered prisms, one sharp-edged roof shape answering another.

This leads you past some free geometric walls on an upper-level terrace that overlooks a court, originally decorated with a brightly painted circular design and watered by a cheap lawn-sprinkler fountain. A balcony behind a thin stud-and-stucco wall (punctured by large cutouts over the court) goes round three sides at this level, leading to spartan guest rooms with high ceilings, skylit showers, and tiny balconies that look out on campus lawns and a lagoon. (The architects added one little third-floor guest room, which allowed them to include a tower in their village.) To the south, behind a wall, are handball courts and a swimming pool.

The prime spectacle of the club comes after you cross the upper deck to the dining-room wing. Here futuristic bridges and stairways fly through open spaces at odd angles and lead down to a triangular dining room. This room is further split by divider walls, which are opened up by angled proscenium-arch cutouts ringed with bare theatrical bulbs. The whole scene was originally a blaze of light, color, and clashing cultural innuendos. Lush burgundy or lipstick-red carpets led to a romanesque-arch fireplace surround and chunks of old Spanish ceilings nailed to the walls—the latter borrowed from Hearst Castle storage. A genuine old tapestry hung under abstract banners made of neon—an image by night of Las Vegas or the Ginza. One heavy old crystal chandelier graced the main freeway interchange of flying ramps and stairs. Cheap-looking metal trusses and corrugated plastic roofing were left on display. On the wall by the entrance the architects mounted seven stuffed animal heads, in conscious mockery of traditional "gentlemen's-club" style. An absurdly steep red staircase led to a wall of liquor lockers in the private bar.

This Piranesi play of passageways and levels, the windows behind windows, the psychedelic light shows and witty allusions guaranteed the building notoriety and worldwide publication. But not all of the Santa Barbara faculty enjoyed being on stage in, or upstaged by, what was supposed to be their home away from home. Many stayed away altogether, feeling mocked by their own $600,000 club and annoyed by all the architectural tourists who kept flocking to seek it out.

As of two years ago, the neon and cloth banners were gone; the deer heads were gone; the painted courtyard fountain was gone. A new chancellor had assumed power in 1978, and his wife (with the support of club members) took on the job of redecorating the club—that is, undoing much of the Moore–Turnbull exuberance. The tapestry, the old fireplaces, and the ceiling bits are still there, as well as the baroque chandelier hanging from a heavy chain over the flying bridge. The little locker room–bar atop the highest stair appears to be unused. A shabby pool table and some overstuffed chairs had been shoved into the room containing the Hearst Castle fireplace. One sensed some resistance to climbing all the spectacular stairs. Many of the intricate array of light bulbs had burned out or been removed. Wood showed peeling paint, metal trusses were blistered with rust, the corrugated plastic roofing looked awful. The flashings over the French doors to the courtyard had been visibly recaulked at their leaky edges. The building is still *used*—in it I have lunched, gone to meetings, stayed overnight, watched a lively college dance—but in the spring of 1981, it looked as unloved as an unweeded garden.

"If you polled the members of the faculty today," Professor Gebhard told me at that time, "you'd find that ninety percent of them dislike it." The lack of affection was tangible and visible. When I first read of, and saw pictures of, this building in 1969, I was favorably excited. It seemed to me an authentic, indigenous instance of "California art" in our time, comparable to the work of Ed Kienholz or Joan Didion. Today, fond as I am of Charles Moore's life-enhancing space-and-light games, I have come to share some of my Santa Barbara colleagues' resistance to this supermannerist fun house, which makes no effort even to pretend to be part of a conservative university's way of life.

THE Santa Cruz campus of the University of California, opened in 1965, is a uniquely Californian blend of Oxford, Antioch College, and a regional park, and anything but conservative. Very early in its lifetime it gained a reputation as an idyllic and uninhibited institution set in two thousand acres of meadow and redwood forest overlooking Monterey Bay, where liberated students and teachers learned and taught unorthodox things in unorthodox ways.

To the architectural community, it's best known as a valuable outdoor museum of the work of the better-known practitioners of the Bay Region style, like the Belvedere lagoon in Marin County. Individual residential colleges and other buildings were commissioned from a roll call of Bay Region masters: Wurster Bernardi and Emmons; Joseph Esherick and Associates; Campbell and Wong; Ernest J. Kump and Associates; John Funk; Reid and Tarics; Marquis and Stoller; John Carl Warnecke; Callister, Payne and Rosse; and Anshen and Allen. Almost all of their buildings blend handsomely with the redwoods and rolling hills, evoke a handsome California domesticity, and take advantage of the distant views. But by far the greatest professional attention has been paid to one that does none of these things. Kresge College, or "Clown Town" as some early students nicknamed it, was commissioned from MLTW/Moore–Turnbull in 1965, but—for a variety of reasons, mostly money—not opened until fall of 1973, at a cost of $3.2 million.

Of Moore's most celebrated and controversial works, I've almost made my peace with the Piazza d'Italia, on the presumption it will one day be properly finished and used. I've voted a qualified no on several of the mannered East Coast mansions. But I'm still having a hard time coming to terms with his two contributions to my own university—the faculty club at Santa Barbara and Kresge College at Santa Cruz.

Bill Turnbull, who was left to fight most of the battles for Kresge between 1965 and 1974, was obliged to offer the university regents two completely different designs, in order to meet their demands for drastically reduced costs and the new student life styles of 1969. Independent apartments without corridors or maid service replaced traditional dormitory rooms. A restaurant and co-op grocery replaced the college dining hall. With the architects' help, Provost Robert Edgar and Professor Michael Kahn offered a course for students who wanted to help design the college. The students came up with all sorts of idealistic, antihierarchical schemes.

By the time the college was finally opened, however, many of these concepts, virtually built into its fabric (a correlation of living and learning styles, "kin-group" associations, student-directed education, a willing surrender of privacy, eight-person communal units) had been superseded by administrative fiat or changing student tastes. The administration no longer allows students, for example, to partition, paint, and furnish their own empty apartments any way they choose, as Moore and Turnbull had intended. But the ideas and images of Kresge College have kept it in the public and professional eye.

The processional uphill tour through the college buildings has become an architectural pilgrim's ritual, a Via Dolorosa between punched-out stage-set walls that insistently keep out the forest. From the outside, Kresge College camouflages itself. You enter at the bottom of the hill, through blah openings in reddish-brown, earth-colored walls. From there on the redwoods and the bay below are very nearly banned, and the college turns in on itself.

As soon as you enter the show begins: an original and mind-boggling combination of innumerable, almost literary allusions, metaphors, and symbols, few of them altogether serious. It's a European village street, an American motel, a lot of thin temporary stage or movie sets made of cheap wood and plaster and painted in bright white and pop primary colors. (Forget all those other architects' timid "natural" tones.) It's full of mock "celebrations" of trivial events—a laundry room, a phone booth made into monuments; Venturi-esque chunks of Vegasy neon; and giant rectangular cuts in freestanding walls that frame nothing but oblongs of sky.

The back of the red-earth-colored entrance wall is stenciled in a bright blue and yellow pattern. The uphill climb begins at a low ring of amphitheater seats and a fountain that never works, where meetings and seminars are supposed to take place, but rarely do. At this, the "town center" end of the college, are located administrative offices, shops, and the mail room, emblazoned with neon and bright colors. You head up the first narrow asphalt "street" between ingenious, vaguely motellike two-story dormitory units faced with rhythmically punctured sunshade facades about five inches thick, in which students sit or lean, and arrive at the "plaza." Here, a yellow-backed laundry room, a rainbow-arched phone booth, and a red, white, and blue rostrum (ever used?) mock the civic monuments of a genuine urban place. The crudely painted rainbow, I was told, was a student protest against the surfeit of white.

A hidden back path then cuts uphill behind the dorms to a rather splendid stage-set portal with cut-out shapes of different sizes staring at the sky and peeking into the trees. On the other side of it, at the foot of the third and last uphill street, are orange-walled seminar rooms and the college library. The small library (which, by student vote, has no books) is a wonderful place, with a fine stairway down, many open levels, unexpected angles and views, and private nooks. The dappled light shining through the redwoods just outside is beautifully varied and modulated by layers of outside and inside windows.

Across from the library is another monumentally and quite madly celebrated phone booth. Finally, this last upper street arrives at an octagonal walled terrace with great high sky frames, which serves as an outdoor foyer for the restaurant, the "town hall," and a room housing electronic games.

It's easy to see why Kresge became the most published and professionally popular of the Santa Cruz gallery of colleges. It's an astonishing experiment in unexpected shapes, vistas, colors, and materials. It incorporates some original notions about place making, symbolism, cultural commentary, and the ritualization of everyday life. But you may also understand why, after a euphoric beginning, the college became in a few years the one *least* applied for among Santa Cruz students, and got itself badly maintained, almost trashed. "Tear it down and do it better," read a men's-room graffito a few years ago. The bright paint faded and peeled, woodwork rotted, holes appeared in the Sheetrock. The university, which had forced cheap building materials by its budget cuts, fought for years with Turnbull's office over who was responsible for the damp and decay. I was told by students a few years ago that they had heard Mr. Moore didn't *want* it to last more than twenty-five years, and they seemed to be doing their best to realize his wishes.

When I was last there, the university had finally got round to repainting Kresge College, and repairing the plaster. Azaleas and trumpet vines were in full bloom, a new Chinese restaurant had taken over the dining room, and the once-scruffy, caricature-hippie students had been miraculously replaced by a scrubbed generation of preppies. Even so, and though I enjoyed all the carefully programmed and composed processional and spatial experiences, I noticed that almost no one else was using them. Kresge occupants just run off to or from class out the nearest escape hatch to the woods, and hardly ever play their designated roles in the Moore–Turnbull Italian village comedy of 1965. These Sicilian "streets" are deserted more often than not, as students retreat into what little privacy they can salvage; far more life is visible through the windows than outside. Many students I talked to wished they were in the more predictable and elegant Wurster- or Esherick-designed colleges, where they felt their lives would be less forced into someone else's fantasies by these insistent and inescapable colors and walls. Other students adore it all, get positively high on the architecture.

As I see it, both the Sea Ranch Condominium and Kresge College grew in part out of a certain set of California ideas of the 1960s—ecological sensitivity, democratic participation, unstructured education, consciousness expansion, communal living. The Sea Ranch Condominium transcends these sources and endures Kresge College still carries, I think, the too-visible signs of its times and its willful, even private intellectual sources.

Moore and Turnbull were playing formalist games here with unexpected shapes and colors and associations, *trying* to shake students up, to change their lives. At one time, the architects justified their love for thin, bright, stage-set architecture by reference to the transiency of college life—as if students passing through Oxford or Yale were harmed by the obvious permanence of their surroundings. Some of the theoretical explanations they gave for their design decisions ("telephone booths are enlarged as street markers to serve as a commentary on the importance of communication in student and faculty life") strike me as absurd.

Although Kresge College has become a favorite of semiologist-critics and foreign architects, it is, in some respects, already a period piece. Its 3-D jokes aren't always funny; its messages don't always read; its celebration of the transient, the cheap, and the trivial can sometimes end up self-defeating and hollow.

For all that, I like being in, walking through Kresge College. It's coming, with each return visit, to seem less insistently odd, more uplifting and enhancing. On a fifth or sixth return, the oasis-white and bright primary colors stop shouting and begin to seem normal. The rich displays of light through cut-out walls become more life enhancing than bizarre. I can find myself feeling more full of joy and potential because it exists and I'm in it.

I've never tried to *live* in Kresge College, I grant, or lead a college student's life (what Moore once described as "an urgently important four-year-long operetta") within its stage-set walls. To do that, one may well crave fewer *Dr. Calagari* kicks and a greater degree of calm. Its buildings are never natural, never an invisible medium between you and nature. They assert themselves—but not, necessarily, *against* the inhabitant.

14 / GOING TO YALE

W ILLIAM TURNBULL and Mimi Weingarten, his partner and his sister, tried to persuade Charles Moore
that, by accepting the chairmanship at Yale, he
would increase his and his firm's reputation among
a national clientele. They were right. Within a few
years after arriving in New Haven, he was established as a "celebrity architect" in New York art-and-architecture circles and was at-
tracting residential commissions, in particular, on a scale he had
never managed to achieve in California.

I find myself less comfortable with the houses Moore designed
for East Coast clients in his early Yale years than with others he
designed before and after. Five large houses he designed between
1967 and 1969 were set on spacious tracts of land; the old problems of difficult sites and tight budgets were no longer part of the
challenge. Each of these clients laid down specific and very different requirements. But all five houses are marked by a fun-house
kind of freedom which suggests to me a lack of healthy constraint—whether that constraint comes from more demanding
and self-assured clients or from questioning equal partners. Although William Turnbull continued as Moore's legal partner during these years, and several younger associates were involved,
these five houses were essentially solo designs.

Moore's escape from the demanding give-and-take of the early
MLTW (and later Moore–Turnbull) design sessions did indeed free
him for the fantasy-making experience of his own New Haven
dream house (and Gordana Murray's remodeled house in Cambridge, which shares some of its wanton hysterics). But the escape
also seems to have left him somewhat rudderless and more than
usually self-indulgent; perhaps (for once) more the willful, mannered artist than the attentive servant of other people's needs.

The personal liberation may well have been an essential stage in

Moore's own growth into a richer and more affecting diversity. But the products of his transitional, intermediate stage (I doubt that he sees it as such, but I do) strike me as less enduringly satisfying than the best houses he designed before and after them. Charles Moore could quit his own personal op-art experiments when he tired of them, move on and let new owners repaint or dismantle them. But the owner of one of his big houses along the Connecticut shore, should he tire of its illusionist devices, may not feel so free.

Each of these houses was built about a visible geometrical conceit. This suggests not so much the *discovery* of an innate and necessary unifying concept as the *imposition* of some daring, distinctive stroke, like the slashing line or curve of an abstract painter's that brings a confused canvas to startling life. Seen in this way, these houses remain able to astonish and in many ways delight. But unlike the best Moore residences of the early sixties and the seventies, they do not feel like forms naturally evolved from their different owners' characters and needs. There is no question of Moore's mastery, by this time, of the manipulation of interior space and light. But he seems not to have discovered a meaningful and appropriate way to transfer his great repertory of inventions, discovered in the design of relatively small houses for a landscape and a tradition he knew well, to the design of very large houses in a less familiar setting. The trick, it seems—which he only began to use after 1970—lay in a conscious evocation of historical forms native to the region, and what feels like a more attentive respect to the private differences of different clients. This is what separates, to my eye, buildings like the Swan, Isham, Rubenstein, and Stanwood houses, the "House near New York" (whose owner prefers to stay anonymous), and his Cold Spring Harbor work—all designed after 1973—from the big, jazzy manors of the early Yale years: the Klotz house in Westerly, Rhode Island (1967–70); the Tempchin house in Bethesda, Maryland (1968–69); the Stern house in Woodbridge, Connecticut (1969–70); the Koizim house in Westport, Connecticut (1969–71)—although this one *does* I think succeed; and the Gagarin house in Peru, Vermont (1969–72).

THE Tempchin house, in section—or seen from the ascending drive—is made of two large blocks sheathed in gray-stained redwood boards, each sliced off at the top of an angle of about thirty degrees. The garage, or right block, points up to the left; the house, or left block, points up to the right. These two sharp-pointed prisms are separated by a low, flat-roofed breezeway fifty feet long, punctured by six square arches in one wall and nine in the other, which set up a syncopated rhythm as they look through to the terrace and trees behind.

As one moves out of the breezeway and into the house, the punctured, parallel stage-set walls of this gallery continue inside, in a dazzling display of light holes, layers, and optical effects. Just past the entry, the walls of this gallery-become-hallway leap up about twenty-five feet (the high side of the roofslope) to accommodate an immense window at treetop height. ("Everyone is completely knocked out when they first walk in," says Mrs. Tempchin.) This vertical window, and three skylights, flood the house with light from above. The oak floors of this central passage descend to a study on the lower floor, surrounded by five bedrooms, a playroom, and three baths. As the hall floors descend, the punctured walls alongside them descend too, following the roofslope. All along their length, high and low cut-out rectangles (or, at the ceiling, triangles) look into other spaces of the house—often through still *other* cut-out rectangles in walls beyond. The effect is spectacular.

The rooms of the upper level—apart from this mind-boggling gallery—are sheltered under a symmetrical, pyramidal roof, all four slopes of which stop at the high-angled light tower over the hall. A large living room, with nonrectangular corners, glass walls, and skylights of its own, opens to an oddly shaped deck floating over the trees. This leads to a second, art-filled study (built over the first), which seems to hover in space over the descending hall. Huge house plants and pointed "effects" (like close-spaced rows of bare light bulbs to delineate ceiling ridges) and an impressive collection of modern art and furniture appropriately fill these spaces. Kitchen and two dining areas (leading to yet another deck), enclosed by more faceted glass walls, are located on a slightly lower level, all visible through the cut-out walls. The sheer play of interior, light-washed vistas in this large house—a marriage of cool elegance and high theatricalism—is almost unequaled. Designed (like the Koizim house) around an impressive collection of modern art, it became itself the most notable item in the collection. "I feel I'm *living* in a work of art," says Barbara Tempchin, still thrilled about the place after fifteen years.

The original budget ($55,000 for thirty-six-hundred square feet of house) was exceeded, but not by all that much. Moore kept trying to persuade Mrs. Tempchin to stop changing her mind, so he could keep costs down. "We had considered hiring one of the local Washington stars, but he was totally inflexible, full of architectural arrogance. He wouldn't dream of letting you shift one of his windows three inches. But Chuck was so incredibly sensitive. The basic design was his, of course; yet everything evolved out of what *we* wanted. We were so lucky. I can't imagine any other architect bringing so much artistry, joy, and consideration. He's sensitive not only to what clients want in a house, but also to what their *feelings* are."

THE Gagarin house (which I have not seen) is a large vacation house in the mountains of Vermont, used in summer as well as winter for large numbers of guests and (I am told) splendid parties. From the outside, photographs show an unreadable jumble, four or five cedar-walled buildings with very odd roofs (one is a light gallery) shoved together around a high concrete fireplace tower, with large windows punched in odd places. The top layer of its double roof is standing seam metal alloy, a "tacky" material, like interior Sheetrock, Moore likes to use in expensive houses. Both planes and elevations run at several confusing angles. Flying balconies connect bedroom wings in the space over a huge high living area, its roof supported on mammoth exposed beams. Interior photos show a color scheme—bright checkerboard squares, orange and yellow diagonal stripes, cartoons and graphics on the walls—matched by mobiles, light fixtures, inside trees, and exposed structural plates to create an effect of superabundant strangeness. One cannot fairly judge a house one hasn't been in, but if this bizarre structure has a unifying principle, I certainly haven't discovered it.

THE Klotz house, hidden among the trees atop Watch Hill near the Rhode Island–Connecticut border—a historic settlement of old stone-and-shingle mansions—was designed around the most highly mannered geometrical concept Moore has ever used: five octagonal towers of space superimposed on a square plan. From the outside, the result is a multifaceted, sprawling wooden pile which (except for a rather splendid open porch—one of the octagons—and the extravagance of cypress siding) I cannot find attractive. Some Vermont neighbors of the Gagarins thought their house looked like a barn with the roof fallen in; the Klotz house reminded me of a big wooden ship, somehow wrecked and beached on its Rhode Island hilltop.

Inside is madness. The octagonal "towers" did not impose any tangible order, the way similarly obsessive patterns do in certain Frank Lloyd Wright houses. What they did instead was provide Moore with a chance to play countless games with angles, corners, and levels, intersecting and bending stairs, cutting innumerable interior view openings that look up or down three, four, five different levels. Carpets crawl up and over built-in seats, then spill down cascades of seating stairs—all this around the ubiquitous forty-five-degree angles. Moore's Yale design students built a chunky fireplace out of great granite chips. The brick chimney above it twists around on its courses to avoid an anticipated angle above. Students painted the kitchen bright blue, yellow, and orange ("We're thinking of redoing it," admitted Mrs. Klotz), including four-foot-high letters reading KITCH. (Elsewhere, a bench is painted BENCH.) Art of loud and various sorts hangs wherever the many glazed and unglazed windows permit it. Moore himself painted a black-and-white breaking wave—an idea he got from a Japanese lunchbox from the New York World's Fair—on the wall of the master bedroom. He covered an exposed beam end first with a Chevrolet hubcap, then (when the owners protested) with a New Orleans street grille.

Rooms and stairs get more and more cramped as one climbs up and up in these puzzling spaces. There is scarcely room to walk alongside the owners' bed; the "study" at the top level is more a finish to the spiral than a notably useful room; bathroom walls do funny things to fit around octagons (and avoid having doors). The rooms of the children's wing, painted more wild colors, seem to suffer more than others from having been inserted into a predetermined geometry.

I find the Klotz house dizzyingly busy, disconcertingly eccentric: a Sea Ranch interior gone completely off its tracks, overfull of ill-assorted gimmicks and designed about a meaningless geometrical premise. The cypress wood, used inside as well as out, looks as expensive as it must have been. ("Moore never designed for someone with our resources before," Mr. Klotz informed me.) The spectacular views up, down, and out of the main (dining-room) octagon, and to a lesser degree of the entry octagon, are joyful and exhilarating. But the insistent vertical circulation seems needlessly constant and cramped, and tranquility is altogether absent. Paul and Nancy Klotz, however (a builder–developer and an arts-and-crafts dealer) seem to be ecstatic, but for a little rain damage, and tell joyful tales of their planning and building days with Moore. They tried first for Louis Kahn, Mr. Klotz told me, then heard of "this new character from California. When we saw slides of the Sea Ranch, we said, 'This is the guy.'" In the end, they felt that, by means of close and constant listening, he came to know them better than they knew themselves and gave them exactly what they wanted. "If you ever said no, he'd redesign it—but somehow it came out the same every time."

PAUL KLOTZ'S law partner married a friend of Harold Stern's, a cardiologist in New Haven. The connection eventually led to Dr. Stern's commissioning Moore (who was now working with Bill Grover) to design *him* a house in Woodbridge, Connecticut, a wealthy, woodsy suburb of large houses on acre-and-a-half-minimum lots. Although a sharp and engaging man, Dr. Stern gave Moore the freest rein of any of his clients. "He just let him go," according to Dr. Howard Stansel, who now owns the house. "'Tell me when it's done,' he said."

"He met our kids; we told him our needs," said Dr. Stern. "We needed a housekeeper, and the master bedroom suite had to be isolated from the children. His first sketch looked like a motel, so we told him no. But it's true, I offered very little advice: what can a surgeon tell a world-famous architect? He and Bill Grover flew over the site in their airplane, then came out with transits to work out the ideal exposure and view. But that crossed-corridors thing was just something he wanted to do."

The "crossed-corridors thing" is the wild geometrical gesture that made the Sterns' house notorious; and in plan it does look monumentally absurd. The house is made up, in concept, of two hallways—each about one hundred feet long—which intersect like airport runways at a 23.5-degree angle in the middle of the house, at which point the whole house is squeezed down to about six feet wide. "Rooms," where they occur, seem distinctly secondary to these exorbitant axes. The major axis corridor, which runs parallel to most of the rooms, is two stories high for much of its length. The skewed secondary corridor that crosses it has a flying balcony in the middle of its upper level. Both sides of both corridors are bombarded by light from an exotic gallery of windows, rendering the house (which, like all these houses, looks queer and lumpy outside) both totally transparent and quite gorgeously bright.

Actually, the visceral fact of being inside the Stern–Stansel house was more wonderful than I could possibly have imagined. Absurd they may be, but those intersecting, sometimes floating, multilevel corridors, surrounded and interpenetrated by so much daylight and air, form one of the most dazzling processionalspatial experiences I've ever known. One corridor starts narrow and high-walled, at the main entrance to the house; its floor then climbs to the "main" level of kitchen, dining room, and deck. The other begins at this level, at a service entrance behind the garage, and leads first past the kitchen. The two cross in the region of the tree-surrounded deck, which makes the deck a splendid place for sitting and looking through the waist of the transparent X-shaped house to the Connecticut hills and the distant Sound. (Inside, their junction is marked by a lozenge of green marble set into the hardwood floor.) A sharp-edged wall then divides their separate paths, down separate stairs, to the two halves of a split-level living room—the ultimate goal of both processionals and very much the "end" of the house. It is illuminated by skylights, sliding glass doors, and a stunning, thirty-foot-high range of vertical windows at the end. Originally, it also contained some of Moore's Mexican souvenirs, his gift to the owners: a big orange ceramic "tree-of-life" nuptial candelabra ("It broke into bits, but Charles glued it all back together"), a lintel salvaged from a demolished church and turned into a mantel.

Other rooms vary in quality. The lovely master bedroom has a great stained-glass window high over the bed and a balcony of its own. The three small children's rooms, on the other hand, miles down the upper hall, perch their beds on little lofts, a fancy of which one might tire. The housekeeper's room adjacent is an island of conservative chintz, with good reason. When Dr. Stern was trying to sell the house after his divorce, prospective buyers kept worrying about what their help would think of it. "I don't mind climbing all those stairs," they would tell him, "but I'll never get my maid up here."

This suggests one reason for my divided feelings about the house. Its undeniable joys remind me of those of Chiswick House or the Villa Rotunda, places designed more as spatial experiences than as houses to be lived in. Here one has not only to keep climbing up and down stairs (a common challenge in Moore houses), but also hiking back and forth along the celebrated "unifying-concept" runways. Mrs. Stansel admitted that she and her husband rarely used the interesting triangular den (once a playroom) near the entrance; the stairs down from the kitchen made it too inconvenient. But the journey from kitchen to living room is more formidable still. Moore says he knew all along that the "crossed-corridor thing" was going to be a gamble, but concluded that it was "a gamble that seems to have paid off."

The original cedar siding had to be pulled off and replaced (water warped it and popped out the nails). Sounds travel all through the house. The demanding design apparently put strains on Harold Stern's first marriage; his second wife simply refused to live here. Moore added warm colors, I was told—mostly yellows—in the hope of counteracting some of these alienating effects. It's a spectacular place to visit, and now in the hands of respectful (if not entirely converted) second owners. But I doubt that many families would be comfortably able to live here long.

MY own favorite among these five houses, where visual splendor seems least at odds with livability, was designed for two avid collectors of large, colorful works of contemporary art from Westport, Connecticut, (they are now also divorced), who wanted to add a famous-name *house* to their collection. They looked up pictures of the Sea Ranch at the Yale library and liked what they saw. Charles Moore was an hour and a half late for their first meeting, but "we were so taken with him we fell for him then and there," Mrs. Koizim

recalls. "At that first meeting I remember whispering to my husband, 'He's the one!'"

They visited the site with Charles—an acre of shoreline carved
from an old estate with smashing views down and across Sau-
gatuck River, out of Long Island Sound—on a cold, windy night.
Ellen Koizim remembers Moore scrambling over the rocks and
brambles in the dark. At dinner that evening he drew up a sketch
plan on a paper napkin. She still has it, mounted and framed, all
the squiggly ink detail oozing and blurring into the paper. Despite
innumerable later changes and refinements, this turned out to be
the basic (and very unusual) form of the house she inhabits today.

The plan (once again) looks weird; the entrance facade hectic
and contrived. It might fit well in a place like the Hamptons, where
the artful rich have commissioned so many strange white architectural statements. But Westport is nothing if not Connecticut
traditional, and the house looks defiantly out of place. (Fortunately
for local sensibilities, it is hidden around a bend of a wooded lane,
in a little enclave of riverfront mansions.)

One's first view of the front comes as a shock. Flat, wide-spread-
ing white-plastered walls rise to a high square center, which breaks
out into odd-angled prisms, a light tower, and a chimney up on a
kind of stalk. Large wall cutouts and windows pop in no discernible
order out of all these walls, prisms, and towers. There is no roof in
view (actually there *is* one, and a shingled one at that, but it slopes
backward toward the river). Through a pair of gigantic, two-story-
high windows in the central cube one can see right through the
house toward the shore. (The river facade, by contrast, is almost
classical in its regularity.)

The plan reveals the side wings to be designed around walls set
at forty-five degrees to the huge central block, most of which is
occupied by a splendid living room—art gallery. (Harvey Koizim
took half of the art with him on their divorce, so large pale patches
alternate with the remaining Warhol, Oldenberg, Kruschnik, etc.)

As with all of his more successful houses, Charles started with
an idea of how it might be unique, a metaphor of its specialness
and difference—which makes this house much more than another
geometrical game. In this case he saw the house as a kind of
southwestern village of four individual white stucco houses inside
one big roof, with high, open wood-framed public plazas in be-

tween, and transparent flying bridges connecting the bedrooms on their upper level. I can't say I read it that way myself, but this ruling metaphor seems to give the Koizims' house a greater degree of coherence and amiability than the others I have just described. All of it is visible and comprehensible from the grand central "plaza" of the living room (one could entertain hundreds here), just as most of the surrounding smaller spaces, upstairs and down, look into and drink from its color, light, and air. The secondary living spaces—an enclosed, low-ceilinged inglenook, a lower tile-floored area off the main room, the breakfast corner, the sumptuous deck—are all pleasant places to be in. The bedrooms are large and handsomely decorated and make good use of their ceiling slopes, angles, and light. High windows and skylights pour down sunlight or moonlight over the entrance and at both ends of the flying corridor upstairs. Colors throughout are both elegant and bright.

With the basic shape and the ruling metaphor worked out—the character of the house—Charles Moore then accepted lists of hundreds of written-out desiderata from the Koizims and their two teenaged sons. He moved the triangular pool further out to save a great six-trunked tree, then built the deck around it. Once the house was framed, he climbed up on the rafters and realized what a fine vista down through the house there could be from the older boy's bedroom, so he cut out a huge inside window. He added two triangular windows in the study upstairs under the roof, and moved the breakfast room into a glassed-in forty-five-degree prow. (The house has a number of these 45-degree—or 135-degree—corners; some are exciting, some inconvenient.) He personally spray-painted a pattern of stenciled designs around the great layered view windows of the living room—then erased a few to keep it from looking like wallpaper. (A *House and Garden* editor presumed the owners had done it themselves and simply botched the job.) He donated a giddy frame of dessert molds to cover a dull door to the basement. You enter the living room through a glamorous curtain made out of hundreds of cheap metal key rings.

This great house, alas, has its problems. It survived a gale a few years ago, but still leaks badly in any storm. It costs thousands of dollars to heat and can get overheated in summer from all the glass. The $1,500 windows in the breakfast-room prow were apparently leaking when I visited, and Mrs. Koizim was counting the cost of replacing them. After her divorce, and her children's growing up, Ellen Koizim found the house much too large, and lived in a couple of rooms so she wouldn't have to heat the rest. Although she found the spaces, the light, and the vistas incomparably fine, she was having to face the possibility of selling this splendid house and moving somewhere else.

15 / PUBLIC HOUSING

"THE individual house is a labor of love," *Newsweek* once quoted Charles Moore as saying. "I've done government-sponsored low-income housing work, and it's like working in the dark. I don't know who the people living there will be."

Given his humanistic, imaginative, and client-centered approach to design, it is not surprising that public housing for anonymous users goes against the grain of Moore's architectural style. Public housing was a specialty of many of the modernist masters. But this may have been because it lent itself so well to their aesthetic preference for pure, machined blocks and slabs made of identical modular units, as much as because of their deep concern for the plight of the homeless and ill-housed.

But it is difficult (as even Frank Lloyd Wright learned) to build a profitable architectural practice out of nothing but custom-designed single-family houses. Given land and construction costs in many areas of the United States, it may soon be next to impossible. "Fascinating as the design of individual houses is," Moore said in 1964, "it includes an appalling waste of time locating contractors, fighting down the bids . . . waiting, arguing with everyone, writing letters, and waiting some more." One of Moore's, Lyndon's, and Turnbull's earliest joint projects—it predates the formation of MLTW—was for a sixty-five-unit condominium in Coronado, California, which tried to give every unit an identity of its own by breaking down the scale of a ten-story building into what looked like several smaller buildings cleverly assembled together. Each resident, it was hoped, would be able to identify (and identify with) his own different set of windows, terrace, views, and exposures. The result, set back from the street, with low buildings and walled garden terraces in front, was meant to fit comfortably into a neighborhood of one- and two-story houses.

West Plaza Condominiums (1961–62), as this building was

called, was an ingenious early attempt to "break out of the box" of anonymous Identikit units in a slab. Although it won a *Progressive Architecture* design citation in 1963, some jurors resisted the apparent disorder of it all, the choppy heterogeneity of forms. It was never built.

The Sea Ranch Condominium came next. But that can only be called "public housing" in a special and limited way. While full of new problems unique to its location and its purpose, this dream project freed the architects from many of the tiresome constraints typical of the design of multiple-unit housing for unknown inhabitants.

Moore's first—and, until 1981, last—opportunity to build a large-scale public housing project came when he took over as chairman at Yale in 1965. The mayor of New Haven (Richard Lee) asked him to take on a long-vacant redevelopment-cleared tract between the train station and the city center, isolated from downtown by part of a busy ring road. For this area, he was asked to come up with a model city for eight hundred low-income households. Other architects—including Ludwig Mies van der Rohe—had already tried and given up.

All architecture, I noted earlier, may be regarded as primarily problem solving. But designing subsidized housing to meet Federal Housing Administration standards and costs, satisfy civic officials, and still prove commercially attractive enough to tempt private underwriters often reduces the architect's job to nothing *but* problem solving, and problem solving of a particularly knotty and frustrating kind. To satisfy all the parties and regulations involved in public housing, and at the same time to please prospective residents—and create respectable architecture—is arguably the greatest challenge in the profession today.

Moore's four years of work on Church Street South (as the New Haven project is called) included the preparation and presentation to official reviewing agencies of thirty-two separate site plans. Architects and officials fought over where to put cars, how to cross the ring road, how high to build. (Going lower than three or four stories used up too much of the land. Going higher required elevators, which are expensive.) Moore wanted pedestrian streets, community gathering places and shops, play areas and vistas, buildings broken into small units and positioned to form small individual neighborhoods. All these things were designed to modify, and if possible humanize, the bleak institutional look that has made the phrase *housing project* a term of scorn and shame in so many American cities.

He and his partners planned to build their basic three- or four-story housing blocks (identical small apartments, identical windows and doors; eighteen dollars a square foot permits only so much variation) out of preformed concrete. But at the last minute the developer informed them that they'd have to shift to cheaper concrete block. In an attempt to add some charm to this radically charmless material, they tried alternating textured blocks with smooth; then painted the door surrounds, railings, and other parts of the facades of individual units with broad bright stripes of color—different colors for different "neighborhoods."

It was important for Professor Moore, as a top Ivy League administrator in 1965, to demonstrate his social-concern credentials through Church Street South. It was important for Charles W. Moore, rising-star architect, to prove that he could succeed where so many others—including Mies van der Rohe—had failed, by spinning the straw of an FHA budget into the gold of distinguished and livable buildings. And it was important for MLTW to win and complete a major East Coast commission of this size. (More than $6 million was budgeted for the first phase alone. Eventually, the whole project cost $15 million.)

"This was my first big housing," Moore told an interviewer in 1972. "I didn't know how far I could go. I went as far as I dared without losing the job, because once I started, I couldn't afford to lose the job. . . . I didn't have the kind of contract that left me ready to back out at any moment without going to jail. I was trapped." (The developer, not the architect, backed out in 1969, leaving one hundred units unbuilt and a large patch of land still empty.)

Two plots—one in a corner near the train station, the other at the far north end—were taken by the local Jewish Community Council, which asked MLTW to design high-rise housing for old people with low incomes. Their two projects, supported by federal loans and the local redevelopment agency, went more smoothly than the concrete-block village of family housing; Moore retains good feelings about his dealings with the JCC. The corner by the train station was filled by the eight-story Robert T. Wolfe building of minimum "efficiency" apartments (ten per floor, off a central corridor). Deprived of much chance to enliven the units themselves (except with large windows), Moore and his associates tried in a number of inexpensive ways to enhance the exterior. Faceted bay windows growing out of several units vary the castlelike facade, as does a shift from plain to dark textured brick.

The northern site is occupied by a twenty-story, 217-unit tower which consciously mimics Roche and Dinkeloo's prize-winning, slightly pompous Knights of Columbus headquarters building across the expressway: same basic shape, same forty-five-degree alignment with the city grid, same number of stories. In place of the K of C's four massive, cylindrical corner service towers (which support essentially transparent floors), Moore & Company shaved off twenty feet from each of *their* corners, making the JCC's Tower One (there is now also a Tower Two) octagonal in plan. As with the Robert Wolfe building to the south, most of the other variations are what might be called cosmetic: a jazzy entry, a variety of colors and brick surfaces. The building itself looks "Ugly and Ordinary," in the Robert Venturi tradition. But the public dining and lounge areas on the ground floor share some of the high-pop excitement of the Santa Barbara Faculty Club, and the building has proved popular with its tenants.

It is less easy for me to evaluate the success of the multifamily housing. Mayor Lee professed himself disappointed. He had hoped Moore would give New Haven a prize-winning architectural statement, and instead got what he thought looked like concrete-block barracks.

They *do* rather look like barracks—although barracks set at some very odd angles and separated by a number of Kresge College gateways and punctured walls, Tivoli Garden lampstands, and decorated pavements. I looked at it, drove around it, and (although Charles Moore advised against this) walked through it. I did not, I must admit, interview any residents. Somehow the idea of a white professor, who lives in his own house in California, asking black residents of a rent-subsidized project in New Haven what they think of their homes struck me as distasteful—perhaps even as asking for trouble. A skillful urban sociologist, even a better (or braver) reporter, could, I'm sure, have done this successfully. As it was, suspicious stares hurried my progress along the nearly abandoned, rather bleak looking mall. I took pictures from my car.

The bright painted facades are now faded and overscrawled with black graffiti. The Tivoli globes are broken; the plazas are empty.

The neighborhood swarms with children—a great source of color and vitality—but so do many inner-city neighborhoods. The lively public outdoor scene Moore imagined has simply not materialized. And the unbuilt area north felt like no-man's-land. Church Street South may well be (or be one day) a more civilized environment than most American public housing projects, but I simply wasn't able to judge.

I TOURED, with the same degree of superficiality, three other East Coast housing projects designed by Charles Moore Associates in the early 1970s: Taylor Townhouses in Norwalk, Connecticut; Maplewood Terrace at Middletown, Connecticut; and Whitman Village in Huntington (Long Island), New York.

Taylor Townhouses (1972) is a set of fourteen two-story units (each about sixteen by thirty-three feet) in an urban-renewal area near Westport, squeezed between two streets on either side of a central pedestrian way, with tiny gardens and parking hidden behind. White-plastered and mock-Mediterranean, it looks like nothing so much as a Kresge College spinoff, with housing units on either side of a sloping pedestrian street: the same stage-set arcades, the large white globes, a miniature cascade of angled steps down the street. It also looks a bit odd in this corner of New England. The narrow central plaza or street seemed more a designer's fantasy than a genuine village place. But the units (this was an early design by Moore Grover Harper) still seemed livable and the residents content. I was pleased when the firm moved out of this exotic idiom into something more indigenous and homey.

Maplewood Terrace (fifty units, 1971) and Whitman Village (260 units, 1975) have in common a return to forms, materials, and details recognizable to their residents as looking like and signifying *houses*. To my outsider's eye, both developments seemed a significant step forward—because, if you will, stylistically backward—in public housing design. Both are built around grassy central spaces, with car parks hidden on the periphery. Both combine long rows of two-story townhouses (each with its individual entry from outside) with boxy, detached four-unit buildings that look very much like big, old-fashioned single-family houses. The exterior walls of both are sheathed with wood shingles, outlined in white trim, generously lighted by classically paned windows; both have roofs (especially in the quadruplexes) just like old-fashioned gables. Intelligent site planning allowed the handsome backs of the long terrace rows to block out adjacent traffic and focus life inward on the greens. Clever interior design enabled the architects to fit interesting split-level plans under a unifying roofslope. Sentimental private gestures of the residents' (scalloped door surrounds, brass eagles and plaques and door knockers, even shutters and plant boxes) look perfectly at home. Some angle-cut arches and sharply sliced roof shapes (plus a few Sea Ranchy space games in the community centers) are all that gave away the identity of the avant-garde architects responsible for this comfortable arrière-garde traditionalism.

Whitman Village—which is Maplewood enlarged—seems definitely worthy of closer study, and (if indeed it is "working," sociologically) of imitation. It is built on a clumsily shaped piece of ground opposite a busy four-lane road and a train-station parking lot, to which it sensibly turns its back. The twenty-one quadruplexes, looking very solid and mid-Atlantic, were built along the inner residential street, across from the old single-family houses they resemble. The idea was to minimize the usual hostility of established middle-class homeowners to the alien intrusion of a "project" into their midst. (Up the road is an older six-story brick project of typical ugliness, which stresses by contrast the humanness and apparent livability of Moore Associates' effort.) Level changes across the site are exploited by stepped paths, narrow townhouse porches connected herringbone fashion, and lanes that run through little clumps of trees. The village green and play area are kept open at the center. Once inside, you are completely unaware of the adjacent traffic and train station.

This may be nothing but a pious illusion created by good design, but life here does look better than in the squat, closed private houses across the street. Whitman Village appears oriented more to "moderate-" than "low"-income residents, and (in spring 1981) appeared to be both racially integrated and well maintained—neither of which was true at Church Street South. (This may, of course, only reflect the difference between social and economic conditions on west Long Island and those in New Haven.) The detectable Moore & Company details add spice and originality. But more important is the thoughtful, noninstitutional design of the whole. Like Maplewood Terrace, it makes use of an undesirable strip of semiurban land, works hard to fit it into an existing neighborhood of single-family houses, and directs most of the design energies involved not to the making of new shapes, but to housing real families comfortably at very low cost, in buildings at once recognizably old-fashioned and secretly new.

THE only other completed low-income project Charles Moore and his associates designed in the 1970s was a pair of "villages" near Orono, Maine (which I have not seen), sponsored by the University of Maine, and made up of two hundred prefabricated, eleven-foot four-inch mobile-home units. These were carefully positioned along curving woodland paths and combined with brightly painted winter vestibules to liven things up. Similar experiments in the very low cost use of prefabricated mobile units were planned for other locations, but never built.

In 1974, Charles Moore Associates designed two well-publicized and influential open-market housing developments—one for the very old town of Williamsburg, Virginia; the other for the new town of Columbia, Maryland. These made extensive use of explicit historical recollections. Roofslopes, facades, dormers, arcades, porches, chimneys, clapboarding, paned windows, and paneled doors were all intended to evoke, in a novel yet genial way, American houses and neighborhoods of the seventeenth through nineteenth centuries. Both (like the completed low-income projects) made praiseworthy efforts to hide extra automobiles, to establish an older-style continuity of pedestrian streetfront, to use real wood and wood shingles, and to enfront meadows and greens—in some cases by playing variations on the classic Charleston (S.C.) house model, which turns sideways to the street and faces its own private garden (or car park). Neither has been built.

In sad fact, most of the housing projects designed by Charles Moore and his partners—whether for subsidized low-income residents (both families and old people) or for open-market sale— have never got further than plans and models. During Moore's ten years at Yale, first MLTW/Moore–Turnbull, then Charles Moore Associates came up with a total of thirty-one multiple-unit-housing designs for public and private clients, of which only the five described above were actually completed. The investment of the firm's time and money in so many unrealized housing projects during this decade—unrealized for a variety of reasons, including the drying up of federal funds—was a major cause of Charles Moore Associates' near-bankruptcy in 1971.

Large, corporate-style architectural offices, still designing in the standardized high-rise-slab models of the 1950s, remain the most financially successful purveyors of subsidized public housing. Smaller firms have been able to capitalize on the desire for village-like public housing and condominium complexes, many of them derived from MLTW ideas. Not until 1981, with the award of the Tegeler Hafen Berlin project to Moore Ruble Yudell, has one of Moore's firms had a chance to experiment again with housing on the scale of Church Street South. But his realized work there, at the Sea Ranch in California, in Middletown, Connecticut, and in Huntington, New York; plus his published but unrealized projects for Coronado and Los Angeles in California, Williamsburg in Virginia, Columbia in Maryland, Kauai in Hawaii, and St. Simon's Island in Georgia have had a significant influence on the unboxing and humanizing of multifamily housing in the United States.

16 / THE PIAZZA d'ITALIA

I T is impossible for me to write of the Piazza d'Italia in New Orleans—Charles Moore's most unusual and most controversial public project—without acknowledging the pathos of its mistreatment. It has been abandoned like an unwanted child for almost all the first five years of its life.

Charles has more than once overestimated the goodwill and good faith of other people, whose active participation is sometimes necessary to bring his buildings to life. Places like Kresge College, the Santa Barbara Faculty Club, and the housing at Church Street South are in part stage sets that stand inanimate until the spontaneous drama of users' active lives is played out within and before them. But nothing he designed before the 1984 World's Fair was ever *more* a stage set, more a theatrical backdrop than St. Joseph's Fountain at the piazza. Unpeopled, unused, it can look as sad as it is spectacular.

Moreover, the City of New Orleans has often refused to turn on the water and replace the burned-out lights, which are as essential a part of the piazza's architecture as marble, slate, and stucco. The local Italian-American Federation (original sponsors of the project) has them turned on whenever it can animate the piazza with festivities—a total of three or four days a year. The federation has also persuaded the city to have the fountain operating and the piazza occupied for other events, perhaps once every two or three months. (There is talk of using the piazza as a setting for a production of Mascagni's Sicilian-village opera, *Cavalleria Rusticana*.) But that leaves a lot of empty days in between. My luck is such that in three visits to New Orleans between 1981 and 1983, I never once saw any water in the fountain and never more than two or three other derelicts or architecture lovers in the piazza. After 1980, I was told, the current mayor refused to spend any money to draw attention to the piazza, a pet project of his predecessor's. (He now seems more willing to help.) I told Joe Maselli, Sr., president of the Italian-American Federation and prime mover of the piazza project, how depressing I had found the absence of life in the piazza on each of my visits.

"*You're* depressed?" he replied. "You get to leave. I have to look at that place every day of my life. Think how terrible I feel! I have to work so hard to keep any enthusiasm going among our people. But I have faith. Soon, it's all gonna come together. We were just five years ahead of our time."

As originally designed, the circular piazza and its Roman-fantasy fountain were to be surrounded by new and reconverted buildings—shops, restaurants, cafés, offices—which would embrace the piazza's bright and illusionistic walls with more solid architecture and surround it by people who could look into and learn to love its world of free classical forms. These shops and offices were to be the start (like those of Ghirardelli Square in San Francisco) of a renaissance in the tawdry, half-abandoned warehouse district of the city. Had this occurred, the piazza would have formed a welcome and colorful open space in a lively area between downtown and the waterfront, filled day and night with workers, shoppers, and tourists either passing through or relaxing, and restaurant patrons sitting at tables around its perimeter.

Instead, for much of 1978–83, it lay quiet and alone behind the twenty-two-story Lykes Building, its space-frame "campanile" (without bells) and mock-temple entrance beckoning tourists in off the street to what looked like the leftover set of a long-finished movie. Without water, lights, or people, a festive fountain makes little sense. Trees and vines meant to shade the piazza (and form living capitals to some columns) were never maintained, so the place can be unbearably hot in a New Orleans summer. Green algae spread over its untended pools. Garbage accumulated along the marble-faced steps. With no real and occupied buildings behind it, the Piazza d'Italia seemed more thin and impermanent than it actually was. Made of steel frame and stucco, slate, marble, granite paving stones, stainless steel, and tile, at a cost of $1.7 million, the piazza *isn't* a transient stage set. It just looks like one. Still surrounded by vacant lots, disused old warehouses, and slummy streets, it seemed to serve no vital social purpose. To admire the stunningly beautiful Lafayette Street archway, one had to walk back down one of the trashier alleys in town. (This street will, I was told, be transformed into a handsome pedestrian mall in time for the 1984 fair, thereby connecting Charles Moore's fairground entrance with Charles Moore's piazza.) As if to force the issue, the architects left two ends of an open upper gallery hanging in space, perhaps hoping to shame someone into financing the connecting promenade in between. The two stub ends are still there, blank and obviously incomplete. "Someday there will be shops around it," Charles Moore wrote in 1978, "like Ghirardelli Square in San Francisco; but for the moment it is just sitting by itself, and a little bit lonesome." That "moment" was to last a long time.

Originally, the City of New Orleans planned to lease out the surrounding rental offices, shops, and restaurants, designed by Perez Associates at the same time as the fountain and piazza (many of them in restored old buildings), and then use this income to support revenue bonds to finance the construction of the project itself. This proved to be unfeasible; so a private developer had to be found. It was presumed that the exuberant piazza would have private developers lining up for the chance to invest in the buildings around it. But costs mounted, recession set in, the area's reputation failed to improve; no developer showed up. The Italian-American Federation, which had worked so long and so hard to make all this happen, raised more than a million dollars of its own to construct an opulent renaissancey palazzo (designed by Charles Moore) to fill one corner of the site. But inflation quadrupled the cost, and the palazzo had to be abandoned. (The federation now occupies one of the old buildings on the east side of the block.) Perez Associates came up with a scheme for a low-rise luxury hotel overlooking, and slightly spilling into, the piazza, which would guarantee it the life and attention it needs. Political delays made it impossible to complete the building in time for the fair, which chilled the interest of a couple of hotel chains and developers.

All this, one hopes, will soon change. Love it or hate it, the Piazza d'Italia is simply too extraordinary a piece of urban design—now historic as well as "historicist"—to exist indefinitely as a ghost of its good intentions or to decay into the self-mocking pretensions of a Venice, California. About half of the old commercial properties had been or were being rehabilitated by 1983. Land and buildings in the area have appreciated greatly in value since 1975. As I write, there are high hopes that an upscale hotelier will exercise his option to build Perez's $30 million hotel, thereby filling the half-empty city block that now surrounds the piazza, and that the 1984 fair will draw tourists (and investors) into its orbit.

Still to come [wrote one enthusiastic critic in 1978] is not only the completion of the buildings that surround St. Joseph's Fountain . . . but also the successful integration of the Piazza into the life of the city. The revitalization of a forgotten neighborhood is an operation as chancy as a heart transplant: unless the right chemistry is present, the organism will reject the new presence, no matter how well-planned or successfully executed the surgery has been.[3]

Let me presume that all the right things will happen, describe the piazza and its fountain as if they were alive and properly used all the year round, and tell something of the story of how they came to be.

In 1973, Mayor Moon Landrieu had asked Joe Maselli, Sr.—"a longtime personal friend"—what he could do for the Italian-American community of New Orleans before he left office. Landrieu suggested a statue of some sort: Garibaldi, Columbus. But Maselli says, "I told him, 'No, Moon. I want something more. I want a *living* monument, not just a piece of stone.' 'O.K., Joe,' he tells me. 'You raise the money; I'll give you the property to put it on.'"

It took Maselli and his friends three persistent years, but they finally got the money they needed, in equal portions from the United States Environmental Development Administration and the State of Louisiana. Mayor Landrieu gave them the land he promised.

The piece of land in question is a large city block (Poydras Street to Lafayette, St. Peter's to Tchoupitoulas) which developer Joe Canizaro, one of Maselli's *compatrioti*, had earlier traded to the city for some alleyways he needed. For its northeast corner, on Poydras Street, Perez Associates had designed in 1972 a standard modern office building and underground parking garage, headquarters of the Lykes Brothers Shipping Company. Its most notable exterior features were the assertive black-and-white vertical stripes (black window bands, white divider walls) on its four facades. After Mayor Landrieu agreed to build a piazza on the remainder of the site for his Italian-American friends (and as a spur to neighborhood re-development), his office investigated more than sixty architectural firms, then invited six of them to submit specific proposals. To no one's great surprise, the office of August Perez and Associates—which had already designed a great number of the innocuous public buildings of New Orleans, as well as work for Canizaro—was declared the winner. The local press screamed of corruption and dirty politics (hardly a novelty in New Orleans), but in fact the Perez submission—by Allen Eskew, a Berkeley grad, and Malcolm Heard, two junior members of the firm—was a thoughtful and re-spectful effort to save the old buildings, fill in the perimeter space with good new ones (incorporating imitations of the old arches), and open up a great circle in the middle, surrounded by super-graphics, a fountain-altar for St. Joseph under a bright Italianate awning, and French Quarter charm and detail.

But what drew the greatest attention was the runner-up entry, from Charles Moore Associates of Connecticut. They too—several members of the firm had participated, along with Charles—began with a great curved interior court, although theirs was elliptical rather than circular, which spread out from the center of the block in eccentric rings of black and white (recycled white granite paving stones and black slabs of slate) that copied the Lykes Building stripes. These ellipses swept around, through, and under buildings to the edges of all four surrounding streets. In the center of their plan rose an open seventy-five-foot multicolored bell tower, below which water spilled over two jagged-edged, contour-map step is-lands (islands one could walk on, water one could wade through), like those of another plaza-fountain Moore had worked on for Port-land in 1965.

At each street entrance, and at several other places about the plaza, Moore Associates' plan showed freestanding sections of ar-cade painted (on the inside) in bright, "groovy" colors. Along the Lafayette Street edge, they proposed a stand of magnolias, live oaks, and crepe myrtles, with white azaleas underneath. The low "infill" buildings around the edges were in part faced with mirror glass, to reflect the older buildings alongside them. Their rooftops zoomed up diagonally for solar-energy collectors, a Grover–Harper specialty at the time. The curving facades facing the court were fronted by arched loggias and interesting windows.

All this impressed the critics, but rather floored the five Italian-American Federation jurors (including Maselli and Canizaro), who opted—against the mayor's representatives—for what they thought was the more salable security of Perez Associates' plan. But as soon as the jury's vote was announced, Mayor Landrieu personally invited Moore to serve as a consultant on the final design. "I think I was supposed to say no, but I said yes." He talked to Eskew and Heard between planes, decided he liked them, and they agreed on the spot to a joint-venture agreement.

By this time Moore was himself relocating in Los Angeles, settling in to both UCLA and UIG (where his chief assistant was an ex-Yalie named Ron Filson). So the official design credits on the completed portions of the Piazza d'Italia read "August Perez and Associates, New Orleans, architects; R. Allen Eskew and Malcolm Heard, project designers," in top billing—they did, after all, win the competition; followed by "Fountain design by Charles Moore, Urban Innovations Group, Los Angeles; Ron Filson, project coordinator." Later publications sometimes reverse the order of the two firms (to the annoyance of the Perez office) and ignore the original contribution of Moore's Connecticut colleagues. Tina Beebe and Richard Peters have their usual credits for color and lighting—no small matters in this case.

Other than the fact that the surrounding commercial buildings haven't yet been built, the major differences between the Moore Associates competition entry plan and the Perez–Moore joint-venture plan that actually got built are five:

1. Moore's elliptical plaza yielded to Heard's and Eskew's circle, with a wide pie-shaped entrance segment (the circular arcs of paving continue through this wedge) reaching in from Poydras Street alongside the Lykes Building.
2. His central tower was abandoned for two skeletal signpost buildings at the north end of the site, designed primarily by Heard and Eskew: a thin-walled, eighty-four-foot tower at the northwest corner, a dramatic study in modern cut-out shapes, illuminated at night by exotic stage lighting; and a small pipe-formed pergola in the shape of a classical temple.

3. The landscaping along Lafayette Street to the south was lost for a proposed buildout to the property line. In its place rose the Lafayette Street arch: an imposing triumphal arch of the most elegant colors and shapes.

4. The contour-map fountain islands were pushed against the east side of the piazza and reshaped to form an abstract, eighty-foot-long relief map of Italy (plus Sicily; most Italian-Americans in New Orleans are of Sicilian origin). The waters pour (when they pour) down three mirrored courses representing the Arno, the Po, and the Tiber rivers, into two basins that stand for the Tyrrhenian and the Adriatic seas. (Charles thought he had come up with this idea on his own. But when Rodolfo Machado, now in Cambridge, reminded him of an earlier "Italy-shaped" design *he* had done, and had published in P/A, Moore willingly yielded prime credit to Perez—"so no one would say I had stolen Rodolfo's idea.")

5. In an extravagant—and to many critics, offensive—outburst of historical eclecticism, the simply arched wall segments of Moore's original design were transformed into mock-historical colonnades—thin segments of brightly colored wall decorated with hysterically free adaptations of the classic Greco-Roman orders (Doric, Ionic, Corinthian), plus two others: the Tuscan and the Composite (Corinthian with an Ionic top). These are arranged as a consciously monumental sequence of screen walls on either side of and behind the map-of-Italy fountain. They rise to a heroic, fifty-foot-high set of arches and columns atop the "Alps" of Italy—the highest part of the peninsula of steps—intended to frame windows of a restaurant that never got built. (The blankness of the climactic rear arch is a little disconcerting.)

Unless you have been told (or are viewing it from above), you may not recognize the terraced and watered portion of the piazza as an abstract map of Italy. (Sicily forms a speaker's rostrum for Italian festival days.) You are more likely, in fact, to see it simply as a strangely free-form series of sharp-angled steps made of granite cobblestones and slate and faced with white marble, and (on lucky days) bubbling over with water.

The freestanding wall segments on the east side of the piazza, which follow the curving lines of its black and white circular rings, are tied together by the fact that they're all made out of columns, capitals (of a sort), and entablatures (the short walls that run along the top of a colonnade). These will probably call to mind, either vaguely or specifically, classical buildings or ruins (or Roman movie sets) the spectator has seen. But each one is a different color and put together in a different way. The effect, like that of the free-form map-of-Italy steps, can be disorienting.

There *is* a logic to the color scheme, which recedes from a saturated brick color at the lowest walls in front, through terra cotta to curry to chamois-ocher (these are Tina Beebe's designations) at the rear, a "Mediterranean" series that grows warmer and more intense as it marches toward the viewer. (The backs of the walls are painted various shades of gray.) But however logical the color scheme may be, it still comes as a shock in this city and this setting. It is frantically at odds with the pretend classicism of its forms and is visually complicated by inlays of stainless steel and glowing bands of neon.

There's a logic, too, of a quirky and Charles Moore-ish kind, to the column and capital forms of these curving segments of wall. But one probably has to have read about it somewhere in order to discern it.

(It's been written about a great deal. One sometimes feels that it was designed *so as* to be written about, like the abstract paintings Tom Wolfe mocks in *The Painted Word*.)

The two foremost screens (the walls recede chronologically and get taller as they go back), the Pompeian-red ones, are supposedly Tuscan—but since the Tuscan order was so austere, they could pass for Kresge College modern. Here, alternate rectangular penetrations in the wall contain circular showerheads designed to create fluted ghost "columns" made of falling water. A row of stainless-steel squares above, washed by more water, becomes then not metopes (the square spaces in a Doric entablature) but "wetopes." (Charles Moore joke.)

Next behind, on the left, is a short Doric wall, pale rusty orange in its punctured entablature, stainless steel for its tin-can capitals and split-open hollow columns. (Water pours down *inside* these columns, visible through the split.) Thin veneers of veined greenish marble, affixed to plaster forms, stand in for solid pedestals below. (All the taller columns behind stand on similar pedestals, like sliced sections of the real thing. Solid marble pedestals were no doubt out of the question, but I find the effect a little strained and cartoonish. Vandals are prying off the marble.)

This fragment of wall has become the most notorious and most photographed of all. Two sculptured ovals on either side of its central stainless-steel arch are carved in the bald, mustachioed likeness of Charles Willard Moore circa 1978, each intended to spit water eternally onto Sicily underneath. This, one is always told, was *not* Moore's idea, but a secret tribute to him contrived by his associates. If so, I would like to have been there the day he first saw it. It makes the red signature tile squares Frank Lloyd Wright affixed to some of his buildings look like a piece of girlish reticence.

The Ionic wall segment, next back, to the right of Italy—an orangey terra cotta, cut for large openings—is surmounted by another entablature of sprinklered stainless-steel squares. The curling capitals are formed of sharp-edged, shiny rolls of steel, like opened tops of sardine cans. Each of these receding screen walls is connected to the one behind it by an arched buttress at one end. The buttress at the end of the Ionic wall reaches up to a proud, gaudy peach-colored Corinthian wall (more intricately faceted stainless-steel capitals; curling squirts of water complete the design), topped by a high and elegantly molded entablature wall on which are carved (in Latin) the words: "This fountain is dedicated as a gift to all the people of New Orleans." The golden-ocher Composite-order wall, on the opposite side of north Italy, rises higher still. Atop it are carved, in still larger Roman relief letters, the words "Fons Sancti Josephi."

The climax of this entire assemblage of walls and steps and water is the high open portico of the Alps building, a sort of powdery yellow-beige, designed to front the never-built restaurant. Two colossal super-Corinthian half-columns frame its sides. The outline of a triumphal arch, cut into a thin wall, stands in its center. A further shadow set of four columns (straight Ionic), with its entablature broken for a central arch, lies within, on the grayish tan back wall of the porch. All this is outlined and banded with blue, green, and red neon tubing.

WHAT is one to make of all this? Professional architecture critics and theorists who have determined in advance that complexity and contradiction, or multiplicity of cultural reference, or literary wit are what matter most in post- (or anti-) modern architecture seize on the Piazza d'Italia as a perfect demonstration case for their ideas. Inevitably, they either ignore or exaggerate its function for the City of New Orleans and what they imagine its "Italian community" to be.

Charles Jencks, the American-British critic who has set up shop as the definer of terms for architecture since 1960, sees the essence of postmodernism as what he calls *double coding*: one style or message for the masses, another for the knowing elite, the two deftly condensed into a single building. The Piazza d'Italia suits his definition perfectly. Italian tourists, or local mamas and papas, can enjoy it, according to this theory, for its high colors and splashing waters and vague recollections (or explicit celebrations) of Italia and traditional culture. The architectural cognoscenti, meanwhile, can smile at the punctured pomposity represented in the neon-edged Serliana and the visual puns on Vitruvius.

I would venture three critical points.

First, unless and until the Piazza d'Italia actually comes into service as a fully public place, it is irresponsible to judge its success. Since 1978, it has shocked and distressed more of the architectural world than it has pleased—including a few people who have actually visited it; a very few who have seen it in use, water gushing, lights blinking, people swarming about; and the far greater number who know it only from impressive photographs in magazines and books. Very few of these people could possibly have been assessing the piazza as anything more than a piece of theoretical, self-indulgent sculpture. It *is* in part that; but it was also intended to be an effective and evocative center of dynamic social activity, and it hasn't yet had the opportunity to prove either its success *or* its failure in those terms.

Second, I find the concept of double-coded architecture—of private jokes or allusions in manifestly public works—to be questionable, even offensive. One may well and wisely mine the whole of the architectural past for ideas in a contemporary building. But to make the game of *spotting* those ideas a major part of one's design intentions strikes me as decadent and trivial. Much too much of what has been written of the Piazza d'Italia (including some texts by Charles W. Moore) has concentrated on these arcane references and Society of Architectural Historians jests. If the Piazza d'Italia had to depend for its success on clever twistings of the tails of past masters, then I would declare it not only a public failure but a patronizing insult. Unlike Hadrian's Villa or John Soane's house in Lincoln's Inn Square—or for that matter Charles Moore's houses—it was commissioned as a civic and public place, and it *must* succeed first on public, not private, terms.

Fortunately, and thirdly, I think it does. (Or will. Or could.) It succeeds even now for me, *in potentia*, stripped of all these allusions and jests, and will succeed even more fully when it is complete. I take great pleasure in, and can imagine others taking pleasure in, the sheer exuberance of its colors and shapes, its illusions and allusions, its water games and steel games, the grandeur and surprise and disposition and finesse of its pieces—whether or not I or they knew a triglyph from a tripod. The proportions of these thin, Hollywood Roman-epic walls are played against and modulated by the subtle color changes and the just-perceptible curve in ways I find exquisitely pleasing. The spaces between columns and openings in each wall, the placings of the walls one against the other are arranged with soul-settling tact and *mesure*. If it is a joke, it is a joke on a monumental scale, but in no way (as some have claimed) an insult to Italy or our noble Western heritage.[4] The immeasurably rich legacy of the region we now call Italy, and of the classic orders of architecture, are things so diverse and so powerful, have nourished so many centuries and regions of good art and good building, that they can easily embrace one Jovian jest.

But the piazza is not just an Olympian joke. It is also—I speak of its potential, not its actual state—a quite beautifully organized and orchestrated public space. Proportions, details, materials, and colors are combined even more scrupulously and (to my eye) pleasingly than all the celebrated references and allusions. It does not depend for its success on semiotic transliterations of its shapes or on the insider's familiarity with architectural history. It is *not*, in its heart, a cynical dig at the classics.

These elements are present, and they may well qualify or on occasion reduce the freedom and healthiness of the overall pleasure of one's experience. Charles Moore, when set free from adult collaborators or control, can be incorrigibly and excessively clever, like other child prodigies who never totally grow up. Some of the jokes here, detached from the context of the pleasurable whole, do indeed appear (as hostile critics have called them) architectural one liners, with a very short half life—as embarrassingly silly as the spitting Charles Moore heads on the mock-Doric wall.

I offer my sincerest best wishes to the Italian-American patriots and New Orleans investors, on whose goodwill and hard work the future of this place depends. If it *is* a stage set, it is the supreme outdoor stage set of our time, and I hope it gets treated with proper respect. It is suited not so much for *Cavalleria Rusticana*, or (as hostile critics might have it) for A *Funny Thing Happened on the Way to the Forum*, as it is for the daily human comedy of thousands of happy Italian Orleanians and their friends.

17 / EARLY LOS ANGELES

ONE reason Charles Moore encounters the resistance he does from some East Coast critics and professionals—despite his ten years' tenure at Yale and notable buildings in all parts of the country—is that he is irrevocably identified with California, and in particular southern California. He not only lives in Los Angeles, which is very shallow and uncultured of him. He also takes it seriously, which is worse. He writes and lectures favorably about it, which only proves his incorrigible frivolousness, and designs buildings intended to celebrate its more shameful characteristics—suggesting that he either shares or admires them or both.

In his forthcoming book *Los Angeles: The City Observed*, Moore frequently makes reference to a favorite Noel Coward remark about the city: "What's phoney is so real there, and what's real is so phoney." Los Angeles, he declares, is not a city of buildings in the standard architectural sense ("tattooed boxes") but a city of *rides*: rides between places, whether on freeways or "surface streets," even rides (as in Disneyland) to nowhere. "You get on some mode of conveyance and then you experience things. This makes Los Angeles very theatrical and experiential, and that interests me a lot. The city doesn't pay much attention to the sterner virtues." Even the omnipresent flora, the natural landscape of southern California, he reminds the reader, is of course not natural.

Northern California, where he first earned his reputation, has at least a sound heart of history and hard work beneath its cultivation of sensual pleasure. The stout timbers, the timeless forms, and the frequently bitter weather of the Sea Ranch evoke this well.

But southern California, as a culture, often appears to the outsider 100 percent devoted to greed, the glittering surface, and instant gratification. And built places designed to cater to or evoke the southern Californian way of life run a serious risk of looking (again, to the non-indigene) as fragile, as depthless, and as narcissistic as the way of life itself. Shame! cries the outsider, brought up on the sterner virtues—on dutiful effort, guilt, and the heavy hand of the past.

Until his Beverly Hills and San Juan Capistrano projects are completed, Charles Moore's greatest tributes to southern California as a culture will remain the Burns house and the faculty club at Santa Barbara. The success (or failure) in both cases depended on what an architect of genius was able to make of local forms, plus evocative objects and colors, not only the simple fact of his using them. Moore can triumph or fail as well with Palladian or log cabin or imperial Roman motifs. But insofar as a "southern California idiom" implies things like this-season's decorator colors and *objets*, the shimmering unreality of a David Hockney swimming pool, and the broad, bright, inch-thick walls of Sunset Strip billboards, I do feel that it appears to be a radical, an essential, but in the end a less valuable part of Charles Moore's bicoastal nature: the part that, were it not counterbalanced with a few sturdier characteristics, might well have made him this century's number one set designer.

I have referred, in passing, to some of the problems he had satisfying two quintessentially southern California clients: the consortium of psychoanalysts who commissioned an office building off Little Santa Monica Boulevard in 1968; and the lecturer in English drama at UCLA who asked him in 1976 for a French farmhouse made of concrete block to go in his Brentwood meadow. Both cases reveal some of the joys and some of the dangers of designing in and for this extraordinary place.

The very idea of a suave, consciously tranquilizing haven for twenty-one different psychoanalysts and their patients, off a semi-crummy west LA boulevard, sounds like a bad stand-up comedian's joke. Architect Richard Chylinski, who was left to fend off the feral analysts and their attorneys whenever Charles escaped to Yale, could not believe the selfishness, greed, and litigiousness of this mismatched collection of clients. They hired and fired their own engineers and contractors, squabbled like little children over who got the biggest piece (of window, toilet, balcony, or planting); they shaved specifications, refused to pay bills, sued the architects for negligence and incompetence—and, in the end, piled praise on Moore and Chylinski. "I want to thank you and Charles for the building," their spokesman told Chylinski when it was all finally over. "Everyone who comes here is happier. I never knew a building could do so much for sick people."

Given the three years of haggling and unpleasantness involved, I find it astonishing that the Psychoanalytic Associates Building—which is just around the corner from Moore's own triplex, should he ever require their ministrations—*did* turn out to be so elegantly ordered and calm. If one needed to see a psychoanalyst, I can't think of a nicer place to do it. Somehow, while making compromises right and left with these difficult clients, Moore managed to sneak in many of his own favorite gestures—and yet keep the end result beneficently serene. The Moore tourist will recognize the single-pitch roof forms, the rich layering of cut-out walls, the very free use of overhead windows, the balcony corridors that become flying bridges and overlook spaces below. He will have seen elsewhere these stairways that widen and turn as they flow, these hallways that take surprising processional jogs. But here all these things are softened and muted, and rendered nonfunny and unaggressive, as befits the building's use and its users. The windows are all large and satisfying rectangles, almost golden in their proportions. The color symphony soothes, makes life instantly easier. The rough stucco exterior, deftly punctuated by big windows, turns from a soft rosy tan to pale beige as it turns a corner. Inside, the office doors are creamy, frosting-like greens and blues and rust reds, against soft off-pastel walls. Mind-untangling accents are provided by geometric wall paintings of the same colors as the doors, rich rosy beige carpets. Large-leafed plants in chrome cylinders rest under rhomboids of light from the clerestories and skylights above.

It remains, basically, a twenty-one-doctor corridor-and-office building, with a central reception desk, a lounge, and a private garage. But it is lifted well out of the medical-office-building norm by the floods of joyful light, the calming chasms of free space to look into, the unexpected but satisfying angles and shapes, and the ever-so-suave palette of colors. The Little Santa Monica facade fits into its very ordinary neighborhood so unobtrusively the building is easy to miss. But on close inspection the play of balconies, planting, and window shapes (especially to one who knows the private wars that lay behind them) forms an abstract pattern of remarkable finesse.

Architectural historian David Gebhard saw all sorts of local "sources" in the building. It is, he once wrote, "partly Spanish Revival in its stuccoed surfaces and its numerous courtyards, *moderne* in such features as horizontal bands of windows, and self-consciously Schindler-esque in its complex anti-high art play of interpenetrating volumes." Professor Gebhard was writing of an earlier and more complicated plan. I don't see all that *he* saw; but I do see in the building something like the work of an architect as psychoanalyst, trying to solve the problems of some troubled and troublesome people by making a place that is both native to west LA and wonderfully appropriate to its purpose. At first sight I thought it almost eerily calm, a touch too decorator-suave. But that may have been a reassuring sign that I didn't require what its owners had to offer.

IF I am too well adjusted to love (or need) the Psychoanalytic Associates Building with whole heart, I may be too clumsily normal to comprehend all the delights of the house Charles designed eight years later for David Rodes—a willful and demanding client with some fixed and unusual ideas.

"Actually, Charles may not *like* this house," Mr. Rodes admitted to me. "It's probably too sober, too cool for him. *I* love it because I can't imagine anyone else living in it but me. Lee [Burns] gave him far more headway than I did; but Lee's house is too insistently witty for me. It's really half Charles. All those doodads. This is all me. I knew Charles's idiom before I hired him, so I knew what I didn't want. I *didn't* want tile floors; I didn't want mirrors; I didn't want a grand staircase. Now I half wish I'd hired someone more venturesome, like the Morphosis Group. But do ask Charles what he really thinks of my house."

Moore was not surprised when I told him what Mr. Rodes had said. "I knew David felt that way. Spatially, I don't think there was any dispute. The arguments were all over finishes. His own attitudes, and the pressure from his friends (some of whom are very rich), led him to look for an elegantly finished and expensive house—without a budget to match. And so I was pressing for things that I guess could be classed as 'witty,' but would have kept the budget down—a little bit more of 'loving hands at home.'"

I found the Rodes house icy and alien, the closest thing to a look-at-me piece of live-in sculpture Moore has ever done. Given the client's romance with architectural history and the theater, however, and his self-conscious aestheticism, the house may well be perfect for him.

It enfronts a broad, flat meadow (planted into orange orchard) as a single, bowed stone-gray stucco wall. In the wall, five French doors, and five square windows above them, broadly framed in cool blue and off-beige, are disposed with perfect symmetry. A little carport to one side, a mirror-image terrace to the other (each topped by a curving metal trellis) extend the insistent symmetry into something like the shape of the *Queen Mary*'s bridge.

Behind this awesomely perfect wall lies an even more awesomely perfect room—a high double-cube space (as at Wilton House in Somerset), curving at the edges and the front, in which the owner has arranged six cushy chairs in soft peaches and powdery greens (:"These are my colors") in two-thirds of a circle. They face a cold gray-tiled box of a fireplace, located precisely opposite the central door. A neat pile of square cushions in the same colors allows him to accommodate more than six guests.

The client requested that the house be painted in cool, recessive, faded colors, and that the palette specifically not include warm earth colors, browns, reds, oranges of any sort, nor should it include any yellows or greens (most particularly avocado). This left the family of grays, taupes, and blues, with the possibility of slipping in some peach or apricot.[5]

The actual decisions about interior color were made on the spot, with the minute attention and fine gradations of a color-field painter, blending and mixing hues to achieve effects of considerable refinement.

The space behind the large living room is also perfect: an octagonal dining room-conservatory open to the roof, lighted by French windows that give on to a stone-walled grotto. It is colored as dream-suavely as the curved double cube, and furnished with the same meticulous austerity. On my visit, a single blue iris rose from a bud vase on a table directly under the one hanging lamp.

Functional, less formal spaces (sleeping, bathing, cooking, study) are fitted into two levels of the two sides of this splayed and bowed rectangle, like the almost afterthought users' rooms in a more precious Palladian villa. Indeed, the house has often been called Palladian—though Mr. Rodes also cites such sources as Scamozzi, the Bibienas, Lutyens, Kahn, and French chateaux. But I feel its Palladianism more as an idea—the idea of a formal, sym-metrical showplace, like Chiswick House—than as anything dis-cernible to the heart or the eye.

The house has a nice big kitchen (Mr. Rodes loves to cook) and an ocean-liner-railed balcony over the fireplace, dividing the two wings. Here visiting actors perform for guests, seated below on those soft Italian cushions and chairs. Opposite the balcony, at-tached to the bowed front wall, is a large theatrical lighting grid (theoretically it continues those outside trellises over the two side wings, as if they pierced the wall). It holds ten ellipsoidal halogen spots, with two others trained upward. An oval terrace in front of the house can serve as an additional stage area for guests who will sit in the orange-grove-to-be.

"Actually," said David Rodes, "theater and stage sets were the central metaphors Charles and I used. You should have seen the house before it was framed in. It was a pure, theatrical space. It's very glamorous, very pretty at night. Tina's colors, the bleached-oak floors, starlight through the windows, all those spots. My friends once proposed aiming one Surprise Pink spot right at my chair."

I love the upstairs bathroom (it has its own inside window) and the light on the bookcase-lined stairs. I can understand what it is the owner and his friends enjoy in the cool, high, powdery spaces, as I can understand the pleasure many people take in an especially elegant modern skyscraper. But I feel that much of Charles Moore's innate vitality, exuberance, and imagination were frustrated, per-haps even misdirected, in straining to meet the fixed demands and unusual needs of a person radically unlike himself.

18 / CONNECTICUT
1973–78

D
URING Charles Moore's last years in Connecticut, and his first years in Los Angeles, he designed a number of houses for East Coast clients very different from those of his early days at Yale. Those first large houses are still remarkably exciting places, with their flying corridors and spiraling stairs, their many-windowed fronts and punched-out white walls, their op-art illusions and dazzling perspectives. But I find myself drawn more easily to the rich, calm works of the later Yale years, which strike me as more selfless, mature, and resolved.

The 1969–72 houses, despite their dynamic individuality, all depend on certain dramatic and recognizable "Charles Moore" gestures, which are probably related to the architect's own fantasies and theories at the time. The Swan, Isham, Rubenstein, and Stanwood houses, and the large "House near New York" (designed 1973–77, completed 1976–78) are, on the other hand, such distinctive expressions of their *owners'* needs and fantasies that one would be unlikely to attribute them to the same architect—unless one understood well Moore's most open and receptive manner. All five of the later homes exude a warm sense of recalled history and geography. They are sensitively carved to fit their inhabitants, inserted into their natural surroundings with great respect, and—in each case—inspired by, and contained within, a unifying concept that is as beautiful to think about as it is to observe.

IN order to guard his family's privacy and safety (he and his brothers were all left immense fortunes), the owner of the "House near New York" asks that the house not be identified in print by his name or by a more specific location. One of the owner's brothers is a successful architect himself, who had remodeled an old barn on the two-hundred-acre estate into a jazzy new guest house. But when it came time to build the manor house itself, the owner knew he wanted something other than his brother's particular style. Generously, his brother offered him a list of alternate names— including Charles Moore's.

According to Richard Oliver, a former student of Moore's who collaborated with him on the project, Charles won the job as much for his sensitivity as for his skills or his style. The owner, an active venture capitalist, philanthropist, and sportsman then in his thirties, devoted husband and father of two sons, had suddenly begun to lose his sight. (A victim of retinitis pigmentosa, he quickly lost vision in the blue range altogether, retaining for a while some sensitivity to reds and to extremes of light and shade.) Of all the architects he interviewed, Moore seemed the most acutely responsive to his and his family's special needs. Charles, in turn, respected the man profoundly: I have heard him discuss only two other clients with such admiration and warmth. He was determined to get the job, even if it meant playing down his usual exuberance. He had the plans vacuum-formed in plastic, so the owner could read the spaces with his fingers. Detailed descriptions of each wall were written up in a large book.

The eleven-thousand-square-foot mansion Moore and Oliver designed is a "great house" in every sense, yet still one that tries to be friendly and unique. The house is unlike anything Moore had ever done before, with costly fieldstone walls and a roof of Virginia slate. One approaches it through a classic country-house park, acres of woods filled with rabbit and deer. Cars arrive in a graveled forecourt, low stone walls topped by urns.

There, the house looms complex and immense. It seems a series of houses, a little village of high-rising wooden forms that narrow as they ascend, ending in chimney towers or high belvederes (actually ventilator housings) atop steeply sloping roofs. These forms, on the tops of three separately roofed pavilions (add garage wing and pool house), and the open central space between them, were a conscious borrowing from Stratford Hall in Virginia, the great Lee family mansion of 1725 Moore had long admired for its clarity and grandeur.

The front of the house is straightforward and welcoming. Other sides of the house—a serpentining walk leads around its perimeter—take on more bizarre configurations; windows march up triangular faces toward the soaring vent towers. The house is, from outside, defiantly independent of its "sources" and slightly intimidating in its size. From one spot at the rear of the house, the highest tower of all rises skyward forty or fifty feet above the level of the path.

This dramatic mixture of the strange and the familiar is kept surprisingly tranquil by the horizontally overlapped cedar siding, stained a thin, creamy beige, with mushroom gray trim, and one fine rust red line under the roofline (Tina Beebe's choices). The answering roofslopes of the separate pavilions create from some angles a welcome sense of balance. The warm orangey brown fieldstone, the dark gray slate roof, the French doors and door-sized windows all seem gestures toward great houses of another day.

Moore seemed torn here between an urge to create a kind of eighteenth- or nineteenth-century grandeur and a perversely modern craving to deform or domesticate: truncating, chopping, pulling things apart, assertively including unbalanced or ungrand details. In the end, the house stands on a tantalizing razor's edge between the grandly conservative (rooms fit into traditional forms) and the eccentrically unique (forms dictated by inner needs, both the owner's and the architect's). The unresolved high drama of this house may well come from the architect's trying to have it both ways.

The owner's inner needs are responded to inside the house, which places closed, formal, old-fashioned rooms around a central street or passageway as exotic and as dreamlike as anything Moore has ever designed. Accepting with high energy the challenge of compensating for one partially lost sense by accentuating others, Moore worked a sinuous, sensory pathway through and around the downstairs core of the house, then upstairs around the bedrooms by way of balconies and bridges. Its entire length is marked by a curving, polished wooden rail mounted on red poles, to lead the master of the manor along. Directly inside the front door, trees rise twenty or thirty feet, their leaves filtering bright light from high windows. The floors of the passage are paved with hard, slightly uneven red tiles, providing contrast underfoot with the hardwood and carpets of the formal rooms left and right. Further on, one passes a small ornamental pool and fountain set into the floor, water playing with its pleasing noises over a sculpted spill of red and blue tiled blocks. The path then curves around past a glazed conservatory of still more exotic trees and plants (and the entrance to a pool and private gym), to the owner's dark office, the master bedroom, then to a carpeted stairway leading up, and a bridge that cuts back across the entry hall. The entire length of this long, two-story circulation street is marked not only by the wooden rail, but by the clear feel of tiled floors and flagstone walls, by brilliant changes of light, by vivid sounds and smells.

The conservative decors, the closed rooms, the luxurious materials, the orangerie and conservatory, the ever-rippling swimming pool (glass enclosed, solar heated) are obviously reflections of the owner's tastes and desires. If they don't seem precisely "Charles Moore," that's because Charles Moore was happy on this occasion to dissolve his needs into those of his client. The sense-alerting, self-guiding trails through and around the house may have begun as concessions to his special needs, but they grew into a series of visual, tactile, aural, and olfactory delights accessible to any one of the family or their guests. All this was then shaped and contained in a series of apparently separate buildings that achieve a kind of country-house grandeur without ever becoming so awesome a mass as to seem uncomfortable to the family or dishonest to the century from which they grew.

THE other four wood-finished houses of 1976–78 I referred to were built on a more normal scale. But each is as individually wrought as the "House near New York," compact of original ideas and suffused with Moore's growing enthusiasm for other times and other places. ("This enthusiasm," he once wrote, "is frequently put down as an unworthy one, limp and nostalgic; but I'm on the edge of pressing for Nostalgia as a Guiding Principle.")

Simone Swan, a genteel, gracefully aging lady who moves like her namesake, had spent a rich life among art and artists. Working with the de Menil family in Houston, she came to know Louis Kahn, whom they had engaged to design a cultural study center there. In 1973, Kahn offered to design Mrs. Swan a house for a small piece of property she owned in the woods of eastern Long Island. "'Oh, no, Mr. Kahn,' I protested. 'I want a modest house.' He replied, 'By a man who I hope is modest.'" On his urging, she bought an old farmhouse so that they might reuse its hand-hewn beams, joists, and flooring.

Unfortunately, Kahn died before he could do either the Texas cultural center or the Long Island house. Mrs. Swan next met Charles Moore, this "huge teddy bear" of a man, at a party in 1974, and agreed to talk to him about doing the job. Her son Eric had recently completed a stay at Findhorn, the ecological commune in Scotland, and he impressed on her the need for radical energy-saving techniques: windmill power, earth toilets, passive solar heating. "Charles insisted, 'But I have an *expert* on solar heating on my staff'—which was a lie, of course. Grover knew nothing about it. He also underestimated the costs by eleven thousand dollars—which I paid. Not to mention the repairs I've had to do since." A demanding but not an impossible client, she preferred working with Mark Simon to working with Bill Grover. She thought Moore and Grover "giggled too much."

"I remember once interrupting one of their silly conversations and saying, 'Could we *please* stop talking about Rona Barrett—whoever she is—and talk about my twenty-eight-foot-high living room? I am going to have to shut it off completely in the winter. How do you propose to do that?' After about a ten-minute silence, Bill Grover came up with one of his clownish ideas: bricking up the space every fall. Then Mark Simon suggested using foam-rubber bricks—which in a way *is* what I ended up with." The twelve-inch-thick foam-rubber pads on her long living-room couch were designed in such a way that they fit exactly into the space alongside the chimney, and allow her to seal off the room and leave it unheated all winter. Insulation, the double fireplace, French doors with jalousies, and provision for future "solarizing" helped meet the rest of her son's and her energy demands.

Simone Swan rejected Moore's first design. "It was flawless conceptually, but it seemed too worldly and ideal for me, too Sunday *New York Times*. It didn't respond to some of my secret needs." Eric thought it wasn't Zen enough: too cozy, too classy suburban. "Charles seemed delighted when I said no." So she told him some more about her childhood in the Belgian Congo, her dreams of living high in the trees, her father, her need for rough wood and a sense of the rural past. He came up with his best small house (bar a few leaks and other functional disorders) since 1965.

Everyone who visits Swan House reads its primal forms differently. I saw it as a tiny medieval German village or a row of houses under a Christmas tree. Others see in it a chapel, a timeless farmhouse, the Parson Capen house of 1683—whatever rural vernacular they may have known as children. "I see it as a gingerbread house without the frosting," says Simone.

It is, to be sure, hidden in the woods, like the witch's house in "Hansel and Gretel." A very steeply pitched roof covers a narrow rectangular box about fifteen by sixty feet in plan. An attached shed roof and open trellis (made partly of the old timbers) shelter part of a wooden porch that runs the length of the house, separating it from a small, separate guest house to the south. The variety of steep roofslopes, the high chimney, and this sheltered streetlike porch, with its row of five French doors, are what prompted me to perceive it as a little village street. The west end of the house (the sealable living room) is open all twenty-eight feet to the roof peak. Seven of those hand-hewn beams reach (nonstructurally) like crossties from one side of the sloping upper walls to the other, above the blades of a wide wooden fan. It's a spectacular high white tent of a room, great for summer parties, and it opens all along to the deck.

The house is divided in two by a high white fireplace wall—itself a piece of prehistoric-looking sculpture—round which is tucked a narrow staircase. Beyond it stretches a low-ceilinged open country kitchen; pots and utensils hang from the antique beams above. Polished boards run the full length of the floor. Above the kitchen are the private quarters of Swan House, a perfect realm of dreams. They contain a mattress up on a stepped and curtained platform, with a moon-viewing skylight and a morning glimpse of Long Island Sound through the trees; an oldtime bathtub out in the open with its own view into the green leaves; yet another secret view from the toilet; mirrors to extend the skylight blue; a tiny winter sun balcony over the deck; and a big interior window from Mrs. Swan's office, looking down into the great living-room space.

IT was Simone Swan who persuaded Heyward and Sheila Isham, who also owned property on the east end of Long Island, to talk to Charles Moore. "They had commissioned a house from this *nobody*. I said, 'Don't waste your time. Hire the number one.'" The three had met in Haiti, where Mrs. Swan vacations with native friends, and Mr. Isham was U.S. ambassador. Mrs. Isham was a professional painter, so they had the art world in common as well—although the two women are as different as bronze and lace. "I would never have chosen Moore on the basis of Simone's house," Mrs. Isham declares.

"I was not very easy to work with," she admits. "I had a reputation for chewing up architects and spitting them out. I had already bought and rejected five other plans." Charles Moore and Mark Simon presented her with four different schemes at once, "to ensure our continued employment." The trick worked.

"It was a real collaboration," according to Sheila Isham—"a marvelous creative partnership. He wasn't afraid to let me design my own house—of course, with his mastermind ideas. He gave me infinite options—'If you do this, this will happen'—and allowed me to erase whatever I wanted. We were still in Haiti then" (after London, Berlin, Moscow, Hong Kong, Paris, and Port au Prince, Ambassador Isham is back again in Washington), "and of course Charles was flying around the world. So we did it all at these *intense* four-hour sessions around dinner at the Barbizon Plaza. Sometimes we wouldn't see him for three months. Mark did all the follow-up work."

This is another cluster or "village" of houses, three neat gray-shingled, unexceptional-looking Long Island farmhouse buildings enclosing (by walls of windows or sliding barn doors) a calm, grassy court—one of the "oriental" elements the owner required. ("Other architects kept giving us all these superficial orientalisms, like wind chimes. Only Charles understood the real Chinese concept I wanted.") Closing off the east end of the compound is a two-story guest house I like very much. To the south is a well-lighted studio with double-height doors to accommodate Sheila Isham's large, spray-painted "metaphysical color field" canvases. Inside the main house, sections of wall roll on barn-door tracks mounted in cedar ceiling beams, allowing her paintings to be displayed and room configurations to be changed. Two of these rolling art walls move together to close off a square Japanese "tea room," with sliding tatami-covered floor platforms, looking into the tranquilizing green court. The western-style living room is twenty-eight feet high and skylit, and looks out into miles of the wild grass and potato fields which roll right up to the house. The master bath boasts a large sunken tub with a view of its own Japanese garden and the green fields beyond.

The house is everything Mrs. Isham wanted: an unassertively local-looking farmhouse in the fields, a place for her to paint and show her paintings, a memory of happy years in Asia, a comfortable and easy family house filled with light, almost timelessly calm. It is logical enough to satisfy Louis Kahn. The courtyard, the large and luminous canvases, the superimposed images of a Long Island farm and an Asian pavilion gave her and her architects the focal points they needed. Except for some exhilarating space games in the guest house, the house is a little *too* tranquil for my tastes; very little beyond some signature angled arches, the roof shapes, and the barn doors identifies it readily as Moore's. But this only proves how willing and able he had become to abandon his own earlier dreams, needs, and preferences on behalf of those of a client with different views.

LEE RUBENSTEIN, a Washington, D.C., engineer and builder, knew of Moore's work through his friends the Tempchins, whose house in Bethesda Moore had designed in 1968. Mr. Rubenstein had bought, in 1976, a 120-year-old barn on the Maryland Eastern Shore, looking south to the Choptank River as it pours out into Chesapeake Bay. He wanted to convert it into an energy-saving vacation house ("It was still filled with animals when I bought it"), while preserving all its fine old features: the thick stone walls and columns of the ground floor, the original walls and roof above, the fantastic array of wooden posts, beams, and diagonal bracers inside, and two truly monumental silos (fifty-five feet high, eighteen feet in diameter) in front.

Since living spaces would have to be inserted into an interior forest of old stone and timber, he felt that the architect would have to be someone who knew how to deal with volumes. What he knew of the Tempchins' house, and subsequent conversations with Moore (who was very excited about this epic remodeling job), convinced Mr. Rubenstein that he was the one.

Moore—working once more with young Mark Simon, the most *simpatico* of his partners at the time—came up with a design that is nothing less than triumphant. The stone-walled first floor, seventy-eight by thirty-two feet (it is actually two "buildings," divided by the old barn-door entrance space), was turned into entry kitchen and dining area to the west, bedrooms and baths to the east. (The Rubensteins had three children, but can comfortably sleep a dozen or more here.) Over the kitchen wing is the master-bedroom suite; over *it* was placed a large loft, with a Ping-Pong table and quiet places to sit or sleep. A spacious living room (the view is better from upstairs), over the children's bedrooms, is built around all the original wood posts and a high fireplace sheathed in rusted metal from the original roof. A steep, final stairway wraps around it to a belvedere under the roof.

Because the dining area, the broad entry staircase, and the whole center section of the house were kept unceiled and open to the roof, and because most of the "third-floor" level is unfloored—except for a flying bridge between the wings—almost every region of this unique house enjoys ever-changing and unfailingly exciting vistas up, across, and through its priceless old timbers. Every room is able to "anticipate" the rooms adjacent. This keeps the Rubensteins' Maryland house a geometrical space trip as uplifting (and as natural) as a great medieval timbered barn, like the early fourteenth-century Abbey Grange at Great Coxwell in Berkshire (which William Morris called "the greatest piece of architecture in England").

Cheaply heating so huge an open space was a challenge Moore, Simon, and Rubenstein undertook together. Even though the family and their friends use the house only an average of two weekends a month, it had (for preservation's sake) to be kept minimally heated (fifty to fifty-five degrees) all the time; and though they wanted to retain the old roof, a century of damp had rotted a number of rafters.

Thriftily, like old farmers, they laid new wood over these old rafters (rather than tearing them out), nailed two-by-six pieces through the old roof, and laid a new metal roof atop them, filling the interstices with insulation. Similarly, they hung new board-and-batten siding (already weathering to "old") outside the original upper frame. Five solar collectors on the south-facing roof generally suffice to maintain the minimal nonresident heat. When the house is occupied, they heat water instead, while two fireplaces and an oil-fired heater keep the house warm. ("We used a total of two hundred seventy-five gallons in 1982," Mr. Rubenstein boasted.)

The best light, and the river view, are to the south, which had been blocked by a shed that ran the full length of the barn. Ingeniously, and beautifully, Moore and Simon simply stripped this shed down to its skeleton, retaining all the handsome structural members for a trellised terrace that extends the life of the house outside and lets in much of the light that does such wonderful things to the "tantalizing fretwork" of wood members inside.

Many of our better architects have become skilled at adaptive reuse. But the Rubenstein house goes far beyond that. An *Architectural Record* House of the Year in 1978, the genius involved in its redesign is at one with the timeless high quality of the original structure: nothing has been lost; everything has been enhanced. Charles Moore, a man who all his life has admired fine old barns and other wooden vernacular buildings—perhaps more than any other type—finally got the chance to honor them not by allusion or imitation, but by opening up a great original to a new and wonderful life.

BOB and Peggy Stanwood had owned a fine piece of property—a rolling wooded hillside near Hartford, Connecticut, with a great view to the east—for fifteen years before they built. All the while her engineer husband was being transferred around the country by his employers, Mrs. Stanwood vowed to return to it one day and build their dream house. In Los Angeles in 1976, they saw Lee Burns's house on a house tour and were so impressed they made an appointment then and there to see the architect.

"Only later did we learn how famous he was. We panicked, and almost canceled. Buzz Yudell ushered us in, warned us that we'd get *at most* fifteen minutes. This was our meeting with the master. But Charles turned out to be more nervous than we were. Once we met, we all relaxed, and he gave us two hours."

In their moves around the country, Bob and Peggy Stanwood (and their two children) had developed a long list of the things they would require in their dream house. They wanted (1) a clapboarded, normal-looking house with proper eaves and trim ("After all, this *is* New England"); (2) a perfect workshop (Bob got one twenty-four feet square); (3) to incorporate timbers from an old barn *they* had bought (they never did, but Moore managed to give them an old barn anyway); (4) total natural daylight; (5) a house that fell down the hill toward the view, "not just on the land but of it"; and (6) total energy efficiency: passive solar, woodburning stoves, the works.

They got all they asked for, but for a while Moore—working again with Mark Simon—felt frustrated by his inability to come up with a unifying image that would add some excitement to this altogether too-sensible scheme. Then he seized on the notion of "old barn timbers" and concocted the fantasy of a house within a house: a two-story "original settlers'" cabin with exposed heavy barn timbers and vertical siding of yellow pine, fitted *inside* a modern, solar-heated white Sheetrock-and-glass house with concrete floors (which is itself enclosed in a dark-brown-stained clapboarded New England shell).

Contractors' estimates, unfortunately, came in $40,000 over their budget. Wretched at the thought of abandoning their dream house, the Stanwoods subtracted everything from the total cost that they could conceivably do themselves, and planned to use weekends and vacations for the next five to seven years to do all the painting and finish carpentry, frame and hang the inside doors, finish the drywalling, install bookshelves and stoves, make the barn doors, and decorate the bedrooms. Along with a modest beach house in Malibu, which is being built entirely by the owners, this makes the Stanwoods' one of two Charles Moore do-it-yourselfers.

19 / COLD SPRING HARBOR

ONE of Moore's favorite East Coast clients is James D. Watson, the double-helix man, the *enfant terrible* from Harvard who shared the Nobel Prize in physiology and medicine in 1962 and then told all about his research, personality, and ambition in a best-selling book. Since 1968, Jim Watson has been the director of an idyllically located laboratory in Cold Spring Harbor, Long Island. This laboratory, founded in the nineteenth century for genetic research, presented Dr. Watson with a formidable challenge. On the one hand, he had under his control a hundred-acre "village" of thirty nineteenth-century mid-Atlantic houses facing an Arcadian blue cove —plus an extensive neo-Georgian estate to the north, recently donated to the lab. On the other, he had somehow to cope with an epic boom in the laboratory's two specialties, neurobiology and the relationship between DNA and cancer, knowing full well that his neighbors around the harbor would not tolerate the least intrusion on their matchless haven of anything that looked like a gigantic new scientific enterprise. How was he to accommodate a six- to tenfold increase in laboratory activity and still keep Cold Spring Harbor looking like a whaling village of the late nineteenth century?

In the summer of 1972, after a controversial conference on DNA research hazards at Asilomar near Monterey, Jim and Liz Watson drove north along the California coast. They stopped for the night at—where else?—the Sea Ranch Lodge, took the real estate promoters' tour the next day, and were fascinated by what they saw. Back in Long Island, they learned that one of the prime movers of the Sea Ranch design was now a near neighbor across Long Island Sound. They met Charles Moore. Like a lot of clients I talked to, Mrs. Watson fell hard. "I *adored* Charles Moore," she told me. "If Jim ever moved, it would have to be to another Charles Moore house."

Redoing the Watsons' own house at Cold Spring was the first

project they gave to Charles and his Essex associates. Airslie House is an eighteenth-century sea-captain's residence, remade into a proper white-painted Victorian with turrets and porches in 1856—and from the outside, that's still what it is. Moore virtually gutted the interior, however, then put it back together in a way that still *feels* very comfortably nineteenth century, with box-shaped rooms and symmetrically placed alcoves that fit neatly into the outside tower bays. The one Moore-ish tour de force—a wedding of Kresge College stage sets and early Americana—is the new, apparently freestanding, three-story yellow stairwell. Thin, non-parallel stud-and-stucco walls with jazzy cutouts support a new-old staircase with the most exquisitely turned rails that runs all through the center of the house. It's one way to Moore-ize your old house and yet feel that you're still preserving it intact.

The next job was to design a waste-treatment facility that fit into a village of old, or imitation-old, houses. Charles's solution was to top it with a little terrace and a neo-Victorian gazebo and disguise it with shingles and scrollwork.

Then came the remodeling of the Jones Laboratory—a high, white-painted-wood Long Island building of 1895. Here, the problem was to preserve both the simple barnlike exterior and the magnificent interior woodwork (the walls and vaulted ceiling had been meticulously planked in thin horizontal strips, like the hull of a clipper ship turned inside out) and somehow to accommodate within it facilities for the most demanding controlled-environment biological research.

First, Moore Grover Harper designed a detached little "dog-house" in back, in the same style as the original, insulated for low-temperature work. Then Charles came up with the idea of inserting five self-contained and sealable space-age modules inside the great timber "hull." This way the interior could be left untouched and still allow the scientists warm, old-fashioned spaces between their little labs to escape to for reading, relaxing, and conferring. Light from the big old windows shines on the polished floors and passes right through carefully lined up cutouts in the aluminum pods. Diamond-paned dormers and views across the green "village" make the regular lab benches outside the pods seem a wonderful blend of nineteenth- and twentieth-century worlds. The project won a national AIA "extended use" award in 1980. (These awards are now given to the best remodelings of old buildings for new uses.) Like all his Cold Spring Harbor work, it demonstrates Moore's recent willingness to submerge the architect's usual impulse to make striking new places on the landscape in the interest of salvaging something beautiful and old.

Several other old structures at Cold Spring Harbor have been similarly and successfully "recycled," as the current term has it, by Moore's younger associates in Connecticut. A large new animal building looks, appropriately, like an old wooden barn. The medium-sized Delbrück Laboratory, housing more genetic engineers, could almost pass for an early nineteenth-century house, if you ignored the oversized vent "chimney" and superscaled windows. Moore himself served as chief designer for the Cancer Lab of 1979: a large new fifty-room state-of-the-art laboratory encased in an outscaled imitation-nineteenth-century house, complete with dormers, eaves, and chimneys, all the elements oversized to make the building look smaller; and a projected new/old-looking $2 million wooden auditorium, with four large eccentric dormers rising from a big shingle-style roof.

Mrs. Watson herself took on the job of redecorating Davenport House, an 1882 building used for staff housing, which a local gas-station attendant described to me as "that ugly green and yellow Victorian at the entrance to the lab." Not all of Cold Spring Harbor is enchanted by the eclectic pluralism of postmodern taste.

To me the most astonishing building at the complex is a new guest house for sixteen conference goers at the former Robertson Estate to the north, called Sammis Hall. Charles's original design—which has been considerably modified by Bob Harper—was inspired by Palladio's 1549 Villa Poiana near Vicenza and dedicated in July 1981. Already it's been included in books, exhibitions, and articles dealing with postmodern classicism.

Most recent historicist adventures by other architects strike me as willful and slightly desperate games; as aggressive ways of drawing attention to oneself in a modernist world; or as simply trendy—"neohistoricism is in"—without much concern for or understanding of the history that underlies these forms and the meanings they evoke. A few, like Philip Johnson's period-style skyscrapers, seem to cackle with cynicism; others, like Thomas Gordon Smith's neo-Roman fantasies, seem closed and solipsistic: private, theoretical fantasies.

But I had no trouble with the obvious Palladianism of Sammis

Hall. There is nothing joky or carbon copy about it. It remains gloriously simple and seems to work very well, both visually and functionally. The facades are elegant and symmetrical. On the front, rectangular wings flank an arched center pavilion; a formal shield hangs over the inset entry. Snug guest suites are disposed in the corners two by two, each with its view of the woods, leaving the whole center open for an uplifting, brilliant foyer. Its stairway is made monumental by a beautiful box of cut-out inner walls, heroic arches and windows, and the light that pours in from a central lantern. The play of positive and negative shapes is exceedingly artful. The sensually rich color blending—of soft mauves and terra-cotta roses and cool grays—strikes me as flawless, the great spill of light as wonderfully high baroque. The nearest thing to it in Moore's *oeuvre* seems to be the biaxially symmetrical, neoclassical Rudolph house (1981) in Williamstown, Massachusetts, for which Robert Harper of MGH is now given primary credit. I have not yet been able to see it.

Coming at Sammis Hall for the first time, I was hit by it as by a bolt out of the fantasy past, a jewel box hidden in the Long Island woods, out of time and out of place. But I never felt it as funny or wrong, as some clever architect's private indulgence. Along with the Piazza d'Italia (and perhaps the Rodes house), it's Charles Moore's most nearly pure-art building, and yet in no way irresponsible. $375,000 for a sixteen-room Long Island guest house was still a bargain in 1981.

20/TWO RECENT HOUSES

I N 1979, Carol Phelan, the wife of a Chicago attorney, was enrolled in the architecture program of the University of Illinois's Chicago Circle campus. She asked Dick Whitaker (head of the program, as well as a friend and former neighbor) if he would design a house for her family. Her husband had discovered, while jogging past it one morning, a $220,000 waterfront lot for sale in Winnetka, with a great cliffside view of Lake Michigan. Whitaker professed to be uneasy about working for friends and begged off. Then Mrs. Phelan heard a joint presentation given by all four former partners in MLTW in the Graham Foundation lecture series. She was so impressed that she went back to Whitaker and asked if perhaps all *four* of them might get together once more, to design a house to fit this impressive piece of property.

And so (at Whitaker's urging) they did. It was to be like all those Beatles reunion concerts that never took place. Lyndon and Turnbull came out to look at the site. Whitaker coordinated operations. In August of 1979 all four of the celebrated Sea Ranch initials (plus Dick Peters) gathered in Turnbull's San Francisco waterfront office, worked for three hours in the morning, broke for lunch, then worked again till six. At the end of the day, they had a house.

"It was like the old days on Heinz Avenue," Whitaker says happily. "All four of us drawing and redrawing on rolls of yellow tracing paper." After four more hours drafting the next morning, they met with the Phelans at ten, and the couple liked what they saw.

"The marvelous moment came that second morning," says Moore. "We had sat around the day before and talked about what shape it might take, and come to what seemed like some very casual agreements. Then we all went off to a nice Chinese dinner.

"The next day we started very early, about six, because the Phelans had a plane to catch. I drew the plans, and Turnbull drew the site plans, and Lyndon drew the elevations, and Whitaker drew the sections. We didn't even look at each other's stuff—more than a little bit—and yet we were all drawing the same house! It was almost uncanny. Because we hadn't done anything, all four of us together, in it must have been fifteen years."

Plans moved immediately into the preliminary design stage, with Carol Phelan later helping to "rethink and fine tune" them, Turnbull's office handling specifications, and Whitaker, in Chicago, running the job.

There followed a couple of years of the usual homebuilder's griefs—hardware that didn't arrive, light fixtures that didn't fit. When I visited the Phelans in June 1981, many rooms were still only partially furnished, and the incomplete landscaping in front (a feature Bill Turnbull regarded as essential) left this costly house looking rather raw from the street, too visibly close to its neighbors.

Like a lot of staged celebrity reunions, this one turned out to be something of a disappointment. I didn't stay very long, and the day was dreadfully humid. But although I could spot the four architects' fingerprints all over the design, I felt the absence of any real electricity, of the magical unifying concepts that illuminated all their work in the early 1960s.

The most notable thing about the Phelan house is a set of broad, processional stairs which runs through the center of the house, lighted by large windows and wall cuts high above. (The spaces over the entry and stairwell are kept open up through two or three floors.) These stairs shift in width, axis, and finally direction, turning back on themselves after descending in easy stages past living room, past lake-viewing deck, to reach the children's bedrooms and family room down below. High walls are left open to allow one to enjoy the elegant fall and turns of this careful cascade of polished wood.

Large windows seem to be punched haphazardly in both south and north facades (a disconcerting design feature of several recent Turnbull and Lyndon houses). Windows look through to other windows (via wall cuts and lattice), doors are made of glass, the broad blue horizon of the lake is unavoidable. By means of high dormer windows, a long slide of outdoor stairs, a sequence of broad decks, a latticed belvedere with hammock, and a winding path down through the trees to a lakeshore gazebo and the beach, Lake Michigan (which is not the world's most exciting spread of water) totally dominates much of one's experience of the house.

Apart from the many-leveled splendors of the central stairs, and a few probably satisfying nooks, the spaces of the house seemed to me uncommonly ordinary—flat-ceilinged cubes decorated with expensive good taste (beige wall-to-wall carpets, creamy marble fireplace walls, a potted tree in the master bedroom), rendered more provocative than they really are by Dick Peters's hidden light sources and Tina Beebe's warm and subtle colors.

Even the boys' trademarks—the visible level changes, the cut-out walls, the caves and bays and belvederes, the frantic fenestration—seemed to lack the aptness, the unified necessity of the best of their early houses. Maybe you can't buy back a golden age—or force a miracle to happen in a day and a half. Then again, maybe I should try the Phelan house again, fully furnished and landscaped, on a cooler, drier day.

CHARLES MOORE'S most lavish house commission to date was completed in 1981, at a cost of more than $1.5 million. It came to him in an unusual way. Gerald D. Hines, the flashy Houston developer and builder, had purchased one of the continent's dream home-building sites, at the convergence of two creeks in Aspen, Colorado, with tall evergreens all around and the Rockies for a backdrop. He went to Philip Johnson (who had designed skyscraper offices for him) and asked whom he should get to design a new vacation pad. Johnson proposed a panel of three: Charles Moore, Michael Graves, or Charles Gwathmey. Gwathmey declined to do a house, so Mr. Hines held a minicompetition between the other two. He flew Moore and Graves out to the site, commissioned two sets of drawings, and in October 1978, decided to build Moore's. Or rather, Moore and Turnbull's: warned by Philip Johnson of Moore's much-divided attention and his reputation for running off, Hines insisted that Bill Turnbull's dependable San Francisco office share with Moore responsibility for both designing the building and seeing it through to completion.

Michael Graves's formal, geometrical designs altogether ignored one dominating feature of the landscape—a splendid forty-foot Engelmann's spruce. Moore and Turnbull, on the other hand, took this tree as their *donnée* and designed the whole house around it. This immense house, accommodated under one great sloping, sheltering roof, has been virtually eaten into to form a courtyard for the great tree. The tree looms over the property from a distance and continues to assert its central presence as you arrive at the carefully hidden drive and move closer into the court.

This is a complicated house, but a coherent and workable one. In the plan, one can trace a twisting stepped corridor that rises and falls around the *inside* of the multifaceted spruce-tree courtyard. This forms the house's second major design motif, and one of its uniquely seductive spatial experiences. Moving up to the living room and dining room, then down to the den and guest bedrooms, you walk inside a high processional space of perfectly matched golden brown woods, lighted as in a dream by high tree-viewing, sun-trapping windows, and an extraordinary series of etched and leaded art-glass panels with wavelike patterns and emerald inserts. Overhead, as you approach the living room, there appears a mad-looking set of trusses and beams. The steep tent of the ceiling is in fact demarcated and decorated by an essentially nonfunctional array of stenciled, parallel "free rafters" in green and large rolling trusses in Pompeian red. The furnishing of the split-level room is luxurious, impeccably suave, and incredibly expensive. The fireplace boasts a huge copper hood; high dormer niches admit the only east light permitted by Colorado's energy-saving codes. The "back" view is out a grand set of Palladian windows to the convergence of the creeks.

To the side, the dining area and kitchen are set off and enclosed by their own similar but smaller-scaled interior pergola and trellis. Beyond the kitchen, stairs descend to a comfortable breakfast room with its own view of the rushing waters. If you return to the ambling, circuitous step corridor, with its astonishing gallery of glass, you descend next to a lower-level, high-ceilinged den, past a comic, make-believe moosehead built and donated by Charles W. Moore.

The master-bedroom wing, which lies to the other side of and below the dining room, is predictably luxurious, with its own split levels, fine woods, woodburning stove, and a private view of the waters. (Unfortunately, the Hineses, like so many of Moore's clients—the Mattersons, Talberts, Johnsons, Sterns, Shinefields, Koizims, Slaters—have split up since their house was designed.) The palatial guest bedrooms each have their own views and fine woods and custom-made quilts and fourposter beds. The rear of the house, quite surprisingly, has a nearly symmetrical facade, in gray-colored stucco, as opposed to the warm redwood and wildly asymmetrical plan and fenestration of the front. It overlooks a hot tub and terraced gardens, down to the fork of the streams. When I visited it with him, Bill Turnbull was planning to plant five hundred wild daffodils and narcissus.

I like this best of all Moore and Turnbull's great houses, in great part because of the exquisite finesse of its woodwork and detailing. I love the symphonic play of light and space, the tangible unity of the design, the great roof, the rising and falling staircase-hall, the beautiful openwork pergola over the dining area, almost every aspect of the furnishing and decoration. My only reservation concerns those big rosy soft-edged trusses—which go nowhere visually, set up a rhythm that is abruptly cut off, and look too obviously joky for so sweetly reasonable a building: a Moore gesture, perhaps, in a Turnbull space. And I'm not quite certain that the plain painted "outside house" ever worked out its juncture with the dazzling, many-edged redwood of the cut-out spruce-tree court.

One's major quarrel with the house, I suppose, might be socioeconomic rather than aesthetic. Do you or do you not believe in the rightness of putting this much time, effort, money, genius, and craftsmanship into one rich man's extravagant vacation home? In the end I decided that if I could take the stately homes of England, or the residences that earlier American architects like Richard Morris Hunt, Frank Lloyd Wright, Bernard Maybeck, and the Greene brothers designed for their wealthier clients, I could live with Gerry Hines's breathtaking pleasure dome in Aspen.

21 / NEW ORLEANS TODAY

S INCE the Piazza d'Italia fountain was finished in 1978, most of Charles Moore's work with Perez Associates in New Orleans has been directed toward portions of the Louisiana World Exposition for 1984. He has also served as consulting architect on two other Perez–UIG collaborations—one for a city park in Gulfport, Mississippi, alongside a new Perez office building; the other for an exuberant hotel remodeling in Natchez.

Moore's fondness for New Orleans is of long standing. He likes its cultural mix, its fine little old buildings, its restaurants, and its air of overripeness verging on corruption. Considering that, and the atmosphere of productive concord and mutual respect that has surrounded his dealings with Perez, there are likely to be more collaborations in the future.

The Gulfport project, completed in 1981, is collaboration so intimate it looks almost like copulation. Moore's sinuous, wriggling park penetrates the stable and upright effort of the Perez regulars, mocking and enhancing it at once.

For a local banker, Allen Eskew of Perez designed the most impressive office building in Gulfport, a hot, slow-moving port city of forty thousand. Fifteen stories of offices, faced with limestone and windowed with reflective glass, were carefully set on top of a three-story "renaissance" base, with elegantly laid brick courses and large, round-arched windows and doors.

Half the remainder of the block was given over to a multistory parking garage. Ivy crawls up the grooves of its scored-concrete walls, which is not a bad way to hide a parking garage. The railing of the uppermost parking level—a Moore and Filson idea—is designed as a colossal section of classical molding, its rolls painted soft mauve, pale blue, and white.

The other quarter of the block was Charles's to play with. Further to civilize the Perez office's already civilized bank building and garage, and to wake up a sleepy downtown, he designed a small city park largely composed of three elements: first, a shallow pond, ambling freely about, with its edges cut to an angular approximation of the Mississippi gulf coastline; second, a metal-trellised walkway covered with wisteria, which bends along the shoreline of the pond, then marches right into the rear of the bank building's lobby and out the other side; and third, a broad, sloping greensward in front of the parking garage, on which he set a two-dimensional house facade in a grove of trees. ("What's *that* for?" asked his banker client. "To make a secret place," Moore helpfully replied.) This simplified concrete wall, with square and arched openings, recalls many detached and punctured stage-set facades Moore and his colleagues have designed. It comments with amusement on the garage wall behind it; it led my imagination off to southern Civil War ruins. Some of the wit and allusion in this Mississippi stroll garden may be more sophisticated than its users require. But Moore was delighted to learn that two workmen were seen identifying their favorite fishing spots along his imaginary coast.

The shaped pond, edged in white marble and dark terrazzo, is related to the map-of-Italy contours of St. Joseph's Fountain. The trellised promenade idea can be seen in the Empress's Walk at the fair. The design of this trellis (mainly by Ron Filson) is particularly witty and seductive. It imagined a hood of greenery before the vines even grew, and formed a shady tunnel out of space. Its path along the water's edge is marked by sixty green metal poles that fan out at the top, like upended lawn rakes. The upper corners of these are joined, either transversely (forming overhead arches) or at angles, by flat, arc-shaped pieces of metal. To the radiating struts of both the fan-shaped capitals and the round-topped arches have been welded beautiful cut-out green metal filigree in an abstract leaf pattern, over which now twines the live wisteria.

I visited Gulfport on a day so hot few chose to amble or pause. The wisteria hadn't grown enough to offer much shade, the pond water was dirty, and most people were avoiding the circuitous path of the garden for more direct routes. But the little park is alive with bright remarks, and the trellised walk along the water is a beautiful thing.

THE remodeling of the Natchez Eola Hotel (1980–82) was another of Perez's downtown high-rise jobs for a small, wealthy southern city, where Charles Moore was brought in to provide magic. The result is the most delightful of the many period hotel restorations undertaken in the United States in recent years, intended to win back to center cities travelers who have begun to tire of Ramada Inns along the highway and to hunger for more elegance, better service, and a denser sense of history. Most of these endeavors (a great number of them have been in the South) take the proud path of total restoration. Murals are repainted, gold leaf is reapplied to moldings and ceilings, stained glass is repaired, hand-sewn carpets are replaced, brass hardware and hardwood floors are polished and repolished. New stone "from the original quarry" is cut. "Exact copies" of old moldings are made to restore facades and grand foyers. Worldwide searches are made for authentic 1920 chandeliers. If need be, *imitation* 1890 salons are created. The results can be Stately Home Spectacular and are much admired by tourists and the National Trust. But they don't call for much imagination on the part of the architect or allow today to impinge in any visible way on this fantasy of yesterday.

The Eola Hotel in Natchez was an L-shaped, seven-story building fronting on two streets, embracing with its brick-faced wings two other lower commercial buildings at the corner of Main Street and Pearl. The social center of this oil-rich, historic Mississippi River town from 1927 until the 1960s, it fell into decay along with the rest of downtown, and was closed in 1976.

Forrest Germany, a young oil man from Dallas who has known and loved Natchez for twenty years (and now owns a fair piece of it), bought the abandoned hotel for a bargain $135,000. He remembered staying there with his father, Norman Germany, during oil-surveying trips in the 1950s, and decided the time was ripe to bring back the past. Having succeeded at the Eola, the Germanys are now gradually restoring Main Street as well. With more historic houses open to the public than most cities ten times its size, little Natchez has become a tourist boom town, with the Germanys—and the redoubtable garden-club ladies who run the house tours—sitting pretty at the center. "Antebellum is real big here, sir," the hotel manager assured me. "Real, real big."

Perez Associates (Allen Eskew was project director) redid 108 guest rooms, leaving the marble in the bathrooms, adding old-fashioned ceiling fans and imitation antiques, and repainting the hotel in chic lavender and pink colors that appalled Mr. Germany. The owners also bought a brick-and-columned mansion across the street, to serve as an annex to the hotel, with *real* antiques in rooms at premium prices. Mr. Germany's niece, Debbie Forrest from Dallas, was hired as a special decorating consultant. Charles Moore's tastes are certainly unpredictable; but I assume that the virile hunting prints, the velvet valences and tasseled swags, and the rose-flowered upholstery fabrics in the lobby are Miss Forrest's contribution.

Along with the old hotel (which retains its old brick-and-stone facades) and the postbellum guest house, the new owners also bought the two corner buildings, gutted one for more rooms, and tore down the other to form a new entrance court on Pearl Street. It's in this court that Charles Moore made most of his contributions.

Moore's central new-old image for the Eola (as in a great deal of his recent work) is a classical, semicircle-topped arch. As you enter the walled courtyard, brick-paved and full of greenery, a white three-story wall punctured with arches and arch fragments (carved out of the old Levy Building) rises to your left. One giant arched wall cut opens two levels of corridors to the air. Directly ahead of you, at the seventh-floor level of the old hotel's west wing, three oversized and elegantly detailed round-topped dormers rise over the new mansard roof. The largest of the three, a blind (windowless) dormer at the Main Street end, simply marks the top of the fire stairs. (Exploring to discover what wonders lay beneath it, I got locked in and had to walk down seven flights.) The two adjacent dormers, with the same thick moldings, central keystone, elaborate cornices and consoles, surround large arched windows. These, I presumed, must look out from splendid suites or lounges. But they simply illuminate the corridor of the new seventh-floor mansard and provide the Natchez Eola with an unmistakable postmodern classical image.

The entrance to the hotel is through a gable-roofed, green wood-and-glass aedicule, like a small guardhouse or chapel, with a glazed-arch doorway whose mullions intersect into more arching forms. Projecting into the garden court is Moore's most significant contribution to the reborn hotel: a conservatory-restaurant under a steep, single-slope roof, enclosed on three sides by faceted walls of glass, and on the fourth (the interior) side by high, deep-cut rose-colored arches off the hotel's central hall. On the interior, this wonderful restaurant uses cool, smoky colors (pearl gray, gray rose, gray blue, a softer blue) to receive and reflect the light that pours in on all sides.

In addition to the glass walls, there are also six square skylights (between more Old South ceiling fans), a high triangular dormer, and a very attractive play of artificial light. The framing and detailing of the glass walls became an elaborate series of variations on the classic southern rising-sun fanlight. The central arc and projecting rays of the fanlight take on different shapes and proportions as the wall sizes change. The effect is at once Natchez traditional, ingenious, and fun.

Up on the seventh floor, this motif provides the central feature of a riverview cocktail lounge. Radiating mullions spread out of two concentric arches, through three adjacent windows, from a twelve-foot-square central sunrise design. The whole affords a stunning prospect across Natchez to (at least at sunset) the silvered Mississippi, the light of Louisiana, and a flaming orange sky. The sensitive tea-rose/terra-cotta/deep-green coloring of this room, with its excellent modern versions of classical moldings, is Miss Forrest's work rather than Mr. Moore's, and worthy of high praise. Fortunes have been spent elsewhere redecorating hotel restaurants and bars, often to execrable effect. The downstairs restaurant and the upstairs lounge at the Natchez Eola (I have mixed feelings about the lobby—except for a nice latticed summerhouse built inside it—and the new Café La Salle) are definitely worth the trip, and the Germanys' $9 million investment.

ANOTHER elegant old-new hotel, not unlike the Natchez Eola, has—as I mentioned—been designed to embrace (and, one hopes, enliven) the Piazza d'Italia. Bill Hersey's renderings show a four-story, two-hundred-room building with an open fourth-floor gallery amid shuttered windows, some with awnings. The walls are colored Vieux Carré rose. A glassed-in conservatory restaurant, like the Eola's, projects into the piazza from the west. But it was designed by Dan Donovan of Perez, not by Moore; the latter, to his chagrin, was not even consulted on the design. And as of this writing, no investor had agreed to undertake it.

Earlier, in 1980, Charles Moore had drawn up plans to fill in the southeast corner of the piazza block with a building for the Italian-American Renaissance Foundation, an offshoot of Joe Maselli's consortium of twenty-three Italian-American organizations in the southeastern United States. His building, borrowing motifs from authentic Italian Renaissance palazzi, would have housed offices (including the local Italian consulate), library, museum, and ballroom. (It was designed in conjunction with Saputo and Rowe, of New Orleans.) Eight stone busts of local Italian leaders were to stand on the exterior walls. A wrought-iron "ducal balcony" would have ornamented the center of the St. Peter's Street facade, in front of a monumental window not unlike the Lafayette Street arch. On Lafayette Street, five large classically detailed windows were to have been surrounded by red, white, and green bands of tile, directly connected to similar Italian-flag bands on the adjacent arch and along the east side.

Inside, a grand staircase was to lead to a ballroom twenty-four feet high behind the great windows, with arches, pilasters, a pedimented entry, a frescoed ceiling, and nude statues. At one point Moore proposed casting the statues live from the more attractive sons and daughters of the local Italian community.

While no doubt fun to design, the building probably had about as much chance of getting built as one of Charles's more fanciful drawings, despite the enthusiasm and fund-raising abilities of Mr. Maselli and his friends.

UNLIKE more sober and permanent structures, the temporary settings for fantasy (stage sets, movie sets, party decors) can go on being designed up to the very moment they're built. So although I am writing this just one year before the 1984 Louisiana World Exposition is scheduled to open, neither the architects nor I know for certain what it is going to look like.

But a number of things *are* fixed. Some of them are the same as, some quite different from, what we saw emerging from the design session of January 1982, described back in chapter 1.

As a rule, I try to resist judging too confidently projects still unbuilt. A great deal can happen between the pencil and the laid-in-place brick. But, since there's a chance that the Moore–Turnbull contributions to the New Orleans fair will result in work as memorable and important as anything they've done, I'll risk describing their designs for the fair as of spring 1983.

It has been decided that the Wonderwall, born at the Sea Ranch design session, will be the central design feature of the fair—along with not one but *two* festive entry colonnades and lagoons the Moore–Turnbull group is designing. (Plans for a 300-foot Tower of New Orleans at the end of the Julia Street axis, where the theme building was originally to have gone, have been abandoned. An aerial gondola ride will ferry passengers, suspended 350 feet high, across the river from the foot of Poydras Street.)

A great deal of the fair's design (including most of the permanent structures) remain in the hands of other men. Both the huge new $92 million civic Exhibition Center with its glass sawtooth-section roof (during the fair it will house the Louisiana Pavilion and other state and industrial exhibits), and the two-story steel-and-concrete International Pavilion which stretches along the riverfront, are being designed by other groups at Perez Associates. These are both to be straightforward modern structures, with no hint of historicism or fantasy in their design. The renovation of 250,000 square feet of existing warehouses on the site into restaurants, shops, and exhibit areas, though a more obviously past-related project, is also out of Moore's hands. After the fair is over, the Rouse Company of Maryland is planning to build a permanent Harbor Place waterfront mall, along the lines of their popular developments in Boston, New York, and Baltimore. Frank Gehry of Los Angeles has designed a riverside amphitheater. Ian Mc-Naughton of New Orleans, in conjunction with Cooper–Lecky of Washington, designed the large United States Pavilion at the southeast corner of the site. The Vatican has been permitted to erect a pavilion of its own (in God only knows what style). Separate industrial pavilions—the imagined "corporate turds" from which Moore and Turnbull kept cringing—will be designed and built by the exhibitors' own choice of architects. Peter Spurney, grand vizier of the whole exposition, must approve all designs. But his tastes are not necessarily Moore's, and he is not likely to say no to many major exhibitors. So something of the "chaos of Brussels" may still appear in certain areas.

Eight major rides, like Disneyland E-ticket adventures, will be positioned in various places about the eighty-two-acre site. The Louisiana Pavilion, in fact, is being designed (by Metaform of Cambridge) as one big Pirates of the Caribbean sail-through excursion. These may come closer in spirit to the efforts of the Moore–

Turnbull atelier. A 180-foot Ferris wheel and a Magic Carpet ride were in fact incorporated into their wall. But the design of these rides will be left to the international engineers and theme-park magnates who specialize in such things.

Moore–Turnbull's specific contributions add up to only about one-eighth the cost of all of Perez Associates' work on the fair (between $10 and $12 million of their $80 million plus). Even so, I think it likely that they will so dominate the fairgoer's visual and imaginative experience that they *will* have created its most enduring image. Because of the unifying force and high visionary power of their designs, and some ingenious site planning by Perez, the Louisiana World Exposition of 1984 seems to me more likely to be remembered as a distinctive and pleasurable architectural event than any other world's fair of the past forty-five years.

The Wonderwall—which has now grown to 2,300 feet long—begins, as planned, at the north entry loop, fills up the whole twenty-two-foot median strip (or "neutral ground," as New Orleanians call it) of Front Street, and extends to the south entrance arcade. Here it bends toward the river and ends with a loop about the Ferris wheel. (This has been relocated from its earlier site. There is no longer a "matching" carousel, but the curve of the Wonderwall here creates something of the same visual effect.)

The Wonderwall, you may recall, began with Moore's fantasy of squeezed-together, mock-historical architectural fragments, in the manner of Piranesi's busy engraving, "Idee delle Antiche Vie Appia e Ardeatina." Since January 1982, the original scheme has lost its specific historical references, but gained in both coherence and wonderfulness.

It is built around a simple concrete "tunnel"—a long roof slab set on columns, ten feet wide and nearly half a mile long. After every twenty-four running feet of this there occurs a modular, ten-foot-square unit, which houses a fountain or similar special event. On top of and alongside this concrete base rises a metal scaffolding. And attached to the scaffolding is a spectacular array of fantastic facades—the wall itself.

These facades—six inches thick, and prefabricated of perforated or corrugated sheet metal on simple steel frames—are composed of twenty-four discrete forms, combined and repeated in hundreds of variations and prepainted in a dreamlike variety of confectionary colors: magic purples and lavenders above, lemon yellows and soft blues in the middle, greens and grays below. The lights (here and throughout the fairgrounds) were designed by Dick Peters: sparkling jewel clusters combined with overall washes of glowing color, a blend of the styles of the 1915 and 1939 San Francisco fairs. The architects opted for metal (rather than wood and plaster) construction in order to simplify erection, to allow for the possibility of waterfalls down the sides, and to fit in with—rather than fight or try to hide—the giant power-line pylons that march down the street.

The catalogue of twenty-four wall elements does have a few historical referents. It includes openwork aviaries like those of the Villa Borghese in Rome, shaped like the Farnese pavilions on the Palatine. There are also a puffy Arabian Nights turban dome; lacy latticework "tree domes" formed by intersecting two-dimensional units (one of Kent Bloomer's contributions); flat sections of arcading in several different configurations (Venetian, palm tree, Art Deco); a round-domed tempietto; and a demountable classic facade, the wings of which can be pulled apart and replaced by alligators rampant. (Louisiana bayou alligators crawl all over the wall, leaping out in sparkling, scary silhouette, holding up roofs. A thirty-foot monster made of gilded sandbags crawls through the tunneling base.)

But the separate elements that make up the wall remind me of nothing so much as those wonderful fantasy kingdoms Charles Moore has been drawing on his Christmas cards and gift sketches for many years. A fair being a fair, and not the troublesome real world, he has finally had the chance to build one full size.

Almost every Christmas, his fantasy drawings included elevations of impossibly top-heavy towers, the uppermost level wider than the next below, and so on and so on down, each level pierced by open arches, the whole crowned by a steep dome or turret and a long flapping banner. That, in fact, will be the tallest of the twenty-four elements (fifty feet from base to banner), allowable only when the looping high-tension power lines rise high enough to permit it. Many of his imaginary rock islands included at least one pavilion perched out on an impossibly cantilevered set of high unsupported stairs, where imaginary Isoldes could scan the seas for their imaginary Tristans. These will form the other dominant element of the wall. A six-inch-thick purple-painted flat on aluminum studs can defy some of the apparent laws of statics.

Kent Bloomer, the sculptor who was Moore's co-teacher and fellow fantasist at Yale, came up with the idea of constructing the Wonderwall so that the lowest level, where people will walk through, under, and along (as well as sit, shop, and watch parades), represented a realm of darkness, something damp and subterranean. "Its quality," he wrote, "should be dripping, squooshy, haptic, powerful, weird, out-of-scale (sometimes oversized, sometimes undersized for children and miniature creatures), earthy in color with purple and neon accents, etc." Here are built fake-stone grottoes, shady seats, tropical plantations, and plenty of fountains. (The linear aqueduct up above was lost to practical considerations.) Mock alligators, chameleons, pelicans, and similar creatures parade between refreshment stands and souvenir stalls.

The middle range, atop the concrete tunnel—visible, but generally inaccessible (the monorail that runs through the fairgrounds is now also separate from the wall)—represents earthly kingdoms. Here rise the make-believe castle walls and arcades and porches and steps in bright colors, with colossal Mardi-Gras-float heads and limbs populating their imaginary rooms, and artificial as well as real flowers and foliage decorating the scaffolds.

The high skyline of the Wonderwall, far over visitors' heads, represents the celestial kingdom: glittery spires and domes and towers, gold and silver banners and balloons, angels and stars, twittering birds in aviary domes.

Handed Bloomer's ideas and Moore's twenty-four easy pieces (I oversimplify design credit), Leonard Salvato and Arthur Anderson first built a white cardboard model of the whole wall at one-eighth-inch scale (which made it twenty-four feet long). This allowed the team to decide how all these units would be multiplied, divided, and disposed. They then built a gorgeously detailed model at four times that scale, representing two long sections of the wall. These were each about five feet long and two feet high, and built out of actual little metal studs and screen walls. They were colored according to Tina Beebe's scheme, and lighted according to Dick Peters's, with thirteen hundred tiny twinkling bulbs. They included intricate filigree domes, silvered busts, fountains, feathers, alligators, balloons, and pelicans decorating the landings and arcades of their little linear magic kingdoms.

Given the irrational intricacy of the Wonderwall—for all its prefab simplicity—Perez is allowing the Moore–Turnbull team to dispense with complete working drawings. Instead they can (to a degree) instruct the men erecting it directly on the site, like medieval master builders, changing their minds about placement and color as they (and the builders) see fit—another of Charles Moore's dreams come true.

The main (north) entrance lagoon is smaller than it was in the 1982 plans, but it retains the same configuration and shoreline. The covered Empress's Walk still skirts the northern shoreline, and the river-god pavilions—deprived of their deities—still surround the lake, all as planned in January 1982. Moore's and Anderson's idea of building these pavilions in different sizes, then positioning them so they would all line up in perspective from a single viewing point near the entrance, has been retained, but improved on. After experimenting with a number of configurations inside peephole box models, the team hit on the recherché notion of having the pavilions come together (visually) to form an image of the main building of the *1884* New Orleans fair—a typical Second Empire pile of high decorated windows and steep mansard roofs. So now the seven lakeshore pavilions—the nearest ones tiny shelters, the distant ones large enough to accommodate brass bands or cafés—compose (when seen from the Instamatic aedicule) into the central entrance, two side towers, two wings, and two end pavilions of a make-believe Victorian manor.

At the south entrance, the Apollonian calm of the Empress's Walk, the Mississippi Trevi (should it stay in), and these Beaux Arts pavilions is replaced by a Dionysiac frenzy. Wild and passionate deities (and alligators and mermaids) leap out, made of metal mesh and live plants. A covered Cajun Walk leads you past jungly bayous. Water squirts out at visitors unexpectedly, the way it did in many seventeenth- and eighteenth-century noblemen's gardens. A spectacular entry structure of Louisiana filigree trusses converges on a mirror-faceted disco ball twelve feet in diameter. In place of the open Roman rotunda through which visitors pass at the north end, the designers seized for their south entry on a local motif. Twenty-two freestanding Corinthian columns on high pedestals (with pineapple-and-pelican capitals) are a tribute to the ruins of Windsor Plantation near Lorman, Mississippi, built in 1860 and burned in 1890. (At the ruins, the columns form a rectangle; here, a circle.) As I write, the exact form of both entry rotundas is still being debated. There will probably be boat rides or concessions of some sort (or performers on barges) using the lagoons and canals. But that too remains to be determined.

No visitor to the New Orleans fair will be able to ignore the Moore–Turnbull fantasy world. On a grander (if less permanent) scale than ever before—and in plain view of 10 to 15 million people—Charles Moore has been able to make some of his wildest architectural dreams come true.

UNEASY associates in Los Angeles persist in fearing that Charles Moore will soon transfer his "permanent" base to the Crescent City, extracting himself from the responsibilities of his own growing fame and financial success at both Los Angeles offices, as well as from his UCLA post. Dean Filson—his former student, protégé, and associate—would, they suspect, be happy to offer him a comparable teaching position at Tulane. Arthur Anderson and Leonard Salvato, according to this scenario, would play the same roles that Grover and Harper or Ruble and Yudell did earlier and elsewhere, and provide Moore with the eager and able young partners he always likes to work with. He would have a desirable old house to play with in the French Quarter and someone to share the problems of keeping it up. For any larger projects he undertook, Perez Associates would be as secure as the mint. Designing first the Piazza d'Italia fountain, then a major portion of the world's fair with their leading firm of architects has already made Charles Moore a considerable celebrity in New Orleans.

But unless serious illness (or some comparable crisis) should intervene, no base for Moore is likely to be more than a temporary perch. His commitments, like his interests, are global. Moving from Los Angeles to New Orleans would probably only mean that he ended up using one airport more than another.

22 / LOS ANGELES TODAY

AFTER the attention gained by his first few southern California projects, Moore's activity in Los Angeles fell into something of a slump. A few costly houses ended up bland or compromised. He and his two offices entered and lost several competitions.

Then, in 1979, Seen Leong Kwee, a wealthy Singapore developer, hired Moore Ruble Yudell to design him a house—for Singapore. (His younger brother, a Cornell architecture graduate, had worked in the MRY office.) The elegant, exotic result, still incomplete as of late 1982, combined a conceptual plan of the most rigorous formal symmetry (eight interlocking rectangles, broken here and there for courtyards and terraces) with fantasies of tropical hedonism.

At the center of the house is a fifteen-by-forty-foot atrium largely given over to a decorative pool filled with fish and tropical plants. It is surrounded by landscaped peninsulas and a lounging terrace under arcades. This interior courtyard rises two stories; grids of wooden latticework fill the upper parts of its side walls, and the roofpeak dissolves into trellis. Lush vines (in the drawings) grow through and over its wood members. At either end of the court one looks through arched and square cutouts in gabled screen walls to still other screen walls and windows beyond. The arches and latticework at the sides also reveal further layers of punctured wall.

This air-cooling courtyard—the innermost of the eight rectangles—is flanked on the south by a broad, stepped entrance court (the whole house sits on a podium) and a long living room; on the north by a formal dining room, kitchen, and servant's quarters. Beyond the pair of screen walls on the east end lies the intellectual center of the house, a symmetrical library with two-story Palladian arches on all four walls. Its upper gallery leads directly to the large, irregular master-bedroom suite.

An asymmetrical private courtyard, open to the sky through latticed holes in the roof, divides this, the formal half of the house, from the two-level family quarters behind it. These contain children's and guest bedrooms downstairs, the master suite (with its two side balconies) above.

The outer form of the house is a simple gabled box with wide overhanging eaves, varied and eaten into when appropriate. The wide overhangs, the trellised roof cuts, the central pool, the essentially closed outer walls are all concessions to equatorial heat and humidity. Outside, a circular dining pavilion sits on a peninsula in the middle of a tiny lagoon, looking across to a classical round tempietto which houses the Kwees' prize dogs.

The apparent formality of this large complex is modulated not only by such self-indulgent gestures, but also by a color plan as subtle and mood enhancing as anything Tina Beebe has ever done. It includes a different tone for the inside and the outside of each of the eight conceptual rectangles, moving from pale blue green at the central pool and blue gray at the library (each "cooler" on the inside wall than on the out) to peaches and yellows and browns as you move toward the outside. (To break the pastel tranquility, trellises and trim are painted in brighter versions of the colors of their rooms.) My research budget didn't reach to Singapore, so I can't quite imagine the sum effect of all this lavish refinement. But plans, models, and sketches evoke something quite wonderful indeed.

Once the house was under way, Mr. Kwee (who has built, among other things, a John Portman hotel in Singapore and has courted other name architects) commissioned from Moore Ruble Yudell plans for several urban-design-competition projects in Singapore, none of which has come to be. They included a fifty-foot square Palladian building, which was to go on the same block as a giant I. M. Pei ice-cube-tray high-rise (the small parcel went to Pei also); a sixteen-story condominium; an "inside-out pyramid garden" (i.e., a block with a pyramid gouged out); and the Forest Building, which looked, in some models and renderings, like one of Moore's more enchanting unbuilt works. Eleven stories tall, the interior of its entrance corner—behind glass—rose into an exotic atrium lobby the full height of the building. Every few floors as it rose, this inner opening was enlarged by setbacks, on which live palm trees were to grow (and multiply) before mirrored walls.

THE most significant completed project of Moore's two Los Angeles offices in recent years (as of 1983) is St. Matthew's Episcopal Church in Pacific Palisades. I have already described the participatory process—the St. Matthew Passion, Charles once called it—that led to this job's taking four years to complete. This—and more particularly the committee process that followed it—led to occasional bitterness, many design changes, and something less than a profit for Moore Ruble Yudell. Although none of them is a Christian believer, their first church obviously meant a great deal to Charles Moore and his partners. Distinguished modern architects (Wright, Aalto, Breuer, Le Corbusier) have often been measured by their response to this sublime and otherworldly challenge.

Although the sometimes bull-headed, sometimes picayune wrangling of parish participants meant that the finished design was going to be theirs no less than the architects'—in many ways conservative, perhaps compromised—Charles Moore, John Ruble, and Buzz Yudell all insist they are pleased with the result. "I'm *very* happy with the result," says Moore. "But I was extremely unhappy with some of the personal relationships. The workshop part was in my opinion a great success and did all the things it was supposed to—producing, I think, a distinguished scheme for a building. I think that's because everyone involved was creative, *doing* something they could put care and attention into, and they improved the building as they did. But the long, the *over*long building-committee process that followed turned many of these creative participants into critics. . . . Now we were in adversary roles. . . . I would try to be agreeable, and then when they'd ride roughshod over poor John, or behave meanly to Tina, I was called in to be Mister Tough Guy. And I got bored with that."

The exterior aspect is striking; possibly, if you care to read it that way, symbolic. Out of one of Charles Moore's most extensive, ground-hugging, California shingle roofs—the favored low-to-high, pyramidally converging slopes, eroded here and there for courtyards, tree holes, and the like—out of this rises, out of this in fact *bursts* a high, cross-gabled, cruciform church. Once planned for wood, it is now surfaced inside and out with plaster. The exterior is a dun adobe color that grows more tolerable in sunlight, and is carefully scored, as if with a ghost of pilasters and entablature. The high roof eaves are underlined with a fine, floating board. The lowest edge of the California roof is supported on fat wooden posts. Extending out to the south, they form an open-roofed pergola or entry porch, which—one day soon—will terminate in a simple belfry tower.

From end wall to end wall, the transept arm of the high structure is about eighty feet long. Each of its end walls is punctured by a high, plain circle of glass, casually intersected by the vertical wood strips that decorate all the interior walls. (Stained glass, one day, is to fill these modern rose windows.) Fore and aft in the nave arm— its dimensions are about thirty by seventy-five feet; the roofpeak is about forty feet from the floor—the gabled ends are fronted with freestanding steel arches, twenty feet up to the turn of the curve, enclosed each within a gabled bent. Although these do support roof trusses, they do not in fact touch the walls or ceiling. Instead, they serve primarily as great frames for the sanctuary at one end of the nave, the organ and choir ranks at the other—as well as hovering reminders of more classical church forms.

Perhaps the words "transept" and "nave" should be put inside quotation marks. From inside, you rarely read them as such, or even note the cruciform plan—unless you stand under the crossing and look *up*: up at the high roofs, with their exposed fir rafters and planking; up at the long steel truss of the transept arm; up at the intricate web of finger trusses directly overhead. But at ground level, the seating arrangement and the brilliant play of light are determined more by the lower, outward-sloping roofs, which are somewhat more ski-lodgey than ecclesiastical, and which give the church the shape (in plan) of a broad rectangle cut off at two corners. The pews, which dictated this shape, form an angled semicircular arc facing the altar.

This interplay of forms is not always coherent. Both inside and out, I felt a traditional, formal church trying to break out of a more casual and sheltering California space—which may be what St. Matthew's is.

The leftover spaces permitted by the large, lower tentlike roof allowed the architects to accommodate, off the wide ambulatory behind the pews, a light-filled side chapel, a baptistry-fountain, and a small off-center narthex or entry vestibule. The heavy-timbered pergola to the south is balanced by a tree-shaded courtyard to the north, tucked under a hole in the same sheltering roof. The low roof ambles around the side of and behind the church proper—always maintaining the proper slope—for sacristy, vestries, and the choir's practice room, built around a separate half-cloister.

Everywhere I felt the tension between ritual traditionalism and the casual California style, a tension not always or easily resolved. ("I'm not as worried as you are about the high-church/low-church compromise," Moore responded. "That's the nature of an Episcopal congregation.") If very little of the building (except the low spreading roof) "looks like" something by Charles Moore, it may be because so much of his effort was spent trying to accommodate these two concepts—both of them, in their different ways, stylistically conservative. It may also be because much of the design and detailing was the work of John Ruble and Buzz Yudell, as well as the building committee, vestry, rector, and parish. Outside, the suavely scored stucco walls sit a little uneasily between cedar shingles and the stout redwood posts. The interior walls, painted (after great debate) two different shades of dusty rose, are overlaid with vertical battens: interestingly milled wooden strips three feet apart that rise from floor to ceiling. These are then joined under the ceiling by little Ruskinian Gothic arches-under-gables, which look to me like a compromise on behalf of parishioners who insisted on more Gothic and more wood.

The church is paved in ruddy Mexican clay tiles, relieved by small shiny blue ceramic tiles set crosswise at occasional intersections. They would have been set at every intersection, but that cost too much. The blue tiles were to placate parishioners who thought that an all-Mexican floor would look too unspeakably Catholic. The interior woodwork—ceiling structure, deep window frames, vertical battens—is all exposed and unstained. Both these rustic features (clay tile floor, unstained wood) worried some parishioners. Both, I feel, *do* contribute to a lack of sensual and spiritual coherence in the church.

Very little in the church design, except the cross form overhead, addresses itself directly to anything one can regard as Catholic, Christian, or even particularly religious. But this may simply be the result of a southern California Episcopal parish defining itself. An impressive lineup of handsomely framed windows rises from the floor, set deeply back in the thick plastered walls. They bring in light and natural views from many angles—most notably a series on either side of the altar, decreasing in height and brightness as they approach the Holy Sacrament. But this seems primarily a concession to tree-loving pantheists. I have experienced more otherworldly feelings in many of Moore's secular buildings.

A large abstract Tree of Life (now *there's* a safe symbol!), nicely cut from flat layers of wood, serves as a reredos or screen behind the altar. It's a handsome thing and was the rector's own idea, but it reminded me more of the logo for a new tract of California ranchettes than of anything divine. Over the altar, hovering in space over the worshippers' heads, hangs a large, vaguely Celtic-looking cross, without a Christ; the donors disliked bodies on their crosses. ("I was very sad about losing that," said Moore.) A little river-of-life fountain trickles through the granite-block baptismal font. Four handsome Book of Kells–type evangelists are inset in the entry doors. (They were once intended, in much larger scale, to take the place of the big oak-tree cutout behind the altar. I wish they had.) The small, off-center entrance has been enhanced by other discreet features, but it still seems an unhappy compromise. The $200,000 organ, for which much of this $1.8 million church was designed, demanded axial pride of place.

The things that disappoint me in St. Matthew's Church (a confusion of aim, a certain shallowness of faith) may well be radical characteristics in its congregation, perfectly realized by their architects. The concept (and aspect) of two imploding symbolic forms remains apt and impressive, from both inside and out. Many of the simplified traditional elements Moore Ruble Yudell devised—the purified rose windows, the freestanding nave arches, the finger trusses of the crossing (which look like a modern *memory* of rib vaulting or fan tracery)—seem thoughtful solutions for a new building designed to serve ancient purposes.

MORE important than St. Matthew's Church may be three large-scale projects now on the boards at Moore's two Los Angeles offices. There is good reason to believe that all three will be completed, in one form or another. They will compel critics to make a major reassessment of Moore's style, work methods, and capabilities. Already they have forced a reorganization of his offices and his working life.

The Internationale Bauaustellung Berlin 1984 (1984 Berlin Building Authority) was the dream child of Joseph Paul Kleihues, a noted architect, critic, and professor who wanted to turn forty different pieces of West Berlin over to leading architects, both German and foreign, in order to demonstrate what exciting things were happening in the architecture of the 1980s. At the same time, he hoped, this would help pull West Berlin out of a slough of substandard housing that had persisted since the war. Earlier IBA programs, in 1933 and 1957, had stressed radical, avant-garde redesign. This was intended to be a more modest postmodern, past-respecting effort.

Competitions were held in 1980 and 1981 for all forty projects. But many of the winners submitted things so far out that no politician or developer would touch them. Then the Berlin senate and individual town councils, suffering from political and economic problems of their own, backed out of major participation.

So most of IBA Berlin 1984 remains paper architecture. Kleihues and his Authority were left with a very few sites over which they retained control and on which they could still hope to cultivate innovative and attention-getting projects. Even so, the finalists asked to draw up plans for these sites included some of the world's best-known postmodern experimenters: Carlo Aymonino, Mario Botta, Peter Eisenman, Ralph Erskine, Vittorio Gregotti, Arata Isozaki, Rem Koolhaas, Rob Krier, Kisho Kurokawa, Aldo Rossi, Peter and Alison Smithson, James Stirling—and Charles Moore.

Charles Moore claims to have been flabbergasted when he learned that the Moore Ruble Yudell plans for the Tegeler Hafen (Tegel Harbor) site—a large project combining housing, an artificial lake, an island sports center, and a cultural complex—won out over other invited submissions from distinguished architects in 1980. "I was sure it was set up for Isozaki." But for a long time, it looked as if this, too, was destined never to grow beyond drawings and models, a victim of German politics and economics.

It now appears that a modified version of Moore's original plan will in fact be built, and that Moore Ruble Yudell will be charged with designing a major portion of the actual buildings.

The full scope of the project is difficult to determine, since many decisions remain to be made. Originally there was talk of $200 million (for an office of a dozen people to design!); then—as the sports center got cut out—of half that sum. Early in 1983, John Ruble guessed the housing total (which now seems fairly certain to be built) at $40 to $60 million, the rest at perhaps half of that. MRY's share of the pie may come to $30 or $40 million. Since that might still be more than the little Santa Monica office could easily whip off, the plan was to work together with a Berlin-based architect who would handle production drawings and on-site supervision.

The design that impressed Professor Kleihues and the IBA judges called for a shallow artificial inlet to be dredged, pulling the existing harbor shoreline further inland; then building in its center a round-ended, 650-foot-long island playground connected to the city by bridges. Along the new south shore MRY designed housing in various configurations: a sinuous row of neat, neoclassical, four-story townhouses, unified like a Nash crescent by pilasters and dormers; handsome three- and eight-unit villas at the end of townhouse rows. These were shown as symmetrical cubes, like little manor houses, with more neoclassical details, pyramidal roofs, gabled dormers, skylights, and some astonishing interior spaces under the roofs. At the west end rise apartment buildings, stepping up ten or more stories, with peaked roofs and intricate fenestration, somehow "relating" to existing tower blocks just across the street.

It now looks as if an ad hoc consortium of Berlin architects will get to design half the housing (probably the terraced rows), and various international celebrities some of the villas, to perpetuate the original IBA-84 idea. Moore and his partners hope to retain overall site control and to design personally a triplex villa at the east end of the terraces, a "place-making" set of four larger villas near the west end, and the towers themselves. (Being considered to design one each of the remaining villas are such architects as Richard Stern, Stanley Tigerman, Ralph Erskine, Paolo Portoghesi, and John Hejduk—a high-powered lineup.)

The central Fantasy Island has lost most ground in the years since Moore's competition victory. Originally, it was a great glassed megastructure housing three swimming pools, palm-tree gardens, a gymnasium, restaurants, and public promenades: one of Charles Moore's typically impossible dreams. Even jurors friendly to Moore's overall scheme were put off by its shape; it looked (as one critic put it) "like a battleship by Jim Stirling"—a famous British architect who once favored such things—"parked in the tiny artificial lake." Moore promised to reduce his colossal conservatory and to turn the island into something more playful and Venetian.

Economic forces almost sank the island completely when the developer who agreed to take on the housing refused to have anything to do with it. In the end, the local town council—which had desperately wanted that elegantissimo swim center—agreed to dredge out the lagoon at its own expense. They gave the developer permission to build the profitable housing *only* if he would also do something with their island. He proposed building a *private* sports club, while guaranteeing public access to some parts of the island. Since the matter remains unresolved, MRY may just turn their island into a park until someone decides what buildings can be built.

In the absence of Berlin senate funds, very little of the cultural complex north of the island may see the light of day. It was a favored part of the original submission, since all its buildings were composed in the keen, clean neoclassically symmetrical style of Karl Friedrich Schinkel, the recently rediscovered hero-architect of Berlin, whose great 1832 Humboldt Mansion lies nearby. At the very least, Moore Ruble Yudell hopes to get the chance to "define the corners" of the area by designing the long, double-vaulted library and central plaza—though Charles doesn't see that happening until at least 1986. The IBA itself has been rescheduled for (or extended to) 1987.

THE second major project now in hand at Moore Ruble Yudell is a resort hotel and conference center for San Juan Capistrano, a small Spanish mission town near the California coast, sixty miles south of their office. Gole Staneh, a wealthy Iranian who lives most of the year in London (but who also has a beach house in San Clemente) decided that the area was ripe for resort development. He commissioned plans for one large and one small hotel on land he owned in the two cities, by means of a minicompetition among Moore Ruble Yudell, Machado and Silvetti of Boston (winner of *Progressive Architecture*'s 1980 first design award), and Michael Graves. Having recently lost a big library job in San Juan Capistrano to Graves (who dropped out of Staneh's contest), Moore and his partners were delighted to capture this far grander commission. (Machado and Silvetti, as runners-up, were awarded the smaller hotel in San Clemente.)

Staneh specifically demanded certain romantic imagery in his competition program—it was to evoke a hillside castle fortress, a Mediterranean village. Moore was more than happy to satisfy him.

The "castle" portion of the complex is represented by the large conference-center block, along with one high round-towered guest wing, both of which look down on the highway and the city from their hilltop site. (Unenthusiastic about such intimidating imagery, the city planning commission forced them to temper this somewhat.) But it is the resort hotel itself—The Parador, it will be called—that will provide the real stuff of romance; more particularly, the long circuit of gardens, plazas, pools, and village streets (all bearing appropriate Spanish names) which leads the favored guest along his way.

The approach road winds gradually up and around the hill, past a separate village of tile-roofed bungalow units, to a circular and arcaded entry court. The reception lobby beyond is meant to be a splendid event: circular, domed, and very high, with grand staircases and elevators enclosed in palm-tree columns. A glass-roofed restaurant stands alongside, between lobby and conference center. Since the hotel is built horizontally rather than vertically (it rarely rises higher than three stories), many guests will have a long walk to their rooms. So the way is made as diverting as possible, with all manner of stage-set happenings en route. Visual and conceptual unity is provided by Mediterranean tile roofs and warm ocher walls, by arches and balconies, lush vegetation, fountains and watercourses; by the peak-roofed square towers that rise over the complex, like the watch towers of an old Italian town; and, most ingeniously, by a long spinal "wall" that runs both inside and out of the buildings. This begins at the lobby as a linear pair of parallel screen walls roofed with a long skylight that brings light into the top-level corridor. When that building ends, the wall breaks outside to become a freestanding double arcade, which bends around gracefully to enclose a courtyard, merges back into the facing guest building, and finally erupts in an erotic set of high, double-curved arcades out of which water pours into a baroque sequence of swimming pools—Los Baños de los Arcos.

Details of The Parador have yet to be worked out, but the overall site plan and the theatrical concept—the tile, the arches, the curves, the spine wall, the open balconies, the village squares, the Mediterranean gardens and towers—all seem satisfactory to the client. Moore has always included Disneyland, San Simeon, and Hadrian's Villa on his list of favored places, and The Parador seems to pay homage to all three. Its intricate, building-wrapped gardens, divided by arched walls and waterways, resemble things he has been trying to build ever since the doomed Xanadune project of 1972. At the start, Mr. Staneh's Dutch investment company will build only two-thirds of the three-hundred-room, $24 million project, deferring the castlelike northern terminus, with its axis-ending plaza. Not San Simeon, perhaps; but still a sizable investment in California romance.

ANOTHER eight-figure project to come Moore's way in the last year has been the opportunity to surround William Gage's Spanish colonial city hall in Beverly Hills (1932) with a new two-block-square civic center that will straddle Rexford Drive. In July of 1982, just back from his annual British hegira (and en route to his Mexican fat farm), Charles learned that his was one of five firms (with Peter Eisenman's, Arthur Erickson's, Frank Gehry's, and Moshe Safdie's) invited to spend two months and $24,000 drawing up plans for the site.

Alongside Moore's incredibly rich proposal, the offerings of the other competitors looked to me simplistic, boring, or inept. Moore came up with something far more than the buildings the program asked for. He also defined a splendid new series of urban places, a diagonal procession of elliptical plazas that starts at one corner of the site, crosses Rexford Drive, and ends at the other.

"What I thought was really freaky (and bad) about the existing civic center," he told me, "was that the buildings formally face every which way; they all turn away from each other. There's no sense of a civic *center*. So it seemed to me that what you had to do to turn that around was to have the clearest possible spatial *something*, in the outdoor space in the middle."

Once his design team had figured out where best to locate the required facilities—a new police headquarters, an expanded fire station (the old city hall and library stayed where they were)—Charles simply drew a diagonal line through the leftover space and decided to turn *that* into his "spatial something," his pedestrian mall. He ordered the others in his group to leave that space alone.

They then set to work trying to satisfy a three-inch-thick schedule of requirements—building heights, parking places, fire-truck access, jail cells, wheelchair routes. The team managed to meet California's strict disabled-access requirements with the most astonishing series of wheelchair ramps; it winds, floats, flies behind arches, across bridges, all through this stairy and watery site.

Charles, meanwhile, fiddled with Churrigueresque wall motifs taken from the old city hall and devised a series of precast three-story units with arches and window moldings and decorative tiles spilling down from the top, a cheap and effective imitation of the original. Thanks in part to this, his proposal not only came in cheaper than any of the competition's ($35 million against Gehry's $45 million—the next lowest—and Erickson's $70 million), but also seemed to evolve most naturally from, to embrace most affectionately, the beloved fifty-year-old "Spanish" city hall at its center.

"Even so, we were about halfway to deadline and had *very* little sense of any overall design," said Stephen Harby, a design captain of the Moore–UIG team. "Just before it was absolutely too late to do anything, Charles came in, and in that cavalier way of his drew a few ellipses along the diagonal mall. He fussed because nobody knew how to draw ellipses correctly, so I went out and bought a machine that does it for you. Once he had that established, we just curved the corners of our buildings to fit his row of elliptical courtyards."

"But why ellipses?" I asked. "Oh, I don't know," said Moore. "I wanted a line, an axis. I needed a geometry that would make a point, and I think I just automatically assumed ellipses would be nice. I couldn't use circles because they don't have any direction. Ellipses point you somewhere, yet they're not too insistent or jagged. I expect now the critics will all say I was copying Sant'Ignazio in Rome, or something."

Charles then sketched some freestanding arched aedicules in different sizes, like toy towers or slim Spanish Arcs de Triomphe, speckled with colored tiles at the top. These could be set around the ellipses in places where there weren't buildings nearby to define their edges and form colonnades.

The requisite buildings of the Beverly Hills civic center—including a new jail, and an 889-car parking garage (this still being Los Angeles)—will obtain grace and favor from their very placement, the curves of their corners, and the way they repeat the pilasters, arched openings, and parapet decor of the old city hall. Unlike

some other competitors, Charles retained the old library, enlarging
and rearranging it, and surrounded it with a new exterior wall,
identical in bay width and facade treatment to the new fire station
across Rexford Drive. To give fire trucks the turning radius they
needed, he bent the station back in an outward curve; then he bent
the library facade back in a matching curve. Together they form a
"welcoming" entrance for northbound cars. At the other end of the
site, a broad, beautifully designed arch spans Rexford Drive, sup-
porting a handsome hall-and-office bridge between the police
station and city hall. These two gestures make the automobile
entrances to the center almost as exciting as the pedestrians'
approach.

But it is the Roman baroque sequence of pedestrian spaces that
is going to turn this into one of America's memorable urban centers. Two little "wing" buildings (the architects found functions for
them after designing them, in good Beaux Arts fashion) splay out
on either side of a first small elliptical court, in front of a splendid
triumphal arch—perhaps slightly more splendid than one requires
to celebrate a walk from the Rodeo Drive shops to one's local library, but then Beverly Hills isn't your ordinary village. This leads
to the next ellipse, shown in plan as laid out in a baroque maze of
turf. It is shaped half by a curved corner of the fire station, half by a
freestanding colonnade which serves as a side entrance to city
hall. Palm trees surround the next small elliptical court. Then
come the tall aedicular units, beginning on one side of Rexford
Drive and continuing on the other. (The idea that car traffic will
continue to penetrate this grand promenade is, I think, a wonderful
LA conceit.) Along with concentric rings of street paving, these
define the grandest plaza of all. This is a magnificent space, cars
or no cars, half encircled by sixty-foot-tall Washingtonia palms,
ramped under the arches and crossed, east of Rexford, by a series
of stepped baroque terraces, which turn into benches for lunching
or sunning. A driveway off Rexford slyly leads cars around this
plaza and into the five-level parking garage.

The next ellipse, through a big round arch, is mostly filled with
water, and surrounded by lush planting. Along one side (in the
drawings) is moored a stone boat, high-stepped fore and aft, like
the one at Villa Vizcaya in Florida—another classical folly Charles
has long wanted to build. Restaurants, he hopes, will look out onto

this pool, and water may cascade into a grotto, down either side of the intricate set of steps and arches that finally leads one out the northeast corner of the site onto Santa Monica Boulevard.

Originally, the processional route ended at the semicircular apse that encloses the car ramp of the parking garage, but the jurors thought that gauche. Realigning the great parade of ellipses so they would indeed end at the northeast corner forced Moore to shrink some of them. But it also freed some more space between the water ellipse, the garage, and the library. The architects had planned all along to fit in a small community theater there. But now Moore decided to make it a perfect jewel box of a theater (seating five hundred), which he hoped to build in tiers of walled rococo boxes, like the eighteenth-century court theaters of Europe—"just the thing for Beverly Hills." But the mayor insisted that was too "elitist" for this bastion of egalitarian democracy.

The whole Beverly Hills project teems with such ideas. Its landscape plan (by Regula Campbell) includes rows of high palms and low palms, a Sevillian grove of orange trees, water lilies, monkey-puzzle trees. (Moore once claimed that the only worthwhile architecture in Los Angeles was the plants.) But his was also the only one of the competition entries that followed the city's complex program precisely, satisfying every requirement. "I know that's not most people's idea of Charles Moore," said Steve Harby. "But he's a totally functional architect *first*. He sets the rules for imagery and design, of course, and we defer to him on that. But he inevitably defers to *us* on function."

IN addition to these three projects, Moore Ruble Yudell was recently awarded the contract to design a new art school for San Antonio ($3 million, forty thousand square feet), and a new civic center for San Juan Capistrano, originally planned to face Michael Graves's new library. For Houston, he and UIG have offered a redesign of Hermann Park, incorporating the exaggerated-perspective waterways of his defunct Indianapolis park project, a higher arch for Sam Houston's statue, and the cubistic 1939 World's Fair elephants of his Best Products Company facade. (Three of these elephants stand hip to hip on an island in the middle of a lake. The middle one is surmounted by an obelisk, like Bernini's seventeenth-century elephant in the Piazza della Minerva.) With UIG also he is designing an Extension and Alumni Center for the University of California at Irvine, based ("although they don't know it") on the three facing facades of a 1607 church, and a country club for Steamboat Springs, Colorado ("That's a maybe"). John Matthews of Dallas recently chose Moore over Michael Graves to design a $20 million, 120-unit condominium for him near Highland Park. The preliminary model showed a monumental, neo-Mayan pile of two-story luxury blocks, each pierced for its private garden, with side wings reaching down to embrace a broad forecourt. Moore was also finally risking a major skyscraper design—the slim, seventy-two-story tower Carnegie Hall wanted to trade its air rights for, on property next to its existing 1891 building on Fifty-seventh Street in New York.

If Moore were to win the Carnegie Hall Tower competition ("It's just a dream at the moment"), he would be obliged to work in concert with a large and established New York firm, able to handle all the drafting, specifications, and supervision involved. Already, during 1982, he has had to redefine his relationship with the Urban Innovations Group of UCLA. "Charles Moore, Inc." now rents space in UIG's building, while continuing to use its services (including UCLA student workers). "His" designers officially work for UIG, in confusing joint-venture agreements. For larger jobs (like Beverly Hills) both his offices sometimes contract with other firms to get necessary drawings done.

For the first time in twenty-five years, we are talking about hundreds of millions of dollars of real work, much of it won in high-level competitions by a man long known as a whimsical designer of funny-looking houses and notorious for never sitting still. As one of his Los Angeles associates (who is reveling in the new prosperity) put it, "All this is going to force Charles Moore to change his way of operating. He will either have to stay in one place longer, or accept the fact that he is going to lose a major portion of design control in buildings that bear his name. His time is finite, and he's just too overexpanded now to retain control."

The young man—who, like several others over the years, has worked his way up from student to slide sorter to general handyman to one of Moore's chief designers—pointed out a questionable corner in the plan of one of the current grandiose projects. "See that? I did that. Charles never even saw it. But we can't wait for him anymore to get things done that have to be done. He complains if we go ahead without him, but then he complains whenever he's expected to put in more time here than he likes. He organizes his life so he can get away as much as possible. He *hates* feeling tied down—as you know. Now that he's finally got all this wonderful business, Los Angeles is becoming oppressive to him. Gayley Avenue has become too much like work. It's no longer his refuge of preference. No wonder he keeps flying off to New Orleans."[6]

23 / UNBUILT AND UNBUILDABLE

I N 1974, Charles Moore designed and built (with the help of young associates in Connecticut) two cardboard dollhouses—one a Tuscan villa; the other a layered, slotted-together castle—which he still includes in his list of collected works. In 1982, he was one of nineteen international architects invited by *Architectural Design* magazine in London to design another dollhouse, for exhibition, publication, and eventual sale. (Two hundred sixty other architects, from twenty-seven countries, submitted dollhouse plans for the accompanying open competition.)

Why, one might ask, would an architect as busy as Charles Moore spend time and money designing dollhouses, when not even normal dolls are ever likely to live in them?

Then again, why not?

These "follies," as I've taken to calling Moore's essentially unbuildable projects, allow him the chance to explore design ideas and space possibilities that might be difficult to work into real buildings for life-size clients. In a way, they're his own version of the fantasy assignments he gives his students. Museums, galleries, and magazines enjoy sponsoring and paying for these theoretical designs, as if to show celebrities at play, famous architects set free from real-world constraints. A surprising number of the world's most highly regarded architects take these commissions with great seriousness and use the resultant models, mock facades, and theoretical plans to make weighty statements about architecture and the world, or to contrive provocative or obscure metaphysical conceits, like built versions of the places imagined by Di Chiricho or Dali.[7]

Charles Moore often seems to be making jokes (some of which elude me) in his designs for these things. An intricate little cardboard model he and Jim Winkler did for a 1980 conference in Stuttgart was intended to be his "answer" to a famous house

Le Corbusier designed for an event in Stuttgart fifty-three years before.

With Alice Wingwall (Donlyn Lyndon's wife), Moore contributed to a centennial exhibition of the Architectural League of New York in 1981, which was intended to provoke fruitful collaborations between artists and architects.

Moore designed and built a wooden red-orange dollhouse in several movable parts, supposedly "alluding" to Stratford Hall. The biggest block was shaped like a section of his "House near New York," split open for a few mirrored stairs; two flat-topped arch-of-triumph aedicules recall those he later devised for Beverly Hills; three tiny staircases on wheels were supposed to pull everything together. Alice Wingwall decorated all this with gilded, Barbie-Doll-sized jeans and shirts, and backed it with a grainy photomontage of the feet of a colossal statue standing alongside a peeling Palladian colonnade; in the distance, Charles had drawn one of his fantasy kingdoms. I liked her contribution; couldn't understand his. (His 1982 dollhouse for London was a mauve-and-rose box that opened up to a elegant Victorian gothic tower and two L-shaped wings, decorated with William Morris-y wallpapers. Like Moore #7, it seems to refer to Frederick Church's 1874 mansion at Olana, New York.)

Best Products Company of Richmond, Virginia, the discount retailer which deals exclusively out of its own large catalogue-sale showrooms, has, in recent years, undertaken a unique form of architectural patronage. Beginning in 1971, it commissioned ten weird facades—but *only* the facades—for its standard two-story windowless showroom-warehouses, from a group of visionary "de-architects" in New York called SITE. Eight have so far been built—attention-grabbing metaphysical jokes (facades that tilt, facades that peel, facades that crumble or fall apart) on a gigantic and permanent scale. In 1979, Robert Venturi decorated a showroom exterior for Best Products with giant red-and-white flowers, and Hugh Hardy's office designed its new corporate headquarters.

Then, for a 1980 display at the Museum of Modern Art, Best Products commissioned six additional facades: not to build, but simply to stimulate thinking about new design possibilities.

In three cases (Michael Graves, Allan Greenberg, Robert Stern) the contributions recalled recent real work done by these well-known postmodern designers. Stanley Tigerman designed a superordinary suburban tract house, gigantically overscaled. Tony Lumsden came up with a spectacular, waving glass canopy floating over and through the eaten-away wall. Charles Moore's offering was totally unlike anything he (or anyone else) had ever done before. Twelve abstract elephants made of mirrored and sharply faceted metal planes, each bearing a howdah in the form of a pile of mirrored tea trays, flank a mirrored and faceted entry portal in the same giddy style. In the splendid model—built by Jim Winkler and Robert Vlock of UIG—these were illuminated in a glowing rainbow of colors.

The design is a direct steal (Moore is the first to admit) from the Mayan-Burmese-Malayan Elephant Towers, designed by Donald Macky, that marked the entrance to the 1939–40 World's Fair on Treasure Island in San Francisco Bay. (Moore attended the fair as a lad of fourteen.) This may be another case, like the Santa Barbara Faculty Club, of Charles Moore's becoming so fascinated by the fake-nostalgic architecture of the recent California past that he—in his nostalgia for *that* nostalgia—decided to enshrine it at a slightly skewed remove.

The architecture section of the 1980 Venice Biennale was devoted to Il Presenza del Passato (the Presence of the Past). It was a powerful propaganda gesture on behalf of *dopo-modernismo*, of architecture as art and theory, and of the postmodern use of historical ideas, instigated by Italian architect and critic Paolo Portoghesi.

In addition to fifty-six architects or firms, from eleven different countries, whose past-respecting works were displayed in a separate gallery (three grand old men—Philip Johnson and two Italians, Ignazio Gardella and Mario Ridolfi—rated special tributes), Portoghesi and his panel of advisers invited twenty antimodern architects to design twenty-by-forty-foot facades. These facades were erected between the nave columns of a restored sixteenth-century rope factory in Venice. With half the facades facing the other half, they formed a stage-set street supposedly representing the newest architectural ideas, which Portoghesi called the Strada Novissima. Eight Americans, including Moore, were among the twenty invited. The popular exhibition later traveled to Paris and San Francisco, where a few new facades were commissioned. Behind each facade (which had to have some sort of real entrance) each architect was invited to display whatever photos, drawings, models, or descriptions of his work that he wished.

I'm not sure what Portoghesi and the Biennale judges had expected; but almost none of the facades looked like the possible front of a real building; and they didn't add up to a "street" of any kind, new or old. Many of the designs were defiantly unreadable, gaga, or ugly; a few seemed to mock the whole affair. Eccentrically trendy and almost hermetically mannered, the exhibition may have warranted mocking. The most crowd-pleasing facade was Thomas Gordon Smith's baroque pastiche of twisted Bernini columns and plaster details against a green "frescoed" wall. The most interesting was Hans Hollein's little essay on columns, three in a row: a foliage-wrapped cylinder, an artificial tree column (also after Bernini), and a ruined classical fragment suspended on wires for visitors to walk under. Most of the American offerings seemed to me either cartoon classicism or embarrassingly lame displays by professionals who ought to have done better—including Charles Moore. He contributed a set of high cut-out arches and arch fragments on layers of painted plywood, which more or less evoke the spectacular entrance plazas he designed for the Bunker Hill project in Los Angeles.

Other Charles Moore follies have included Moore Ruble Yudell's "late entry" in the Chicago *Tribune* Tower competition of 1922–23, a clever stunt orchestrated by Stanley Tigerman and some friends in 1980, which attracted sixty-eight designs. (The original competition, in 1922, drew 263 entries—but then a real commission and $100,000 in prizes were at stake.)

The 1980 "late entries" included a few genuinely buildable, even handsome, modern and postmodern designs; but most took the form of unbuildable jokes, comments, or symbols of one kind or another. There were some very explicit statements (a flag-wrapped tower to mock the *Tribune*'s chauvinism; a giant tommy gun to represent Chicago; Walter Gropius's 1923 entry falling over sideways). The sillier putdowns included a mammoth baby's bottle and a twenty-one-story Tuscan column (another of the 1923 entries) sheathed in a transparent condom. Moore Ruble Yudell's gorgeous rendering showed Eliel Saarinen's 1923 runner-up design (which many critics preferred to the winner) split open to reveal a futurist fantasy city inside and turned into a colossal flashlight by a powerful beam that shone through the open top.

The 1980 Castelli Gallery exhibition of eight utopian Houses for Sale insisted that the plans and drawings were in fact available for clients to buy and build. But the contributions of several of the participants, better known for their theoretical than their actual houses, are certain to remain "art" and not architecture. (One could purchase the drawings alone.)

Charles Moore, shattering expectations once again, came up with a house design I can actually imagine building and happily living in. He began with a steep, creek-edged ravine in Texas. For it, he created a house that maintains a lively, livable tension between classical archetypes and the forms of a comfortable southwestern ranch house.

The house, to be made of cheap and standard materials, has rectangular rooms and a shady Texas porch. Against this are played things like a semicircular piazza and grotto from the Villa Giulia, the pavilion shapes of the Farnese gardens on the Palatine, a touch of Schinkel, a formal canal, a round pool, a great arched entry, and a look, at least, of symmetry. Two showy Palladian windows and a few big arches are set among straight-edged double-hung windows and French doors. A curving glazed gallery surrounding the amphitheatrical pool court is pure C. W. Moore. A decent jungle planted in the gallery, he suggests, plus the shady veranda and some ceiling vents, should "make the place efficiently energy saving, though it sidesteps the better known imagery of that persuasion."

I should mention, finally, a great House for Schinkel Moore designed with Bill Hersey and John Kyrk for a Japanese competition in 1979. The whole thing is splendid and silly and knowing and full of wit, a sage blending of two centuries by a man at home in both. "Mr. Schinkel is a splendid client," they wrote on their entry, "not afraid of the classical past nor ashamed of romantic sensibilities. He looks forward to what he calls the 'thrill of denial' of 20th Century architecture but feels no need to burden himself with its stylistic enthusiasms."

ALMOST every architect's collected works include some serious projects that, for one reason or another, were never realized in bricks and mortar. Buildings are designed on speculation and then find no takers. Competitions are entered and lost. A client commissions a plan for a building and then decides he doesn't like it, or discovers he can't afford it, or fails to obtain the necessary permits and financing.

I've made reference already to several of Charles Moore's unrealized designs which fall into one or another of these categories: the 1962 condominiums for Coronado, the numerous housing schemes designed from Yale, the Italian-American Federation Building in New Orleans, the several Singapore projects for Mr. Kwee, the library competition in San Juan Capistrano he lost to Michael Graves.

Sometimes unbuilt projects become almost as famous as an architect's finished buildings. The Saarinen and Gropius entries in the Chicago *Tribune* Tower Competition have been reproduced in books on architecture, I'm sure, more often than Howells and Hood's winning design. Le Corbusier's Ville Radieuse for Paris, Wright's Mile-High Skyscraper for Chicago, and Paolo Soleri's monstrous "arcologies" never got built either (thank God); but their notoriety has been considerable all the same. Wright's catalogue lists 433 executed works, but even more that were designed and never built. Among the latter are some of his best-known plans.

Charles Moore hasn't wasted that many good designs. But at least three of his unbuilt projects warrant particular attention.

The Xanadune condominium project for St. Simon's Island in Georgia (designed 1972) would, I think, have been one of his major works. It was to contain three hundred apartment units, of seven different configurations, in what looked from the surrounding beach like one big old shingle-style Cape May hotel, with a giant, low-sloping, pyramidal roof broken open for dozens of dormers. The hope was that the building, from the outside, would either blend into the sand dunes or at least look as old-fashioned and domestic as the single-family residences around it.

Actually, the four roofslopes never met in the center. The whole inside of the seven-building complex was to be opened up for a garden full of strange and wonderful things: a swimming pool, a jogging track, a trellised promenade, a handball court, gazebos, palm trees, freestanding arcades. The cut walls facing this lavish and secret interior space were painted, in the model, bright oranges and fuchsias, and unified by a motif of paired quarter-circle (or half-circle) arches over rectangular openings.

The idea of a pyramidally roofed building open at the center was first devised by Moore for the Jenkins house scheme (1961) in California's Napa Valley. This house did eventually get built, but in a comparatively timid Japanese-pavilion fashion: the owner rejected the central hole. (Converging ceiling slopes, high triangular dormers, and freestanding room units still provide some excitement; but it's not a house Moore is proud of.) The Slater house at Stinson Beach (1964) successfully realized the idea on a small scale. The huge, low-sloping pyramidal roof of Xanadune, cut away for courtyards, was first ventured in 1960, in a competition entry for the California governor's mansion by Moore and Peters—another major unbuilt project. This plan combined grandeur, casualness, and local historic reference even more successfully than the "House near New York," mainly (I think) because it possessed a rigorous order the larger scheme lacks. Some of the fantasy world of Xanadune's interior court seems to have been recycled into the gardens and promenades of The Parador resort hotel in San Juan Capistrano.

A second Moore project I am sorry never attracted sufficient financial support was the Indianapolis River Park design of 1980. This was to be a hundred-acre theme park on both sides of the White River, which (at one stage of the design) also included a thousand-foot tower—an inverted cone of open steel grillwork—by Cesar Pelli, a performing-arts center, a new bridge, and a relocated zoo. Moore worked out his original scheme during his stay at the American Academy in Rome in the fall of 1980. Streets radiate from a focal point in the northeast, then splay out in reverse perspective, so that you start out feeling like Alice in Wonderland (after her first drink) or Gulliver in Lilliput, much larger than the buildings. The buildings and streets gradually get bigger and bigger, until *you're* the one that seems small. Landfilled wedges between the radiating streets, split for an artificial river canyon and connected by bridges, were to create make-believe mountains up to one hundred feet high. Pedestrians could walk on, under, or over the streets, or alternately snake around them in boats gliding through a series of canals like those at Hadrian's Villa. Moore had even hoped to continue the paddleboat canal *over* the river, on an old cattle bridge, as an alternative to crossing by cable car, ferry boat, or the ordinary bridge.

I found the drawings mad and fascinating when I saw them in spring 1981, but I felt sure that never in a million years would Indianapolis accept it. Moore had done dozens of sketches for this project, working in hundreds of ideas, which Steve Harby and Jim Winkler then drew up for him to revise, complicating things more and more while holding tight to the Wonderland logic of his radiating streets and built-up mountain blocks. These gradually grow from twenty-by-thirty-foot chunks with very low facades, to superblocks three hundred by four hundred feet faced by grand walls. At the end was tethered a hot-air balloon designed to carry passengers a thousand feet up in the air. Disengaged facades with agricultural-motif columns celebrating Indiana's farms (apples, ears of corn, soybean leaves) sheltered cafés and refreshment stands. Dance halls, beer gardens, aquarium tanks visible from land or sea, an aviary, Roman baths, an oval skating rink—there was no end to the wonders Charles kept sketching in. But so far the whole multi-million-dollar project has come to nothing.

The best-known loser in which Charles Moore has been involved was a huge redevelopment project for downtown Los Angeles. In the last twenty years, this area has been transformed from a hilly neighborhood of rundown old houses and shops (most of them demolished in the late fifties, when the hills were regraded) to an intense and oppressive forest of gray or glass skyscrapers, most of them bank headquarters, the tallest forty to sixty stories high. The area—called Bunker Hill, though not much of the hill is left—lies adjacent to the three banal theaters of Welton Becket's Los Angeles Music Center (1969) and one of John Portman's glitziest mirrored-cylinder hotels (1978).

Having failed in earlier attempts to attract developers, the Los Angeles Community Redevelopment Agency put its last remaining major parcel (razed and partially leveled twenty years before) up for bids in 1979. This was an eleven-acre, three-and-a-half-block segment between Grand Avenue and Olive Street, which also included the area back and downhill of Olive that had previously been connected to the hilltop by a funicular railway called Angels Flight. (The funicular was to be restored.) On this site, the CRA asked for 4.5 million square feet of offices, shops, housing, a hotel, and—when the city decided it needed one—a new modern-art museum, plus a city park. Each developer was to submit a proposal that included both financing ($700 million to $1 billion) and architectural design.

Five proposals were received, and in July 1980 the CRA board voted for that of Bunker Hill Associates (primarily Cadillac–Fairview), whose architect was Arthur Erickson of Vancouver, working in collaboration with two Los Angeles firms. (Arata Isozaki of Tokyo has since been added, to design the new museum.) The design is almost classically modernist, and includes some of Erickson's famous play with transparent walls: a biaxial, symmetrical, and icily monumental parade of glass-walled skyscrapers in a park, connected at the base by sloping glass galleries.

Many in the architectural press lamented the choice, since they had fallen in love with the runner-up design, from Maguire Partners of Los Angeles. (The choice of the winner had as much to do with financial resources and profitability as with design.) The second-place scheme vigorously rejected any effort at overall formal unity by inviting seven different architectural offices—a "parade of stars"—to participate, each doing his own piece his own way, all kept in a kind of harmony of discords by the UCLA–UIG team of Harvey Perloff, Barton Myers, and Edgardo Contini. Cesar Pelli, once of Los Angeles, now at Yale, got the biggest office tower; Robert Kennard (a black Los Angeles architect), the second biggest; Barton Myers and Frank Gehry of Los Angeles, the two apartment blocks; Ricardo Legoretta of Mexico City, the hotel; and Hardy Holzman and Pfeiffer of New York, the museum. The hotel was to be a sort of triangular ski slope, a wedge set on edge; the museum looked like three chunks of the hotel that had fallen off into the street.

Charles Moore opted for the "little buildings at the feet" of the others' giant towers, in the downhill plot surrounding the funicular, and, in collaboration with Larry Halprin, for the "cosmetics of formal gateways and plazas" that tie together the whole Grand Avenue front, behind one of Halprin's people-oriented promenade-parks.

Both of these would, I think, have been unique and extraordinary urban events, whatever the buildings above and behind them may have looked like. Moore's block of housing (366 condominiums and rental apartments, moderately priced to be eligible for federal subsidies) looks in the drawings like at least eleven different buildings, ranging from six to twenty-three stories tall, all designed with great gusto and imagination. They are intricately disposed around the steep-rising funicular, a series of small parks and stepped baroque plazas, and a swimming pool; and are enlivened by open balconies, arcaded loggias, corner towers and turrets, peaked and mansarded roofs, and hanging-garden terraces on the upper floors. The north-curving tops on three of the buildings contain penthouses with spectacular light and views. The intricacy, variety, and romantic busyness of it all look like some especially desirable corner of San Francisco or New York in the 1920s, grown together accidentally but congenially over many years, rather than a block of downtown Los Angeles designed by one man in 1980. Angel's Flats, as it was called, was designed to help assure the total revitalization of the project by bringing back into it ordinary people who would live there full time.

The original program called for a one-and-a-half-acre city park. Halprin and Moore reinterpreted that into a European series of urban piazzas, courts, and promenades, another of those stage sets where they hoped real people would get together and do interesting things, at the feet of their peers' lofty towers. Grand Avenue itself, in their scheme, became a ninety-five-foot-wide linear plaza (for pedestrians and some cars; through auto traffic was to go under the street), with fountains, greenery, sculpture, lights, and places to sit. The high buildings were to be kept from creating an intimidating cliff of glass at streetside by a thirty-foot-wide strollers' arcade and trees with shops and cafés underneath, interrupted in two places by spectacular pavilions designed with all of Moore's world's fair virtuosity at theatrical effects. These would contain layers of high freestanding arches, palm trees and other planting, ranges of amphitheater steps and seats, and streams or cascades of water. The architects hoped that these magic places would somehow make downtown Angelenos lighthearted and festive.

The North Court featured a series of stream-divided steps, a high arched stage for theatrical events, and (behind it) the mirrored image of a Victorian house enclosing an upper-level restaurant, flanked by mammoth vine-bearded heads in niches. The South Court was to contain a spectacular waterfall fountain fed from an aqueduct that ran along the top of the open-arched colonnade and curving rotunda behind it. Restaurants and sidewalk cafés were to spill into the plaza of this, the Los Angeles Trevi fountain.

It's not going to happen, any of it—at least not here. But Moore has never designed anything more aggressively joyful. At Bunker Hill, moreover, the joy would have been all open to the public and not have had to end when the fair was over.

CONCLUSION: HOW MUCH DOES HE MATTER?

I N many ways, it's more comfortable to be an art historian—one who analyzes and evaluates the work of artists safely dead—than an art *critic*, who must come to terms with the works of artists, like Charles Moore, still very much alive. And as a critic, it's simpler to put together and defend opinions on the work of *pure* artists, whose works pretend to no other end but expression or symbolic meaning or delight, than on the work of impure, quasi-artists like Moore, who must somehow also shelter students or families, or persuade people to spend money, or keep out wind and rain, or allow for convenient cooking and comfortable sleeping, and so forth.

A lot of architectural criticism, until fairly recently, contented itself with regarding buildings as oversized relief sculptures stuck together at the corners: at most, as walk-through sculptures; at least, as abstracted and reduced diagrams (plans, elevations, sections) of their real and living selves. By not only visiting, but also talking to the residents and users of almost a hundred Charles Moore buildings—and, whenever possible, "living" in them, however briefly—I've tried to force myself out of those habits.

I've come, for instance, to know a great deal about leaky ceilings and dangerous stairs, about gaudy colors and supergraphics the mind's eye grows weary of, about bizarre one-of-a-kind houses one cannot live long with or easily resell. Dr. Stern's house in Connecticut—those two diagonal corridors that intersect at a weirdly sharp point—stayed on the market for years after his divorce, until a colleague finally bought it at a bargain price. Other houses have been stripped and rebuilt. When Charles Moore next decides to move on, I wonder who will be found to pay good money for the cramped spaces and tin boxes and that long cascade of stairs in his present Los Angeles pad. (His two neighbors, I was told, already have plans for dividing up his space.)

But I've also come to a more refined understanding of other human needs and the ways in which an architect of genius can interpret and satisfy them. Insofar as buildings *are* more than paintings or sculptures, the needs they may satisfy are deeper and more essential for most of us than the "needs" met by objects in a museum display. This explains, I think, why many people who can respond with excitement and pleasure to unconventional works in an art gallery *cannot* do so to unconventional buildings: too many basic memories and impulses are at stake. People tend to judge homes, I have found, on the simple standard of what *they* have happily lived in—or think they want to live in—themselves. For many people, enclosed box rooms with flat ceilings, closable doors, and symmetrically disposed windows are so much a part of their lives that they feel personally—and quite reasonably—disoriented by, threatened by, hostile to anything different. High spaces (except in grand public buildings), oddly placed holes, confusing levels, acute angles, the "wrong" materials or colors, are not simply arguable possibilities in building art. They are unfamiliar, uncomfortable, and hence personally and aesthetically *wrong*.

So I must grant anyone the right to disagree with me absolutely as I try to catalogue the things I admire most in the work of Charles W. Moore, what I see as the unique difference or specialness of his contribution to the architecture of our time.

First, Charles Moore has demonstrated that punched-out holes in solid walls, whether glazed or open, can go more places and do more things than anyone before in the history of architecture ever imagined. He has embarked upon a full, open exploration of the sensory and emotional potentials of skylights and light traps, view frames, light-washed walls, magical space enlargers, dappled and reflected light, plus the sheer joy of peeking through holes and the wonderful negative shapes that cut-out spaces can make.

He can, and sometimes will, arrange windows for their exterior effect. But more often he seems to let interior decisions—what the light or view holes will do for the inhabitants—determine the exterior elevations. Sometimes this creates crazy or "ugly" faces that antagonize traditionalist neighbors. Other times—as at the Sea Ranch—the "accidental" outside result seems surprisingly right.

Two of the richest results of Moore's lifelong exploration of light holes are (1) the conceptual wonder of transparent, see-through houses, like Reverdy Johnson's, or Ellen Koizim's, or the Stern–Stansel house; and (2) the modulations both of light and the eyes' own games of dimension and discovery he and his partners achieve by what they call *layering*—placing a screen of unglazed openings, of one shape and rhythm, in front of a further, usually glazed, set of openings of another. There are dozens of examples of this; the Tempchin house and the little library at Kresge College are two of the best.

The emotional effects of Moore's natural-light channels, one should note, have often been enhanced by the supersubtle color games of Tina Beebe and by Dick Peters's mastery of artificial illumination.

Second, Charles Moore has exploited, as no architect since the more awe-inspiring Beaux Arts eclectics, the exhilarating effects of internal *vertical* space. He has been doing this by means of shaftlike ascents or great downhill dramatic slopes—usually in contrast to adjacent *low*-ceilinged spaces—ever since the wee breakthrough cabins of 1961–62, made spectacular by their heavenly reach upward from petite ground plans. Nowadays, I pretend to sympathize as owners complain to me about heating bills for their "needlessly" high Charles Moore living-room ceilings. Ah! I think, sipping their wines, my spirit soaring aloft—Reason not the *need*!

This grows into something more than the uplifting sense of surplus overhead space. It grows, as in the Talbert house or the Sea Ranch Condominium, into the visual play of seeing and the kinesthetic sense of imagining oneself moving or flying to other levels—two, three, four levels of horizontal space visible at once —and into the primal joy involved in looking down on active life from balcony perches or peering through *interior* windows. The whole building space, thus carefully managed, becomes at once visible and coherent—and yet unprecedentedly rich in spatial terms.

Vertical extension, I grant, is unnatural to man taking his domestic ease. We don't fly, and climbing is hard work: we tend to reach and move *out* rather than up. This, I think, is why Frank Lloyd Wright's horizontally designed and accented buildings are so satisfying, so soul settling to most people. Moore's are *unsettlingly* dramatic. But yielding to them, if one can, I honestly believe enlarges one's perceptions, one's imagination, and one's self.

A third insight or specialty of Moore's involves staircases. He obviously loves the gravity-defying, self-enhancing, view-changing effect of an erect human body proceeding upward or downward on a magic geometric waterfall of levels. He has, throughout his professional life, devised means of celebrating and magnifying this act. Some of his ascending-descending "stages," perhaps because they are simply hard for me to negotiate, I think foolish and extreme. Others, like those in the foyer of Sammis Hall or the corridor of the Hines house, are as voluptuously satisfying as the Scala Regia in the Vatican, the winding stairs of a medieval church or castle tower, the stepped streets of an Italian hillside town. No other living architect is quite such a virtuoso of stairs.

Fourth, an extension of this is Charles Moore's deeply rooted devotion to processional movement, which some ascribe to his early experience of oriental architecture. This may not relate to the ways in which we as tenants actually *use* his buildings; the space-after-space sequences may sometimes seem forced (Kresge College, the "House near New York," the Stern–Stansel corridors). But I'm willing to believe that one's awareness of them is still "enlarging." It seems to help to place us, cosmically—like the chain of salons at Syon House near London or most large Christian churches. In fact, I'm almost certain that Moore's rich awareness of historical archetypes—probably unparalleled among practicing architects—lies behind this antimodern but apparently correct intuition.

One favorably disposed toward his work could carry this further, fifthly, and assert that Moore's understanding of the deepest, most universal emotional needs of human beings—needs that can in *any way* be satisfied by the place-maker's art—is more sensitive and refined than that of any other practitioner: that he is, in fact, in his less ego-assertive, most *homo universalis* efforts—profoundly in touch with his own, and thereby *our*, instinctual cravings, which students I take through his buildings often translate into Freudian or Jungian terms. He *knows* we want to crawl under tables or hide in caves, peer down on others or into secret places; knows that we love the surprise of light from secret sources; knows that altars and canopies and skylights and grand staircases and window seats, nooks and crannies, organized vistas, the sound of moving water touch and transfix us in profound and prerational places. He knows, moreover, how to orchestrate and achieve these deep-lying satisfactions in real buildings designed for real people.

Two extensions or aspects of this come, perhaps, closer to private obsessions of Moore's than to universal insights. Number six is an obsession with moving water. Remember the story of that great multilevel waterfall he built near his parents' home in Battle Creek at a very early age. His Ph.D. dissertation at Princeton—a book he is now trying diligently to finish—dealt with water in architecture. The Lovejoy Fountain in Portland, on which he collaborated, seems about as primal as a man-made place can get. But how *much* of his work depends on the presence of living water—at Monterey Bay, the Sea Ranch, on Long Island Sound, along creeks near Big Sur or Aspen—one is *forced* to attend to. The mock rivers of Italy which may one day yet flow over the Piazza d'Italia; the bubbling fountains (now turned off) designed for a sightless but otherwise hypersensitive client; the fountain, dried and stifled, at Kresge College—the world seems determined to thwart his craving for running water. The extraordinary fantasy canals and lagoons he has dreamed up for Berlin and Indianapolis and the New Orleans fair, the imaginary shoreline at Gulfport Plaza, the interior ponds and fountains that cool the Kwee mansion in Singapore; his long-standing obsessions with the waters of Hadrian's Villa, of the Alhambra: here again, I believe, Moore's private needs, realized in actual or potential built places, come very close to the needs of all men.

This extends to number seven, perhaps more private still—Moore's penchant for sheer sybaritic sensual indulgence, uncommon in any major architect since Wright, and totally at odds with the icy-classic puritanism of most of the modern movement. From this one may well recoil if the disposition seems alien and wrong. But total orchestrations of exotic, perhaps even erotic, body-enhancing colors, textures, lights, positions, and feelings abound in his work—in the flying bridges and blood-red colors of Santa Barbara, in window-seat chaise longues one *cannot* sit up straight in, in Gerald Hines's living room at Aspen; sublimely in the locker rooms of the Northern Recreation Center at the Sea Ranch. Give that place to a really keen architectural psychoanalyst, and he just might be able to plumb the wellsprings of Charles Willard Moore.

Let me signal just two other aspects of Moore's work that strike me as important, both far too complex to go into in any detail. Number eight is his compulsion to make referential connections to other buildings and places, both neighbors of his own build-ings—the old barns of Sonoma County, Santa Barbara Spanish—and other buildings and places in history, which he knows so well. Architects all over are suddenly doing this again, after fifty or sixty years of antihistorical independence. Moore is neither the first nor the most assertive neohistoricist, and some of his allusions are either too obvious or too subtle even for me. But many—like the honorable Palladian reference at Sammis Hall, the gestures to Schinkel at Berlin, the Spanish colonial fantasies for Beverly Hills and San Juan Capistrano, the centuries of allusion compacted into the New Orleans piazza—do seem to make present sense as well and enrich *our* world by their artful remembrance of things past.

Finally, I remain impressed by his almost metaphysical impulse and ability to follow the path of Louis Kahn—one of his early men-tors—in finding for each new building a unique center of meaning, an *architectural* raison d'être. "*What* is this building, what does it want to *be*?" Kahn demanded of his students. Not just, Why does this go here? or How does it solve the needs of the program? but What *is* it, uniquely, as a design: does it speak, assert itself, make some kind of separate and coherent sense?

For each successful Charles Moore building there is a crystal, a core visual idea or image, a catalytic agent—often expressed as a metaphor—which, quite independent of any rational program or problem-solving process, both generates and then unifies the final, often very complex design. Sheila Isham's Japanese medita-tion garden, Simone Swan's medieval wooden village wrought in a single building; the inside log cabin of the Stanwoods' clap-board house; David Rodes's dream of an elegant French provincial farmhouse; Lee Burns's dream of a hedonistic Mexican–Holly-wood haven.

Charles Moore cannot be identified with a single type of build-ing, repeated and refined over and over—no organic, horizontal prairie houses, no lucid series of precisionist cubes. I can conjure up an imaginary building by Johnson or Roche or Stirling or Bar-ragan—but what does a "Charles Moore building" look like? For each project he pulls ten thousand ideas out of that encyclopedic store; driven by who knows what inner impulses, he then rushes off halfway around the world. He so willingly accepts and then uses the ideas and suggestions of clients and colleagues—in fact, *insists* on their contributions—that it is often difficult to say how much of *any* Charles Moore building *is* Charles Moore's. When the collaborators find themselves trapped by clashing demands, he will dash back impatiently—or simply telephone—and cut through to a solution in minutes. I have heard this tale over and over, as if he honestly did own a magic wandlike pencil. Though he clearly has a repertoire of favored gestures, he has hated to repeat himself in any fundamental way; and he apparently has no serious objection to the remodeling or even demolition of his own works.

He does care about posterity—his place, his reputation. But by carrying on in the butterfly way he does, he makes it difficult for even admiring critics to fashion one for him. His detractors, meanwhile, can always decry this very changeability, this lack of repose or obvious development.

I've touched more than once on possible subconscious sources for Moore's *oeuvre*, which is really presumptuous of me. But there is about him a sense of a huge, radically lonely genius fixed forever at a magically open preadolescent level, still building houses under the dining-room table or damming the neighborhood creek into magic cascades: *open*, that is to say, in a way we other adults are not, to primal impulses; to the usefulness and wonderful difference of all people, all styles, all times, all possibilities. There seems to be very little in him of the typical grownup's censoring mechanism, by which both our prejudices and our definably different personalities are formed. In the mind of this fifty-eight-year-old "child genius" are stored, as in a prodigious, near-photographic memory bank, millions of images waiting to be used. He can pull them out as required and solve virtually any design problem in computer-fast time.

Involved with this are the incorrigible humor; the itch to keep traveling, to see more things, to see *all* things; the wish to design and build hundreds of unique and different works, even if it means that he can never sit still to see even *one* through to a flawless realization. This makes him dependent on a legion of attendants and acolytes, who must pick up the pieces, turn his napkin sketches into working drawings, mollify clients, meet budgets, take him to the airport, prepare his meals, sort his slides, wash his socks. They kick at their dependent and "exploited" position, all hundred or two hundred of them. But all profess to love him: to know all his childish and irresponsible ways and weaknesses, but also the rarity of his genius and imagination and the basic goodness of this extraordinary man.

Acknowledgments

I SPENT large parts of two of the most enjoyable years of my life working on this book. One of the things that made that time so enjoyable was the fact that I was able to spend so much of it looking at and being in (even occasionally living in) houses designed by Charles Moore and his friends.

But even more enjoyable, in the long run, was getting to *know* Charles Moore and his friends—including more than a hundred of his relatives, teachers, colleagues, collaborators, clients, and students. They not only made it possible for me to write this book; they also greatly enriched my life. (In one instance, enriched it very specifically and tangibly. Frustrated by returning home from each Moore tour to a decent but very ordinary house, I asked Donlyn Lyndon, one of Charles Moore's original partners and oldest friends, if he could turn my house into a special place too. He could, and—with the help of master builder Charles Goettsche—he did.)

Anyone who has read this book will understand why meeting, observing, and talking to Charles Moore was such a prize adventure. He gave up many hours of his time to answer my questions, housed me and fed me at his own homes, and helped me obtain access to many other people and places. At the same time, he willingly accepted my position of critical distance. This book, with all its faults (and its assessments of *his* faults), will have to serve as my thanks.

Charles Moore's many collaborators and colleagues were similarly gracious, hospitable, and helpful. Bill Turnbull and Don and Alice Lyndon, three excellent people, were very nearly co-authors of much of the book, through the assistance and criticism they provided. Bill Grover, Bob Harper, and their partners in Connecticut; Buzz Yudell, John Ruble, and Tina Beebe in Santa Monica; Stephen Harby and Richard Best in Westwood; Arthur Anderson, Leonard Salvato, Allen Eskew, and Ron Filson in New Orleans; and

Dick and Sue Whitaker in Chicago were all wonderful hosts (what great eating and drinking Moore people do!) and free-flowing fountains of information. I can think of this whole enterprise, in fact, in terms of memorable conversations (some carefully recorded, some too good to record) over fine meals in wonderful places: with Gerry Allen in a Park Avenue apartment; with Dick Oliver at a restaurant in Chelsea; with Jim and Sandy Righter at the Lawn Club in New Haven; with the New Orleans gang at Moran's and Antoine's; with several of the partners of Moore Grover Harper at La Fine Bouche in Essex; with Kent and Nona Bloomer at their wonderful old house with its windmill along the Connecticut shore; with the Rubles and Yudells, eating couscous in Santa Monica; with Nick Pyle and Paul Helmsley in the Hollywood hills.

Many others who have known and worked with Charles Moore over the years shared their thoughts and memories with me, the bitter and the sweet: Dmitri Vedensky, Marvin Buchanan, Bill Mitchell, Roger and Betty Bailey, Hugh Hardy, Dick Chylinski, Vernon De Mars, Joe Esherick, Harvey Perloff, Peter Becker, John Echlin, Bill Hersey (an unusually candid and eloquent source), Kay Le Clercq, Eric Horner, and a number of students. Alfred Boeke, Morley Baer, and Joe Maselli filled in important details by telephone. A long talk with Lawrence Halprin turned out to be almost too personal to use; never has anyone I've interviewed told me so much, so well, in such a short time. Like several of these good people, he began as a source and stayed on as a friend.

I must particularly thank Dick Peters, a colleague of mine on the Berkeley faculty, who, learning of my interest in the work of his old friend and one-time collaborator, arranged my first meeting with Charles Moore and helped make possible subsequent encounters.

Three people uniquely close to Charles—his sister and brother-in-law, Mimi and Saul Weingarten, and his very special friend, Dona Guimaraes—were more helpful and friendly than I had any right to expect. Brad Neal, who began a Ph.D. dissertation on MLTW at Berkeley in 1977, generously lent me all the tapes he had made of his interviews with the principals. I had useful conversations (over more good food and wine) with three California architectural critics, who knew far more about Charles Moore and his work than I did: Sally Woodbridge, David Gebhard, and Tom Hines.

Considering how frequently the inhabitants of celebrated buildings must be bothered by architectural tourists, it is remarkable how hospitable most of the Moore owners I contacted were. For a great many of them, I discovered, their experiences with Charles and his partners remain one of the happier memories of their lives—and the results of those experiences are now a daily joy they seem only too willing to share. (There are others, I should add, whose experiences were not happy and who remain justifiably discontented with the results. To these people I offer thanks for their honesty as well as their hospitality.)

Leland Burns not only opened his joyous house to me, but allowed me to share the experience of living in it, to listen to his wonderful organ, and to enjoy his genial and civilized company. Reverdy Johnson let my family borrow his classic house at the Sea Ranch for a weekend. Simone Swan, a woman of rare charm, served me lunch on her veranda; my wife and I dined with Martin and Elaine Knutsen one Sunday in Sonoma. David Rodes, Miriam Licht, Paul and Nancy Klotz, Hans and Claire Rogger, Ellen Koizim, Sheila Isham, Dr. Horace Stansel, Elizabeth Watson, Duane Matterson, and Peggy Stanwood all offered hospitality as well as tours and reminiscences. Others who generously allowed me to see and ask about their houses included Cy Jobson, Carol Phelan, Ray Fabrizio, William Jewett, Richard Perry, Richard Larson, Nancy Boas, Bea Slater, Dr. June Dunbar, Carol Shinefield, Hope Cahill, Don and Dallas Lee Clark, Emil Hoffman, Mark and Leslie Smith, Bill Clement, George Wickstead (two fine sources on Sea Ranch history as well), Deborah Halvonik, and James Heady. Right up to deadline, I hoped to get to the Washington, D.C., area to see two celebrated houses there; but that proved impossible, so I had to depend on published descriptions and helpful telephone interviews with Dr. Stanley and Barbara Tempchin and Lee Rubenstein. In only three instances was I told I would be unable to see buildings I had hoped to inspect.

Some former owners, like Marilyn Bonham Campbell, Wilkie Talbert, Dr. Harold Stern, Edie Karas, Elaine Budge, and Jean Hubbard, answered my questions about their relationships with the architects, the evolution of the design, and their own experiences in the houses, either in person or by telephone or mail. Teresa Yuen and Robert Edgar of the University of California at Santa Cruz filled me in on some of the problems and joys of Kresge College, as did a number of current students. Reverend Arnold Fenton and

John Davis helped me to understand the unique design process that led to the new St. Matthew's Church in Pacific Palisades. Eleanor Szymanski, formerly with Gunwyn Ventures in Princeton, made it possible for me to see the celebrated "House near New York," as well as the portions of the Gunwyn offices redesigned by Charles Moore.

Finally, I would like to offer my thanks to Emay Buck in Essex, Connecticut, and my very special thanks to Marilyn Zuber in Los Angeles. These two women, who have helped Charles Moore keep his life and his records in some sort of order, were indispensable for me in my work. My travels were in part paid for by grants from the Committee on Research at the University of California in Berkeley, for which I am most grateful. The library of the College of Environmental Design at the university is an inexhaustible and well-run source of published material on architecture, which Chris Goodrich helped me sort through and collect. Erika St.John ably organized my travels, Lyn Heffernon typed the final manuscript, and Jane Lamb and Diane Wong helped me out typing earlier drafts during a period of pressure.

I thank my wife and children for tolerating my obsession and my absences, and I am pleased that they have been able to share with me some of the pleasures and fruits of my work. No author could ask for a better editor than William Abrahams, a better agent than Lois Wallace.

Berkeley, California
March 1983

Notes

INTRODUCTION: WHO IS CHARLES MOORE?

1. Thomas Jefferson, Benjamin Henry Latrobe, Charles Bulfinch, William Strickland, Alexander Jackson Davis, Frank Furness, Henry Hobson Richardson, James Renwick, Louis Sullivan, Bernard Maybeck, Stanford White, Richard Morris Hunt, Frank Lloyd Wright, Walter Gropius, Ludwig Mies van der Rohe, and Eero Saarinen.

2. A still earlier resistance to modernism may be traced to certain influential architects and building authorities in Britain in the mid-1950s. One eloquent early case was that made by Norman Mailer, writing in E*squire* in 1963:

    [Totalitarianism] proliferates in that new architecture which rests like an incubus upon the American landscape, that new architecture which cannot be called modern because it is not architecture but opposed to architecture. Modern architecture began with the desire to use the building materials of the twentieth century—steel, glass, reinforced concrete—and such techniques as cantilevered structure to increase the sculptural beauty of buildings while enlarging their function. It was the first art to be engulfed by the totalitarians who distorted the search of modern architecture for simplicity, and converted it to monotony. The essence of totalitarianism is that it beheads. It beheads individuality, variety, dissent, extreme possibility, romantic faith, it blinds vision, deadens instinct, it obliterates the past. Since it is also irrational, it puts up buildings with flat roofs and huge expanses of glass in northern climates and then suffocates the inhabitants with super-heating systems while the flat roof leaks under a weight of snow. . . . By dislocating us from the most powerful emotions of reality, totalitarianism leaves us further isolated in the empty landscapes of psychosis, precisely that inner landscape of void and dread which we flee by turning to totalitarian styles of life. . . .

    People who admire the new architecture find it of value because it obliterates the past. They are sufficiently totalitarian to wish to avoid the consequences of the past. . . . Yes, the people who admire the new architecture are unconsciously totalitarian. They are looking to eject into their environment and landscape the same deadness and monotony life has put into them. [Reprinted in *The Presidential Papers of Norman Mailer* (New York, 1964)]

    Frank Lloyd Wright, it should be noted, despised the austere and unromantic new European style from the start.

3. In *Architecture Today* (London and New York, 1982), Charles Jencks—who claims

339

credit for first using the term *postmodern* ("in its usually accepted sense") in 1975—insists that a distinction should be made, when discussing nonmodernist architecture since 1960, between *postmodern* and *late-modern* manifestations. Both he sees as reactions against the boredom and oppressive "dumbness" of the basic blank box. Late modernists *exaggerate* the technological and abstract characteristics of modernism, according to Jencks, with more and more aggressive structural members and joints, more extravagant displays of pure geometry, mirrored shapes, exposed pipes, and so forth. Postmodernists, in his definition, reject the dominion of technology and pure rationalism altogether. They seek frames of expressive reference that are more interesting and complex than those of the modernists, more humane and accessible. They look for these in the architecture of the past, in neighboring buildings and local traditions, and in popular activities and literary references.

Jencks distinguishes the first category from the second (and both from classic modernism) according to a list of thirty characteristics. He then further subdivides late modern and postmodern into thirteen subcategories, and positions some two hundred architects and their works into sub-subcategories under these. Many of them (including Charles Moore, to whom he refers more frequently than any other architect) are placed in several different groups. Twenty-five architects, in fact (*not* including Moore, who is exclusively postmodern), appear on *both* his late-modern and postmodern lists.

Jencks's effort at classification is prodigious, but I can't see that it does much to dispel the chaos to which I refer.

4. See Charles Moore and Nicholas Pyle, eds., *The Yale Mathematics Building Competition* (New Haven, 1974).

5. *MLTW/Moore, Lyndon, Turnbull and Whitaker: The Sea Ranch, California, 1966–,* edited and photographed by Yukio Futagawa, text by William Turnbull, Jr., "Global Architecture" series, no. 3 (Tokyo, 1970); *Houses by MLTW, Moore, Lyndon, Turnbull and Whitaker,* vol. I, 1959–75, text by Donlyn Lyndon, edited and photographed by Yukio Futagawa (Tokyo, 1975); *The Work of Charles W. Moore,* extra issue no. 5, A + U, A *Monthly Journal of Architecture and Urbanism* (Tokyo, May 1978), a 324-page catalogue edited by Toshuo Nakamura, texts by Charles Moore and others; Gerald Allen, *Charles Moore,* "Monographs on Contemporary Architecture" series (New York, 1980; London, 1981); *Charles Moore & Company,* special issue no. 7, GA Houses (Tokyo, 1980), a 235-page survey edited by Wayne N. T. Fujii, texts by Richard Whitaker and others. Two of Moore's and his colleagues' own books include photos, plans, and discussions of several of their works: Kent C. Bloomer and Charles W. Moore, *Body, Memory, and Architecture* (New Haven and London, 1977); and especially Charles Moore, Gerald Allen, and Donlyn Lyndon, *The Place of Houses* (New York, 1974).

6. From "Schindler and Richardson," in Charles Moore and Gerald Allen, *Dimensions* (New York, 1976); originally published in *Progressive Architecture* (January 1973).

7. Moore, Allen, and Lyndon, *The Place of Houses.*

8. Ibid.

PART ONE: The Life

1. From "Schindler and Richardson," in Charles Moore and Gerald Allen, *Dimensions* (New York, 1976); originally published in *Progressive Architecture* (January 1973).
2. Among them: Wurster Bernardi and Emmons, Joseph Esherick, Mario Corbett, Charles Warren Callister, John Funk, Ernest J. Kump, Hardison and De Mars, Campbell and Wong, Henry Hill, Anshen and Allen, George Rockrise, Marquis and Stoller, John Lord King, John Lyon Reid and Partners, Mario Ciampi, Henrik Bull, Jones and Emmons, and the early John Carl Warnecke.
3. F. Andreas Burr, "Learning Under Moore," in Wayne N. T. Fujii, ed., *Charles Moore & Company*, special issue no. 7, GA *Houses* (Tokyo, 1980).
4. It was finished and published late in 1983: Charles Moore and Katherine Smith, eds., *Home Sweet Home: American Domestic Vernacular Architecture* (New York, 1983).
5. From "Schindler and Richardson," in Moore and Allen, *Dimensions*; originally published in *Journal of the Society of Architectural Historians* (December 1975).
6. Henry-Russell Hitchcock, *The Architecture of H. H. Richardson and His Times* (New York, 1936; revised 1961).

PART TWO: The Works

1. "The End of Arcadia," in Sally Woodbridge, ed., *Bay Area Houses* (New York, 1976).
2. Charles Moore, Gerald Allen, and Donlyn Lyndon, *The Place of Houses* (New York, 1974).
3. Martin Filler, "The Magic Fountain," *Progressive Architecture* (November 1978).
4. "The jocular triteness and flamboyant emptiness of those effects seems quite intentional, as though Moore meant to parody not only the Disneyland emptiness of Americans, but also the seriousness of architecture and art itself."

   "In my mind, no amount of pseudo-classical vocabulary, neon decor, magic mountains, etc. can turn 'eclectic appreciation' into a creative act."

   "Differences of opinion notwithstanding, a put-on is a put-on. . . . Another joke in extremely poor taste by someone who obviously hates Italy and/or New Orleans. . . . I can't help but agree with one of the joke's authors, who uses his own sculptured head as a gargoyle. While Moore's sculptured face is laughing, he's puking too." [Letters to the Editor, *Progressive Architecture* (January, 1979)]

   "I am certain other Americans of Italian descent feel as I do that the committee which selected this 'clothesline' design should apologize to the Italian-American community for this insult to their heritage."

   "I can usually manage to perceive some humor in Italian jokes if they aren't too brutish, but this place is surely the unkindest cut of all."

   "The Piazza d'Italia is a melange of architectural sterility and smart-aleckism further vulgarized at night by neon lights. It is incredible that $1.65 million of taxpayers' money . . . should have been spent on such a project. If the City of New Orleans intended to honor its large population of Italian descent, it has failed to do so. The Piazza is a refined Coney Island exhibition of inanity, with the two faces of Charles W. Moore spouting water into the square below. . . ."

"The humblest Italian descendent in this community, unaware as he may be of the artistic glories of his ancestors, possesses an instinctive love of beauty to which the Piazza d'Italia is an affront. . . ." [Letters to the Editor, the New Orleans *Times-Picayune and States-Item* (1979)]

5. Tina Beebe, "Coloring Space," in Wayne N. T. Fujii, ed., *Charles Moore & Company*, special issue no. 7, GA *Houses* (Tokyo, 1980).

6. "Already Richardson was too busy, apparently, even to see and criticize all the work that went out from his own office. . . . Over-production already was lowering the level of production in Richardson's office. Had he lived, his reputation must soon have suffered from such work signed with his name. . . . His office force, in putting through drawings he had no chance to revise, was saving him efforts that he could not make. To a large extent, they thus saved him at the expense of his reputation." [Henry-Russell Hitchcock, *The Architecture of* H. H. *Richardson and His Times* (New York, 1936)]

7. To give an idea of the level and range of architects who are willing to devote time and talent to these unbuildable events, I list the participants in the recent invitational celebrity architecture shows in which Moore has been involved. Unless noted, they work primarily in the United States.

Best Products Company Facades (Museum of Modern Art, New York, 1979): Michael Graves, Allan Greenberg, Anthony Lumsden, Charles Moore, Robert A. M. Stern, Stanley Tigerman.

Venice Biennale 1980, Strada Novissima Facades (Venice, Paris, San Francisco): Ricardo Bofill (Spain), Costantino Dardi (Italy), Frank O. Gehry, Studio GRAU (Italy), Michael Graves, Allan Greenberg, Hans Hollein (Austria), Arata Isozaki (Japan), J. P. Kleihues (West Germany), Leon Krier (UK), Rem Koolhaas (UK/U.S.), Charles Moore, Christian de Portzamperc (France), Franco Purini (Italy), Massimo Scolari (Italy), Thomas Gordon Smith, Robert A. M. Stern, Stanley Tigerman, Oswald Mathias Ungers (West Germany/U.S.), Robert Venturi.

"*Late Entries*" *in the 1922 Chicago Tribune Tower Competition* (Museum of Contemporary Art, Chicago, 1980): A large number of the sixty-eight invited and uninvited entries were from Chicago-based architects, university professors, and younger Rome Prize–winners of the American Academy. Among the better-known invited participants were Architectonica of Miami (three submissions), Thomas Beeby, Frank O. Gehry, Helmut Jahn, Donlyn Lyndon, Rodolfo Machado, Moore Ruble Yudell, Walter Netsch, Cesar Pelli, Jorge Silvetti, Thomas Gordon Smith, Peter and Alison Smithson (UK), Robert A. M. Stern, TAFT Architects of Houston, Susanna Torre, William Turnbull, Jr., and Ben Weese.

Houses for Sale (Castelli Gallery, New York, 1980): Emilio Ambasz, Peter Eisenman, Vittorio Gregotti (Italy), Arata Isozaki (Japan), Charles Moore, Cesar Pelli, Cedric Price (UK), Oswald Mathias Ungers (West Germany).

Collaboration: Artists and Architects (the Architecture League of New York, 1981): Emilio Ambasz, James Freed, Frank O. Gehry, Michael Graves, Hugh

Hardy, Richard Meier, Charles Moore, Cesar Pelli, Robert A. M. Stern, Stanley Tigerman, Susanna Torre.

Formica Corporation Furniture Design (1981–82): Emilio Ambasz, Ward Bennett, Frank O. Gehry, Charles Moore, SITE Architects, Stanley Tigerman, Robert Venturi, Massimo and Celia Vignelli.

Architectural Design Doll's House (London, 1982). Invited submissions; Takefumi Aida (Japan), Tadao Anda (Japan), Doug Cleland and Paul Sutton (UK), Theo Crosby (UK), Francis De Vallee (France), Terry Farrell (UK), Michael Gold and Paul Wellard (UK—first prize), Ron Herron (UK), Bruno Minardi (Italy), John David Mooney, Charles Moore, Jean Nouvel (France), Eduardo Paolozzi (UK), Gustav Peichl (Austria), Franco Purini and Federica Ottone (Italy), TAFT Architects, David West (UK), Colin Wilson and M. J. Long (UK), and John Zerning and Isabel Sutton (UK).

The House for Schinkel competition sponsored by *Japan Architect* (1979–80), in which Moore, working with Bill Hersey and John Kyrk, received an honorable mention, was an open event which attracted 384 entries, judged anonymously. Moore's was the only name I recognized among the twenty cited by judge James Stirling of Britain.

Index